GROUP
DYNAMICS
for TEAMS

SAGE was founded in 1965 by Sara Miller McCune to support the dissemination of usable knowledge by publishing innovative and high-quality research and teaching content. Today, we publish more than 850 journals, including those of more than 300 learned societies, more than 800 new books per year, and a growing range of library products including archives, data, case studies, reports, and video. SAGE remains majority-owned by our founder, and after Sara's lifetime will become owned by a charitable trust that secures our continued independence.

Los Angeles | London | New Delhi | Singapore | Washington DC

5th
edition

GROUP DYNAMICS *for* TEAMS

DANIEL LEVI

California Polytechnic State University, San Luis Obispo

$SAGE

Los Angeles | London | New Delhi
Singapore | Washington DC

Los Angeles | London | New Delhi
Singapore | Washington DC

FOR INFORMATION:

SAGE Publications, Inc.
2455 Teller Road
Thousand Oaks, California 91320
E-mail: order@sagepub.com

SAGE Publications Ltd.
1 Oliver's Yard
55 City Road
London, EC1Y 1SP
United Kingdom

SAGE Publications India Pvt. Ltd.
B 1/I 1 Mohan Cooperative Industrial Area
Mathura Road, New Delhi 110 044
India

SAGE Publications Asia-Pacific Pte. Ltd.
3 Church Street
#10–04 Samsung Hub
Singapore 049483

Acquisitions Editor: Lara Parra
Development Editor: Nathan Davidson
Editorial Assistant: Morgan McCardell
Production Editor: Veronica Stapleton
    Hooper
Copy Editor: Janet Ford
Typesetter: Hurix Systems Pvt. Ltd.
Proofreader: Dennis W. Webb
Indexer: Sheila Bodell
Cover Designer: Rose Storey
Marketing Manager: Shari Countryman

Copyright © 2017 by SAGE Publications, Inc.

Leading Virtual Teams icon from iStock 16635106.

Printed in the United States of America

ISBN: 978-1-4833-7834-3

This book is printed on acid-free paper.

15 16 17 18 19 10 9 8 7 6 5 4 3 2 1

Brief Contents

Detailed Contents

Acknowledgments

Many people helped shape this book. My understanding of work teams, including both manufacturing and professional teams, was fostered by the many opportunities I had to study and consult with actual teams in industry. Andrew Young, Margaret Lawn, and Don Devito created a number of opportunities for me to work with teams in the United States and abroad. Most of my research and consulting on work teams was performed with Charles Slem, my partner at Cal Poly, San Luis Obispo. As a teacher of group dynamics, I learned by coteaching with Fred Stultz and Robert Christenson. In addition, I had the opportunity to work with engineering teams at Cal Poly as part of a NASA-supported program to improve engineering education. Daniel Mittleman, associate professor of Computing and Digital Media at DePaul University, helped me understand the impacts of virtual teamwork and contributed to the Leading Virtual Teams sections of the book. David Askay, assistant professor of Communications Studies at Cal Poly, wrote the Communication chapter (Chapter 6) and contributed ideas and sections on the impacts of diversity and the use of technology by teams. Finally, the psychology, business, and engineering students in my group dynamics and teamwork classes have helped teach me what is important about how teams operate.

The support of various editors at SAGE Publications has been invaluable. I have also benefited from the many anonymous academic reviews of the book and proposed revisions. In addition, Kathy Johnston and Sara Kocher labored diligently to improve my language and make the text more readable. My wife, Sara, deserves special credit for her thoughtful reviews and supportive presence throughout this process.

For comprehensive reviews of the manuscript, I would like to thank the following reviewers:

Mark A. Arvisais, Towson University

Kerrie Q. Baker, Cedar Crest College

Anita Leffel, The University of Texas at San Antonio

Russell O. Mays, Georgia Southern University

Kevin L. Nadal, John Jay College of Criminal Justice

C. Kevin Synnott, Eastern Connecticut State University

About the Author

Daniel Levi is a professor in the Psychology and Child Development Department at Cal Poly, San Luis Obispo, California. He holds an MA and a PhD in environmental psychology from the University of Arizona. He teaches classes in teamwork and in environmental and organizational psychology. His teamwork class was designed primarily for engineering and business students at Cal Poly. He has conducted research and worked as a consultant with factory and engineering teams for companies, such as Nortel Networks, TRW, Hewlett-Packard, and Philips Electronics. In addition, he has worked on international team research projects in Europe and Asia.

Dr. Levi's research and consulting with factory teams primarily focused on the use of teams to support technological change and the adoption of just-in-time and quality programs. This work examined a variety of team issues, including job redesign, training, compensation, supervision, and change management approaches. His work with professional teams primarily was accomplished with engineering design teams. These projects examined the use of concurrent engineering, self-management, and the globalization of teams. The topics of this work included the impact of information technology on teams, facilitation and training needs for professional teams, and the impacts of organizational culture and leadership.

Early work on the present book was sponsored by an engineering education grant from NASA. This project focused on the development of teamwork skills in engineering students working on multidisciplinary projects. This project led to the development of cases and activities for learning teamwork skills and research on teamwork training, and evaluating and rewarding student teams. Recent research on student teams examines gender and cross-cultural issues, social support within teams, and bullying and hijacking in student teams.

David Askay is an assistant professor in the Communications Studies Department at Cal Poly, San Luis Obispo. He earned a PhD in Organizational Science from the University of North Carolina at Charlotte (2013) and teaches in the areas of groups, organizations, and technology.

Introduction

There are two sources of information about teamwork. First, there is a large body of research in psychology and the social sciences called group dynamics that examines how people work in small groups. This research was collected over the past century and has developed into a broad base of knowledge about the operation of groups. Second, the use of teams in the workplace has expanded rapidly during the past three decades. Management researchers and applied social scientists have studied this development to provide advice to organizations about how to make teams operate more effectively. However, these two areas of research and knowledge often operate along separate paths.

The purpose of this book is to unite these two important perspectives on how people work together. It organizes research and theories of group dynamics in order to apply this information to the ways in which teams operate in organizations. The concepts of group dynamics are presented so they are useful for people who work in teams and also to enlarge their understandings of how teams operate. It is hoped that this integration helps readers better understand the internal dynamics of teams so they can become more effective team leaders and members.

The larger goal of this book is to make teams more successful. Teams are important in our society, and learning teamwork skills is important for individual career success. This book presents many concepts related to how teams operate. In addition, the chapters contain application sections with techniques, advice for leading virtual teams, case studies (called Team Leader's Challenge), surveys, and activities designed to develop teamwork skills. The appendix contains tools and advice to help students in project teams. Teamwork is not just something one reads about and then understands; teamwork develops through guided experience and feedback. This book provides a framework for teaching about teams and improving how teams function.

Overview

The seventeen chapters in this book cover a wide range of topics related to group dynamics and teamwork. These chapters are organized into four parts: characteristics of teams, processes of teamwork, issues teams face, and organizational context of teams. An appendix provides advice and tools to support student project teams.

Part I: Characteristics of Teams

Chapters 1 and 2 provide an introduction to group dynamics and teamwork. Chapter 1 explains the differences between groups and teams. This chapter also examines the purpose of teams in organizations and why they are increasing in use. It concludes with a brief history of both the use of teams and the study of group dynamics.

Chapter 2 explores the characteristics of successful teams. It explains the basic components necessary to create effective teams and examines the conditions and characteristics of successful work teams. It presents both traditional perspectives toward team success and a positive psychology perspective. In many ways, this chapter establishes a goal for team members, whereas the rest of the book explains how to reach that goal.

Part II: Processes of Teamwork

Chapters 3 through 6 present the underlying processes of teamwork. Chapter 3 examines the processes and stages that relate to forming teams. Team members must be socialized or incorporated into teams. Teams must establish goals and norms (operating rules) to begin work. These are the first steps in team development.

Chapter 4 presents some of the main processes and concepts from group dynamics that explain how teams operate. Working together as a team affects the motivation of participants both positively and negatively. Team members form social relationships with one another that help define their identities as teams. Teams divide tasks into different roles to coordinate the work. The behaviors and actions of team members can be viewed as either task oriented or social, both of which are necessary for teams to function smoothly. Teams are dynamic entities that adapt to changes and learn how to work together more effectively.

One of the underlying concepts that define teamwork is cooperation. Teams are a collection of people who work cooperatively together to accomplish goals. However, teams often are disrupted by competition. Chapter 5 explains how cooperation and competition affect the dynamics of teams.

Team members interact by communicating with one another. Chapter 6 examines the communication that occurs within teams. It describes the communication process, how teams develop supportive communication climates, and the effects of emotional intelligence on communication. The chapter also presents practical advice on how to facilitate team meetings and develop skills that help improve team communication.

Part III: Issues Teams Face

The third part of the book contains seven chapters that focus on a variety of issues that teams face in learning to operate effectively. Chapter 7 examines conflict and conflict resolution in teams. Although conflict often is viewed as a negative event, certain types of conflict are both healthy and necessary for teams to succeed. The chapter explains the dynamics of conflict within teams and discusses various approaches to managing conflict in teams.

Chapter 8 describes how power and social influence operate in teams. Different types of power and influence tactics are available to teams and their members; the use of power has wide-ranging applications and effects on teams. In one important sense, the essence of teams at work is a shift in power. Teams exist because their organizations are willing to shift power and control to teams.

The central purpose of many types of teams is to make decisions. Chapter 9 examines group decision-making processes. It illustrates operative conditions when teams are better than individuals at making decisions and the problems that groups encounter in trying to make effective decisions. The chapter ends with a presentation of decision-making techniques that are useful for teams.

Chapter 10 presents leadership options for teams from authoritarian control to self-management. The various approaches to understanding leadership are reviewed, with an emphasis on leadership models that are useful for understanding team leadership. The chapter examines self-managing teams in detail to illustrate this important alternative to traditional leadership approaches.

The different methods that teams use to solve problems are examined in Chapter 11. The chapter compares how teams solve problems with how teams should solve problems. The chapter presents a variety of problem-solving techniques to help improve how teams analyze and solve problems.

Creativity, which is one aspect of teams that often is criticized, is discussed in Chapter 12. Teams can inhibit individual creativity, but some problems require teams to develop creative solutions. The chapter examines the factors that discourage creativity in teams and presents some techniques that foster team creativity.

Chapter 13 examines how diversity affects teams: the problems, causes, and effects. In one sense, if everyone were alike then there would be no need for teamwork. Teams benefit from the multiple perspectives inherent in diversity; however, group processes need to be managed effectively in order to realize these benefits.

Part IV: Organizational Context of Teams

The final section of the book presents a set of issues that relate to the use of teams in organizations. Chapter 14 examines the relationship between teams and culture. Culture defines the underlying values and practices of a team or organization. Teams develop cultures that regulate how they operate. Work teams are more likely to be successful if their organization's culture supports them. International culture has many impacts on teamwork. Transnational teams need to develop a hybrid culture that mediates the cultural differences among its members.

Although teams often are thought of as people interacting directly with one another, Chapter 15 examines the impacts of teams that interact through technology. Virtual teams comprise members who may be dispersed around the world and use a variety of technologies to communicate and coordinate their efforts. The selection and use of these technologies changes some of the dynamics of the teams operations.

Chapter 16 examines approaches to evaluating and rewarding teams. One of the keys to developing effective teams is creating a mechanism to provide quality feedback to teams so they can improve their own performance. Performance evaluation systems help provide feedback, while reward programs motivate team members to act on this information.

Team building and the various approaches for improving how teams operate is the focus of Chapter 17, the final chapter. Organizations use team-building techniques to help teams get started, overcome obstacles, and improve performance. Teamwork training helps develop people skills so that everyone can work together more effectively.

Appendix: Guide to Student Team Projects

One of the reasons students want to learn about group dynamics is to improve the effectiveness of their teams at work and school. As a teacher of group dynamics and teamwork, I require students to work on a large project throughout the course. Working on their team project provides the students with an opportunity to try out the ideas they are learning in the course.

The Guide to Student Team Projects contains some of the tools and advice that students need to successfully complete a team project. The appendix covers topics, such as how to start a team, plan a team project, monitor the progress of the team and project, write as a team, and end the team. This is practical advice on techniques and activities to help improve the team's performance.

The student project teams in my classes range from five to seven members who are randomly appointed to the team. They are given a large and poorly structured assignment, requiring them to clarify and negotiate the specifics. The teams must conduct periodic group process evaluations so that they regularly discuss and try to improve the teamwork process. Although I grade the quality of the team's final product, the students grade the performance of the individual team members. (This is a very important step, and we spend class time discussing how to do this.)

Although this is a guide for student projects, the tools in the appendix are useful for many types of project teams.

Learning Approaches

Learning how to work in teams is not a matter of simply reading about group dynamics. Fundamentally, teamwork is a set of skills that must be developed through practice and feedback. In addition to presenting information about how teams operate, this book contains four other types of material that are helpful for developing teamwork skills: application sections, case studies, surveys, and activities.

Many chapters in the book incorporate application sections. The purpose of these sections is to provide practical advice on applying the concepts in the chapters. These sections focus on presenting techniques rather than theories and concepts. These techniques can be applied to the existing teams or can be used with a team in a class to practice the skills. In addition, most of the chapters contain an application section called Leading Virtual Teams, which provides practical advice for dealing with the group dynamics problems created by working in a virtual team setting.

All chapters end with case studies and teamwork activities. The case studies, called Team Leader's Challenge, present a difficult team problem and contain discussion questions for providing advice to the team's leader. The cases use a variety of student and work teams. By using the concepts in the chapter, the cases can be analyzed and options for the team leaders developed.

Eight of the chapters contain brief psychological surveys that examine a personal orientation toward a teamwork issue presented in the chapter. Survey topics range from attitudes toward teamwork, to cooperativeness, to preferred conflict styles, to opinions about team rewards. Discussion questions after the surveys help students and other team members understand the impact of individual differences on teamwork.

The teamwork activities examine a topic in the chapter and then include a set of discussion questions designed to apply what has been learned to actual teams. Some of the activities are structured discussions or small-group exercises. However, most of the activities are structured observations of how teams operate. One of the most important ways to improve both one's teamwork skills and the operation of teams is to learn how to be a good observer of group processes. These observation activities are constructed to develop these skills.

There are several options that can be used for the observation activities. If the observers belong to functioning teams, then they can observe their own teams. For example, a teamwork class might have students working on project teams. Use the observation activities to study and provide feedback to the project teams, or create groups in class settings and give group assignments. There are many books on small-group activities to use to create assignments for the groups. Small-group discussions of the Team Leader's Challenges provide an alternative activity to observe how groups interact. A class can use several groups with an observer assigned to each group or a single group that performs while being surrounded by many group process observers. Finally, ask students to find a team that they can observe as part of an ongoing class project.

Each of the activities includes objective, activity, analysis, and discussion sections. The structure of the activities makes them suitable for homework assignments or for entries in group dynamics journals. The basic structure of the written assignments includes answering the following questions: What did you observe? How did you analyze this information? How would you apply this knowledge?

By working through the applications, cases, surveys, and activities presented here, team members gain practical skills and knowledge that can be directly applied to improve the operations of their teams and the ultimate success of teamwork.

PART I

Characteristics of Teams

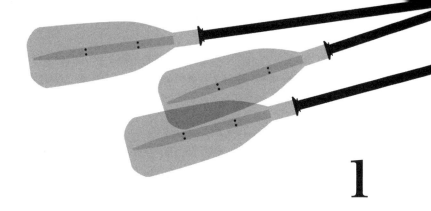

1

Understanding Teams

A team is a special type of group in which people work interdependently to accomplish a goal. Organizations use many different types of teams to serve a variety of purposes. The use of teams to perform work has a long history, but during the past few decades organizational teamwork has changed: It has expanded rapidly because of changes in the nature of jobs and the structure of organizations. The scientific study of group dynamics provides useful insights about how teams operate and how they can be improved.

Learning Objectives

1. What are the characteristics of a group?
2. How is a team different from a group?
3. How are teams used by organizations?
4. How are work groups different from teams and self-managing teams?
5. Why is the use of teams by organizations increasing?
6. What are the main historical trends in the use of teams?
7. How has the study of group dynamics changed over time?

1.1 Defining Groups and Teams

A group is more than just a collection of people. There is a difference between the people who are in a park, the work group that is assembling a product, and the team playing football. To define the differences between collections of people, groups, and teams, researchers use several approaches that vary depending on which features are considered important.

One approach is to describe the social characteristics of a group (see Table 1.1). A group exists for a reason or purpose and has a goal shared by the group members. The people in a group have some type of relationship or are connected to one another. They recognize this connection, and it binds them together so they collectively share what happens to fellow group members. From a teamwork perspective, this interdependence is probably the most important characteristic of a group. Group members interact and communicate with one another. Often, communication is viewed as a central process of a group. The people in a group recognize and acknowledge their membership in a collective. Formal and informal rules, roles, and norms of the group control the interactions of group members. The people in a group influence one another, and the desire to remain in the group increases the

Table 1.1 Characteristics of a Group

Goal orientation	People joining together for some purpose and to achieve some goal
Interdependent	People who have some type of relationship, see connections among themselves, or believe they share a common fate
Interpersonal interaction	People who communicate and interact with one another
Perception of membership	Recognition that there is a collective to which one belongs
Structured relations	Roles, rules, and norms that control people's interactions
Mutual influence	Impact people have on one another because of their connections
Individual motivation	Satisfaction of personal needs through membership in the group

SOURCE: Johnson, D., & Johnson, F. (1997). *Joining together: Group theory and group skills* (6th ed.). Boston, MA: Allyn & Bacon.

potential for mutual influence. Finally, a group satisfies members' physical and psychological needs such that individuals are motivated to continue their participation in the group.

From a psychological perspective, two processes define a group: *social identification* and *social representation* (Hayes, 1997). Social identification refers to the recognition that a group exists separately from others. It is the creation of a belief in "us versus them." Identification is both a cognitive process (classifying the world into categories) and an emotional process (viewing one's group as better than other groups). Social representation is the shared values, ideas, and beliefs that people have about the world. Over time, belonging to a group changes the ways its members view the world. The group develops a shared worldview through member interactions.

Most definitions of teamwork classify a team as a special type of group. To some theorists, the distinction between groups and teams is fuzzy. They consider teams to be simply groups in work settings (Parks & Sanna, 1999). Other theorists focus on how the behavior of teams differs from that of typical groups. Teams have been defined as structured groups of people working on defined common goals that require coordinated interactions to accomplish certain tasks (Forsyth, 1999). This definition emphasizes one key feature of a team: that members work together on a common project for which they all are accountable. However, other qualifiers can be used to distinguish groups from teams.

One common distinction relates to application. Teams typically are engaged in sports or work activities. They have applied functions, and the roles of team members are related to their functions. For example, members of sports teams have specific assigned roles, (such as a pitcher or shortstop on a baseball team.) Teams usually exist within larger organizations. Their members have specialized knowledge, skills, and abilities related to their tasks. This is why researchers typically do not talk about a family as a team; in a family, roles are inherited and not directly related to tasks. This distinction appears in research on groups and teams. Research on groups typically is conducted in laboratory settings, whereas research on teams typically is done in field studies that focus on the use of teams in the workplace (Kerr & Tindale, 2004).

Group is a more inclusive term than *team*. Groups range in size from two to thousands, whereas teams have a narrower range of sizes. A dating couple may be considered a group, but not a team. Political parties and social organizations are groups, but not teams. A team typically is composed of 3 to 12 people who interact with one another directly (although this interaction may occur through communication technology). A team is not simply people who belong to the same group or who are jointly functioning in the same place.

Katzenbach and Smith (1993) focus on performance in their definition of teamwork. In addition to team members having a common purpose, performance goals are connected to this purpose, for which everyone in the team is held mutually accountable. They also believe the concept of a team should be limited to a fairly small number of people with complementary skills who interact directly. This helps distinguish teams from work groups, whose members jointly do the same tasks, but do not require integration and coordination to perform the tasks.

Hayes (1997) focuses on power in her definition of teams. She believes a team must actively cooperate to achieve its goals. For this to occur, a team must have independence, responsibility, and the power to operate. A team is not a group of people who perform a task under the rigid control of an authority figure. For a group to become a team, it must be empowered and must have some authority to act on its own. In addition, team members are more likely to work together cooperatively and provide assistance to one another than are members of other types of work groups.

Because there is no firm dividing line between a group and a team, the use of these terms in this book is somewhat arbitrary. When referring to research on group dynamics, especially laboratory research, the term *group* is used. When talking about applications in work environments where people are interdependent, the term *team* is used. For the in-between cases, *group* and *team* are used interchangeably.

1.2 Purposes and Types of Teams

Organizations use teams in a variety of ways. Because of this variety, there are many ways to classify teams and these classifications help explain the psychological and organizational differences among different types of teams. One important distinction is the relationship of the team to the organization. Teams vary depending on how much power and authority they are given by their umbrella organizations.

How Teams Are Used by Organizations

Teams are used to serve a variety of functions for organizations. The day-to-day operations of organizations can be shifted to teams (e.g., factory production teams, airline crews). Teams can be formed to provide advice and deal with special problems. For instance, teams might be created to suggest improvements in work processes. Teams can help manage coordination problems by linking different parts of organizations. Budget or planning committees might be composed of members from several departments, for example. Finally, teams can be used to change organizations by planning for the future or managing transitions.

Obviously, a teams' configuration can be very mixed. Concurrent engineering teams are teams composed of members of an organization whose task is to oversee the design, manufacturing, and marketing of new products. Affiliation in a concurrent engineering team is normally part of the day-to-day activity of people working in research and development. However, other members of the team may be there on a part-time, temporary basis to deal with coordination, special problems, and implementation of change. Research and development staff may define the characteristics of a new product, while representatives from other departments may comment on issues related to production and marketing.

Sundstrom (1999) identifies six types of work teams on the basis of the functions they perform:

1. Production teams, such as factory teams, manufacture or assemble products on a repetitive basis.

2. Service teams, such as maintenance crews and food services, conduct repeated transactions with customers.

3. Management teams, composed of managers, work together, plan, develop policy, or coordinate the activities of an organization.

4. Project teams, such as research and engineering teams, bring experts together to perform a specific task within a defined period.

5. Action or performing teams, such as sports teams, entertainment groups, and surgery teams, engage in brief performances that are repeated under new conditions and that require specialized skills and extensive training or preparation.

6. Finally, parallel teams are temporary teams that operate outside normal work, such as employee involvement groups and advisory committees that provide suggestions or recommendations for changing an organization.

Classifying Teams

Teams can be classified by ways other than the types of activities they perform (Devine, Clayton, Philips, Dunford, & Melner, 1999). Researchers have suggested classifying teams by whether they are permanent or temporary, how much internal specialization and interdependence they require, and how much integration and coordination with other parts of the organization are needed (Mohrman, 1993; Sundstrom, DeMeuse, & Futrell, 1990).

One of the most important distinctions among types of teams is how much power they are allocated (Hayes, 1997). When an organization uses teams rather than individual workers to perform tasks, it is giving the teams some power and authority to control the operations of its members. This shifting of power affects leadership, decision making, and how the work activities of team members are linked.

There are three options for organizing people into work groups: a work group, a team, or a self-managing team. The differences among these options are presented in Table 1.2. Work groups are part of the organization's hierarchical system. Supervisors or managers who control the decision-making process lead these work groups. Group members typically work on independent tasks that are linked by the supervisor's direction or by the work system.

Teams are given some power and authority so they are somewhat independent of the organization's hierarchy. Their leaders are selected by management and given some managerial power. Team leaders can use a variety of techniques for making decisions, such as using the teams to provide advice about decisions (consultative), having the teams vote, or using consensus to make decisions. Team members' work activities are interdependent and coordinated by the leaders.

Table 1.2   Organization of People Into Work Groups

	Work Group	Team	Self-Managing Team
Power	Part of organization's hierarchy, management controlled	Linked to organization's hierarchy, some shift of power to team	Linked to organization's hierarchy, increased power and independence
Leadership	Manager or supervisor controlled	Leader, with limited managerial power, selected by organization	Leader, the team facilitator, selected by the team
Decision making	Authoritarian or consultative	Consultative, democratic, or consensus	Democratic or consensus
Activities or tasks	Independent	Interdependent, coordinated by leader	Interdependent, coordinated by team members

SOURCE: Adapted from McGrath, J. (1984). *Groups: Interaction and performance.* Englewood Cliffs, NJ: Prentice Hall.

Self-managing teams are given significantly more power and authority than traditional work groups and are more independent of an organization's hierarchy. Team members typically select their leaders; as a result the leaders have limited power and must facilitate—rather than control—their teams' operations. The leaders must rely on democratic or consensus decision making because they have no authority to make teams accept decisions. The work of team members is highly interdependent, and all team members work together to coordinate activities.

1.3 Why Organizations Use Teams

The traditional approach to organizing people to perform a task is called *scientific management* (Taylor, 1923). In this approach, managers or technical experts analyze a task and divide it into small activity units that are performed by individuals. The system is designed such that each activity unit is linked to other activity units, and individuals work separately to complete the entire task. It is the role of management to design the system and control the operations of the workers. It is the role of the workers to perform a specific activity. In other words, managers think and control and workers act.

This traditional approach works very well under certain conditions. It requires that the task remain the same for some time because it is difficult to change the system. It requires that the process not be too complex or easily disrupted because the workers doing routine activities are unaware of what happens in other parts of the system. It focuses on productivity and often ignores concerns about quality and customer service because these factors require more commitment to the job. It assumes that there are workers who are willing to perform routine activities under controlled situations. Under these conditions, scientific management is the best approach, and the time and expense of developing teams is not needed.

Teams are important, however, when the goal is to improve the way a product is made or a service is provided; when the job is complex; when customer service and quality are important; or when rapid change is necessary. These are the conditions that create the need for teams (Helper, Kleiner, & Wang, 2010). Modern organizations are shifting to teamwork because of changes in the characteristics of jobs and organizations.

Job Characteristics

Many jobs are changing from routine to nonroutine work (Mohrman, Cohen, & Mohrman, 1995), which encourages the use of teamwork. Nonroutine jobs involve more complexity, interdependence, uncertainty, variety, and change than routine jobs. Jobs of this type are difficult to manage in traditional work systems, but are well suited for teamwork.

Nonroutine jobs are found in a number of contemporary work settings. Teams are a good way to handle factory jobs that have become increasingly complex because of technology or other factors (Manufacturing Studies Board, 1986). The individual factory worker operating a single machine all day is being replaced by a team of workers who monitor, troubleshoot, maintain, and manage a complex and integrated work system. Because the technology is integrated, the workers must be as well.

These changes also affect professional work. Imagine designing a new product for the marketplace. Design, manufacturing, marketing, and sales of the product require expertise from a variety of disciplines and support from many parts of an organization. Given that few individuals possess all the necessary knowledge and expertise to bring a product to completion, a diversity of knowledge is gained by using a team approach. In addition, using team members from several departments enhances support within the organization for the new product. The team members help coordinate the project throughout the organization.

The complexity of a problem or task often requires multiple forms of expertise. No one person may have all the skills or knowledge to complete a task or solve a problem, but a team may have sufficient expertise to deal with the task or problem. Complexity also implies that problems may be confusing or difficult to understand and solve. Here, the value of teamwork is not in multiple forms of expertise, but rather in multiple perspectives. People learn from the group interactions in teams, which helps them to gain new perspectives in analyzing problems and developing solutions.

Organizational Characteristics

The rate at which change is increasing in business and society is phenomenal. Markets are expanding, and competition is progressively more global. It is difficult to keep up with these changes using traditional approaches to organizational design; the changing business environment is forcing organizations to change the way they operate. Communications technology allows organizations to create new ways to integrate their operations. Businesses know they need to reduce costs, improve quality, reduce the time spent creating new products, improve customer service, and increase their adaptability to an increasingly competitive environment.

As organizations change to meet contemporary demands, new organizational characteristics increase the importance of teamwork (Mohrman et al., 1995). One significant new characteristic of this change is a shift to simpler organizational hierarchies, a transition driven by the desire to save costs and increase flexibility by reducing layers of management. To a certain extent, teams have replaced managers, and teams now often carry out traditional management functions.

Teams provide a way to integrate and coordinate the various parts of an organization and do this in a more timely and cost-effective manner than traditional organizational hierarchies. Teams execute tasks better, learn faster, and change more easily than traditional work structures, which are all characteristics required by contemporary organizations.

1.4 History of Teams and Group Dynamics

The use of teams in organizations has changed significantly over the past century. During that period, the scientific study of group dynamics has evolved into an interdisciplinary research field.

Foundations of Teamwork

The Industrial Revolution shifted most work organizations to a hierarchical approach that used scientific management to design jobs (Taylor, 1923). Manufacturing jobs were simplified, and professionals and managers were brought in to ensure that the production system operated efficiently. Scientific management was a system that worked well, but that also created problems: It alienated workers, who then became increasingly difficult to motivate. It became more difficult to set up as technical systems increased in complexity. It was inflexible and difficult to change. Finally, it was difficult to successfully incorporate new goals other than efficiency (such as quality).

The scientific management model of organizations began to be questioned during the 1920s and 1930s because of social problems in the workplace. The Hawthorne studies—research projects designed to examine how environmental factors, such as lighting and work breaks affected work performance—inadvertently revealed that social factors had an important impact on performance (Mayo, 1933). In some cases, because people were being studied, they tried to perform better (what social scientists now call the "Hawthorne effect"). In other cases, group norms limited or controlled performance. For example, studies of the "bank wiring room" showed that informal group norms had a major impact on the performance of work groups (Sundstrom, McIntyre, Halfhill, & Richards, 2000). The "group in front" frequently engaged in conversation and play, but had high levels of performance, while the "group in back" engaged in play, but had low levels of performance. The work groups enforced group production norms: Members who worked too fast were hit on the arm by coworkers, a practice known as *binging*. In addition to the substantial impact on productivity of these informal work group norms, work groups were able to effectively enforce norms, resulting in positive or negative benefits to the organization.

During the 1960s and 1970s, organizational psychologists and industrial engineers refined the use of teams at work. Sociotechnical systems theory (STS) provided a way to analyze what people do at work and to determine the best way of organizing them (Appelbaum & Batt, 1994). According to STS, teams should be used when jobs are technically uncertain rather than routine, when jobs are interdependent and require coordination to perform, and when the environment is turbulent and requires flexibility. Many jobs today meet these criteria. The most famous applied example of STS was at the Volvo car facilities in Sweden. The assembly line approach to work was redesigned to be performed by "semiautonomous groups." Although there were several successful demonstrations of the value of using teams at work, this teamwork approach did not become popular.

The contemporary emphasis on teamwork has its origins in another change that occurred during the 1970s. The rise of Japan as a manufacturing power resulted in the distribution of high-quality inexpensive products into the global marketplace. When business experts visited Japan to see how Japanese goals had been achieved, they found that teamwork in the form of *Quality Circles* seemed to be the answer. Quality Circles are parallel teams of production workers and supervisors who meet to analyze problems and develop solutions to quality problems in the manufacturing process. Throughout the 1980s, companies in the United States and Europe experimented with Quality Circle teams (and later Total Quality Management teams). The jobs performed by workers were still primarily individual, but workers were organized in teams as a way to improve quality and other aspects of production.

The focus on quality in manufacturing launched the teamwork movement, but other factors have sustained it. The increased use of information technology, the downsizing of layers of management, business process reengineering, and globalization have all contributed to the use of teams. Teamwork in U.S. companies expanded rapidly during the 1990s and included more professional and managerial teams. Research shows that 85% of companies with 100 or more employees use some type of work teams (Cohen & Bailey, 1997). In addition, some organizations are restructuring and using teams as a central element in the integration of various parts of their organizations (Mohrman et al., 1995).

Because of the changing nature of teams, three issues are increasingly important: dynamic composition, technology and distance, and empowerment and delayering (Tannenbaum, Mathieu, Salas, & Cohen, 2012).

Teams now operate in a more dynamic and complex environment. Rather than stable teams that work together for long periods of time, contemporary teams are often more transitory with changing membership. Teamwork can be done by people working together in one place or distributed around the globe. In either case, teams are relying on technology to support their communications and work. As organizations rely more on the use of teams, power is shifting from traditional organizational hierarchies to teams. Teams are replacing many traditional management functions.

Two current movements within psychology are affecting the study of teamwork. Multiculturalism and diversity are becoming increasingly important as our society and the global workforce becomes more diverse. Diversity research examines the variety of effects of the different types of diversity within teams. Because of communications technology, the study of transnational teams combines research on international diversity with the impacts of technology. The second movement is the rise of positive psychology, which is the study of people's strengths and how to promote positive functioning. Many positive psychology factors relate to the study of teamwork, such as supportive personal relations, reflexivity and learning, empowerment, and appreciative inquiry. In addition, positive psychology provides an alternative perspective on the meaning of team success and how to achieve it.

Foundations of Group Dynamics

An unfortunate gap exists between our understanding of work teams and the study of group dynamics. The scientific study of groups began at the turn of the twentieth century with the work of Norman Triplett (1898). Triplett's research showed the effects of working alone versus working in a group. For example, he observed that bicycle racers who pedaled around a racetrack in groups were faster than those who pedaled around alone. This effect is called *social facilitation* because the presence of other people facilitates (or increases) performance. (Later research showed that performance increased for well-learned skills, but declined for less well-developed skills.)

Early studies in psychology had a similar perspective in that they were designed to show how groups affected individual performance or attitudes. Although this was group research, the focus was on individuals. Psychologists did not treat groups as an entity appropriate for scientific study. This perspective changed during the 1940s, however, because of the work of Kurt Lewin and his followers (Lewin, 1951). Lewin created the term *group dynamics* to show his interest in the group as a unit of study. For the first time, psychologists took the study of groups seriously rather than simply looking at the effects of groups on individuals. Lewin's innovations in research methods, applications, and focus still define much of the study of group dynamics today.

Lewin developed a new approach to research in psychology. He began with a belief that "There is nothing so practical as a good theory" (Lewin, 1951, p. 169). His innovation was in refining how theories in psychology should be used. He developed an approach called *action research,* where scientists develop theories about how groups operate, and then use their theories in practical applications to improve the operations of groups. The process of applying a theory and evaluating its effects is then used to refine the theory and improve the operations of groups.

One of Lewin's primary concerns was social change. He believed it is easier to change a group than it is to change an individual. If the behavior of individuals is changed and the individuals return to their everyday life, the influence of the people around them tend to reverse the behavior change. If the behavior of a group of people is changed, the group continues to reinforce or stabilize the behavioral change in its members. Lewin developed models of organizational change and group dynamics techniques that are still used today.

Mainstream social psychologists returned to their focus on theory-oriented laboratory studies during the 1950s and 1960s. Their research primarily examined topics, such as conformity and helping behavior that focused on the effects groups have on individuals rather than on group dynamics. Research on group dynamics shifted to sociologists like Robert Bales, who used the study of small groups as a way to understand social systems. Their research used laboratory groups and led to the development of various systems for categorizing the group process, such as Interaction Process Analysis.

During this period, organizational and humanistic psychologists studied a special type of laboratory group called *t-groups* (also called *encounter groups*). These were small, unstructured groups that were encouraged to engage in open and personal discussions, often over a series of days. Participation in these groups was supposed to increase self-awareness, interpersonal communication skills, and group process skills. Their popularity decreased as concerns with ethics and transfer of training issues raised questions about their value. (See Chapter 17 for a further discussion of these issues.)

By the 1990s, research on teamwork moved from social psychology studies of small groups in laboratories to other disciplines (Stewart, 2010). Researchers from sociology, anthropology, political science, communication, business, and education now study aspects of group dynamics. Although psychological research is still dominated by laboratory research on how groups operate, many other disciplines emphasize applied research and study teams in real-world settings. Theory on group dynamics is changing and becoming more sophisticated (Hackman, 2012). Rather than simple models that look at cause-effect relationships, new models focus on the conditions that help teams manage their own processes. Instead of looking at group behavior as the sum of individual variables, there is a focus on the emergent properties of teams. The search to find the best approach to manage a team has been replaced by the recognition of what is termed *equifinality*—that there are many ways for teams to operate successfully.

LEADING VIRTUAL TEAMS: VIRTUAL MEETINGS AND VIRTUAL COLLABORATION—SELECTING TECHNOLOGIES TO USE FOR YOUR TEAM

Problem: Virtual meetings are mediated by communication and collaboration (shared problem-solving) tools. How does a meeting leader know which tool (or set of tools) to use for a given meeting? And once the tool type is chosen, how does a meeting leader select which product to use?

Solution: Not all virtual meeting tools are alike. Just as a hammer, saw, and screwdriver serve different purposes in a carpenter's toolbox, virtual meeting tools are of different types and serve different purposes. Selecting the wrong virtual meeting tool is akin to trying to hammer in a nail with the back end of a screwdriver: You may get it to work, but it is going to be very difficult and it is unlikely to do a good job.

To determine the appropriate tool for the task, consider: In our meeting, what kind of interaction do we want participants to have during each step of our agenda? Is one person talking to many people? Are people displaying images? Are people building ideas together (perhaps generating a list or writing a document)? Will people need to vote to make a decision? List the specific interactions for each agenda step.

To determine the appropriate product to use for the task, consider: Will one product support the interactions for many or all our agenda items? What products are available to the participants? Are the participants already familiar with a particular product that fulfills our needs? If we have to use multiple products, does the information transfer easily among the products we will use? For any new product: Is it stable and reliable? Is the learning curve for using it short and simple?

Summary

Groups are more than just collections of people. Groups have goals, interdependent relationships, interactions, structured relations, and mutual influence. Individuals are aware of their membership in groups and participate in order to satisfy personal needs. Although the distinction between groups and teams is not completely clear, the term *teamwork* typically is used to describe groups that are parts of sports or work organizations. Team members work interdependently to accomplish goals and have the power to control at least part of their operations.

Organizations are shifting away from individual work performed in hierarchical work structures and toward team-based operations. The changing goals in organizations that must deal with the evolving work environment are driving this shift. Jobs are becoming increasingly complex and interdependent, and organizations are finding that they must be more flexible. All these changes encourage the use of teamwork.

Organizations use teams in a number of ways. Teams provide advice, make things or provide services, create projects, and perform specialized activities. Teams also vary according to the power they are given, their types of leadership and decision-making processes, and the tasks they perform. These factors define the differences among traditional work groups, traditional teams, and self-managing teams.

Working in small groups was common before the Industrial Revolution, but scientific management simplified jobs and created hierarchical work systems. The Hawthorne studies of the 1930s demonstrated the importance of understanding the aspects of work related to social relations. Following World War II, researchers began to experiment with work teams. During the 1960s, STS presented a way to analyze work and identify the need for teams. However, it was the rise of Japanese manufacturing teams during the 1980s that led to the increased use of teamwork in the United States. Paralleling this growth in the use of teams, the social sciences developed the field of group dynamics, which focuses on understanding how groups operate. Today, group dynamics is a scientific field that provides information useful in improving the operations of teams.

Team Leader's Challenge 1

You have just become the manager of an insurance office with five professional agents and several clerical assistants. The office is part of a larger company headquartered in another city. Your office handles both sales and the processing of insurance claims. The office has been traditionally organized, with the manager running the office and supervising each employee individually.

You have heard a lot about the advantages of shifting to teamwork—it is popular in the business press. Shifting to teamwork is supposed to improve customer service, make the office more responsive to changes, and improve morale. However, you have also heard that it can be difficult to create and manage teams. You are comfortable and capable as a traditional manager, but think maybe you should try something new, such as teamwork.

What are the pros and cons of reorganizing the office into a team?

Who should be on the team? Should the team include both the professionals and the clerical assistants?

How much authority or control should you maintain over the team?

SURVEY: ATTITUDES TOWARD TEAMWORK

Purpose: Understand your attitudes about the use of teams at work. Do you believe that teams are an effective way to work? Do you enjoy the social aspects of teamwork? The answers to these questions may help you decide how you want to participate in teams.

Directions: Think about the last time you worked on a team project. Use the following scale to show how much you agree with the list of statements about teamwork:

Strongly Disagree	Disagree	Neutral	Agree	Strongly Agree
1	2	3	4	5

_____ 1. Using a team was an effective way to do the project.

_____ 2. My team was good at resolving internal conflicts and disagreements.

_____ 3. The project the team performed was challenging and important.

_____ 4. I made new friends while working on the team.

_____ 5. My team developed innovative ways of solving team problems.

_____ 6. I really liked getting to know the other members of the team.

_____ 7. Management provided adequate feedback to the team about its performance.

_____ 8. Personal conflicts rarely disrupted the team's functioning.

_____ 9. My team had clear direction and goals.

_____ 10. Team members treated each other with respect.

_____ 11. My team was good at implementing the plans it developed.

_____ 12. The members of my team worked well together.

_____ 13. The assignment my team worked on was well suited for teamwork.

_____ 14. There was rarely unpleasantness among members of the team.
_____ 15. I learned a lot from working on this team.
_____ 16. Participating in the team helped develop my social skills.
_____ 17. My team was good at regulating its own behavior.
_____ 18. I felt supported by my teammates.
_____ 19. My team had good leadership.
_____ 20. The longer we worked together, the better we got along with each other.

Scoring: Add the scores for the odd numbered questions to obtain the score for how you view the task aspects of teamwork. Add the scores for the even numbered questions to obtain the score for how you view the social aspects of teamwork.

Discussion: What does this survey tell you about your attitudes toward the task and social aspects of teamwork? How should you deal with team members who have a negative attitude toward teamwork? What is the relationship between social and task aspects of teamwork?

SOURCE: Adapted from Levi, D., & Slem, C. (1995). Team work in research and development organizations: The characteristics of successful teams. *International Journal of Industrial Ergonomics, 16,* 29–42.

ACTIVITY: WORKING IN TEAMS

Objective: What is it that you like and dislike about working in teams? Use your past experience working on team projects to understand the benefits and problems with teamwork.

Activity: Think about your good and bad experiences working in teams. Meet with other class members and create a list of the good and bad aspects about working on teams.

Analysis: Once your group creates lists of the good and bad things about teamwork, review the items and classify them as *task* or *social aspects* of teamwork. Task issues concern the team's work, while social issues are the social and emotional aspects of working in teams. How does this task or social analysis relate to what you like and dislike about teams? You may also want to compare this analysis with the results of the Attitudes Toward Teamwork survey.

Discussion: There are benefits and problems with working in teams. What can be done to make teams more effective and more enjoyable?

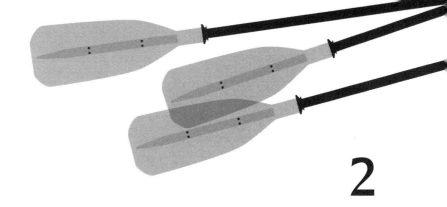

2

Defining Team Success

A successful team completes its task, maintains good social relations, and promotes its members' personal and professional development. All three of these factors are important for defining team success. To perform effectively, a team requires the right types of people, a task that is suitable for teamwork, good internal group processes, and a supportive organizational context. Team members need both an appropriate set of task skills and the interpersonal skills to work as a team. Although teams can perform a wide variety of tasks, appropriate team tasks require that the work of all members is integrated into the final products. The group process should maintain good social relations while at the same time organizing members to perform the task. Finally, the organizational context needs to support the team by promoting cooperation, providing resources, and rewarding success.

Researchers have conducted a number of studies on work teams to determine the characteristics that predict success. Successful teams have clear goals, good leadership, organizational support, appropriate task characteristics, and mutual accountability with rewards. However, the characteristics that predict team success vary depending on the type of team studied. Teams are increasingly being used in the workplace. Teamwork provides many benefits to organizations and their employees, but it is a challenge for organizations to use teams successfully.

Learning Objectives

2.1 (P.20~22)

1. What are the three criteria used to define team success?

2. Why is team success more than just completion of the task?

3. What factors determine whether a team has the right set of people?

4. What types of tasks are better suited for teams than for individuals? Why?

5. How does an organization provide a supportive context for teams?

6. What are the characteristics of successful teams?

7. How does positive psychology define team success?

8. What are the benefits and problems of using work teams?

9. What are the implications when the use of teams becomes a fad?

2.1 Nature of Team Success

One of the prerequisites to studying and understanding teamwork is defining the nature of team success. Existing research on groups and teams uses a variety of measures to study the functioning of teams. Often, research examines these internal measures of team functioning and tries to relate them to external measures of team success.

Measuring the success of teamwork can be difficult. The characteristics that team members and leaders believe are important for success might not be the same characteristics that managers believe are important (Levi & Slem, 1995). Team members focus on the internal operations of the team; they look at the contributions that each member brings to the team and how well members work together. Managers focus on the team's impact on the organization; they are concerned with results, not with how the team operates. There is a danger in using too simplistic a view of success because it may focus on the wrong factors when trying to evaluate and improve a team.

According to Hackman (1987), there are three primary definitions of team success, relating to the task, social relations, and the individual. A successful team completes its task or reaches its goals. While completing the task, team members develop social relations that help them work together and maintain the team. Participation in teamwork is personally rewarding for the individual because of the social support, the learning of new skills, or the rewards given by the organization for participation.

This multiple definition of team success can be seen in action teams, such as fire crews. Obviously, completing the task or putting out the fire is an important criterion of success. However, it is also important that the crews maintain a good working relationship and the crew members do not get injured in the process. Extinguishing the fire is important, but so is preserving the ability of the team to fight future fires.

Completing the Task

From a management perspective, the obvious definition of team success is successful performance on a task. A successful team performs the task better when compared to other ways of organizing people to perform the same task. Although this definition may seem simple, measuring the performance of teams can be difficult. For certain complex tasks, there may be no alternatives to teamwork, making it impossible to compare team and individual outcomes. For professional tasks requiring creativity or value judgments, there may be no clear ways to determine which solutions are best (Orsburn, Moran, Musselwhite, Zenger, & Perrin, 1990). One approach to such measurement problems is to determine whether the products or outputs of the team are acceptable to the owners, customers, and team members. However, these three perspectives may not agree with each other (Spreitzer, Cohen, & Ledford, 1999).

Completing a task successfully as a team is a measure of success, but project success is not a demonstration of team success. Could the task have been completed without a team? What was the benefit of using a team for performing the task? For a particular task, there is often little advantage to using a team. In fact, there are disadvantages because time is "wasted" in developing the team rather than focusing on the task. The advantages of using a team to perform a task occur when unforeseen problems arise and when the team works together on future tasks.

If a project runs smoothly, people working individually under supervision often can perform the necessary task. If a project encounters difficulties, however, the value of a team is demonstrated by the ability of team members to use multiple perspectives to solve problems and motivate one another during the difficult period. Although a team takes time to develop, as people learn to work together they are better able to handle future projects. Many of the benefits of creating a team occur over the long run rather than during the first project the team performs.

Developing Social Relations

Measuring the results of a team's task performance does not completely capture the definition of team success. A successful team performs its task and then is better able to perform the next assigned task. This is the social relations, group maintenance, or viability aspect of teamwork (Sundstrom, DeMeuse, & Futrell, 1990). An important value of teamwork is building the skills and capabilities of the team and organization. For this to happen, the team must have good internal social relations. Performing in the team should encourage participants to want to continue working as a team in the future.

A team must develop social relations among its members. The social interactions necessary for teamwork require group cohesion and good communication. Cohesion comes from the emotional ties that team members have with one another. Good communication depends on understanding and trust. When team members fail to develop good social relations, they do not communicate well, have interpersonal problems that interfere with task performance, and are unable to reward and motivate one another. This limits the ability of the team to continue to operate.

A good example of the problem created when there is too much focus on task performance and too little on social relations is in the computer development team described by Kidder (1981). The team successfully developed a new computer system. However, in the stress of competition and time pressure, the team members burned themselves out. At the end of the project, everyone was happy about the success, but the team members no longer wanted to work together. Was the team a success? Yes, it completed its task, but it failed to develop social relations that encouraged successful teamwork in the future. The capabilities of the team were lost at the end of the project because of its exclusive focus on the task. The organization benefited by getting a new computer system, but it did not improve its ability to use teams to successfully design computer systems in the future. This type of project burnout is all too common in contemporary technology companies.

Benefiting the Individual

The third aspect of team success concerns the individual. Participating in a team should be good for the individual. Teamwork should help improve an individual's social or interpersonal skills (Katzenbach & Smith, 1993). In the workplace, being in a team with members with different expertise or skills should broaden an employee's knowledge and make him or her more aware of other perspectives. In addition to personal development, participating in a team should further an employee's career. Successful contributions to a work team should be reflected in the employee's performance evaluations (O'Dell, 1989).

Working in teams helps satisfy people's social and growth needs. People enjoy working in teams because it increases the social and emotional support they receive. Teams can be great learning experiences. Team members share their knowledge and expertise. As they learn how to be good team members, they also develop communication and organizational skills.

Obviously, these personal benefits are more important to some people than to others. People vary in their social needs; those low in social needs will be less rewarded by teamwork. Some people already have good teamwork skills, whereas others are not interested in learning these skills. Also, the social and learning benefits from teamwork primarily come from successful teams. Working in dysfunctional teams may teach members only how to avoid working in teams in the future.

In addition to personal benefits, participating in a team should help an employee's career in the organization. Unfortunately, this often is not the case. Most organizations focus on managing individuals rather than on managing teams. Even when most of an employee's time is spent collaborating in a team, the typical performance evaluation system focuses on what an individual produces rather than on the success of the team. Being a good team player may go unrecognized, while people who distinguish themselves and stand out are rewarded. This conflict between individual and team success is a major unresolved problem for teamwork in many organizations. (Approaches for dealing with this conflict are discussed in Chapter 16.)

2.2 Conditions for Team Success

The success of a team depends on four conditions (Figure 2.1). First, the team must have the right people to perform the task. Second, the task must be suitable for teamwork. Third, the team must combine its resources

Figure 2.1   Model of Team Interaction

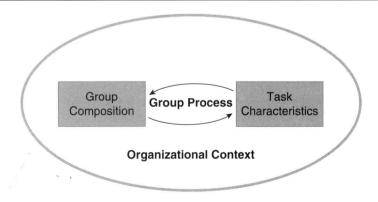

effectively to complete the task. Fourth, the organization must provide a supportive context for the team.

Team Composition

A team's performance depends on the qualities of the individuals performing the task. First, the team must contain people with knowledge, skills, and abilities that match the task requirements. However, the team's members must also have the necessary group process skills to operate effectively. This relates to the social skills and personalities of the team members. Although there are many factors to consider, team leaders are often constrained in their personnel selection options.

Some teams fail because their members do not have the needed knowledge, skills, and abilities to perform their tasks. Good teams have good team members. In their study of highly successful groups, Bennis and Biederman (1997) determined that much of the success of these groups was due to the leaders' ability to recruit highly competent team members. High-performing leaders are not afraid to hire people who are more skilled than they are themselves.

Part of creating an effective team is making sure it has the necessary diversity of knowledge and skills. Interdisciplinary research teams are more productive than teams whose members have similar backgrounds. Teams whose members have differences of opinion are more creative than like-minded teams. Management teams whose members have different backgrounds are more innovative than are homogeneous teams (Guzzo & Dickson, 1996). However, diversity alone is not always a benefit to teams. The advantages of diversity are seen when members are both highly skilled and committed to their team's goals.

There is no guarantee that having many highly talented team members will lead to a high performing team (Swaab, Schaerer, Anicich, Ronay, & Galinsky, 2014). For example, in studies of basketball and other sports teams, having many high performers can lead to conflict and coordination problems that reduce performance compared to teams with fewer high performers. In interdependent sports, such as soccer and basketball, performance can decrease when there are too many high performing athletes, while in more independent sports like baseball, performance increases with more high performing athletes. This is why team member selection should consider both task-related and teamwork-related skills.

Teams require that team members have the skills to work together as a team. Interpersonal skills, problem-solving skills, and teamwork skills may be used as selection criteria for team members, may be taught to team members, or may be inducted through the use of facilitators (Carnevale, Gainer, &

Meltzer, 1990). Interpersonal skills are communication techniques, such as interviewing, active listening, providing feedback, and negotiating. Problem-solving skills improve the effectiveness of teams by providing approaches to analyzing problems and making decisions. Teamwork skills promote an understanding of group processes and provide skills to manage the group processes effectively.

Team members' personalities relate to both their task and social skills (Morgeson, Reider, & Campion, 2005). Conscientious people are task and goal focused; they avoid social loafing and are more likely to engage in cooperative team behavior. Extraversion is a benefit in a team member because he or she likes to work with others and has better social and communication skills. Agreeable individuals are more likely to work cooperatively with others (rather than competitively), and they are better at resolving conflicts. Emotional stability in a person relates to his or her ability to handle stress, maintain a positive perspective, and be cooperative and helpful.

Sometimes, the competency and personality of the weakest or strongest member is most important (Mathieu, Tannenbaum, Donsbach, & Alliger, 2014). For instance, certain technical or leadership skills may be very important to the team's success, and having a team member with these skills is crucial. On the other side, having a very negative team member can lead to dysfunctional group processes, hurt team morale and cohesion, and create conflict within the team. A team member who socially loafs can create inequity problems that lower the motivation of the entire team.

Although team composition is important, team leaders rarely have the information, time, or ability to select an optimal team (Mathieu et al., 2014). Trade-offs need to be made in personnel selection. When replacing a few team members, selection is often based on needed task skills, rather than on teamwork skills. An alternative to focusing on team member selection is the use of other team-building approaches, such as teamwork training, coaching and mentoring, after-action reviews, or teamwork facilitation to develop a team's ability to work effectively together.

Characteristics of the Task

Teams can be used to perform a variety of types of tasks, and tasks vary in how well suited they are for teamwork. A good team task motivates team members and requires coordinated activity. Teams require both appropriate tasks and organizational support for those tasks.

McGrath (1984) developed a system to describe the different types of tasks that teams perform, based on four team goals—generate, choose, negotiate, and execute. Generation includes tasks that focus on the creative generation of new ideas and tasks that develop plans for behavioral action. Choosing deals with intellective tasks, such as problem solving, when there are correct answers and decision-making tasks when there are no correct answers. Negotiation includes tasks aimed at resolving conflicting viewpoints and mixed-motive tasks aimed at resolving conflicts of interest. Execution refers to competitive tasks that help resolve conflicts of power and performance tasks designed to make things or provide services.

McGrath's system explains the different types of tasks a team actually performs. A team may perform only one or two types of tasks. An example is a factory team that primarily performs a physical task and might do some problem solving. Other types of teams may perform many different types of tasks: An example is a project team that both designs and produces a product. Understanding the range of tasks performed by a team is important in selecting and training team members.

Steiner (1972) created a system that explains the different ways that team members' efforts can be combined. The team's work can be added together, limited by the last member, averaged, selected, or combined in any way the team desires. Additive tasks combine team member contributions together, such as when a team paints a house. The productivity of a team will exceed that of the individual team member, but production is often less than the sum of individuals working alone. Conjunctive tasks are not completed until all team members have completed their parts. An example of this is assembly-line work. Although the worst-performing member limits team performance, the team can compensate by providing support to the poor performer. A compensatory task averages the input of team members to create a single solution, while in a disjunctive task the team must generate a single solution that represents the team's product. The decisions of juries and problem solving by technical teams are examples of disjunctive tasks. A team usually performs better than individuals in these types of tasks, but not necessarily better than the best individual in the team. When the team is able to decide how it wants to perform a task, the task is discretionary.

Steiner's system shows that a team performs a variety of tasks that can be combined in different ways, and is useful to explain the benefits of and problems with different ways of combining tasks. For some types of tasks, organizing work into teams can create synergies that improve performance over that of individuals. However, using teams may also reduce performance because of coordination and motivation problems. (These performance losses are discussed in more detail in Chapters 4 and 9.)

A team's task should be aligned with the team's goals and be motivating to the team members (Hackman, 2002). The task should be an identifiable and meaningful piece of work that allows team members to understand their

contributions. Team members need to have the authority and responsibility to exercise judgment about their work practices. The team needs regular and trustworthy feedback about its performance so it can learn how to improve its operation. Finally, the task requires the collective and coordinated efforts of the team members in order to be completed.

The benefits of teamwork are realized only when teams are working on tasks that are suited for teamwork and organizations are willing to support them. Table 2.1 presents a set of task and organizational characteristics that are necessary conditions for the use of teams.

Group Process

Having the right people and the right type of task does not guarantee success for a team. Team members must be able to combine efforts successfully. Teams may not reach their potential if their internal processes interfere with their success. Effective teams organize themselves to perform tasks, develop social relations to support their operations, and assign leaders who can provide direction and facilitate team operations.

Teams communicate in order to make decisions and perform tasks. For both these activities, internal group processes may limit success. Teams may encounter problems with decision making. Teams are imperfect

Table 2.1 When Are Teams Appropriate?

1. The work contains at least some skilled activities.

2. The team can form a meaningful unit with the organization, with clearly defined input and output and stable boundaries.

3. Turnover in the team is minimal.

4. Valid performance evaluation systems exist for both the team and its members.

5. Timely feedback is possible.

6. The team is capable of measuring and controlling the important variances in the workflow.

7. The tasks are highly interdependent so members must work together.

8. Cross-training is supported by management.

9. Jobs can be designed to balance team and individual tasks.

SOURCE: Adapted from Davis, L., & Wacker, G. (1987). Job design. In G. Salvendy (Ed.), *Handbook of human factors* (pp. 431–452). New York, NY: John Wiley.

decision makers and do not always fully use their collected knowledge and skills. Team decisions may be disrupted by personal bias, distorted by the desire to maintain good relationships, or impaired by the desire to make decisions quickly. Teams often become prematurely committed to the first acceptable solution instead of taking a structured approach to problem solving.

Even when teams are organized for the sole purpose of performing certain tasks, group process issues may have both positive and negative impacts on performance. Highly effective teams have task-oriented goals and norms, and these teams outperform collections of individuals. But, things can go wrong. A team can have unclear goals or norms that do not encourage performance of its task. Working in a team can lead to reduced effort by individual members rather than encouraging performance. (This problem, called *social loafing*, is discussed in Chapter 4.)

Internal social relations should provide support for the team. Team members must communicate well, work cooperatively together, and provide emotional support for one another. Teams with high levels of group cohesion and good social relations are the most effective teams. If a team is riddled with conflict and divided into cliques, or if it acts competitively rather than cooperatively, communication can break down.

It is the leader's responsibility to provide direction for the team and facilitate its internal processes. There is no set of rules that a good leader can mechanically follow. Depending on the tasks and team maturity, groups require different types of leadership. The use of teams often changes the nature of leadership because team leaders do not have the same power and authority as traditional managers. The role of the team leader is not to control the team's behavior, but to help create the conditions that allow the team to manage its processes in a changing environment in order to be successful (Hackman, 2012).

Organizational Context

The organizational context has a significant effect on whether teams operate successfully (Guzzo & Dickson, 1996). Teams may be used to improve the operations of organizations, but teams are sensitive to their organizational environments and need the right conditions to succeed. The organizational context relates to the culture of the organization, the support it provides for teams, and its evaluation and reward systems.

Teams are more likely to be successful in organizations with supportive organizational cultures. Supportive cultures encourage open communication and collaborative effort. Power and responsibility are given to teams so they can control their own actions. Although the use of teams can help change an

organization's culture, it can be difficult to initiate change when limits are imposed by the existing culture.

A number of organizational supports should be provided to help teams function more effectively (Hackman, 1990b). Teams perform better when they have clear goals and well-defined tasks. They must be provided with adequate resources, including financial, staffing, and training support. Reliable information from the organization is required for teams to make decisions, coordinate their efforts with other parts of the organization, and plan for future changes. Finally, technical and group process assistance should be available to the teams. They need technical help to solve their problems and facilitation or coaching to deal with interpersonal difficulties.

Building effective teams requires the efforts of both team members and the organization. To improve on the way team members operate, a team needs feedback on its performance and an incentive to change. To an extent, the team can evaluate itself, and team members can provide support for one another, but an effective team requires feedback from the organization and rewards for good performance. Without this, team members cannot focus on the goals the organization has established for the team.

2.3 Characteristics of Successful Teams

What makes successful teams? Many researchers have tried to answer this question. Their typical approach is to find examples of successful teams and use interviews and surveys to determine what makes those teams successful. Although research approaches are similar, the types of teams that researchers investigate often are different. In addition, the types of questions used to examine teams differ depending on the backgrounds of the researchers. The following are several examples of attempts to define the characteristics of successful teams.

Hackman (1987) is an organizational psychologist whose specialty is job design. His research examined a wide variety of teams both at work and in the laboratory. He lists five factors necessary for the successful development of teams:

1. Clear direction and goals. Teams need goals to focus efforts and evaluate performance.

2. Good leadership. Leaders are needed to help manage the internal and external relations of teams and orient teams toward their goals.

3. Tasks suited for teamwork. Tasks should be complex, important, and challenging, requiring the integrated efforts of team members, and the tasks should not be capable of being performed by individuals.

4. Necessary resources to perform tasks. These include material, training, and personnel resources.

5. Supportive organizational environment. Organizations must allocate sufficient power and authority to allow team members to make and implement decisions.

Levi and Slem (1995) are psychologists who examined teamwork in high-tech companies. They studied factory production teams and engineering research and development teams to determine factors related to team success. These are the factors they found necessary for the successful development of teams:

1. Evaluation and rewards. Teams need fair and objective criteria for evaluation, team member performance evaluations should relate to their team contributions, and members should be rewarded when their teams are successful.

2. Social relations. Teams need training in social skills so they can resolve internal conflicts and function smoothly.

3. Organizational support. Management, the organizational system, and the organizational culture must support the use of teams.

4. Task characteristics. Teams need clear direction and goals, tasks that are appropriate for teamwork, and work that is challenging and important.

5. Leadership. Leaders need to facilitate team interactions and provide assistance to teams when problems occur.

Larson and LaFasto (1989) are experts in group communication. They studied a variety of teams from business, sports, and government. Just as in the studies mentioned above, they found that clear goals with standards of excellence, principled leadership, and external support and recognition were important factors in successful teams. In addition, their research indicated that a results-oriented structure, competent team members, a unified commitment, and a collaborative climate were important.

Katzenbach and Smith (1993) are management experts who studied upper-level management teams, primarily in large organizations. They found that clear performance goals, common approaches and methods for completing tasks, and a sense of mutual accountability were factors related to success. In addition, they observed that a team performs best when there are a small number of team members, members have adequate levels of complementary skills, and there is commitment to a common purpose.

Table 2.2 presents a typical list of the characteristics of successful teams. Teams require clear, well-defined goals to provide direction and motivation

Table 2.2   Characteristics of Successful Teams

	Hackman	Levi & Slem	Larson & LaFasto	Katzenbach & Smith
Clear goals	X		X	X
Appropriate leadership	X	X	X	
Organizational support	X	X	X	
Suitable tasks	X	X		X
Accountability and rewards		X	X	X

and to allow for performance evaluation. Leaders keep teams focused on goals and facilitate, but do not control, the teams' activities. The organization's culture and systems must be compatible with teamwork, and organizations must supply teams with the necessary power and resources (e.g., personnel, financial means, training) for task performance. Tasks must be suitable for teamwork. Tasks should require coordinated effort and be both challenging and motivating. Finally, team members should have a sense of common fate or mutual accountability, and their efforts must be evaluated and rewarded in a fair manner.

Although it is useful to try to determine the factors that characterize successful teams, investigations of this type are limited. The differences found by researchers reflect both different research approaches and different types of teams studied. Cohen and Bailey (1997) conducted a meta-analysis of work teams during the 1990s. Their review of 54 studies of work teams shows that the factors important for success are different for production, professional, and managerial teams. For example, for self-managing production teams, the amount of organizational support is very important, but the quality of leadership is relatively unimportant. On the other hand, professional project teams often are dependent on high-quality leadership because of the nonroutine nature of their tasks.

For example, a study of student teams performing a variety of tasks identified a "collective intelligence" factor that predicted successful team performance (Woolley, Chabris, Pentland, Hashmi, & Malone, 2010). Collective intelligence was not correlated with intelligence of the team members, but with three other factors: social sensitivity, equality of communication, and proportion of females. The most important factor predicting team success was social sensitivity, which was a measure of the average level of emotional intelligence of the team members. Equality of communication showed that when team members took turns communicating or when a few people did not dominate the team's communications, they performed better. Increasing the proportion of females on the teams improved performance, although this factor overlapped with the social sensitivity of the teams.

In the past decade, there has been a substantial increase in research on teamwork conducted in applied settings (Mathieu, Maynard, Rapp, & Gilson, 2008). However, this research has not led to a set of rules about how teams should operate. Different types of teams face different challenges, so they need to adopt alternative strategies to be effective. Even for similar types of teams, there are multiple ways for the team to successfully operate. (This is called *equifinality*.) There is no one best model of effective teamwork. In fact, some research suggests it may be more important for team members to share similar models of how to work together than for the model of teamwork used to be especially accurate (Smith-Jentsch, Cannon-Bowers, Tannenbaum, & Salas, 2008).

2.4 Positive Psychology View of Team Success

Positive psychology is a recent and important movement within psychology that studies people's strengths and how to promote positive functioning (Mills, Fleck, & Kozikowski, 2013). Many positive psychology factors are examined in the study of teamwork. Because of its focus on personal development, positive psychology provides an alternative perspective to the meaning of team success and the factors that contribute to it.

Most models of team success focus on task performance, and then include social relations and individual development as support factors. A positive psychology perspective toward team success starts with team member well-being. When team members are fully engaged in the task and they have developed positive and supportive relationships with other team members, then the team is poised for successful performance (Richardson & West, 2010). The positive psychology approach to teamwork attempts to develop teams that help its members satisfy their social and emotional needs while working together to meet the team's challenges and goals.

An overview of the inputs, processes, and outcomes of teamwork from a positive psychology perspective is presented in Figure 2.2. This input-process-output model assumes that a set of team inputs leads to the development of team processes, and these team processes create the conditions for successful performance. From a positive psychology perspective, a team's outcomes

Figure 2.2   Positive Psychology Model of Team Success

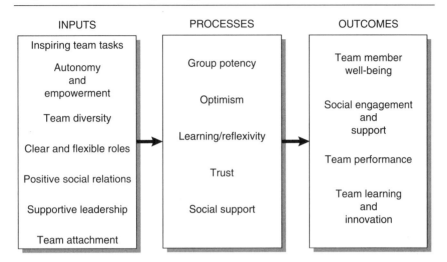

SOURCE: Adapted from Richardson, J., & West, M. (2010). Dream teams: A positive psychology of team working. P. Linley, S. Harrington, & N. Garcea (eds.) Oxford Handbook of Positive Psychology and Work (pp. 235–249). New York: Oxford University Press.

include team performance and emotional, cognitive, and social benefits for individual team members (Richardson & West, 2010). Successful teamwork also provides other benefits to the organization, including better relationships among teams and increased altruism (cooperation and helping behavior) with other parts of the organization. Finally, successful teams are learning teams that seek creative and innovative ways to improve how they operate.

There are several important inputs that create the foundation for positive team performance (Richardson & West, 2010). Teams need to have an inspiring task that motivates team member participation. The task should encourage interdependent work, require members to employ their skills, be perceived as a meaningful activity, allow the team a high degree of autonomy, and provide timely feedback about performance. Teams should contain diverse members and create a safe environment that supports participation by all team members. Team members need clear work roles and the ability for roles and responsibilities to evolve as the team progresses. The team needs to develop supportive personal relationships among its members, through regular interactions, management of conflicts, and encouragement of mutual assistance. Supportive leadership helps to create an inspiring vision for the team and uses monitoring, coaching, and feedback to guide team performance. Team members should develop a healthy attachment to the team by encouraging the development of trust and social relations among members.

These team inputs lead to a set of positive team processes that support enriching teamwork interactions (Richardson & West, 2010). Team members have a sense of group potency where they collectively believe that they have the skills and abilities to succeed. Team members are optimistic about their abilities to cope with adversity and meet their objectives in the future. Team learning becomes an ongoing activity, which is supported by reflexivity—taking time to reflect on their performance and strategies and to learn from their experiences. Team members have a high level of trust to support clear communication and to coordinate activities. Team members provide each other with social support to help provide assistance with performance, and emotional support to counter stress.

The positive psychology approach to teamwork leads to better team performance by focusing on the emotional and cognitive benefits to team members. It provides an alternative perspective on the meaning of team success and how to promote more effective teamwork. Many positive psychology factors are examined in the study of teamwork, such as the impact of supportive personal relations, reflexivity and learning, team efficacy, empowerment, supportive leadership, and appreciative inquiry (Mills et al., 2013).

2.5 Using Teams in the Workplace

Work teams are an important way of improving organizational effectiveness. The transition to use of work teams in factories and offices is considered necessary to help corporations remain competitive (Gwynne, 1990). In fact, the implementation of work teams is one of the most common organizational interventions in manufacturing firms (Sundstrom et al., 1990). It is also one of the most effective interventions for improving organizational performance (Guzzo & Dickson, 1996). In addition to increasing the financial success of companies, teamwork programs improve personnel issues, such as reducing turnover and absenteeism.

Although there are many benefits to using teams at work, developing work teams is not always easy. Organizations encounter a number of problems shifting from traditional work systems to teamwork. Because of the popularity of teams, they are sometimes used in situations where traditional approaches are more appropriate. This can make it difficult to evaluate the success of teamwork in organizations.

Benefits of Teamwork

Teamwork is increasing because teams are an effective way to improve performance and job satisfaction. Large-scale studies on the use of production work teams show their effectiveness (Guzzo & Dickson, 1996). Teams improve both the efficiency and the quality of organizational performance. Using teams provides the flexibility needed to operate in today's rapidly changing business world. When work teams are widespread in an organization, the organization tends to show improvement in other performance areas, such as employee relations. However, teams may develop performance problems that limit their effectiveness, and the initial transition to teamwork may be a difficult process for organizations.

In addition to increasing organizational effectiveness, the implementation of work teams often leads to improvements in job satisfaction and quality of work life (Sundstrom et al., 1990). Teams have these beneficial characteristics because they provide social support to employees, encourage cooperation, and make jobs more interesting and challenging. Furthermore, the transition to teamwork requires training that improves employees' technical and interpersonal skills. Employees view this additional training as a personal benefit.

Problems of Teamwork

Although there are benefits to both organizations and employees, some problems are created by the use of teams and the transition to teamwork. Research on teamwork in work settings provides mixed results. Many of the studies on quality circles (i.e., temporary teams that provide suggestions about how to improve quality) show that these teams are not effective, whereas studies of factory work teams have widely variable results (Guzzo & Dickson, 1996). One of the problems is that teamwork programs are implemented with little consideration for their applicability. Rather than attempting to make existing programs work better, new programs are introduced.

Teamwork programs like quality circles provide only limited power to teams. Such programs often lead to small short-run improvements in performance, but not to long-term improvements (Guzzo & Dickson, 1996). The shift to self-managing work teams often results in significant long-term performance improvements. However, the transition to self-managing teams can be difficult in organizations with traditional management control systems.

Effective work teams have norms that support high-quality performance and a level of group cohesiveness that provides social support for members. Nevertheless, work teams may have problems with norms and cohesiveness. Teams with poor performance norms may not be effective and may be highly resistant to change. Low levels of group cohesion may limit team members' ability to work together, whereas high levels of group cohesion may lower members' performance orientation and impair decision making (Nemeth & Staw, 1989).

Implementing work teams often creates problems. Conflicts exist between team development and the traditional management systems in many organizations (Hackman, 1990a). Teams suffer from implementation problems because of resistance to change. Teamwork requires a supportive organizational context to foster team growth and development.

When the Use of Teams Becomes a Fad

Many managers and employees overrate the effectiveness of teamwork (Allen & Hecht, 2004). People often overemphasize the success of work teams because of the psychological benefits of teamwork, which assumes that teams are high performing. Although research on the effectiveness of work teams is mixed, these mixed findings are not synchronous with the positive view of teamwork held by many managers. The implementation of work teams has been one of the most common organizational changes of the past 20 years. Team use and the benefits of teamwork have become a business fad and organizations now suffer from the subsequent problems of overuse (Charan & Useem, 2002). (—)

One result of the overly positive view of teamwork is that use of teams has expanded beyond the point where they are valuable (Allen & Hecht, 2004). They are used to solve every organizational problem, regardless of whether teams are an appropriate way to organize the work. This means that many teams operate in organizational contexts that are inappropriate for teamwork. The strong belief in the effectiveness of teams also leads to implementation of teams without the organizational changes needed to support the team (Charan & Useem, 2002). Managers implement teams, looking for benefits without considering the costs of training teams and other ensuing organizational changes (Paulus, 2002).

What is needed is a better understanding of where and when teams should be deployed and what actions are required to deploy them effectively. Teams are not the solution to every organizational problem, and they are not automatically successful. They need a purpose, an outcome that requires joint efforts, complementary skills, and mutual responsibility (Katzenbach & Smith, 2001). Organizations get in trouble when the goal of a team is promoting teamwork (a process goal) rather than an identified performance outcome.

Summary

The definition of team success relates to team tasks, social relations, and impact on team members. Successful teams complete their tasks and do so in a collective way that is better than when only individuals perform the tasks. Teams must develop good social relations to support task activities and maintain the existence of the team. Participating in teams should be a benefit to team members, both in terms of learning new skills and in advancing individual careers.

The success of a team depends on the composition of the team, characteristics of the task, the group process, and the organizational context. There are three important aspects of team composition. A team must have members with the right set of knowledge, skills, and abilities to complete its task. For some types of teams, members must represent the relevant parts of an organization to ensure a sense of participation in the decision and support for its implementation. Finally, team members must have the interpersonal skills to work together as a team.

Teams perform a variety of tasks that require different sets of skills. The tasks that teams perform may be analyzed by examining how a member's input relates to the products. For a task in which the team's work is simply added together, the team performs no better than the same number of individuals working alone. When the poorest performing member limits completion of a task, the team performs better because it can compensate for individual problems. For a task that requires the team to make a quality decision, the team often performs better than individuals working alone. A good team task is one that is motivating to the team and requires a coordinated effort to perform.

The group process connects the members of a team to its task. Successful group processes organize the group to complete the task, develop supportive social relations, and assign leaders to provide direction and facilitation. For each of these steps, the team must overcome obstacles that interfere with its interpersonal dynamics.

The organization provides a context for the team. The organization's culture supports the team by creating an environment that encourages collaboration and allows the team to control its internal operations. The organization's systems support the team by providing direction, resources, information, and assistance. One of the most important aspects of the organizational context is the willingness of the organization to provide feedback on a team's performance and to reward successful performance.

Researchers from a variety of perspectives have identified several common features of successful teams: Teams have clear goals that provide direction and motivation. Team leaders structure tasks and facilitate group processes. Their organizations provide supportive contexts for the team's growth. The tasks that teams perform are well suited for teamwork. Finally, team members are held mutually accountable for the success of their teams, and they are rewarded for their efforts. Although these are characteristics of successful teams, the importance of these various characteristics changes depending on the types of teams.

Positive psychology provides an alternative perspective toward team success by focusing on the individual. When team members are fully engaged in their tasks and feel supported by other team members, then the team's performance is likely to be successful.

The use of work teams is increasing because of the many benefits they provide to organizations. Teams help make the organization more productive and flexible, while improving employees' job satisfaction. However, teams are not the solution to every organizational problem. Organizations need to provide a supportive context for teams to be effective. Because of the popularity of work teams, they are sometimes overused. This makes it difficult to evaluate the success of teams at work.

Team Leader's Challenge 2

You are the team leader of a quality improvement team for your school district. For the past several months, the eight high school teachers on the team have analyzed problems and developed recommendations for improving the operation of the school system. You are proud of the team. They responded well to teamwork training and learned how to operate effectively as a team. In addition, social relations among the teachers on the team have been very good and several strong friendships have developed.

You presented the recommendations (developed by the team) to the superintendent of the school district. After waiting for several weeks, the superintendent thanked you for your efforts, but told you that none of the team's recommendations would be implemented at this time because of budget constraints. You feel rejected by the superintendent and discouraged. It is time for your last team meeting. You need to prepare what you are going to tell the team.

How should you (the team leader) handle the last meeting with the team?

In what ways was the team successful and unsuccessful?

How can the organization better use improvement teams in the future?

ACTIVITY: UNDERSTANDING TEAM SUCCESS

Objective: Why are some teams successful while others are unsuccessful? Use your experience with teams to answer this question.

Activity: Think about a time when you were on a successful team. Using Activity Worksheet 2.1, write a description of the team at that time. (What was it like being on the team? What was the team like?) Think about a time when you were on an unsuccessful team. Write a description of the team at that time.

ACTIVITY WORKSHEET 2.1
Successful and Unsuccessful Teams

Successful Team:

Unsuccessful Team:

Analysis: Compare the two descriptions of successful and unsuccessful teams. What characteristics may explain the differences between these two teams? Compare your answers with those of other group members. Are the characteristics similar? Develop a group answer to the following question: What are the characteristics of successful teams?

1. _____

2. _____

3. _____

4. _____

Discussion: Using your list of the characteristics of successful teams, what advice would you give a team leader about how to establish and run a team?

PART II

Processes of Teamwork

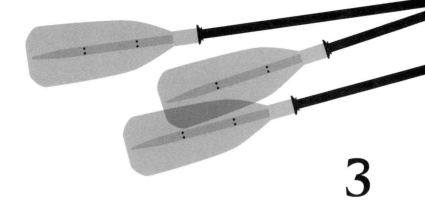

3

Team Beginnings

Teams develop through a series of stages that reflect changes in their internal group processes and the demands of their tasks. This perspective of team stages produces one of the most important insights about teams: They often are not productive at the beginning of projects.

To become more effective, teams should address several issues early in their development. First, the team should socialize new members into the team. This socialization process assimilates new members while accommodating their individual needs. Second, the purpose or objective of the team should be defined through the creation of team goals. Developing team goals is an important process that helps avoid problems, provides direction, and increases motivation. Third, the team should develop rules or team norms for its operation. These norms define appropriate behavior for team members.

There are techniques to help teams form social relations, clarify tasks, develop team norms, and create a team contract. If these techniques are used at the beginning of a team project, teams are more likely to be effective.

Learning Objectives

1. What are the main stages of group development?

2. How do the demands of a project change the way a team operates?

3. What are the implications of team development stages?

4. How do changes in team membership affect team performance?

5. What are the main characteristics of team goals?

6. What are hidden agendas? How do they affect a team?

7. What are the main functions of group norms?

8. What are the positive and negative effects of group norms?

9. What can a team do to help improve the beginning stages of a team project?

3.1 Stages of Teamwork

Research on project teams shows that the start-up activities take longer than anticipated. For many professional design projects, most of the design work occurs during the last half of the allotted time (Gersick, 1988). The main reason for this slow start is that it takes time to clarify the definition of the project, develop social relations, and create effective operating rules. An understanding of group development can help speed up this process and reduce frustration caused by what members often perceive as a sluggish start.

Several approaches exist to explain the changes that teams experience during their operation: Stage theories of group development focus on how internal group processes change over time. Project development theories attempt to describe how teams change based on the tasks that they perform. Finally, cyclical theories explain group process changes as cycles rather than as stages.

Group Development Perspective

There are many stage theories of group development, but most of the theories contain similar elements. The theories try to explain why it takes time for a group to develop before it becomes productive and why the group goes through periods of conflict during its development. Table 3.1 presents the best-known group development stage theory, developed by Tuckman and Jensen (1977). This theory focuses on the development of internal relations among the team members.

A group begins with the forming stage, where little work occurs. Group members get to know one another and learn how to operate as a group. Members tend to be polite and tentative with one another and compliant toward the leader. They often feel uncomfortable and constrained because

Table 3.1   Stages of Group Development

Stage	Activity
Forming	Orientation: members getting to know one another
Storming	Conflict: disagreement about roles and procedures
Norming	Structure: establishment of rules and social relationships
Performing	Work: focus on completing the task
Adjourning	Dissolution: completion of task and end of the group

SOURCE: Adapted from Tuckman, B., & Jensen, M. (1977). Stages of small group development revisited. *Group and Organizational Studies, 2,* 419–427.

they are unfamiliar with the other members. Group members are uncertain about how to act, and they spend time planning how to perform their tasks. This stage ends when the group members become comfortable interacting with one another.

The storming stage that follows often is characterized by conflicts among group members and confusion about group roles and project requirements. Disagreements over procedures can lead to expressions of dissatisfaction and hostility. Group members begin to realize that the project is more difficult than anticipated, and they may become anxious and defensive. Conflict about their roles and the task expands. Although this conflict might be unpleasant, it is important that it occur because it promotes the sharing of different perspectives. Resolution of this conflict clarifies the group's goals and often leads to increased group cohesion.

The group begins to organize itself to work on the task during the norming stage. Here, the group becomes more cohesive, conflict is reduced, and team confidence improves. The group has established some ground rules (or norms) to help members work together, and social relations have developed enough to create a group identity. Increased levels of trust and support characterize group interactions. Although differences still exist and continue to arise, they are handled through constructive discussion and negotiation.

During the performing stage, the group has matured and knows how to operate, so it focuses on its task. If the group has developed norms and successfully built social relations, it can easily handle the stress of approaching deadlines. Studies of groups show that most performance occurs during this stage, near the end of the group project (Hare, 1982). However, not all groups get to this stage and may get bogged down in conflict at earlier stages.

The final stage is the adjourning stage. Some groups have planned endings, while other groups may continue indefinitely. When teams end, they should spend time evaluating their performance and using this feedback to prepare for the future (Wheelan, 2005). However, team endings often are not learning experiences for the team; members may be more interested in celebrating their success or finding excuses for their failures than they are in learning from the team experience (Hackman & Wageman, 2005).

Project Development Perspective

An alternative view of team stages is based on the characteristics of projects rather than on the development of group processes. These theories are based on research on work teams, whereas group development theories often are based on research on therapy or learning groups. For example, McIntyre and Salas (1995) present a model of team development based on the skills that team members develop while completing a project. In their model, a team works on role clarification during the early stages, moves on to coordinated skills development, and finally focuses on increasing the variety and flexibility of its skills as a team. This model uses the changing relationship between the team and the project as the driver of change throughout the stages.

McGrath (1990) proposes a model of how project teams operate over time. The team performs four types of functions: inception (selecting and accepting goals), problem solving, conflict resolution, and execution. During the inception stage, the team is focused on planning activities and collaborating. During the conflict resolution stage, social relations are strained because the team is dealing with conflict. The problem-solving and execution stages focus on coordinating the ideas or actions of the team members. A team does not necessarily need to perform all these functions to achieve its goals. For example, on simple problems the group may go directly from inception to execution without the middle functions.

Ancona and Caldwell (1990) present a model of group development for new product teams. Their three stages of development are based on the changing nature of the tasks and how these changes affect internal processes and external relations. During the creation stage, a team's activities are a mixture of internal and external processes. The team is developing new ideas and creative solutions while organizing the team. External relations include gathering information and building links with relevant organizational units. During the development stage, the team's focus is primarily internal. The project's idea has been approved by the organization, and the team is focused on the technical details of the project. The final stage is diffusion, where external relations become the primary focus of the team. The project is nearly complete, and coordinating its transfer to manufacturing and marketing is the focus of the team's activities.

Cyclical Perspective

Although stage theories of group development are popular, not all teams follow the patterns found in these theories. Some teams skip stages, others get stuck in certain stages, and still others seem to travel through the stages by unique routes. The boundaries between the stages are often less clear-cut than the theories suggest.

Rather than emphasizing a sequence of stages, some team theorists believe that groups go through cycles that can be repeated throughout the life of the team. Marks, Mathieu, and Zaccaro (2001) developed a recurring phase model of teamwork showing how teams perform in temporal cycles of activity that create a rhythm for the team. These cycles may vary from the hourly tasks of production and service teams to project teams with multiyear cycles. The length of the cycle is determined by the task. Teams operate in action cycles (when they are performing their tasks), interpersonal cycles (when they are managing social relations), and transition cycles (when they are evaluating their performance and planning for the future). These cycles can occur in various patterns as needed or at designated times. For example, military teams have formal debriefings (transition cycles) that occur after major activities.

From her research on project teams, Gersick (1988) developed a theory of punctuated equilibrium. Each team had its own pattern of development, but all the teams experienced periods of low activity, followed by bursts of energy and change. In addition, each team had a midpoint crisis when its members realized that half their time was gone, but the project was still in its early stages of completion. This led to a period of panic, followed by increased activity as the team focused on completing the task.

The Gersick punctuated equilibrium model argues that the main reason teams change is when they are faced with external challenges that cause them to reevaluate their current practices (Humphrey & Aime, 2014). One implication of this model is that making the team focus on task strategy is beneficial during the midpoint crisis, rather than at the beginning of the team's development. When teams encounter disruptive events or challenges, they are more willing to reevaluate their routine practices and make changes.

Implications of Team Development Stages

Understanding the stages that teams typically go through can help team members better recognize what is happening to the team and how to manage it. Stage theories explain why most of the team's work gets done at the end of the project and why it is important to build social relations and team norms at the beginning of the project. However, it is important to remember that stage theories of team development do not always apply. A team's life is often a roller coaster of successes and failures. Activities may increase or decrease at different points in time, but they may not fully stop and go away (Humphrey & Aime, 2014). Some teams get stuck at one of the stages or even break up—they never get to the performing stage because they have not worked through their earlier problems (Wheelan, 2005).

Can competent teams skip these development stages and just start performing? Sometimes, a team's early successes can cause them to ignore the task of developing team processes. Highly self-confident project teams may simply focus on the task without adequately debating how they should perform their work (Goncalo, Polman, & Maslach, 2010). Early process conflict not only helps a team develop better work processes and strategies, but it teaches the team how to manage conflicts (Tekleab, Quigley, & Tesluk, 2009). This is why early process conflict is a predictor of later success for project teams. When these teams encounter problems in the later stages of a project, they have the skills to manage the conflict and develop alternative solutions.

Several lessons are important here. First, emotional highs and lows are a normal part of team development. Second, developing the team is important. Time must be spent developing social relations and socializing new members, establishing goals and norms, and defining the project. Third, the team may go through periods of lower task performance as it tries to resolve conflicts over relationship and task issues. This is a normal part of team development as well.

3.2 Group Socialization

A person becomes a member of a group through a process referred to as group socialization. Traditional approaches to group socialization explain how new members are recruited and integrated into relatively permanent groups or teams. Contemporary approaches examine how work teams deal with constantly changing team membership.

In the traditional approach to group socialization, an individual goes through a series of role transitions—from newcomer to full member—during the socialization process. At each step in this process, the individual is evaluating the team and deciding on his or her level of commitment (Moreland & Levine, 1982). Evaluation is the judgment whether the benefits of participation in a team outweigh the costs. Commitment is the desire to maintain a relationship with the team. These processes are mutual. The individual evaluates the team and decides on a level of commitment, and the team evaluates the individual and decides how committed it is to him or her.

The socialization process starts with the investigation stage, where the team attempts to recruit the individual while the individual decides whether to join the team. The socialization stage determines how the individual is integrated into the team. The newcomer spends time seeking out what is expected of him or her by the team, and team members provide information through both formal and informal orientation activities (Wanous, 1980). At the beginning, the newcomer often is anxious about his or her role in the team and tends to be passive, dependent, and conforming. This style actually increases the newcomer's acceptance by established team members (Moreland & Levine, 1989). The newcomer is a threat to the team because he or she brings in a fresh and objective perspective that can be unsettling to existing members. The passive approach adopted by many newcomers reduces the potential threat of criticism of the team and thereby encourages acceptance of the new member.

During the maintenance stage, the individual is fully committed to the team. Even though the individual is a full member of the team, there is an ongoing process of negotiating his or her role and position in the team and the team's goals and practices. Although many members stay in this stage until they leave the team, members may diverge from the team and reduce their commitment because of conflicts between their personal goals and the team's goals.

Keeping teams together for longer periods of time can help to improve performance (Huckman & Staats, 2013). Teams experience a learning curve; they do better as members become familiar with each other. Teams with more experience are better at communicating and coordinating their activities. They have a greater understanding of the knowledge and abilities of individual team members, so they are more effective at applying information to problems. They are better able to respond to stress and change. In research on project teams, teams with greater familiarity were better able to gain the benefits of diversity from team members.

However, in many work organizations, teams have a dynamic composition where frequently new members join and others leave during the life of the team (Tannenbaum, Mathieu, Salas, & Cohen, 2012). Rather than the presence of permanent teams, it is now increasingly common to find temporary teams that have to quickly adjust to new members. There are even "flash" teams, such as emergency surgery teams, airline crews, or disaster relief teams, that are quickly formed to address a need. Many professionals work in multiple teams (Maynard, Mathieu, Gibson, & Rapp, 2012).

These teams can be central or peripheral to the team member's role in the organization. Peripheral team members, who only allocate a small percentage of their time to the team, are less likely to be committed to the team and less aware of how the team operates.

Turnover of team members can have positive and negative effects on a team (Levine & Choi, 2004). The introduction of newcomers requires the team to spend time and energy socializing them. New members may reduce the team's performance because they do not fully understand how the team operates (Bell, Villado, Lukasik, Belau, & Briggs, 2010). However, newcomers may improve the team's operations by providing a fresh perspective. In essence, as the team socializes new members, those newcomers may encourage the team to rethink how it operates (Tannenbaum et al., 2012).

Although turnover may negatively impact team performance, there are approaches teams can use to manage this issue (Higgins, Weiner, & Young, 2012). For some action and professional teams, the stability of team roles, but not membership in those roles, is what is important for team performance. This focus on roles rather than on team members has implications for team socialization. Socialization of new team members focuses on their roles in the team instead of on a particular individual's fit or social relations in the team. This approach toward team roles is used in performance teams, such as orchestras, military, and athletic teams. Although the team membership changes, the team itself remains intact.

3.3 Team Goals

Team goals are "a desirable state of affairs members intend to bring about through combined efforts" (Zander, 1994, p. 15). A clear understanding of a team's objectives through well-articulated goals is one of the most common characteristics of successful teams (Larson & LaFasto, 1989). Research on work teams shows that clear project goals help improve team performance and internal team processes (McComb, Green, & Compton, 1999). A team with shared goals is more likely to complete its tasks on time and involve less internal conflict.

Goals are only one way a team can define its purposes: There are other ways. Teams often create mission statements that in general terms define their purposes and values. A mission statement articulates a team's values, but does not say how the team's purposes will be fulfilled. A team's goals must be consistent with the mission statement, but goals should be objective, defining the accomplishments that need to be completed for success. A team also can create subgoals or objectives that serve as signposts along the way to completion of their goals.

Value and Characteristics of Goals

The value of team goals is to provide the team with direction and motivation. Good team goals are clear and specific, so team members can understand them and relate the goals to their own performance (Locke & Latham, 1990). Progress toward the goals should be measurable (Zander, 1994). If progress toward the goals is not measurable, the team cannot receive adequate feedback on its performance. Without measurability, one might as well tell the team to "go out and do your best"—a nice motivational expression that does not lead to improved performance.

Goals should be moderately difficult. That is, they should be motivating, but not impossible to achieve (Locke & Latham, 1990). Team goals work best when the task is interesting, challenging, and requires that team members work together to succeed. The team feels a sense of accomplishment when it reaches the goals (Zander, 1994). However, care should be taken not to establish goals that are too difficult. When a team repeatedly misses its goals, members become embarrassed, begin to blame one another and outside factors for problems, and may refuse to commit to goals in the future (Zander, 1977).

Teams perform better when they are able to participate in setting challenging performance goals (Kerr & Tindale, 2004). Participation helps gain acceptance and support for the team's goals. The goal-setting process helps the team better understand the task. Participation also encourages collective efficacy, or the belief that the team is capable of meeting its goals.

Goals serve a variety of functions for a team. Table 3.2 lists several of these functions. Goals help direct and motivate the team and its members,

Table 3.2   Functions of Team Goals

1. Serve as a standard that can be used to evaluate performance

2. Motivate team members by encouraging their involvement in the task

3. Guide the team toward certain activities and encourage integration of team members' tasks

4. Provide a criterion for evaluating whether certain actions and decisions are appropriate

5. Serve as a way to inform outside groups about the team and establish relationships with them

6. Determine when team members should be rewarded or punished for their performance

SOURCE: Adapted from Zander, A. (1994). *Making groups effective*. San Francisco, CA: Jossey-Bass.

but they also serve functions outside the team. They help establish relationships with other parts of the organization and criteria for evaluation from the surrounding organization.

It is important to note that a team is not always free to set its own goals. Rather, team goals are often defined by their organizations. There are times when a team is faced with a situation where the goals are unclear or team members have differing views of the goals. For a project team, sometimes understanding the problem the team is trying to solve (i.e., defining the goals of the project) is more difficult and time consuming than developing a solution. Improving the quality of team goals through goal-setting activities is a solution to these problems and is discussed in Chapter 17.

Goal setting is not a onetime activity for a team. One of the values of using teams is their ability to adapt to changing situations and to learn how to improve their performance. When the situation changes, a team needs to reevaluate its goals and objectives. Reflexivity occurs when a team overtly reflects on its goals, strategies, and processes in order to adapt them to current or changing conditions (West, 2004). Periodically meeting to review the team's objectives, strategies, and processes can improve a team's long-term performance.

Hidden Agendas

Team goals provide a number of valuable functions, but they also can be a source of problems. Problems arise from hidden agendas, which are unspoken individual goals that conflict with overall team goals (Johnson & Johnson, 1997).

The most basic type of hidden agenda relates to the motivational aspect of goals. Although the team may decide to commit itself 100% to doing a high-quality job on a project, some team members may not perceive the team's activities as important. They might decide to slack off and spend more time and effort on other activities. Their goal is to help the team succeed with the least amount of effort on their part.

A second type of hidden agenda relates to the directional aspect of goals. Some team members may not agree with the goals of the team, or they may have individual goals that are incompatible with the team goals. For example, in an organization budget committee, team members must deal with the potentially conflicting goals of doing what is best for the organization versus doing what is best for the departments they represent.

Within a team, hidden agendas can create conflict that is difficult to resolve. For example, a low motivated team member will create excuses rather than tell the team he or she is unwilling to work hard on the project.

A team member with conflicting loyalties will hide this conflict, leading other team members to distrust what the team member says. The overall effect of hidden agendas is to damage trust within the team, which reduces communication and makes conflicts more difficult to resolve.

Directly confronting people about hidden agendas often does not work, because it simply forces defensiveness and denial. Rather than directly confronting a team member about a hidden agenda, the team can strengthen its processes to reduce the impacts of hidden agendas. The team can reevaluate its goals so they are acceptable to all team members. Team members' roles can be renegotiated so that expectations are clear. Teams can build trust through better documenting and monitoring of work commitments. Team leaders can help create a safe and open communication climate so that conflicts are more easily addressed.

3.4 Team Norms

Team norms are the ground rules that define appropriate and inappropriate behavior in a team. They establish expectations about the behavior of team members. These rules may be explicit (e.g., use consensus decision making) or implicit (e.g., team members take turns when talking). Although most teams do not formally state their norms, members typically are aware of the rules and follow them.

There are four main functions of team norms (Feldman, 1984). First, team norms express the team's central values, which help give members a sense of who they are as a team. Second, norms help coordinate the activities of team members by establishing common ground and making behavior more predictable. Third, norms help define appropriate behavior for team members, allowing members to avoid embarrassing or difficult situations, thereby encouraging active participation in the team. Fourth, norms help the team survive by creating a distinctive identity; this identity helps team members understand how they are different from others and provides criteria for evaluating deviant behavior within the team.

A number of factors affect the power of team norms to control the behavior of team members (Shaw, 1981). The clearer and more specific a norm is delineated, the more members will conform to it. If most team members accept and conform to the norms, others are more likely to conform. The more cohesive a team becomes, the more conformity there will be to team norms. Teams are more tolerant of deviance from peripheral norms than from norms that are central to their operations (Schein, 1988). For example, technical experts who are valuable contributors to the team may be allowed to violate peripheral norms concerning dress codes or rules of social etiquette.

How Norms Are Formed

Team norms often develop unconsciously and gradually over time. They are created by mutual influence and develop through the interactions of team members. Even though people obey these norms, they may be unable to articulate them. In addition, team members typically obey norms even when there is no external pressure to comply, such as the threat of punishment. This example shows that team members have accepted the norms and are using them to guide their own behavior.

Team norms come from a variety of sources. Teams can develop norms based on those from other teams they previously joined. Norms can be based on outside standards, such as those outlined by other social or organizational teams. Norms also are strongly influenced by what happens early in the team's existence, and they are most likely to develop in situations where members are unsure of correct or acceptable behaviors. For example, when a team is having problems with members showing up late for meetings, the team is likely to develop explicit norms for attendance.

Many teams simply ignore the notion of team norms. They assume that everyone knows how to behave in a team and that there is no need to take the time to articulate norms. It is not until a team starts to have problems that it becomes apparent that different members are operating under different norms. Teams benefit from discussing and establishing explicit team norms, which prevents the development of inappropriate norms (e.g., it is acceptable to be late in submitting one's part of the project) and makes everyone aware of the behaviors that are expected. Table 3.3 presents some issues to consider when establishing team norms for team meetings. When new teams are created, it is useful for the team leader to discuss and obtain agreement about norms. This can be done as part of the process of creating the team's contract. (See Appendix for an example.)

Because teams often rely on information and communications technology, it is important to develop norms about the use of technology (Duarte & Snyder, 2006). Teams need to decide which technologies to use for task and social communication and how electronic documents are shared and managed. For example, technology norms may address issues, such as the expected speed of response to messages, when the entire team is included in a message, who is allowed to edit shared documents, and what is the appropriate size of email and text messages. Finally, teams need to decide when face-to-face communication is necessary. (See Appendix for activity related to establishing technology norms.)

Table 3.3 Norm Issues for Team Meetings

Decisions	How should decisions be made? Must everyone agree for consensus? Should anyone have veto power?
Attendance	What are legitimate reasons for missing meetings? How should the team encourage regular attendance?
Assignments	When assignments are made, what should be done when team members do not complete them, or complete them poorly?
Participation	What should be done to encourage everyone to participate?
Meeting times	When should meetings occur? How often should the team meet? What should be the length of a team meeting?
Agendas and minutes	Who should be responsible for these activities? What other meeting roles should be set up?
Promptness	What should be done to encourage promptness?
Conversational courtesies	How should the team encourage members to listen attentively and respectfully to others? Should the team have rules to limit interruptions or prevent personal criticisms?
Enforcement	How should the team enforce its rules?

SOURCE: Adapted from Scholtes, P. (1988). *The team handbook: How to use teams to improve quality*. Madison, WI: Joiner Associates.

Impact of Team Norms

Team norms have positive and negative aspects. Because they control the team's interactions, norms allow fairer communication, maintain respect among members, and distribute power to weaker members of the team. For example, decision norms like using consensus can limit the power of the leader; equal participation norms can prevent team meetings from being overwhelmed by talkative people; and courtesy norms can prevent bullying and intimidation. These are a benefit to the internal workings of the team. However, norms enforce conformity, which can be a problem from the organization's perspective.

The Hawthorne studies of teamwork showed the benefits of and problems with team norms. In a factory setting, team norms controlled the amount of work people performed. When the team had high performance norms, norms were a benefit because they kept laggards in line and encouraged workers to help one another. When the team had low performance norms, however, the ability of management to change the team's behavior was limited because group norms were resistant to outside influence.

3.5 Application: Jump-Starting Project Teams

Organizing people into teams to complete projects often leads to initial drops in performance because it takes time for teams to develop their internal social processes and approaches to the task (Katzenbach & Smith, 1993). When new teams are formed, techniques can be used to help speed their development. Improving teamwork requires effort at the beginning of the project. Teams that start off well often perform better over time (Hackman, 1990a). This statistic validates why spending time designing and launching a new team is important. The aim is to improve social relations, better define projects and plan a team strategy, and create a team contract that articulates goals, roles, and norms. These starting activities are important predictors of long-term team success (Mathieu & Rapp, 2009).

Team Warm-Ups

One of the problems with teams is the tendency to focus almost exclusively on tasks. It is equally important to recognize the value of developing a team's social relations. Most stage theories of group development state that social relations precede the team's performance stage. Developing social relations among team members aids in socializing new team members. For that reason, it is important to focus on developing social relations early in the team's existence.

Team warm-ups are social "icebreakers" conducted at the start of team meetings (Scholtes, 1988). They are crucial to first team meetings and should be used at meetings during the early stages of team formation to develop social relations within the team. Warm-ups are social activities designed to help team members get to know one another and improve communication during the team project. Warm-ups can be as simple as spending five minutes sharing favorite jokes or chatting about what team members did over the weekend. Common team warm-up exercises that are useful during the early stages of a team's life are included in the Appendix.

Project Definitions and Planning

Teams often jump into projects and then have to back up to earlier stages when problems arise. In the rush toward task completion, a team may spend too little time understanding the assignment (Pokras, 1995). Everyone on the team should have the same understanding of the assignment, and this understanding should conform to the organization's intention.

Many professional teams find the project definition stage to be the most difficult and important stage.

There are many reasons why teams try to skip over the project definition stage. Team members may feel socially uncomfortable at the beginning, so they want to quickly focus on performing the task. Task assignments are often ambiguous, and this ambiguity causes discomfort. Making quick decisions to clear up a problem is emotionally satisfying. Such actions may help address the emotional aspects of a problem, but they often result in a team heading off in the wrong direction, leading to conflict and delays later in the project.

Teams can use several techniques to improve their ability to define a problem and understand its underlying causes. These are discussed in Chapter 11. A team should use these techniques at the beginning of the project to better understand their assignment.

Once the team agrees on the definition of the project, it should spend time developing a performance strategy or plan about how team members will work together. Task-related team planning at the beginning of a team's existence helps promote team effectiveness (Mathieu & Rapp, 2009). Formalized plans provide guidance for the work of team members. Developing performance strategies that outline performance objectives and tactics help direct the team's actions and create a shared mental model of how the team should operate.

Team Contract

A proper team launch includes developing common team goals and objectives, clarifying roles, creating appropriate team norms, and defining performance expectations. An effective way to do this is to develop a team contract or charter (Herrenkohl, 2004). A team contract is a plan for how the team will manage its teamwork activities (Mathieu & Rapp, 2009). It helps clarify role expectations and work norms that support collaborative work. Because contracts help outline members' roles and work processes, they facilitate team members focusing more easily on the task.

The contract explicitly states the agreements the team has reached on how to operate. The act of developing a contract helps the team identify and resolve conflicts and misunderstandings. It is a valuable technique for getting started in the right direction. A more complete description of the components and uses of team contracts and a sample outline of a team contract are presented in the Appendix.

LEADING VIRTUAL TEAMS: STARTING A VIRTUAL TEAM

Problem: Face-to-face communication is a process everyone has been using and practicing since infancy. Virtual communication and collaboration mediated by technology is less familiar to some participants and natural to many others. This presents both a problem and opportunity when starting a virtual team.

Solution: Starting a virtual team can be a problem because team members differ in their experience and skills using communication technology. If not properly addressed, these differences may contribute to motivation and satisfaction differences among team members. However, the differences can be an opportunity because the team leader may be able to influence team norms and culture through the introduction of communication and collaboration processes. The virtual communication and collaboration patterns introduced to the team during initial meetings will be difficult to change once they become established. To this end, a virtual project leader must plan how to start the team.

Team members are typically selected to fulfill team roles based on their skills and experience. When selecting virtual team members, there are other factors to consider: the ability to communicate using technology, the ability to work independently, and their attitude toward working on virtual teams. Beyond these personal issues, technological considerations include availability of technology for each team member, communication access (bandwidth), and experience using the technology.

Most of the literature on virtual teaming suggests getting the team together face-to-face if at all possible to start the team's project. There is value in this suggestion. Face-to-face interaction—and the informal interactions that often accompany it—can help build trust, establish a team identity, and solidify team norms and culture. However, the communication patterns that get created during an initial face-to-face meeting may complicate later attempts to establish virtual norms and culture. The leader must undo the initial set of norms and establish new ones for virtual meetings.

The initial virtual team meeting lays the foundation for the virtual team. During the meeting, the leader needs to create the following: a clear sense of the team's goals and objectives; a clear sense of team member roles; the team contract and norms; virtual meeting protocols, processes, and technical support channels; and collective virtual spaces for storing and sharing information. The leader should model appropriate behaviors (ways to interrupt during videoconferences, kinds of emails that are acceptable, etc.) for the team. Don't assume that all participants know these appropriate behaviors.

Create a virtual social space for team members and strongly encourage its use. Creating a social space, such as a team website for sharing information, is a useful approach for building social relations in a virtual team. Team members should be encouraged to use the site for sharing non-task information. It is important that the leader participates by sharing social information on the site. If necessary and appropriate, set boundaries on use of the site (e.g., forbidden topics, perhaps politics and religion). Encourage sharing of personal photos and discussion of hobbies. The use of this social space is intended to replace the sort of informal conversation that takes place during the off hours of a face-to-face offsite meeting. Participants from different cultures may be more or less comfortable sharing personal information, so do not coerce anyone to participate.

Summary

Teams develop through a series of stages from formation to adjournment. These stages relate to the time needed to develop a team's internal processes and the changing demands of its tasks. The developmental perspective shows the different types of challenges teams face during their existence. Rather than a smooth progression, teams go through periods of low activity followed by bursts of achievement and from periods of smooth relations to conflict. Understanding these stage theories helps explain why teams do most of their productive work during the later stages of projects.

The group socialization process describes the changing relationship between a team and its members. The team and its members evaluate one another to determine reciprocal levels of commitment. Socialization proceeds through a series of stages, from investigation to maintenance. Many types of teams have dynamic team membership, which makes socialization an ongoing activity for teams. This increase in team member turnover has positive and negative impacts on team performance.

Goals define a team's purpose and values and are an important factor in the team's success. Goals often are divided into objectives that are linked to performance criteria. Effective team goals are measurable in order to provide feedback on performance and moderately difficult in order to motivate performance. One common goal problem for a group is hidden agendas. Hidden agendas occur when individual team members have unspoken goals that conflict with the team goals. These can create conflict and distrust in the team and must be managed carefully.

Team norms define appropriate behavior for team members. They help the team operate more smoothly and create a distinctive group identity. Norms often evolve gradually. A team should formally establish its operating norms, however. The impact of team norms can be both positive and negative. Norms help a team operate better internally, but teams can develop norms that do not encourage high performance.

One of the values of viewing the ways teams evolve is that it illustrates the problems teams have at the beginning of projects. Teams must address the problems of undeveloped social relations, ill-defined projects, and ambiguous goals and norms before they can focus on performing their tasks. The operation of teams can be improved by focusing on these problems at the beginning of the team.

Team Leader's Challenge 3

It is the first meeting of a new product development team. The team's goal is to create the next generation of kitchen appliances for the company. The team is composed of members from engineering, product design, marketing, manufacturing, and finance. This project will be the main work activity for team members for the next 8 to 10 months.

As the team leader, you need to get the team started quickly on the project. Management has given you an overall goal for the project, but you have had limited time to plan how to manage it. Because of the limited time for completing the project, you are concerned about getting the team off to a good start.

What are the three most important issues for you (the team leader) to focus on at the beginning of the team project?

How much project planning should you do before meeting with the team?

What should happen at the first meeting?

ACTIVITY: OBSERVING TEAM NORMS

Objective: Norms define the rules for appropriate and inappropriate behavior. Although team members often follow norms, most teams do not develop a formal set of norms. Teams may have norms for a variety of issues. Norms may be enforced by official sanctions (e.g., a fine for a violation) or by informal pressure from the leader or team members.

Activity: Observe a team meeting or a group discussion of the Team Leader Challenge. Using Activity Worksheet 3.1, note the norms being used to make decisions, manage participation, and encourage conversational etiquette. For example, does the team make decisions democratically, such as by voting? Is everyone required to participate before a decision is made? Are there rules to prevent people from interrupting each other?

An alternative norms activity (suggested by Burn, 2004) is to have four-person groups play a card game. After playing for half an hour, they should identify the formal and informal norms that are operating.

Analysis: After developing a set of norms that the team is using, note how well the team follows them. Do the team members consistently follow norms? Are there examples of people violating norms? How does the team respond to violations?

Discussion: Does the team you observed have effective norms? Are the norms explicit or implicit? If you were asked to provide advice to the team, would you recommend that it develop formal norms? What norms do you think the team should formally adopt? Why?

ACTIVITY WORKSHEET 3.1
Observing Team Norms

Decision-Making Norms
Participation Norms
Conversation Etiquette Norms

Activity: Developing a Team Contract

Objective: Team contracts help establish the goals, roles, norms, and performance expectations of a team. Developing a contract is an important first step in establishing guidelines for the operation of a team.

Activity: Form groups of four to six students who are asked to plan and conduct an event. The event could be a charity fundraiser, concert, or party. This is the start-up meeting for the event team. Using Activity Worksheet 3.2, develop a team contract for the event team.

Analysis: Are the goals clear and specific enough to provide direction for the team? Do the roles adequately define each team member's responsibilities? How will the team enforce its norms? Do members feel confident they know what is expected of them?

Discussion: What is the value of developing a team contract? Was it difficult to define the goals, roles, norms, and expectations for the team? How can the team get members to commit to the contract?

ACTIVITY WORKSHEET 3.2
Developing a Team Contract

Team Goals: What are the goals for the team? What does each team member hope to achieve from working on this team?

Roles: What are the primary roles and responsibilities of each team member?

Norms: What are the operating rules for the team? (Consider establishing norms for decision-making, attendance, assignments, participation, and courtesy.)

Performance Expectations: What criteria will be used to evaluate the team and each member's performance?

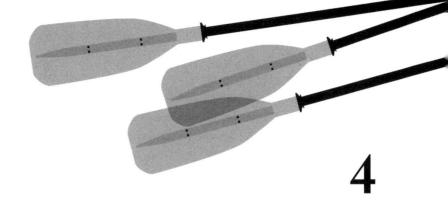

4

Understanding the Basic Team Processes

Motivation, group cohesion, role assignments, task and social behaviors, and team learning are the basic building blocks of successful team performance. Team members working in a team may be motivated to work harder, but sometimes individual effort decreases when individuals work in a team. This phenomenon is called *social loafing*. Developing challenging tasks that require interdependent actions, improving the reward system, fostering team efficacy, and increasing commitment to the team can help reduce social loafing and motivate the team.

Beyond motivating a team, successful performance depends on other factors. Group cohesion is the bond that ties the members together. Cohesive teams generally perform better, but cohesion also can cause performance problems. Like the roles in a play, people perform roles in a team. Poorly defined roles can lead to stress and inefficiency, while clear roles help teams operate with less stress and more efficiently. Although task behaviors typically dominate in work teams, social behaviors are necessary to build relationships among team members. Teams sometimes suffer from a lack of activities aimed at building relationships among members. Teams need to adapt to changing situations and learn how to improve their performance. Learning requires setting aside time to reflect on how the team is doing.

Learning Objectives

1. What factors cause social loafing in a team? How can social loafing be prevented?

2. What motivates a team?

3. What factors encourage group cohesion?

4. How does cohesion affect team performance?

5. What are the causes of role ambiguity and role stress?

6. What are the formal roles commonly played by team members?

7. How do task and social behaviors affect team performance?

8. How can leaders promote team learning?

9. What is the value of group process observations?

4.1 Motivation

The potential of teamwork lies in the fact that a whole is greater than the sum of its parts. That is, the collective work of a team of people is greater than the work that its individuals could accomplish separately. However, team synergies, the creativity in conflicting ideas, and the motivating impact of team spirit should give a team an advantage over a collection of individuals; it does not always work out that way. In some circumstances, working together causes a decrease in motivation that may be due to social loafing. Understanding this motivation problem can suggest to teams the ways to increase team motivation.

Social Loafing

One of the biggest motivation problems for teams is social loafing, which is the reduction of individual contributions when people work in groups rather than alone (Latane, Williams, & Harkins, 1979). A simple experiment demonstrates social loafing. Ask individuals to shout as loud as they can when they are alone, and record the volume. Next, ask two individuals at a time to do the same task and record the volume; the volume will be 34% less than when two individuals shout alone. Finally, ask individuals to perform the same task in six-person groups and record the volume; it will be 64% less than when six individuals are shouting alone.

Social loafing is related to several other group phenomena. People can become "free riders" who perform little in a team because they do not believe their individual efforts are important, and they know they will receive their share of the team's reward regardless of their efforts (Sweeney, 1973). The "sucker effect" (Johnson & Johnson, 1997) is when good performers slack off in teams because they do not want others to take advantage of them. This can lead to all team members reducing their contributions to the task.

A variety of factors contribute to social loafing (Karau & Williams, 1993). If the tasks the team is performing are just a collection of individual tasks, why does the team need to perform in a coordinated way? This reduces motivation because of the lack of a perceived need to work as a team. Individual performance can be hidden in the team's collective effort, leading members to reduce their effort because they are no longer concerned about what others think of their performance. Finally, team members might be unaware of how much effort others are putting into the task. As a result, they do not know whether they are doing their fair share. Unfortunately, people tend to overestimate the extent of their contributions to the team.

One of the best ways to understand social loafing is to look at a situation where it rarely occurs, such as a championship basketball game. Only the team's score counts in determining the winner, but every individual's participation is observable and measurable. The task is motivating by itself and becomes more motivating through the social aspects of performance. The task requires an integrated and coordinated performance. One player cannot win the game by himself or herself, so each player is dependent on the coordinated efforts of the team to win. Winning is important, and success is highly rewarded. There is no social loafing in basketball or in other tasks that share these characteristics.

Research on work teams shows that these sports principles apply to work. When work teams are given challenging tasks, when they are rewarded for team success yet have identifiable individual performance indicators, and when there is commitment to the team, social loafing does not occur (Hackman, 1986).

Increasing Team Motivation

The discussion of the impact of social loafing on a team helps identify the factors that encourage motivation in the team. Increasing a team's motivation depends on multiple factors: the task it performs, how performance will be evaluated and rewarded, the team's belief in its ability to succeed, and the team members' sense of commitment or belonging.

Task

A team is more motivated when the task it performs is interesting, involving, and challenging. Probably the best description of how to create this type of task comes from the job characteristic model (Hackman & Oldham, 1980). A satisfying job creates three critical psychological states: experienced meaningfulness, responsibility for outcomes, and knowledge of results. A task is meaningful when it provides the opportunity to use a variety of skills, to complete an entire piece of work from beginning to end, and to affect others with its completion. Responsibility is experienced when given autonomy or the freedom to design, schedule, and carry out the task as desired. Knowledge of results comes from feedback on the effectiveness of one's performance.

However, a good team task is more than just a good individual task. A good team task requires task interdependence; team members must work together to successfully complete the task. Task interdependence is an additional factor that can be added to the job characteristic model (Van der Vegt, Emans, & Van de Vliert, 1998). It is a shift from individual responsibility to experienced team responsibility for outcomes. To be successful, team members must feel responsible for both their own work and the work of the other team members. It is only when team members experience both types of responsibility that they work in a cooperative way.

Task interdependence can come from the distribution of skills among team members and the work processes of the team. It is one reason why action teams (e.g., sports teams) and cross-functional teams (e.g., design teams where members have different skills) often are more successful than student project teams. In a sports team, the players need one another to succeed. In a cross-functional team, working together is the only way to complete a project. However, in a student team, the students typically all have the same skills and knowledge, so they do not need one another to complete the task.

Interdependence helps motivate team members in several ways. When team members depend on one another to complete a task, power is shared among the members (Franz, 1998). The more team members need one another to complete a task, the more power each team member has over the team. Task interdependence affects how factors, such as conflict, cohesiveness, work norms, and autonomy relate to team effectiveness (Langfred, 2000). When teams are highly interdependent, these variables have a more powerful effect on how well teams perform. Interdependence also encourages members to believe that their contributions to the team are indispensable, unique, and valuable, thereby making them more willing to put effort into the team's task (Kerr & Bruun, 1983).

Evaluations and Rewards

Interdependence relates to both the task and the outcome of the team's work. The task may require coordinated effort, but team members may believe their evaluations and rewards are primarily based on individual performance rather than on the success of the team's effort. Research shows that a belief in outcome interdependence is important because it helps motivate members to work together (Van der Vegt et al., 1998).

To be successful, team members must feel responsible for both their own work and the work of other team members. Team goals and team reward systems encourage this dual sense of responsibility. For example, managerial teams often do not perform well because managers are more concerned about what happens in their respective departments than in the organization as a whole. One of the values of companywide profit-sharing programs is to make organizational success an important goal. When it is achieved, each member of the management team is rewarded. This encourages the managers to think about what is good for the organization rather than only about what is good for their departments.

A balance of individual- and team-based rewards is necessary to encourage both a commitment to the team and an incentive for individual performance (Thompson, 2004). Finding the right balance can be difficult for an organization. In addition, the performance evaluation system must fairly identify both team success and an individual's contribution to that success. When individual contributions to the team are identifiable and linked to the reward system, motivation is increased (Harkins & Jackson, 1985). (The topic of evaluating and rewarding teams is discussed in more detail in Chapter 16.)

Team Efficacy

Teams evaluate their ability to succeed by examining their personal resources and their ability to work together (Hirschfeld & Bernerth, 2008). *Team efficacy* is the perception that the team is capable of performing well at a given task, while *team potency* is the perception that the team is capable of successfully performing across various tasks. Increasing a sense of team efficacy helps increase motivation. Teams with higher collective efficacy have higher levels of motivation to perform, greater staying power when they encounter difficulties and setbacks, and improved performance (Bandura, 2000). Both team efficacy and team potency relate to team performance, especially when there are high levels of task interdependence (Mathieu, Maynard, Rapp, & Gilson, 2008).

Team efficacy has a reciprocal relationship with team performance. In other words, successful performance increases team efficacy and vice versa (Ilgen, Hollenbeck, Johnson, & Jundt, 2005). Team efficacy is influenced by a number of factors (Burn, 2004). Teams that have been successful in the past have higher levels of team efficacy. Leaders who believe their team is competent create teams with higher collective efficacy. Teams with higher collective efficacy are more likely to set higher performance goals, which encourage greater performance (Goncalo, Polman, & Maslach, 2010). Teams with a stronger group identity, whose members more highly value their membership in the team, also have greater team efficacy (Lee, Farh, & Chen, 2011).

Commitment and Cohesion

The more people value membership in the team, the more motivated they are to perform. The increased sense of commitment and attraction to a team is called *group cohesion*. Cohesive teams are less likely to experience social loafing (Karau & Williams, 1997). Group cohesiveness includes a commitment to the task that the team is performing. In a highly cohesive team, members like the task the team is performing, enjoy working together on the task, have personal involvement in the task, and take pride in the team's performance. Highly cohesive teams have more commitment to their tasks and perform better (Wech, Mossholder, Steel, & Bennett, 1998). Because group cohesion has important effects other than motivation, a more complete discussion of it is presented next.

4.2 Group Cohesion

Group cohesion refers to the interpersonal bonds that hold a team together. Cohesion is a multidimensional concept (Beal, Cohen, Burke, & McLendon, 2003). To many theorists, team pride or social identity is the core of group cohesion. Members of a cohesive team have a shared social identity. Membership in the team is personally important, so they define themselves as members of the team (Hogg, 1992). Others view cohesiveness as a type of social attraction (Lott & Lott, 1965). Members of a cohesive team like one another and feel connected because of this relationship. Cohesiveness also can come from the team's task. The joining together to work as a team can create a sense of cohesiveness (Guzzo & Dickson, 1996).

The sense of identification with the team that occurs in cohesive teams has important implications (Hayes, 1997). A team is better able to manage stress and conflict among its members if it has a firm sense of itself as a distinctive team. The creation of a sense of insiders and outsiders to the team causes people to view the members of the team as similar and at the same time different from members of other teams. In work teams, members may have very different skills, professions, and even statuses. Such differences do not prevent development of a cohesive team, however.

How Cohesion Affects the Team's Performance

Group cohesion affects the team in a number of ways. People who are part of cohesive teams are more satisfied with their jobs than are members of noncohesive teams (Hackman, 1992). Group cohesion also helps reduce stress because members are more supportive of one another. The interpersonal effects of group cohesion are generally positive, but the effects on a team's performance are mixed.

Group cohesion has a generally positive impact on team performance (Mullen & Copper, 1994). This is especially true for smaller teams. This relationship goes in both directions: Cohesion can help improve performance, and performance can help improve cohesion. When a team is successful in its task, its level of cohesiveness increases. However, when a team is not successful, members often blame each other for the failure, which reduces group cohesion (Naquin & Tynan, 2003). Cohesion based on commitment to the task has a larger impact on performance than does cohesion based on team attraction or social identity. The effects of cohesion are more important when the team's task requires high levels of interaction, coordination, and interdependence (Beal et al., 2003).

Members of a cohesive team are more likely to accept the team's goals, decisions, and norms. The increased interpersonal bonds among team members amplify the pressure to conform to team norms. As was seen in the discussion of team norms, norms can either support or hamper team productivity (Sundstrom, McIntyre, Halfhill, & Richards, 2000). Effective work teams have norms that support high-quality performance and a level of group cohesiveness that provides social support to its members. However, cohesive teams that lack good performance norms may be ineffective and highly resistant to change (Nemeth & Staw, 1989).

Cohesiveness affects a team's social interactions, which can affect performance and decision making. Low levels of group cohesiveness limit a team's ability to work together. Because they know one another better, cohesive teams are better able to communicate and coordinate their actions (Beal et al., 2003). However, high levels of cohesiveness can impair a team's decision-making ability. Sometimes, team members will "agree" to a decision not because they truly agree with it, but because they do not want to upset the team's relationships (Janis, 1972).

An important aspect of group cohesion relates to conflict resolution and problem solving. A team with poor social relations will avoid dealing with problems until they disrupt the team's ability to perform the task or threaten its existence as a team. A team with good social relations is better equipped to handle problems when they arise. The team can do this because its more open communication allows team members to manage conflicts constructively. This is one reason it is important to develop group cohesion and good social relations early in the team's existence. Forming good social relations early means a team has a better ability to solve problems and manage conflicts throughout the team's work.

Building Group Cohesion

Research on organizations has identified several factors that encourage cohesion in work teams (McKenna, 1994). Team members in a cohesive group tend to have similar attitudes and personal goals. They have spent more time together, which increases their opportunity to develop common interests and ideas. A team's isolation from others may help produce a sense of being special and different. A smaller team tends to be more cohesive than a larger team. Having strict requirements to join a team increases cohesion. Finally, when incentives are based on group rather than individual performance, the team becomes more cooperative and cohesive.

Several approaches can be used to increase cohesion in work teams (Wech et al., 1998). Training in social interaction skills, such as effective listening and conflict management, can improve communication and cohesion. Training in task skills, such as goal setting and job skills, improves the team's ability to work successfully. Team success, and reward for success, improves cohesion. The team leader can enhance cohesion by promoting more interactions among team members, reducing status differences, ensuring that everyone is aware of one another's contributions, and creating a climate of pride in the team. For virtual teams that are located in different places and interact primarily via technology, social media may be a valuable technique for keeping the team together socially, especially for younger team members (Thompson & Coovert, 2006).

There are a variety of team building activities that can be used to increase group cohesion like wilderness experience programs. These approaches are discussed in Chapter 17. But, one of the strongest predictors of group cohesion is team success. Creating opportunities for successful performance and rewarding these successes improves a team's sense of efficacy, increases a sense of pride in the team, and builds cohesion among team members.

4.3 Team Roles

Roles are one of the basic building blocks of successful team performance. A role is a set of behaviors typical of people in certain social contexts. Roles within a team are similar to roles in a play: They describe what people are supposed to do and how their parts relate to what others in the team are doing. Team members can negotiate the roles they want to play, and they have a certain amount of freedom in the performance of their roles.

A team can deliberately create roles for members to perform. These roles are task-related and allow the team to operate more efficiently. Even without deliberately creating formal roles, team members assume informal roles within the team, which emerge over time as the team interacts. These roles can be task-related (e.g., expert, facilitator) or social (e.g., supporter, clown).

The selection or allocation of roles may occur in a variety of ways. The organization, team, or individual may select roles. For example, management in the organization may assign the team leader, the team may elect its leader, or the team may have no official leader (however, an informal leader may eventually emerge in the team). The type of role also affects the selection process. The team often selects members to perform skill-based tasks, whereas social roles often emerge by self-selection.

Definitions of roles also vary. The team explicitly defines some role behaviors, whereas the person filling the role defines other behaviors. For example, the recorder is the person who takes notes prior to writing up the minutes, but whether these are funny or solemn, general or detailed depends on the particular recorder fulfilling the role.

Role Problems

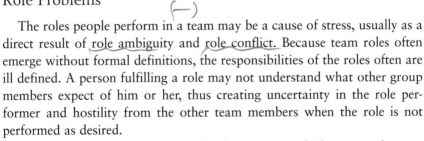

The roles people perform in a team may be a cause of stress, usually as a direct result of role ambiguity and role conflict. Because team roles often emerge without formal definitions, the responsibilities of the roles often are ill defined. A person fulfilling a role may not understand what other group members expect of him or her, thus creating uncertainty in the role performer and hostility from the other team members when the role is not performed as desired.

Team members also occupy several roles at a time, which may involve conflicting demands. Interrole conflict occurs when a person has several incompatible roles. For example, when a person is promoted, he or she often experiences conflict between being a manager and being a friend to former coworkers. Conflicts also may occur within a single role (i.e., intrarole conflict). In a task force with team members from different areas of the organization, members may experience a conflict between roles that are good for the team and/or roles that are good for their organizational areas.

Role ambiguity and conflict have a negative impact on people in an organization. These role problems can create higher levels of stress, decreased satisfaction and morale, and increased job turnover (Kemery, Bedeian, Mossholder, & Touliatos, 1985). Role problems also decrease commitment to the organization and reduce involvement and participation in the team's interactions (Brown, 1996).

For a project team, role problems often appear to worsen near the end of the project. As team members rush to complete their assignments, they become more aware of the different expectations members have about who performs what role. These different expectations of the roles members should be performing lead to conflicts when the team is already stressed about the project deadline.

To address role problems, a team may make explicit the important roles in the team. The tasks that the group is performing may be prioritized so that team members can decide what to do when there are conflicts among tasks.

Types of Team Meeting Roles

Team meetings provide an example of how roles are useful for a team. Meetings operate more efficiently when major task roles are explicitly defined and team members are assigned to fulfill them (Kayser, 1990). One of the main meeting roles is that of leader or facilitator. The leader is responsible for structuring the team's interactions to ensure that the team completes its goals. The leader manages the structure of the meeting, but not its content. The primary activities of the leader are to (a) develop the agenda to help structure team meetings; (b) ensure that information is shared, understood, and processed by the team in a supportive and participative environment; and (c) remove internal problems that hinder the team's operations.

The recorder takes notes on key decisions and task assignments (i.e., who agreed to do what) and writes up the minutes. The minutes focus on the main points rather than capturing the entire discussion. Good documentation of team actions is important. It makes information available for future use, provides a fixed point of reference, and provides documentation of the reasons behind decisions.

Sometimes the recorder acts as the team scribe, noting comments of team members on a blackboard or flip chart during a discussion. After the discussion, the recorder notes any conclusions reached by the team. Some teams assign the role of scribe to another member or to the leader.

Another role is team timekeeper. When the agenda is presented at the beginning of the meeting, teams may identify the time allotted for each item. The timekeeper reminds the team when it has used the time allotted for an agenda item. The team may continue on that topic, recognizing that to do so will extend the meeting longer than planned.

These team meeting roles should be recognized and filled at the outset of a team's existence. However, team members need not be permanently assigned to these roles. It is often better to rotate people through roles, giving everyone a chance to try them out, before the team assigns permanent roles (Kayser, 1990). There are several benefits to this rotation. Every team member has the chance to practice roles. It is a good learning experience, enabling members to fulfill other roles later if there are team absences. In addition, the team has a chance to see how everyone performs. After team members have tried out roles for several meetings, the team is better able to select who should fill them on a more permanent basis.

4.4 Task and Social Behaviors

Teams perform two basic types of behaviors: task behaviors and social behaviors. Task behaviors focus on the team's goals and tasks, while social behaviors focus on the social and emotional needs of the team members and help maintain social relations among them. To function effectively, teams need both task and social behaviors.

Task and social behaviors are used to support the members of the team and are important factors in team success (Huffmeier & Hertel, 2011). Task-related support includes both information sharing and behavioral assistance. Giving ideas and advice and explaining how to perform a task are examples of information sharing, while helping another team member with work tasks and providing supportive backup behaviors are types of behavioral assistance. Social support includes social recognition, such as expressing acceptance and encouraging a sense of belonging to the group, and encouragement, such as rewarding others and listening to their personal issues.

Figure 4.1 shows how task support and social support relate to team performance. Task support increases the collective efficacy of the team and improves coordination among team members. Social support increases group cohesion and helps motivate team members. Both of these factors interact to improve team performance.

The optimum balance between task and social behaviors depends on the characteristics of the task and the team (Belbin, 1981). In task-oriented teams,

Figure 4.1   Task and Social Support in Teams

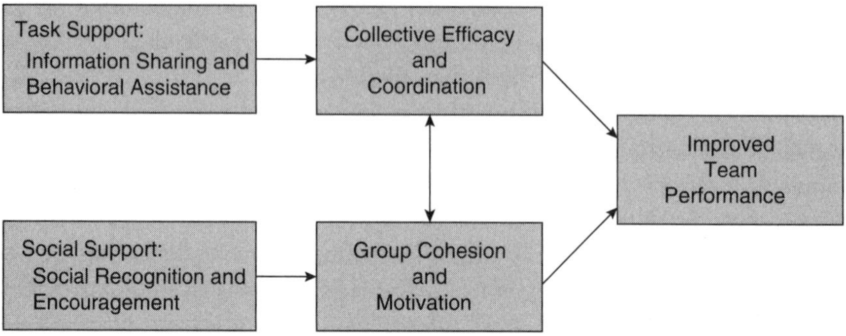

SOURCE: Adapted from Huffmeier, J., & Hertel, G. (2011). Many cheers make light the work: How social support triggers process gains in teams. *Journal of Managerial Psychology*, 26(3), 185–204.

task-oriented behaviors will dominate the team's interactions. A study of engineering teams found that more than 90% of a team's interactions were task oriented (Levi & Cadiz, 1998).

When technical teams are under time pressure, they may not have time to devote to group process issues. Under these conditions, teams may fall back on traditional management methods rather than using teamwork to get the job done (Janz, Colquitt, & Noe, 1997). In general, effective work teams spend about 80% of their time working on the task (Wheelan, 2005).

The right mix of task and social behaviors also depends on the maturity level of the team. When teams are in the forming stage, they must engage in more social-oriented behaviors to develop the social relations of the group. Teams in the performing stage will be dominated by task-oriented behaviors. When a work team develops good social relations early in a project, the team is better able to handle the time pressure at the end because it has developed the working relationships it needs to complete the project.

Value of Social Behaviors

Often, a team tends to focus on the task and ignore the social or relationship aspects of teamwork. Not only does that team fail to promote social relations, but many team members do not even believe they are necessary. It is important to recognize that a team needs a balance. Social behaviors are important for building trust in communication, encouraging the team to operate smoothly, providing social support, and rewarding participation. Negative social relationships among team members can hurt team cohesion and team performance (Jong, Curseu, & Leenders, 2014). When a team runs into problems, it often blames individual team members and does not recognize that poorly developed social relations in the team may have caused these problems.

Although team members and managers often state that task skills are more important than social skills or likeability, they do not select new team members on that criterion. Teams more often select likeable people with limited skills than competent people who are difficult to work with (Casciaro & Lobo, 2005). Social relations are vital in work teams. Members who like their teammates will try to get the best possible performance out of those individuals. On the other hand, it can be so challenging or unpleasant to get information and assistance from difficult people that members avoid asking them to participate.

There is no formula for the right balance of task and social behaviors. Some teams operate well when most of their behaviors are task oriented. A team is out of balance when emotions or personality conflicts become disruptive to team operations. Such behaviors indicate a breakdown in social relations.

Observation studies on task teams show that one deficit in team communication is lack of praise, support, and positive feedback (Levi & Cadiz, 1998). All team members are responsible for this lack of positive communication. Members are quick to criticize another member's idea if they do not like it, but they are reluctant to praise a team member for a good idea or even for good performance. Increasing positive support by team members greatly helps improve social relations within the team and increases its effectiveness.

4.5 Team Adaptation and Learning

One of the main benefits of using teams is their ability to adapt to changing situations (Burke, Stagl, Salas, Pierce, & Kendall, 2006). Teams not only perform tasks, but also change how they operate when their environment changes. Team adaptation is a form of problem solving where the team analyzes the situation, plans and implements solutions, and learns from the experience. Team resilience is a positive psychology concept that refers to the ability to recover from adversity and failure by learning from one's mistakes through reflexive activities (Mills, Fleck & Kozikowski, 2013). Team learning is an ongoing process of action and reflection that leads to a better understanding of team processes and task performance (Mathieu et al., 2008).

Team learning leads to the development of shared mental models of how to operate. Teams have mental models related to the task and social characteristics of the team. A team mental model is knowledge about how to operate as a team to complete a task (Hirschfeld, Jordon, Field, Giles, & Armenakis, 2006). It is related to the type of task, not the specific members of the team. A team's transactive memory system is awareness of the knowledge possessed by the members of the team. It develops over time through interactions within a team and is specific to the team.

Team mental models differ from transactive memory in several ways (Mohammed, Ferzandi, & Hamilton, 2010). Team mental models focus on the shared or common memory of the team; team members are "on the same page," they know other members' roles, or they have a common explanation of how the team operates. In contrast, transactive memory is about the task knowledge that individual team members possess. The knowledge is distributed among the team members rather than shared by the team as a whole. For example, in an airplane flight crew, their team mental model includes an understanding of the different roles of the crewmembers and how those roles need to be coordinated to fly the plane and handle emergencies. The crew's transactive memory is an understanding of the skills and knowledge of the team members. Who on the crew can speak French? Who is most knowledgeable about first aid?

A team mental model is a common understanding by team members about the team's tasks and the operation of the team. There are two main considerations about team mental models: the accuracy of the model and the degree of agreement among team members about the model (Hirschfeld et al., 2006). When teammates hold similar mental models, they are better able to coordinate their activities, solve problems the team encounters, and perform effectively. Since there are many ways for teams to successfully operate (equifinality), there may be many possible accurate team mental models (Smith-Jentsch, Cannon-Bowers, Tannenbaum, & Salas, 2008). Research shows that both the accuracy and degree of agreement about the team's mental model are important for team success (Mathieu et al., 2008).

A transactive memory system includes both the knowledge that particular team members possess and awareness of who knows what (Wegner, 1986). It allows team members to understand who possesses specialized knowledge, how credible that knowledge is, and how to coordinate its use by the team (Lewis, 2004). When team members are aware of the types of knowledge and expertise of the other members, they are better able to coordinate their activities and bring information together to solve problems and make decisions

(Moreland, Argote, & Krishnan, 1996). This helps the team deal with problems, especially on complex and nonroutine tasks where the coordination of team members' skills and knowledge is needed (Zhang, Hempel, Han, & Tjosvold, 2007).

Team learning occurs when team members reflect on how they have dealt with the challenges they faced and adapted by implementing alternative approaches to how they operate (Wiedow & Konradt, 2011). Leaders can encourage team learning by fostering cooperative goals and creating a climate that supports open discussion about the team's processes and tasks. Teams need to set aside time to reflect on their actions and learn from feedback about their performance. Teams also learn by using group process observations to better understand how they operate.

Reflexivity

Reflexivity is the process of taking time to reflect on a team's performance and to develop strategies to improve (West, 2012). Systematic reflection about a team's performance is a powerful tool for learning from experience (Ellis, Carette, Anseel, & Lievens, 2014). Systematic reflection has three functions: develop explanations of why the behaviors occurred, verify team members' perspectives about what occurred, and receive feedback about the success or failure of actions. Reflection is valuable for both successful and failed experiences. It is important for teams to understand their problems and erroneous actions, but it is also important to understand what works by examining the team's correct actions.

After-action reviews, debriefings, and other types of formal team performance reflections started out as a military training approach, but their use has spread to other types of action teams, from airline crews to surgical teams (Villado & Winfred, 2013). These reflexivity actions help to motivate teams to learn, increase understanding about performance, and lead to improvements in performance, team efficacy, and cohesion.

Team reflexivity can also be useful for temporary teams without consistent membership (Vashdi, Bamberger, & Erez, 2013). After-action reviews are common in some types of action teams, like surgical teams, who change membership after completion of their mission. Even though their membership changes, surgical teams benefit from team debriefings and other types of reflexivity experiences. The focus of the learning activities is not about the team members, but about the roles performed by the team. The impacts of these learning experiences manifested in shorter surgeries, more team members helping, and less surgical errors.

Using Feedback

Team learning requires teams to use feedback effectively. The best type of feedback about a team's performance includes both positive and negative information (Smith-Jentsch et al., 2008). Sometimes cohesive teams only discuss positive feedback in order to preserve group harmony. Team leaders may only give negative feedback because they believe that it is best to focus on improvement. One of the major complaints team members have about their leaders giving them feedback is a focus on negative feedback (West, 2004). However, when teams have both positive and negative feedback, they develop better team mental models about how to operate effectively.

The key to obtaining and using feedback is to create a safe environment where people are willing to raise questions and issues without fear of retaliation (Edmondson, Bohmer, & Pisano, 2001). Team members who feel safe are more willing to provide feedback and reflect on their performance in order to learn how to improve the team's operation. For example, surgical teams with a higher level of team safety had team leaders who were more inclusive; they helped minimize status differences among team members and encouraged participation in discussions about how to improve. These teams learned more from each other, were more engaged in their work, and had superior performance than the teams with less psychological safety.

Teams can use feedback in a variety of ways to promote learning. Action teams like military teams often use structured team debriefings as a way for members to process feedback about their performance (Smith-Jentsch et al., 2008). For most teams, reflecting on past performance is a more informal process that occurs after major points in a project or performance cycle, such as a midpoint review.

Group Process Observations

Group process observation and analysis may be used to improve a team's interactions. The group process observer provides valuable support by observing and commenting on how the team is operating. Many team-building programs use outside group process observers to evaluate team interactions and advise the team on improving its performance. Although this is a valuable function, it is better if the members of the team conduct these observations themselves (Dyer, Dyer, & Dyer, 2007). Developing group process observation skills among members allows the team to work on its problems when they occur rather than waiting for an outside consultant.

When a team analyzes its group process, several common problems emerge (Hayes, 1997). In most cases, the team uses only a limited range of available behaviors. For example, team members might frequently give opinions, but only rarely provide support for the ideas of others. Team members also can become stuck in behavioral patterns rather than responding to the needs of the team. For example, one member may become the team's critic and rarely provide information to foster decision making. The team's performance improves when people are more flexible, using behaviors more suited to team needs than to their personal behavioral styles. The use of group process observations may help group members see what is lacking in their interactions, and may encourage team members to adjust their personal styles to enable the team to operate more effectively.

Many of the activities in this book are structured approaches to group process observation. By having a team member observe the team's use of task and social behaviors or conflict resolution styles, the team can obtain feedback about how it is functioning. This feedback can be used to analyze the team's operation and develop more effective ways of interacting within the team.

LEADING VIRTUAL TEAMS: MOTIVATING PARTICIPATION IN VIRTUAL MEETINGS

Problem: People in virtual meetings often multitask (do other things while participating in the meeting) or free ride (have their computer on yet don't participate). These problems tend to be more common in virtual meetings because there is less social presence (individual visibility) encouraging people to engage in the discussion.

Solution: There is no foolproof solution to this problem. People will multitask in virtual meetings if there is no camera on them detailing their activities to other meeting participants (and putting everyone on camera may not be productive for many reasons). Taking the following actions can minimize multitasking and free riding:

1. Prior to the meeting, the leader might communicate with each team member (by telephone, perhaps) to discuss the objectives of the meeting and the unique contribution that individual is able to provide. If the member genuinely agrees to the importance of the objectives and to their unique role, then motivation toward active participation should increase.

2. During the meeting, the leader might use a facilitative process that encourages team members to actively contribute rather than passively listening to meeting activities. When members are engaged by actively contributing to the outcome, they are much less likely to multitask. Active participation is possible even if the meeting consists of presentations. Team members can be asked to actively react to the presented

material by taking notes, framing questions, or summarizing the material presented.

3. Virtual meeting agenda items should be designed to be short and focused. Multitasking increases gradually during long periods of single activity. Breaking the agenda into short segments keeps virtual team members focused and aware of the task at hand.

4. The leader of the virtual meeting should actively engage distributed members by evoking their names on a regular basis. The leader might hold a list of all team members' names and use those names while giving instruction and intermittently check in with distributed participants. Nothing brings a multitasking member back into focus faster than hearing his or her own name called.

Summary

Motivation is a problem for many teams. Working in a team can encourage social loafing, which is the reduction in individual effort that occurs when the individual is performing in a group. Free riders and the sucker effect are related motivational problems. These motivation problems may be caused by tasks that do not require coordinated efforts, inability to identify individual contributions to the team's work, and the false belief that individual members are doing their fair share.

Improving group motivation requires countering the negative effects of social loafing. The team's task should be involving and challenging and should require coordinated effort to complete. The team evaluation and reward system must recognize and reward both individual and team performance. The team's goals should create the belief that motivated effort leads to success. Finally, strengthening commitment to the team by increasing cohesion helps increase group motivation.

Group cohesion is the interpersonal bond that forms within a team. It can emerge from feelings of belonging, social identification, interpersonal attraction, or commitment to the team's task. In most cases, a cohesive team performs better than a noncohesive team because of improved coordination and mutual support. However, high levels of group cohesion may sometimes encourage conformity and impair decision making. One of the main ways to develop group cohesion is to improve communication within the team.

Roles are sets of behaviors that people perform in teams. They may be deliberately created and filled, or they may operate on a more informal basis. Ill-defined roles (i.e., role ambiguity) and conflicts among roles may create stress for team members. Formal team roles (e.g., leader, recorder, or timekeeper) help a team operate more efficiently.

Team members perform task behaviors and social behaviors. Task behaviors help the team perform its task, whereas social behaviors maintain the team's interpersonal relationships. Work teams often ignore the importance of social behaviors, leading to reduction in interpersonal support and an increase in stress. Team interactions may be improved by better balancing the types of behaviors performed.

Teams have the ability to adapt and change how they operate to deal with changes in their environment. Team learning occurs when teams reflect on these changes and develop new action models. These models include a shared understanding of how to perform as a team and an awareness of the knowledge and skills within the team. Both positive and negative feedback are important for team learning. Also, team members must learn how to act as process observers to improve the team's interactions.

Team Leader's Challenge 4

You are the student team leader in a senior-level engineering lab course. The team has seven members and is halfway through a semester-long project that is not going very well. Although some students are highly motivated, a few slackers are creating a discouraging atmosphere for the rest of the team. At the last team meeting, a project discussion turned into a heated and personal argument. Since then, relations among several students have been strained.

One aspect of the argument among the students was about who is responsible for various tasks. Multiple team members are addressing some tasks, while some tasks are being neglected entirely. As the team leader, you are uncertain who is responsible for these missing assignments. You need to intervene to get the team back on track.

What problem should the team leader focus on first?

How should the leader try to improve the performance of the team?

Is the primary cause of the team's problems social or task issues? Explain why.

ACTIVITY: OBSERVING TASK AND SOCIAL BEHAVIORS

Objective: To operate effectively, a team needs both task and social behaviors. Task behaviors help the team complete its goals. Social behaviors foster communication and maintain team social relations. Team members often vary in how much they participate and in the types of behaviors they perform.

Activity: Observe the communication in an existing team or a group discussion of the Team Leader's Challenge. Using Activity Worksheet 4.1, note whether each communication is task oriented or social oriented. Record each communication by noting how frequently task communications and social communications are contributed by each team member.

Analysis: How does the frequency of task communication compare with the frequency of social communication? Was there a balance between these types of behaviors? How is the use of task communication and social communication distributed among team members? Are there people who are primarily task oriented or social oriented? Is the leader primarily task oriented or social oriented?

Discussion: What is the right balance between task behaviors and social behaviors in a team? What factors cause this balance to change? What type of behaviors should the leader perform?

ACTIVITY WORKSHEET 4.1
Observing Task and Social Behaviors

ENR Team : Red Floor	Team Members					
	1	2	3	4	5	6
Task Behaviors: Gives opinions or information, asks questions, or organizes the discussion.		✓	✓	✓		
Social Behaviors: Shows support or acceptance, encourages communications from others, or tries to reduce tensions.	✓				✓	

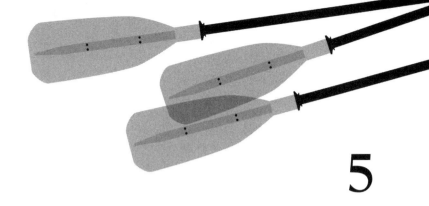

5

Cooperation and Competition

Cooperation is necessary for teams to operate smoothly and effectively, and a cooperative atmosphere offers many benefits for team members. However, many team members find themselves in mixed-motive situations that include both cooperation and competition. Team members may be competitive for cultural, personal, and organizational reasons. Cooperation can be encouraged through strategies focused on team goals, communication, and interpersonal actions. However, if teams become too cooperative then over-conformity and poor decision making can result. Competition can create negative effects on the team, even when the team is successful.

Learning Objectives

1. What is the impact of a mixed-motive situation?

2. Why do people act competitively in teams?

3. How are cooperators, competitors, and individualists different?

4. How does competition hurt a team?

5. How does competition between teams affect a team?

6. What are the benefits and problems of cooperation?

7. How do teams respond to competitive versus cooperative rewards?

8. How can a team deal with the negative effects of competition?

5.1 Teamwork as a Mixed-Motive Situation

The essence of teamwork is the cooperative interactions of team members. Cooperation is limited by competition, especially when goals are not shared. Team members should be working together toward a common goal, but competition makes team members work against one another when their individual goals become more important than the team goal. In a competitive relationship, the goal is to outperform others, and when this rivalry occurs among members in a team, the team is prevented from focusing on its common goals.

Being a team member should encourage people to act cooperatively, but team members often find themselves in a mixed-motive situation. Consider the following examples:

> You are the member of a budget committee that must allocate funds to various departments within the organization. As a committee member, you want to do what is best for the organization, but you also want to make sure your department gets more than its fair share of funds.
>
> As a student working on a group project, you want to do a good job so you can get a good grade. However, you have other classes and demands on your time. What you really want is to put in the least amount of effort and still get a good grade.
>
> As a basketball player, only the team's score determines the winner. You should be focused on coordinating your plays with the other team members. However, there is a scout in the audience, and being the game's high scorer will get you the attention you need to be noticed.

Often, team members find themselves in these all-too-common mixed-motive situations described above. These examples are neither cooperative nor competitive situations, they are both simultaneously. They create "social dilemmas" for the participants. Each member wants to maximize his or her rewards and minimize his or her costs. Selfish behavior may be the best strategy for each individual, but if people act cooperatively then the team and everyone in it is better off.

Unfortunately, many people decide to be competitive in a mixed-motive situation. Once they start acting competitively (or putting in reduced efforts for the team), others respond in the same way. The result is poor team performance. This is one of the reasons why students complain that the worst problem with group projects is that not everyone does his or her fair share (Wall & Nolan, 1987).

Cooperation in a mixed-motive situation is encouraged by several factors. When team members believe their contributions to the team are valuable and important, they are more likely to contribute (Kerr & Bruun, 1983). Members are more prone to act cooperatively if they believe others are likely to act in the same way (Dawes, 1988). Smaller teams tend to be more cooperative than are larger teams (Kerr & Bruun, 1983). Finally, the more members trust one another and believe that others will work for the team, the more committed they become (Parks, 1994).

5.2 Why Are People in Teams Competitive?

Even though working cooperatively on a team should prevent competition, competition may occur anyway. Team members may misperceive the situation and turn a cooperative situation into a competitive one, or may choose to act competitively even when it is in their best interests to act cooperatively. Why do people misperceive a cooperative situation and turn it into a competitive one? The explanations for this phenomenon have to do with culture, personality, and organizational rewards.

Culture

One way to view cultural differences is along an individualist-collectivist dimension (Hofstede, 1980). Individualists tend to be more competitive with their coworkers than collectivists. The United States has an individualist culture that promotes competition. Our emphasis on individualism, freedom, capitalism, and personal success all support the value of competition. Although we are not "anticooperation," we glorify the winners in a competition. Some Americans consider it un-American to say that competition is bad.

Clearly, this cultural value affects the ways in which people respond to situations. Some Americans even have a negative attitude toward teamwork because they believe the individual is more important than the team. To them, a focus on the team means a loss of individual freedom and autonomy.

From a cultural and business perspective, the Japanese have developed a sound approach that combines cooperation and capitalism (Slem, Levi, & Young, 1995). Their collectivist culture promotes cooperation. In Japan, cooperation is highly encouraged and rewarded, and commitment and loyalty are the keys to success in Japanese corporations. At the same time, Japanese businesses have a keen competitive sense. They believe that they are in a competitive fight for survival with other organizations. The key to this struggle is for employees to band together to overcome external forces.

The Japanese and other collectivist cultures have developed a strong inside-outside perspective toward working in teams. It is important for them to act cooperatively with their team members, but also to act competitively with those outside of their team.

Personality

Some people are more competitive than others and act more competitively regardless of the situation. They misperceive situations and redefine them as opportunities to act competitively. This individual difference can be explained as a personality difference. Researchers have identified three personality types to explain why some people are competitive (Knight & Dubro, 1984). These personality types affect how people interpret the situations they are in and how they define success. Figure 5.1 shows how these personality types relate to individual concerns.

Cooperators focus on the team. They are concerned with both their own outcomes and those of others. They attempt to make sure the team is successful and that rewards are distributed equitably among team members.

Competitors view a situation as an opportunity to win. They define success not in terms of their individual goals or the team's goals, but rather relative to others' performances. To a competitor, success means performing better than others. Whether they succeed or the team succeeds is less important than whether they excel more than the other members of the team.

Individualists define success relative to their own personal goals. Unlike competitors, they do not evaluate their performance relative to others. They may or may not care about the success of the team. The team's success is important only if they have adopted the team's goals for themselves.

A cooperative personality type is correlated with many of the standard personality traits used in psychology (Morgeson, Reider, & Campion, 2005). Conscientious people are focused on successful performance, so they are more willing to cooperate with others in teams. Extroverts enjoy cooperation because they like working with others. Agreeable people are more

Figure 5.1   Personality Type and Competition

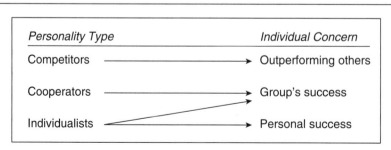

cooperative because they want to avoid the conflicts that competition creates. Finally, people with higher levels of emotional stability tend to be more cooperative and helpful with others.

Organizational Rewards

In many organizations, the shift to teamwork conflicts with the company's human resources practices. Although managers say they want all employees to work as a team, organizational practices often do not encourage or reward teamwork. In most organizations, performance evaluations are based on individual performance, and evaluation is relative to the performance of the other employees. Employees receive a mixed message: Do what the manager says is important (engage in teamwork) or do what you will be rewarded for (stand out as superior to your coworkers). It does not take a psychologist to determine how most employees are going to respond to this mixed message.

The inability to share rewards is probably the factor that most encourages unhealthy competition within organizations (Hayes, 1997). It affects both individual employees and organizational units. For example, departments within an organization often act competitively because they believe they must fight for their share of the organization's resources. Working interdependently to succeed should encourage cooperation over competition (Cheng, 1983). However, many employees are concerned that what is good for the organization overall might not be what is best for them.

Culture, personality, and organizational rewards may all encourage competition when it is not appropriate; however, the most useful of these factors for team leaders is organizational rewards, partly because that is the easiest to change. Although it is tempting to blame American culture, there are many successful team-oriented organizations in the United States. Personality traits are difficult to change, so explaining competition as a personality trait implies there is little the team can do to change the inherent makeup of their team. However, organizational rewards can be changed and used to encourage teamwork and discourage individual competition. (Evaluation and reward approaches are discussed in Chapter 16.) Think about professional football players. These are highly competitive Americans who act very cooperatively with their teammates in order to compete against other teams. They are not driven by personality or culture, but it is the rewards of the situation that orient their behavior.

Shifting a team to cooperative rewards may not change team members' behaviors if they have already established competitive relationships (Beersma et al., 2009). The "cutthroat competition" effect explains that it is harder for teams to change from a competitive to a cooperative relationship when the rewards change than it is to move in the opposite direction. The problem is that once competitive roles have been firmly established, team members do not trust each other to change their behaviors. To change their relationships to reflect more cooperation, team members need to renegotiate their roles and improve coordination. This helps build trust, reduce conflicts, and encourage cooperative behaviors.

5.3 Problems With Competition

What is wrong with competition? Why should competition not help motivate a team? Problems with competition occur on both individual and team levels. Individual competition disrupts the team's focus on its common goals. Team competition creates problems regardless of the team's success. Understanding the dynamics of competition can help explain when and where competition is appropriate.

Communication and Goal Confusion

When individuals or teams in an organization compete against each other, changes occur that prevent the team from being successful (Tjosvold, 1995). Individual competition creates confusion about goals. Eventually, this creates distrust that reduces communication within the team.

A successful team has members who work together to reach a common goal. This common goal provides a focus for the team. However, when team members compete against one another, individual goals can conflict with the team goal. Conflict exists between doing what is best for the individual to succeed (by being better than the others) and doing what is best for the team, which further creates confusion about the goals of the team. Team members then distrust one another because they are uncertain of one another's motives.

The distrust created by mixed goals leads to reduced communication within a team. Communication requires trust; without trust, there is no reason to communicate with others. Over time, internal competition reduces communication within the team.

This goal confusion and breakdown in communication caused by competition can be seen at the organizational level. The managers in an organization must get together and decide on budget allocations. Should a department manager try to do what is best for his or her department or what is best for the organization as a whole? If the departments are competing for limited resources, should the managers request what their departments need, or should they assume that all the other departments are trying to get ahead and aggressively bargain to get as much as they can? Is there any reason to trust the budget estimates from other departments? These questions lead to budget battles where false numbers are used to justify competitive positions.

Intergroup Competition

Intergroup competition can be as much a problem for a team as is individual competition. The classic research project on intergroup competition is Sherif's (1966) studies of boys at summer camp. Researchers divided the boys attending the camp into two groups. For a few weeks, these groups of boys competed against each other in a variety of activities. The effects of competition were negative for both groups. The boys who were arbitrarily divided began to see the members of the other group in negative terms. They formed prejudices—that is, negative beliefs about the abilities of the other group and the personalities of its members. Conflicts became a regular occurrence and required intervention by camp counselors.

The example of how competition can lead to conflict and hostility is even more pronounced in the intergroup situation. Groups are more likely to act competitively with each other than are individuals (Insko et al., 1994). One explanation for this observation comes from social identity theory (Tajfel & Turner, 1986), which reports that a person's sense of self-worth is connected to the groups to which he or she belongs. Consequently, it becomes necessary to view one's group as superior. This translates into an in-group bias, where group members view their own group in overly positive terms, and consequently out-groups in overly negative terms. When the superiority of the group is challenged, members rally to support it and attack the out-group. The conflict escalates easily because group behavior is more anonymous, with fewer interpersonal connections between members and the out-group.

Sherif's (1966) classic study demonstrates several important points about the effects of competition. The main focus was to show that competition led to prejudice. However, the study also revealed the effects of external competition on a team. When a team enters a competition, the team experiences an increase in cohesion and group spirit. Team members become more task focused and tolerate more autocratic leadership. As the competition continues, more loyalty and conformity are demanded from team members. In the short run, these changes may increase productivity and efficiency. In the long run, however, problems arise for the team, regardless of its success.

A team in a competition focuses on its task to the exclusion of social and emotional issues. Over time, ignoring these social issues can lead to the breakdown of the team. Demanding loyalty and conformity from team members may hurt the team's ability to adapt to change. Creativity and innovation may be stifled by competition.

These negative effects of competition occur for both winners and losers. When teams compete, the winners attribute their success to their own superiority (Forsyth & Kelley, 1996). This causes the winners to ignore their problems, which go unsolved. The losing teams often enter into a period of blaming and scapegoating (Worchel, Andreoli, & Folger, 1977). Team members first blame their losses on the situation, then on one another. Eventually, if the teams survive the internal emotional turmoil, they can move to the next step to recognize and solve their problems.

One of the amazing things about the Sherif (1966) study is how easy it is to replicate. In a couple of hours in a workshop, a group of people can be divided into competitive teams. All the negative emotional effects of competition (e.g., prejudices, conflicts, and misperceptions that disrupt performance) soon emerge. This occurs regardless of whether one is studying boys at camp or executives in training programs (Blake & Mouton, 1969). People fall easily into these negative behavior patterns and even accept the negative effects of a competition, if they win.

When Is Competition Appropriate?

Competition is the basis of capitalism because competition encourages innovation, lower prices, and motivation. Given the negative effects of competition, how can this be true? It is important to recognize the difference between internal and external competition. Capitalism is based on competition between organizations, not within organizations. It is useful that Ford competes against General Motors in producing high-quality, low-cost automobiles. It is not useful for Ford's accounting and manufacturing departments to compete with each other within the organization.

To understand how competition affects teamwork, it is important to make this distinction between what occurs within and what occurs outside the team. Competition between organizations can help improve productivity (Hayes, 1997). Competitors provide motivating goals and feedback about performance. However, competition inside an organization can be devastating. It does not matter if the marketing department at General Motors does not give accurate information to Ford; Ford does not expect it. But, when departments within an organization lie to each other to get ahead, the negative impact can be substantial.

Competition may be positive within an organization when jobs are independent rather than interdependent. For example, an organization may sponsor competitions among its sales staff and reward the best performers.

This works when salespeople do not depend on one another to make sales (and when rules are in place that prevent the sabotaging of sales by others). However, most jobs within an organization are interdependent. This is especially true when the organization uses teams. Internal competition among teams within an organization can lead to sabotaged work, unjustified criticism, and withholding of information and resources (Tjosvold, 1995).

5.4 Benefits of and Problems With Cooperation

Cooperation offers many benefits to both the team and its members. However, in some situations, too much cooperation can disrupt a team's performance and decision-making abilities. It is necessary to understand how teams respond to the use of competitive and cooperative rewards.

Benefits of Cooperation

Competition is good for the winners. In other words, for the majority of people in a competitive situation, competition is not a good thing. When members of a team compete, the winners are motivated by the competition. Some members who believe they have a chance of winning are also motivated. However, over time, most group members (about 90%) stop believing they will win. Therefore, they stop being motivated by competition.

Cooperation has the opposite effect on team members. In a cooperative team, all team members are motivated by the team's goals. This motivation is mutually reinforced or encouraged. Team members help and learn from one another. Not only does the team perform better, but so do most of the individual members.

Research on cooperative education demonstrates the benefits of cooperation and competition (Johnson, Maruyama, Johnson, Nelson, & Skon, 1981; Slavin, 1985). In cooperative education classrooms, the best performers still perform at a high level, but the performance of average and lower performers improves. The high performers spend time helping others, and they learn from this experience. Overall, the groups have higher performance, better social relations, higher self-esteem, and a better attitude toward school.

The benefits that accrue to individuals in a cooperative situation have a positive impact on teamwork. Cooperation encourages supportive rather than defensive communication (Lumsden & Lumsden, 1997). Team members are more willing to talk to one another, and this encourages more communication. Increased communication improves coordination on tasks, satisfaction with working together, and overall team performance (Cohen & Bailey, 1997).

The benefits of cooperation at work depend in part on the task. Cooperation is more important when tasks are ambiguous, complex, or changing (Tjosvold, 1995). Such tasks require substantial information sharing to determine the best way to perform them. Because they require coordination, cooperation also is more important when tasks are interdependent and team members need to rely on each other.

Cooperation provides the foundation for the social relations of team members. Teams that work cooperatively have less tension, fewer conflicts, and fewer verbal confrontations (Tjosvold, 1995). They also enjoy a stronger sense of team spirit and greater group cohesion.

Many of the benefits of cooperation for teams are due to the way that conflicts are managed (DeDreu, 2007). To make better decisions, teams need to be motivated to process information and manage differences of opinion in a constructive manner. Cooperation, trust, and safety are preconditions for allowing constructive controversy to occur. When teams handle conflicts constructively, they learn more from each other and perform more effectively.

Problems With Cooperation

Cooperation has its own problems. A team can be too cooperative. It can become so focused on maintaining its internal social relations that it loses sight of the team's goals. Problems with cooperation affect both performance (conformity) and decision making (unhealthy agreement).

Conformity

Highly cooperative teams tend to become highly cohesive. Over time, team members become socially and emotionally connected to one another, which improves communication and coordination. However, this can also create problems because the team becomes too oriented toward itself.

A highly cohesive team is self-rewarding. It rewards contributions and discourages behavior that is not accepted by the team. This means that the team demands conformity from its members. Conformity can help the team operate, but it also can make the team resistant to outside influence and resistant to changing the way it operates (Nemeth & Staw, 1989).

When a team is functioning well and has good performance norms, conformity is a benefit. However, conformity can make it difficult for outsiders to influence the team and change its direction. Even a highly cohesive and cooperative team can perform poorly. Sometimes a work team has norms about not doing too much work (e.g., some of the work teams in the Hawthorne studies mentioned in Chapters 1 and 3). These norms are enforced by the team and can be resistant to change from the organization.

Unhealthy Agreement

Another negative impact of cooperation involves a team's ability to make decisions. Decision making should be focused on making the best decision, given the constraints of the situation. Cooperation can help decision making by establishing trust, which encourages open communication. However, when a cooperative team is cohesive, then the fact that members like one another can disrupt the decision-making process.

The Abilene paradox describes a problem with group decision making caused by members trying to be friendly and cooperative (Harvey, 1988). This occurs when group members adopt a position because they believe it is what other members want. The members fail to challenge one another because they want to avoid conflict or they want to achieve consensus. In the end, they support a proposal no one really wants because of their inability to manage agreement. For example, a project team may continue working on a design strategy that no one thinks will work. However, everyone believes the other team members support this approach, so no one raises objections during team meetings.

The Abilene paradox is an example of unhealthy agreement within a team. In the Abilene paradox, the team's desire to reach agreement on an issue becomes more important than its motivation to find a good solution (Dyer et al., 2007). Team members look for the first acceptable solution or just go along with the leader's solution to avoid disagreements and conflict. This search for quick solutions and avoidance of conflict can lead to poor decisions that cause problems and time delays later in the project. The team is suffering from unhealthy agreement.

Following are some symptoms of unhealthy agreement:

- Team members feel angry about the decisions the team is making.
- Team members agree in private that the team is making bad decisions.
- The team is breaking up into subgroups that blame others for the team's problems.
- People fail to speak up in meetings or fail to communicate their real opinions.

Competitive Versus Cooperative Rewards

There are benefits and problems with both competitive and cooperative reward systems (Beersma et al., 2003). Competitive rewards are effective in motivating individual performance, while cooperative rewards promote trust, cohesiveness, and mutual support, which in turn promote team performance. When a task requires coordinated effort, cooperative rewards are more effective than competitive rewards. However, this simplistic view of cooperative and competitive rewards ignores several important factors that influence work.

What is the primary performance goal? Accuracy and speed of performance are separate, unrelated criteria. Most complex tasks in organizations require both speed and accuracy, but the relative importance of these two factors may vary. A manufacturing team may be encouraged to produce as fast as possible, but this is likely to negatively affect the quality of their performance. Emergency medical teams often must work quickly. At the same time, they must be concerned with the accuracy of their performance. Competitive rewards are strong motivators, especially for encouraging speed (Beersma et al., 2003). Cooperative rewards encourage discussion, collaboration, and information sharing, which may improve accuracy, but will slow the speed of performance.

One of the arguments against using cooperative rewards is that they may encourage social loafing by the team's poor performers (Beersma et al., 2003). High performers are often internally motivated and knowledgeable about how to perform the task, while poor performers have either motivation or skill problems. One of the purposes of organizing people into teams is to enable team members to share their workload and help one another (Ilgen, Hollenbeck, Johnson, & Jundt, 2005). When a member performs poorly because of skill or ability problems, team members will provide assistance and share their knowledge, especially when there are cooperative rewards. When a low-performing member is engaging in social loafing or has motivation problems, competitive rewards may help motivate him or her. Even with cooperative rewards, team members may not provide assistance to someone whose performance is low because of a lack of motivation.

Sometimes, it is the combination of cooperation and competition that works best (Tauer & Harackiewicz, 2004). In a basketball shooting experiment, there was no difference between a cooperative and competitive approach on motivation or performance when performing individually. However, when people worked together to compete against another team, they had higher levels of motivation, satisfaction, and performance. Cooperation encourages participants to be more enthusiastic about working together, while competition focuses participants on the task and challenge. The combination of cooperation and competition rewards accomplishes both objectives.

5.5 Application: Encouraging Cooperation

The central issue in cooperation is the beliefs that team members hold about team goals and the motives of other members (Tjosvold, 1995). Cooperation is based on mutual goals that encourage trust and the ability to rely on others. This encourages team members to combine and integrate their efforts, thereby promoting successful teamwork. Incompatible goals create suspicion and doubt about other team members, thereby leading to a breakdown in communication. Once team members start to compete against one another, the other team members tend to respond in kind (Youngs, 1986).

Encouraging cooperation within a team requires counteracting the negative effects of competition. Competition can lead to confusion about the goals of team members and a breakdown in communication, therefore strategies for dealing with these effects should focus on developing common goals and rebuilding trust and communication (Figure 5.2). Positive social relations among team members can lead to the development of cooperation as a norm. In addition, when teams are in a competitive relationship, team members can develop a strategy for negotiating cooperation in the future.

Common Goals

Research on race relations shows that equal status interactions can help reduce a sense of competition between groups, but that contact by itself is insufficient to reduce the drive to compete (Triandis, 1994). Groups need some reason to work together in order to break down inevitable competitive situations. One approach to forming bonds between groups is through the use of superordinate goals (Sherif, 1966). A superordinate goal is a common goal that all the groups accept as important. By working together on this common goal, prejudice and conflicts between the groups decrease. In the Sherif summer camp studies, counselors brought the boys together to work on common problems that affected the entire camp. Companies focus on the

Figure 5.2   Dealing With the Negative Effects of Competition

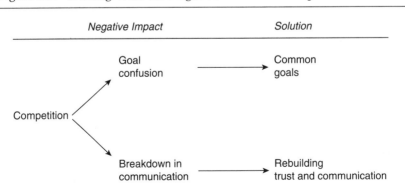

competitive threat from outside as one strategy to encourage the various parts of their organizations to work together.

Working together cooperatively encourages cooperation in the future. Cooperation encourages a redefinition of the group. Rather than viewing the situation as composed of competing parts, people come to believe that they all are part of the same group or team. However, this works only when the cooperative activity is successful. Failure leads to blaming and scapegoating, thereby furthering the competitive relationship among group members (Worchel et al., 1977).

Rebuilding Trust and Communication

Cooperation is encouraged by trust; competition leads to a breakdown in trust (Smith, Carrol, & Ashford, 1995). Trust has both cognitive (Is someone telling the truth?) and emotional (Do I feel I can trust this person?) components (McAllister, 1995). Cooperation primarily relates to the emotional component of trust. Honesty, the number of interactions between team members, and the number of helping experiences they have all lead to greater trust among team members. (Specific approaches to building trust in a team are presented in Chapter 6.)

Cooperation encourages constructive controversy, whereas competition reduces communication and encourages avoidance (Tjosvold, 1995). Constructive controversy allows for open feedback, the raising of questions, and increased communication. Cooperation improves decision making because it increases task-related conflict. Members are able to express a conflict openly without creating social problems within the team. By contrast, conflict is avoided in competitive situations because it is too destructive to social relations. Table 5.1 presents a set of communication rules to foster constructive controversy within a team.

Encouraging Altruistic Norms

Cooperation can develop within a team through positive social interactions. Once established, it becomes a norm for the team. Team altruism is defined as team members' voluntary actions that benefit others (Li, Kirkman, & Porter, 2014). These actions are cooperative and helping behaviors that benefit others or the entire team that are not required by the team or leader. Team altruism can be driven by two different motives. Altruism can be somewhat self-serving, which is when its motives are impression management or social approval. Team altruism is also driven by prosocial motives, such as concern and empathy for others or moral principles (doing the right thing).

Table 5.1   Rules for Constructive Controversy

1. Establish openness norms.	Encourage all team members to express their opinions and feelings.
	Do not dismiss ideas because they appear at first too impractical or undeveloped.
2. Assign opposing views.	Assign a person or subgroup the role of critically evaluating the team's current preferences.
3. Follow the golden rule of controversy.	Discuss issues with others the way you want issues discussed with you. If you want others to listen to you, you should listen to them.
4. Get outside information.	Search for information from a diverse set of outside sources to help the team make a decision.
5. Show personal regard.	Criticize ideas, if you want, but do not attack a person's motivation or personality.
6. Combine ideas.	Avoid either/or thinking, and try to combine ideas to create alternative solutions.

SOURCE: Adapted from Tjosvold, D. (1995). Cooperation theory, constructive controversy, and effectiveness: Learning from crisis. In R. Guzzo & E. Salas (Eds.), *Team effectiveness and decision making in organizations* (pp. 79–112). San Francisco, CA: Jossey-Bass.

A developmental perspective shows how altruism develops and spreads within a team through social interactions. Team members may initiate altruism due to individual motives, such as social approval or concern for others, but then these acts of altruism encourage team coordination and model the value of cooperative behaviors. These positive consequences encourage team altruism to become a norm for the team, which encourages all members to act altruistic toward each other. Thus, the motivation for altruism shifts from personal motives (concern for others) to following the team's norms.

Negotiating Cooperation

Research on the negative effects of competition has examined the various strategies that can be used to encourage cooperation with an opponent. There is an entire research field that uses simulation gaming, such as the prisoner's dilemma, to explore the various options. This research has found a fairly simple strategy for encouraging cooperation (Axelrod, 1984).

The problem for people in a competitive situation is how to make the transition to cooperation. Once competition starts within a team, it tends to continue. If a member tries to threaten the competitors, they become defensive and increasingly hostile. If a member tries to always cooperate with the competitors, then exploitation normally follows. An effective strategy must resolve this dilemma.

The most effective strategy has two rules. First, when the opportunity arises, a team member signals his or her desire to form a cooperative relationship by acting cooperatively. The team member should always start by acting cooperatively and creating opportunities to start over again during transition points in the team's existence. Second, the team member should always respond in kind to his or her competitors' moves (i.e., the tit-for-tat rule). If the competitor acts cooperatively, then the member should respond cooperatively. However, if the competitor acts competitively, the member should respond competitively. This is necessary because an individual who always acts cooperatively is usually exploited.

LEADING VIRTUAL TEAMS: BUILDING TRUST AND SOCIAL RELATIONSHIPS

Problem: Participants in virtual teams may have a more difficult time building trust and social relationships than members of collocated teams.

Solution: Building trust and social relationships among virtual team members can be addressed by focusing on the communication process. In face-to-face communication, the feedback loop for message transfer usually occurs nonverbally. For example, if the meeting leader says "we will finish this section of the agenda in five minutes," the leader can judge from eye contact, facial expression, and body language whether the participants likely received and understood that simple message. In a virtual meeting without high quality videoconferencing, this nonverbal feedback is absent. Even with high quality videoconferencing, the nonverbal information may be difficult for the leader to interpret. Without completion of this feedback loop, we do not know if we were understood, let alone heard.

Building trust requires knowing that our teammates have both heard and understood the meaning of our messages. In virtual meetings this form of trust building does not happen automatically even when videoconferencing. Therefore, the communication feedback loops must be intentionally built into the meeting process and supported by the technology tools employed.

The meeting leader might consider the following activities during the meeting:

1. Reflect back to the team key statements made verbally by distributed members and elicit verbal confirmation from the speaker that the message was reflected back properly. This ensures that the feedback loop is completed between the leader and original speaker and provides other meeting participants with observation of the full loop to support their understanding of the message.

2. If the message is complex or critical to the meeting objective, the leader can request another team member to reflect back the message, perhaps a representative of a different place than the original speaker.

3. Have members of different subgroups jointly clarify and refine key ideas and decisions made during the meeting.

Building social relations can be accomplished in several ways; some of these were discussed in Chapter 3. If possible, meet face-to-face for the first meeting and periodically during the team's life. This allows an opportunity for social and informal communications. Start each virtual team meeting with sharing personal, non-work-related information. These team warm-ups help team members get to know one another. Create a social website for the sharing of photos and personal information. This may be similar to your team's personal Facebook site. It is important for the team leader to participate by using this site; however, team members should not be required to post personal information about themselves.

Summary

Cooperation is the essence of teamwork. However, team members often find themselves in mixed-motive situations that are a combination of cooperation and competition. This is caused by the conflict between individual goals and the team's goals.

People in teams become competitive for three reasons. First, our culture emphasizes the value of competition. Second, people may be competitive rather than cooperative or individualist due to their personality traits. Third, the organization may reward competition among team members. Although all these encourage competition, the organization's reward system is the most useful explanation of the source of competition.

Competition hurts a team by creating goal confusion. Competitive team members focus on individual rather than team goals to guide their behavior.

This leads to distrust, which eventually disrupts communication within the team. Competition with other teams also can create problems leading to hostility and conflict. Although competition with outside organizations may be appropriate, internal competition can be destructive to the team and organization.

Cooperation provides benefits for both individuals and the team. Individuals are motivated and supported in cooperative situations. Cooperation encourages communication and interpersonal support in the team. However, cooperation can cause problems. A cooperative team has high levels of conformity that can reduce performance and creativity and lead to unhealthy agreement, where team members make bad decisions in order to preserve group harmony. Cooperative rewards are more effective in promoting quality work and encouraging the team to help poor performers.

Several team tactics can be used to deal with the negative effects of competition and to build a cooperative environment. A commitment to common goals helps unite team members. Trust building activities can be used to help rebuild any breakdown in a team's communication. Finally, certain negotiation tactics can be used to respond to inappropriate competitive behavior in the team.

Team Leader's Challenge 5

Last year, the manufacturing plant where you work reorganized into self-directed work teams. You are the team leader for one of several teams in the assembly area. The transition to teamwork was difficult, but recently things have been working fairly well. Several months ago, upper management announced a new team incentive program that rewards each team for exceeding production targets. This incentive program had mixed effects on team performance and created some problems at the plant.

Your team is now highly motivated to maximize production, but this has created conflicts with other teams. You find yourself competing with the other manufacturing teams for access to the company's technical support staff. The team has been ignoring machine maintenance issues in order to spend more time producing. There have been several arguments with other teams in the plant who supply parts for your assembly area, and communication with these other teams has deteriorated. You think that the cause of these problems may be the new reward program, but upper management is very supportive of the rewards program.

How should you (the team leader) help the team deal with their internal problems?

What can be done to improve relations with the other teams at the plant?

How can you explain your team's problems to upper management?

SURVEY: COOPERATIVE, COMPETITIVE, OR INDIVIDUALISTIC ORIENTATION

Purpose: To make you aware of your orientation toward others in the team. People vary in their orientation toward other members of the team because of personality differences and different past experiences working on teams. You can develop a cooperative or competitive relationship with other team members or have a more individualistic focus within the team.

Directions: Use the following scale to rate how well these statements describe you:

1 = Not at all   2 = Somewhat   3 = Moderately   4 = Greatly

_____ 1. I like it when everyone on the team works together so we all succeed.

_____ 2. It is important to me to be the best performer on the team.

_____ 3. I don't care how well others do, as long as I succeed at the task I am working on.

_____ 4. I enjoy working on team projects where people share ideas and resources with each other.

_____ 5. Even on a team project, I am motivated to do better than others.

_____ 6. I want to get a good grade in this class regardless of the grades that other students receive.

_____ 7. I learn a lot by working with other people on a team.

_____ 8. I often compare myself with other team members to see who is best.

_____ 9. Even on a team project, I like to spend most of my time working by myself.

_____ 10. I like work situations where people help each other to do a good job.

_____ 11. Most team members evaluate their performance by comparing it to others.

_____ 2. I don't like it when I have to work with others on a project.

_____ 13. I am more productive when I can work with other people.

_____ 14. People perform best when they are encouraged to outperform others.

_____ 15. I would rather work alone than have to coordinate with others.

Scoring:

Add questions 1, 4, 7, 10, and 13 to obtain your Cooperative orientation score.

Add questions 2, 5, 8, 11, and 14 to obtain your Competitive orientation score.

Add questions 3, 6, 9, 12, and 15 to obtain your Individualistic orientation score.

Discussion: How did you compare with other members of your team? If you are highly cooperative or highly competitive, what can you do to make yourself a better team player? What is the impact to the team of having highly cooperative or highly competitive members? How should the team deal with members who are very competitive in their orientation?

SOURCE: Adapted from Johnson, D., & Johnson, F. (1997). *Joining together: Group theory and group skills* (6th ed.). Boston, MA: Allyn & Bacon.

ACTIVITY: UNDERSTANDING COMPETITIVE VERSUS COOPERATIVE GOALS

Objective: Teamwork should be a cooperative activity. Whether team members act cooperatively or competitively depends on how they are evaluated and rewarded. This activity lets groups experience working under competitive and cooperative conditions.

Activity: The class is divided into groups and instructed to make two construction projects. The first project (tower) has a competitive goal, while the second project (arch) has an individualist or cooperative goal. Activity Worksheet 5.1 contains instructions for this activity. It may be useful to assign observers to note how the groups perform these two activities.

Analysis: How did the groups behave differently during these two activities? What were some examples of cooperative and competitive behaviors that occurred in or between the groups? How did group members feel about participating in the two projects?

Discussion: How do competitive and cooperative goals affect behavior within and between groups? What is the impact of quantity (and/or production) versus quality goals on teamwork?

ACTIVITY WORKSHEET 5.1
Competitive Versus Cooperative Goals

Construction Projects

1. Divide the class into groups of four or more members.

2. Give each group a box of supplies, including colored paper, one or more magazines, cardboard, tape, scissors, markers, and paper clips.

Project 1—Construct the Tallest Tower

- Groups have 15 minutes to construct the tallest, free-standing tower possible.

- The group with the tallest tower wins an award (such as candy).

Project 2—Construct a Beautiful Arch

- Groups have 15 minutes to construct an attractive, free-standing arch.

- Groups are allowed to share ideas and materials with one another.

- Judges will give awards (such as candy) to all beautiful, free-standing arches.

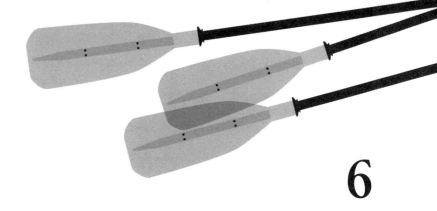

6

Communication

David Askay

Central to any team's actions is communication. People respond both to the content of a message and how a message is communicated. Communication climate, psychological safety, social processes, and trust influence the flow of a team's communications, which impacts both the team's productivity and cohesiveness. Additionally, the emotional intelligence of the team and individuals in the team help make the team's communications more sensitive and effective. Improving communication requires building trust within the team, facilitating team meetings, and developing good communication skills.

Learning Objectives

1. Why is communication important in teams?

2. What contributes to miscommunication in a team?

3. What biases does a team have when processing information to make a decision?

4. How can one avoid dysfunctional group decision making?

5. How are communication and gender interconnected?

6. How can one build trust within a team?

7. What are the characteristics of supportive and defensive communication climates?

8. How does perception of psychological safety affect a team's communications?

9. What is emotional intelligence? How does it affect a team's communications?

10. What are some of the important activities of the facilitator of a meeting?

11. What are the basic communication skills that are useful to facilitate a team meeting?

6.1 Communication Process

Communication in teams can be viewed as a transaction (Barnlund, 1970). This perspective emphasizes that communication is more than simply the transmission of a message from a sender to a recipient. Rather, the transactional model of communication recognizes that people are both simultaneously senders and recipients of messages—both verbal and nonverbal feedback provided by a recipient continuously influences the message that a sender sends. Consider a team member beginning a meeting with an enthusiastic update about the team's progress, only to have blank stares from others in the team. Such nonverbal communication might be interpreted as disinterest, leading to a loss of enthusiasm and change in the direction of the discussion. A second component of the transactional model is that all parties involved in communication influence and are influenced by each other. For example, we often change our communication depending on the recipient of our communication—your communication around your coworkers is likely different than your communication when your manager is present.

Taken together, the simultaneous sending and receiving of messages and the mutual influence of team members illustrate how team communication is a dynamic process that is constantly changing. Consider what occurs when a professor suddenly appears to check in on a group discussion during class; the student's discussion might shift from the previous night's events to quickly blurting out praise and intrigue about the concepts from the lesson. However, members are not the only dynamic affecting communication in teams—levels of trust, power, status, and motivation also change over time and have consequences for the cohesiveness and productivity of a team. These dynamics emphasize that not only *what* you communicate, but *how* you communicate is influenced by and influences the functioning of a team. It is important, then, to be aware of how your communication positively or negatively impacts the team, while also attending and adapting to how others are influencing the team.

Verbal Communication

When communicating verbally, we use language in an attempt to share meaning with others. This might include determining the purpose of your team project, sharing information, or deciding on a solution. While this may appear rather straightforward, the nature of language often makes sharing meaning difficult. This is because the meanings of words are often highly subjective. Language is based on words (like *dog*), which are themselves symbols that refer to something else (a four-legged carnivorous mammal that is often a pet). While the reference of some words is concrete, many others—particularly those involved in problem solving and innovation—are ambiguous. Overlooking this communication element can lead to frustration, failed projects, and wasted time. Consider a team wanting to expand healthy food options on a university campus. There are various contested understandings of what *healthy food* means—such as low calorie, not processed, locally-sourced, organic, non-GMO, vegan, raw, meat-free, and so forth. It is likely that each member of a team will have a different understanding of what is and what is not healthy food. The team must collectively define precisely what they mean in order to effectively research and implement their goal of expanding healthy food options on campus.

However, team members often assume that everyone understands the same meaning for a word. This is called *bypassing,* and it can be a source of much misunderstanding and conflict when engaging in activities, such as assigning tasks and processing information. Consider the coordination of a team assignment. The leader may instruct the team to email their section of the report by Thursday so that she or he can put them together for class on Friday. While the leader may have been expecting the sections by noon, some team members may wait until 11:59 p.m. This delay could prevent the leader from effectively combining the sections and lead to decreased team productivity, as well as conflict between members. Similarly, senders of information often have poor perspective-taking and overestimate a receivers' familiarity with the information being discussed (Keysar & Henly, 2002). This lack of perspective-taking is one reason why technical professionals, such as engineers, have difficulty sharing specialized knowledge in a team—they assume that the receivers have sufficient background information to make sense of brief messages. To avoid verbal miscommunications, team members need to disambiguate their words with clear definitions.

Nonverbal Communication

In addition to using verbal language to share meaning with others, nonverbal cues, such as body language, vocal tones, gestures, touch, eye contact, facial expressions, and use of time and space, can also communicate meaning to others. Moreover, nonverbal messages can replace, emphasize, or even contradict our verbal communication. For example, members can assert dominance over the team through their posture and vocal tones or express contempt through arriving late to a meeting and sarcastically apologizing. Just like verbal communication, nonverbal communication is also ambiguous and easily misunderstood (e.g., is a member not participating because they are tired, disinterested in the project, or angry at another member?). Additionally, nonverbal communication is also continuous—we are always communicating something nonverbally, whether intentionally or unintentionally. Effective team members need to develop awareness as to how their nonverbal communication might be influencing the team and also develop sensitivity to the nonverbal messages of others in the team. As will be discussed later, sensitivity to the nonverbal messages of others and attentiveness to your own nonverbal messages is an essential component of team emotional intelligence.

Communication Within Teams

The simultaneous sending and receiving of verbal and nonverbal communication and the mutual influence of all members have widespread implications for the development and functioning of a team. Poor communication can lead to dysfunctional processing of information and unnecessary conflict among team members. However, by developing the knowledge and skills of effective and appropriate communication (Spitzberg, 1983), teams can foster trust, establish appropriate team norms, and develop a collaborative and creative climate. More importantly, it is through *continued* effective and appropriate communication that these benefits are realized. Trust, for example, is not something that is simply attained and lasts forever. Rather, it is continuously affirmed and reaffirmed through the ongoing interactions between team members: Communication is a transactional process through which we are constantly defining and redefining our relationships with group members. Attention to the flow of communication in a team can empower you to make informed communicative choices that maximize productivity and foster cohesiveness among members.

6.2 Flow of a Team's Communications

Communication plays a vital role in the functioning of a team. Members need to be aware of how to communicate in a manner that is both effective and appropriate for reaching team goals and maintaining the relationships. Ineffective communication can contribute to dysfunctional processing of information, leading to poor decisions. Misunderstandings can also emerge from differences in gender communication styles. Similarly, inappropriate communication can damage the cohesiveness between team members and impede the development of trust. Choices in how you communicate can establish and maintain a safe communication climate that encourages team members to express their knowledge, opinions, and feelings in difficult situations. Interpersonal processes influence the willingness of team members to share information in team discussions. Trust provides the foundation for open and honest communications in the team.

Dysfunctional Information Processing Within the Team

The use of teams creates the potential to make better decisions because members can pool information from diverse backgrounds and experiences. This benefit of using teams occurs only if members share their unique information with the team. However, teams can engage in dysfunctional information sharing and processing that can lead to poor decision making. For example, teams spend most of their time discussing the information already shared by all members rather than combining the unique knowledge and perspectives of members (Gigone & Hastie, 1997). This focus on common rather than unique information also explains why teams often overlook technical information. This type of information is likely to be known to only a few team members, so the team rarely discusses it. Consequently, the information held by most team members before a discussion has more influence on a decision than information received during a meeting, regardless of whether this information is accurate.

Biases in the ways a team processes information may prevent the team from making good decisions because important information that one member holds is ignored by the team (Stasser, 1992). For example, confirmation bias is the prevalent tendency for people to seek information that confirms their beliefs and attitudes, while ignoring information that contradicts their currently held beliefs and attitudes (Nickerson, 1998). In other words, team members often find what they expect to see when processing information. One study found that the auditory perception of a patient's breathing (a critical symptom that distinguishes between two life-threatening conditions) by teams of physicians was influenced by the diagnoses they had anticipated (Tschan et al., 2009)—these physicians heard a breathing pattern that was consistent with the presumed diagnoses even though this breathing pattern was not objectively present. The patient was misdiagnosed because the physicians ignored information that disconfirmed their beliefs. Likewise, design teams may not seek out information that disconfirms the assumptions and beliefs of the team. However, teams that actively process disconfirming information can produce more creative designs, or at the very least, avoid implementing poor solutions. To combat confirmation bias, members should actively find and passionately present disconfirming evidence and information to the team. It can be helpful to assign a member the role of "devil's advocate" to help establish a norm of challenging the team's assumptions.

Information can be also be processed poorly by a team if they discuss topics in terms of false dichotomies. A false dichotomy is the tendency to view options as two opposing extreme possibilities (e.g., either/or, for/ against, etc.) when other possibilities exist (Rothwell, 2015). In other words, perceiving the world in absolute terms (e.g., you are either with me or against me) is often false, since much of reality (and creative solutions) exists in the grey area between these extremes. However, despite this sounding rather obvious, it is often difficult to quickly and easily communicate about these grey areas because our language lacks appropriate words. While we can immediately think and speak in terms of opposites (e.g., short-tall, loud-quiet, etc.), the words to describe the midpoint between these concepts are often vague and nonspecific to the word pairing (between *short* and *tall* is *average*, between *loud* and *quiet* is also *average*, etc.). This illustrates how our language often predisposes us to think in extremes.

False dichotomies can influence the nature of solutions that teams design. Consider the example of a group of students who wished to address the skate-boarding ban on campus by advocating for the ban to be repealed—a clear 'allow-ban' dichotomy in devising a solution. Given the university administration's concern for the safety of both pedestrians and skateboarders, the entire proposal was rejected and the group was unsuccessful in achieving their goal. However, a more fruitful solution might have been to advocate for a middle ground position between banning and allowing, such as for permissible times and locations for skateboarding to be allowed on campus (which incidentally is how bicycling on campus is often regulated). Such an integrative solution allows for the needs of both parties to be met. To battle the false dichotomies that emerge in group discussions, it is useful to question absolute statements made by members and to use the language of provisionalism (e.g., sometimes, often, etc.) when discussing information. This provides the communicative space in a discussion to explore alternate solutions.

Gender and Communication

Research examined group interactions in mixed-sex teams and revealed that men and women tend to exhibit a preference for different communication styles (Tannen, 1991). Masculine communication styles emphasize gaining *status*, which means that talk embodies independence, competition, exerting control, and reporting knowledge in an effort to elevate their position in the group. Consequently, men tend to speak more, focus on task-oriented information, interrupt, offer advice, and make jokes more often than women in mixed-sex groups. In contrast, feminine communication styles emphasize building *connection*, which means that talk embodies interdependence, cooperation, and empowerment in an effort to facilitate agreement, interest in others, and participation. Women, then, tend to share feelings, invite others to speak, and listen in order to foster bonds between members. While labeled masculine and feminine, both of these communication styles are used by both sexes—rather there is a *tendency* for the communication of women to embody connection and the communication of men to embody status.

By understanding these styles of communication, members can better adapt their communication to the group and minimize misunderstandings. For example, the masculine tendency to focus on task-oriented communication may lead a member to consider the sharing of feelings to be a waste of meeting time and discourage a feminine speaker from sharing her emotions with other members. In this scenario, the feminine speaker's desire to foster connection among members is being marginalized, contributing to a less fulfilling and supportive environment. Likewise, a feminine speaker may share their emotions about a difficult day with the desire of gaining comfort and sympathy from teammates; however, a masculine member may instead offer suggestions on how to fix the cause of their problems. Here, these two communication styles are misaligned and a member is not meeting the communication needs of another member. Such misunderstandings may decrease the trust and cohesiveness of team members. Rather than privileging either feminine or masculine communication styles as superior, team members should seek to respect the need for both to coexist. Indeed, instrumental and relational aspects of teams need to be appropriately managed and understood.

Building Trust

Trust can develop differently across different cultures. For instance, a basis for trust in the United States is through having a shared category membership with group members (e.g., both went to the same college), while in Japan, trust is impacted by sharing interpersonal ties with group members.

Trust is also key to fostering communication in a team. For team members to trust, they must believe the team is competent to complete its task (team efficacy) and the team environment is safe for all members (Ilgen, Hollenbeck, Johnson, & Jundt, 2005). Trust is the expression of confidence in the team relationship—that is, the confidence one has that other team members will honor their commitments (Thompson, 2004). It is built on past experiences, understanding the motives of others, and a willingness to believe in others. Trust within a team encourages communication and cooperation and makes conflicts easier to resolve.

Trust is based on social relationships (Uzzi, 1997). People make investments in developing and maintaining their relationships; ties among people encourage cooperation and trust. At the beginning of a social encounter, people take a chance on trusting the other person, while observing how the other responds. The experience of future trust is determined by what happens in the relationship. Trust is built and maintained over time through social interactions—through the sharing of feelings and thoughts.

Trust has many impacts on interpersonal communication, cooperation, and teamwork (Jones & George, 1998). When teams have high levels of trust, people are more willing to help others in a variety of situations. The free exchange of information is encouraged, and there is increased participation in the team's activities. People are more willing to commit to team goals (and to ignore personal goals) when the level of trust is high, plus people are more willing to become involved in the team's activities.

Trust is an individual behavior, but can be viewed at the team level (DeJong & Dirks, 2012). Although one can talk about the overall level of trust, there is a substantial amount of variability in how much team members trust each other. The lack of trust by only a few members of the team can break down the positive relationship between trust and team performance. Team leaders need to build trust among team members and be aware of specific relationships within the team where trust is low. When there are problems with a lack of trust between particular members, procedures for them to monitor each other's performance and ensure obligations are met can help the team rebuild trust in specific relationships.

Building trust in a team involves two types of behaviors: trusting and trustworthiness (Johnson & Johnson, 1997). Trusting means being willing to be open with information and sharing with others by providing help and resources. Trustworthiness means accepting the contributions of other team members, supporting their actions, and cooperating in assisting them.

Although building trust is a slow process, trust is quickly and easily destroyed, often by a single incident. Reestablishing trust after it has been broken may be difficult. The following are some techniques to help (re)build trust:

- Apologize sincerely for actions that destroyed trust in the team.
- Act trusting and demonstrate your support for others in the team.
- Promote cooperation in the team.
- Review the team's goals and gain commitment to common actions.
- Establish credibility by making sure that actions match words.

Psychological Safety

Trust is closely associated with psychological safety in teams. Psychological safety is the perception that members are free to take interpersonal risks and to express their thoughts and feelings without fear of consequences (Edmondson & Lei, 2014). It is a climate of interpersonal trust and mutual respect where team members are able to offer ideas, provide feedback, raise issues, admit mistakes, and ask for help without fear of retribution. This is particularly important to teams where the sharing of diverse information and integration of perspectives is a central activity. Indeed, research consistently shows that psychological safety is associated with higher levels of learning from mistakes (Hirak, Peng, Carmeli, & Schaubroeck, 2012), success in diverse teams (Caruso & Woolley, 2008), creativity (Baer & Frese, 2003), and team performance (Edmondson & Lei, 2014). Virtual teams also benefit from psychological safety, as this mitigates the negative effects of geographical dispersion, electronic dependence, and national culture on innovation and performance (Gibson & Gibbs, 2006).

The value of psychological safety can be seen in the operation of cross-functional teams that are composed of members from a variety of technical backgrounds (Edmondson & Nembhard, 2009). The diversity of viewpoints in these teams is crucial for their success, but this only happens if team members are willing to share their knowledge and learn from each other. These teams encounter communication problems, such as socially induced silence, unproductive communication, and differences in professional language. Members of some cultures may also withhold questions, feedback, or disagreement due to cultural norms dictating politeness or face-saving behaviors.

To overcome the problems created by diversity, teams need to develop an environment of psychological safety to mitigate the interpersonal risks of interacting. Team leaders play an important role in establishing psychological safety by inviting input and feedback, while showing openness to receiving critical information. They can also encourage members to speak up by facilitating communications and minimizing status differences. Assigning the role of devil's advocate can help to legitimize disagreement in teams. Leaders also demonstrate that failure is an opportunity for learning rather than threatening punishment for communicating about problems. While psychological safety is generally viewed as a cognitive phenomenon, it is manifested through communication (Gibson & Gibbs, 2006). This indicates that all team members can foster psychological safety through promoting a supportive communication climate.

Communication Climates

Closely related to psychological safety is the communication climate of groups. Gibb (1961) identified six patterns of group communication that increase or decrease the degree of defensiveness exhibited by members. How one communicates can influence whether team members focus on the content (what they said) or structure (how they said it) of the message. A defensive climate occurs in response to perceived threats to one's self-esteem and shifts mental attention away from the message content and team tasks to instead defending oneself and distorting information. In the short term, this decreases team productivity and erodes cohesiveness. In the long term, a defensive climate can led to burnout and turnover (Becker, Halbesleben, & Dan O'Hair, 2005). By contrast, a supportive climate emphasizes the content of a message and yields increased cooperation and trust, which is essential for the development of psychological safety. Team members establish and maintain a supportive communication climate through choices of how they structure their communication. Gibb offers the following patterns of communication that can contribute to a defensive versus supporting climate.

Evaluation Versus Description

Messages with evaluations contain judgments, accusations, you-statements, contempt, fault finding, and criticism (e.g., *You haven't contributed enough to this presentation*), which are often met with efforts to absolve oneself from blame (e.g., *But, I came to every meeting! Besides, you never gave me clear directions*). By contrast, descriptions that involve framing comments in a manner minimize unease and consider the perceptions and feelings of the sender (e.g., *I'm concerned that our presentation won't go well and have some requests that I'd like you to consider*). Strategies to adopt more descriptive language include using "I-statements" rather than "You-statements" and providing genuine praise before negative feedback (Hornsey, Robson, Smith, Esposo, & Sutton, 2008).

Control Versus Problem Orientation

A defensive climate can emerge from communication aimed at controlling other people by telling them what to do. Indeed, research on psychological reactance reveals that efforts to control one's behavior are often met with resistance or even the opposite behavior (Brehm & Brehm, 1981). This can be illustrated by imagining the typical response of a child being told to clean his or her room. Similarly, members in teams often respond negatively to demands placed on them by others. For example, demanding that a team member skip a planned social event in order to finish an assignment might lead to resistance. However, a more effective pattern of communication is to focus instead on the problem and invite ideas for solving the problem (e.g., *What can we do in order to finish this project by tonight?*). This allows for a productive conversation aimed at how to solve the problem, rather on placing demands on specific team members.

Strategy Versus Spontaneity

People are sensitive to strategies employed to manipulate or deceive them, such as members excusing themselves from a meeting by calling in "sick" or leaving a meeting early because they suddenly have an "appointment." While certainly there are times when such reasons may reflect reality, they contribute to a defensive climate when perceived to be strategic ways of evading uncomfortable questions, withholding information, or not participating. Instead, employing spontaneous communication that is honest, assertive, and contains true self-disclosure can promote an atmosphere of trust in a team (e.g., *I did not sleep well last night and can't meaningfully contribute to this meeting. Can I make it up somehow?*).

Neutrality Versus Empathy

When people communicate, they want to feel heard and to have their perspective considered. In team discussions, however, members may respond with indifference or make little effort to acknowledge others. An example of neutrality is responding to a member's concern about the ethics of a group decision with a dismissive, *"No, it's fine. Don't worry. Let's move on."* Other times a member's email or text message to the team might be completely ignored—even professors can feel devalued by students that fall asleep in class or are distracted by technology. Such behaviors are frustrating and disrespectful, which can contribute to a defensive climate. A supportive climate can be fostered by communicating with empathy—taking another's perspectives and feelings into account. This can be achieved through positive nonverbal behaviors (e.g., listening, putting away a phone during conversations) or verbal behaviors (e.g., *Let's devote the next five minutes to discussing your concern about the ethics of our decision*).

Superiority Versus Equality

Teams often are composed of members possessing differences in power, intelligence, knowledge, skill, wealth, and so on. Despite these differences, messages that are communicated in a superior, belittling manner (e.g., *You're taking too long, I'll just show you the right way to do this*, or *No, I'm the one who has done this before. I know best*) evoke defensiveness that can stifle trust and even promote hostility. This defensiveness can impede the psychological safety of the team by limiting the ability or desire of members to provide meaningful feedback or ask for help that they may need. Instead, adopting communication that embodies a tone of equality (e.g., *I can show you what worked for me, if you'd like*, or *I'd like to hear all of your thoughts on this matter*) and even self-deprecating humor (Greengross & Miller, 2008) encourages harmony and productivity in a team.

Certainty Versus Provisionalism

Few things in life are absolutely certain. On standardized exams, answers containing absolute statements (e.g., always, never, impossible, won't, etc.) are often the incorrect choices and can be a source of frustration for students failing to recall this test-taking strategy. Similarly, team members that communicate with absolute certainty can come across as narrow-minded and unwilling to acknowledge other points of view. Communicating with certainty may shut down discussion (e.g., *That idea will never work!*) and decrease motivation (e.g., *We'll never finish this presentation by tomorrow!*) in the team. Instead, qualifying messages through provisional language by using words like *possibly, might*, and *sometimes* can contribute to more supportive climates where issues can be openly discussed and explored (e.g., *That idea might work, but I have a few concerns*).

These six patterns of communication offer guidance in fostering a supportive communication climate. A communication climate develops in cycles (Lumsden & Lumsden, 1997). When team members communicate with supportive statements, others tend to reciprocate with supportive statements, which encourages trust and openness, and increases their willingness to communicate again. This cycle further increases trust and maintains a supportive climate. However, defensive communication begets defensive communication from others and can quickly spiral into criticism, conflict, and decreased trust. This underscores the importance of quickly recognizing and breaking dysfunctional cycles of defensive communication when they emerge in teams. Adopting supportive patterns of communication can help to establish and maintain psychological safety and promote trust in the team. Still, these should not be expected to work in all situations. Moreover, there are times when defensive strategies are needed, such as using control when dismissing an underperforming member from a team.

6.3 Emotional Intelligence

Feelings and emotions pervade the fabric of teams. *Emotional intelligence* (EI) is the ability to solve emotional problems (Mayer & Salovey, 1997). EI is an important aspect of communication in team discussions and is associated with enhanced levels of team performance (Quoidbach & Hansenne, 2009) and reduced team conflict (Yang & Mossholder, 2004). Additionally, emotional intelligence in members is consistently associated with leadership emergence in teams (Côté, Lopes, Salovey, & Miners, 2010). It includes the following four components:

1. Self-awareness—the ability to identify, understand, and discuss one's emotions;

2. Empathy—the ability to perceive, recognize, and experience others' emotions;

3. Emotional regulation—the ability to regulate one's emotions and control the expression of emotions; and

4. Relationship management—the ability to respond to others' emotions with respect and concern for the relationship. (See Figure 6.1.)

Although EI can be viewed as a skill of individual team members, EI can also be viewed as a part of the team's communication climate. Team EI is about building norms that support the awareness and regulation of emotions

Figure 6.1 Components of Team Emotional Intelligence

	Focus	
	Self	*Other*
Awareness	Self-awareness	Empathy
Behavior	Emotional regulation	Relationship management

SOURCE: Adapted from Greenberg, J. (2011). *Behavior in Organizations* (10th ed.). Boston, MA: Prentice Hall.

within the team (Druskat & Wolff, 2001). Our relationships with team members are not the product of any single interaction, but rather are constantly being defined and redefined during ongoing communication exchanges (Parks, 1977). The ability to recognize and regulate one's emotions and the emotions of others during these ongoing interactions can enhance the relationships of team members. Regulating ones' expression of emotion is important because emotions are contagious in small groups (Ilies, Wagner, & Morgeson, 2007), often occurring without members even being aware of it (Hatfield, Cacioppo, & Rapson, 1993). In particular, team leaders have the most influence over team emotions (Visser, van Knippenberg, van Kleef, & Wisse, 2013).

The development of emotional awareness of a team is influenced greatly by norms. Indeed, collectively endorsed team norms (Diefendorff, Erickson, Grandey, & Dahling, 2011) can shape the emotions felt and displayed in teams (Barsade & O'Neill, 2014). Consequently, team norms can develop that suppress emotions (Menges & Kilduff, 2015), require expression of specific emotions (Van Maanen & Kunda, 1989), or encourage open expression of a range of emotions (Martin, Knopoff, & Beckman, 1998). One way to foster team EI is through developing emotional awareness norms, such as taking time to get to know each other in order to increase interpersonal understanding and to ensure equal participation so that all perspectives can be considered. Emotional regulation norms include setting ground rules for conversational courtesy, providing emotional support to help team members, creating outlets to express emotions, and developing a positive communication environment. These behavioral norms help build trust among team members, create a strong team identity, and develop a sense of team efficacy.

Emotionally intelligent teams are aware of the emotional reactions of team members and develop norms that encourage both confrontation and caring. For example, when a team is trying to make a decision and one member disagrees, it is easy for the team to vote and move on to the next issue. However, an emotionally intelligent team would pause and try to better understand why a team member objects to the decision. They would engage in perspective taking to help understand the issue from alternative views. This shows that the team appreciates and has respect for this perspective, and it may lead to a consensus decision that is acceptable to all team members.

Team EI has many positive impacts on team processes and performance. Emotionally intelligent teams are better able to work through emotional problems, which motivates team members and increases group cohesion

(Ayoko, Callan, & Härtel, 2008). They have higher levels of team trust, which is important for developing a collaborative environment and promoting creativity (Barczak, Lassk, & Mulki, 2010). EI teams are more effective when working in demanding and stressful situations because they have better coordination, fewer conflicts, and use more collaborative conflict resolution approaches (Farh, Seo, & Tesluk, 2012).

One of the most significant results of team EI is the way conflicts are managed. In interdisciplinary teams like medical teams, teams with low levels of EI have poorer social skills, more disruptive behaviors, and use more coercive power tactics (McCallin & Bamford, 2007). Conflicts in these teams threaten the psychological safety of members. Teams with higher levels of EI have fewer conflicts and the conflicts are less intense (Ayoko et al., 2008). These teams are more likely to use a collaborative approach to resolve conflict, while teams with lower levels of EI are more likely to use avoidance as a conflict resolution strategy (Jordan & Troth, 2004).

Teams can improve their EI in several ways. Emotionally intelligent team leaders can model appropriate behavior and facilitate sensitive team communications (Koman & Wolff, 2008). Teams can develop behavioral norms to guide how they manage emotions. Team settings are a good way to teach people how to act with emotional intelligence (Ferris, 2009). Experiential group activities can be used to learn how to perceive emotions, manage one's emotional responses, and act effectively in emotionally challenging social situations. Team-based learning approaches also help build social bonds within the team by creating a psychologically safe context for applying the newly learned emotional abilities (Clarke, 2010).

To discover your own level of EI and discuss how emotionally intelligent norms impact team communication, take the team EI survey at the end of this chapter.

6.4 Facilitating Team Meetings

"So, what are we doing?" These are perhaps the five most frightening words to hear at the beginning of a team meeting. It indicates that the next sixty minutes will probably be spent figuring out why you are meeting for sixty minutes. No wonder that team meetings are often viewed negatively as a waste of time (Rogelberg, Shanock, & Scott, 2012)—many of the meetings you have attended in the past likely *were* a waste of time if they were poorly structured, started late, lacked purpose, went off topic, were dominated by a few individuals, and/or ended late (Rogelberg, Allen, Shanock, Scott, &

Shuffler, 2010). Luckily, bad meetings are not inevitable. By introducing a structure that helps control and facilitate communication, meetings can make more efficient use of everyone's time.

Meetings are where teams share information, make decisions, solve problems, and make sense of their purpose. While a well-structured meeting can actually save time and improve effectiveness of a team, many teams choose not to invest the time in preparing an effective agenda nor managing the participation of members. Instead, poorly structured meetings are often dominated by a few members—in a typical four-person group, two people do more than 70% of the talking; in a six-person group, three people do more than 85% of the talking (Shaw, 1981). Equal participation is an important predictor of success in a variety of team tasks (Woolley, Chabris, Pentland, Hashmi, & Malone, 2010), while unequal participation contributes to dissatisfaction and frustration. Moreover, effective meetings can actually improve attitudes toward meetings and the team as a whole.

In general, meetings start with a review of the agenda and warm-up activities designed to get people talking socially. The body of the meeting focuses on managing the communication process and making the team's decisions. The meeting ends with a summary of decisions and assignments and an evaluation of how well the team is operating. (See Figure 6.2.) Research provides additional guidelines for organizing and conducting effective meetings:

1. *Only have a meeting when there is no other alternative.* Consider the tasks that need to be accomplished and determine if a meeting is truly necessary. Use alternatives when appropriate (e.g., voting via email, quick discussion via teleconference, etc.). You may even set standards for when you have a meeting, such as only when there is a compelling agenda or unresolved issues that impact interdependent tasks (Rogelberg, Scott, & Kello, 2007).

2. *Distribute an agenda several days before the meeting.* Meetings function more effectively when they are planned in advance (Rogelberg et al., 2007) and meeting participants enjoy meetings more when they have a clear objective (Allen et al., 2012). Several days before the meeting, send members an agenda that includes the location, time, duration, and purpose of the meeting. Most importantly, include a concise list of discussion topics, time estimates for topics, and reading materials so that members can come prepared. Some meeting coordinators may solicit additional topics from members to be included in the agenda.

3. *Keep the meeting on time.* People often dislike meetings because they go off topic and run late. Assign a team member to be a timekeeper whose job is to keep the meeting on schedule and end on time. Determine a time limit for individual members to speak so that everyone has an opportunity to contribute to the discussion.

4. *Manage disruptive behaviors.* Disruptive team members may dominate the discussion, be overly talkative, or be rude to other team members. All team members share responsibility for handling difficult members; it is not just the job of the leader to maintain the flow of the meeting. The leader should acknowledge and verbally reward acceptable behaviors. If problem behaviors persist, the leader should talk privately with repeat offenders. If none of these approaches work, assistance from outside the team (e.g., a manager responsible for supervising the offender) may be required.

5. *Summarize important discussions and decisions.* The leader must keep team members focused on the agenda topics. To keep the group process flowing, the leader should stop after discussion of each major agenda item and summarize the team's conclusions. This allows for a check on whether all team members agree with what has happened at the meeting.

6. *Evaluate the group process at the end of each meeting.* The team should evaluate the effectiveness of meetings to identify how the meeting operated, whether there are areas for improvement, and if the meeting objectives were achieved. It is important to gather perceptions from all meeting attendees about the meeting quality because leaders tend to have more positive perceptions of the meeting than those who are not in a position of power (Cohen, Rogelberg, Allen, & Luong, 2011). These group process evaluations provide feedback to the team about its performance and help deal with problems before they get emotionally out of hand. (See the Appendix for a discussion of the use of group process evaluations.)

Figure 6.2   Facilitating a Team Meeting

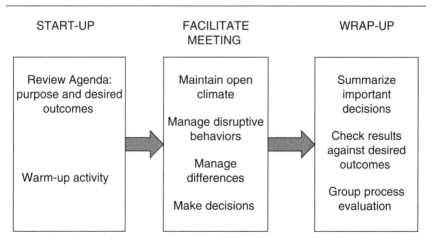

SOURCE: Adapted from Kayser, T. (1990). *Mining group gold.* El Segundo, CA: Sherif.

7. *Distribute minutes of the meeting.* Lack of follow-through on what is discussed is another predictor of dissatisfaction with team meetings (Rogelberg et al., 2010). Indeed, it can be frustrating when a member assigned with completing a task comes to the meeting and announces that they forgot they were supposed to do that. This can be alleviated by assigning someone to create a summary of what was discussed, what decisions were made, what needs to be deliberated, and what actions are expected of members before the next meeting. This not only keeps team members accountable for their assigned tasks, but also updates members who may have been absent from the meeting.

6.5 Communication Skills for Team Meetings

There are many communication skills that are useful for team members. This section reviews four skills.

1. *Ask questions.* Many types of questions are useful for promoting team discussions (Hackett & Martin, 1993). In general, open-ended questions encourage discussion, whereas close-ended questions (e.g., yes/no questions) tend to limit discussion. It is better to ask the team to discuss the pros and cons of an idea than to ask team members whether they agree or disagree with it. After someone has answered a question, it is often useful to ask follow-up questions to clarify the issues. When questions are addressed to the leader, they should be redirected back to the team, if possible, to promote discussion.

When an individual member of the team is asked a direct question by the leader, it can be a threatening experience that reduces discussion. Leaders should try to ask questions of the entire team whenever possible. After asking a question, the leader should remember to give team members sufficient time to respond. The leader should reward participation by acknowledging responses. If no one responds, the leader should try rewording the question or going around the room and having everyone comment on it. A lack of response may mean that the question has a bias or is putting some team members on the defensive.

2. *Listen actively.* The goal of active listening is to provide feedback to the sender of a communication to clarify the communication and promote discussion (Johnson & Johnson, 1997). Good listeners communicate their desire to understand the message and improve their understanding rather than being a conversation narcissist. When listening to a team member, you can respond with either a support response or a shift response (Vangelisti, Knapp, & Daly, 1990). A shift response can erode a supportive climate through refocusing attention from the speaker to oneself by changing the topic of discussion, therefore disregarding the concerns of the speaker. By contrast, a support response demonstrates your awareness by keeping the team's attention on the speaker and their topic. For example, the leader of your team mentions that they are frustrated with the meetings

frequently starting late. A shift response is, "Well, I am frustrated that we never have food here. We should do something about that." A support response is, "That is frustrating. What do you think we should do about it?"

Active listening is another approach to improving communication. In this approach, the listener paraphrases what he or she heard and asks the sender if this is correct. The paraphrasing should convey the listener's understanding of the communication rather than a simple parroting of the message. This sends a message that the listener cares about understanding the message and allows the sender to clarify the communication if needed. Although this is a useful technique, it can become tiresome if used all the time.

3. *Give constructive feedback.* Everyone needs feedback to improve performance. However, receiving feedback (especially negative feedback) may be an uncomfortable experience. Improving one's ability to give constructive feedback is an important teamwork skill (Scholtes, 1994).

The first step in learning to give constructive feedback is recognizing the need for it. Both positive and negative feedback are important. Before giving feedback, examine the context in order to better understand why the behaviors occurred. If a situation is emotional, it is best to wait until things calm down before giving constructive feedback. A team member or leader giving feedback should describe the situation accurately, try not to be judgmental, and speak for himself or herself. When receiving feedback, one should listen carefully, ask questions to better understand, acknowledge reception of the feedback, and take time to sort it out.

If a member is giving solely negative feedback, he or she is not being constructive. Expressing solely negative feedback on the performance or ideas of other team members makes the receivers defensive and discourages communication. It is better to reward desired ideas and behaviors rather than punish the undesirable ideas and behaviors. When giving negative feedback to a team member, corrective alternatives should be offered. Also, negative feedback should be given privately to avoid embarrassing the recipient.

There are several techniques that can improve a team's ability to accept feedback about its performance:

- *Focus on the future.* Focusing on the past makes people defensive. Focus the information on how to improve future performance.
- *Focus on specific behaviors.* Providing general information does not help the team identify the changes needed in its behavior.
- *Focus on learning and problem solving.* The information provided should help the team improve, not just focus on its deficiencies.

4. *Manage feelings.* When emotions become disruptive to the operation of the team, they must be managed effectively (Kayser, 1990). People cannot be prevented from becoming emotional. When emotional issues are related to the team's task, the issues should be addressed in the team meeting. Emotional conflicts related to personal issues may need to be handled in private. All team members should learn how

to handle emotional interactions in the team. The following is an approach to managing feelings during team meetings.

- *Stay neutral.* People have a right to their feelings. The team should encourage and acknowledge the expression of feelings.
- *Understand feelings rather than evaluate them.* All team members should be sensitive to verbal and nonverbal messages. When dealing with emotional issues, it is best to ask questions and seek information to better understand the feelings.
- *Process feelings in the group.* When the team's operation is disrupted by emotions, the team should stop and be silent briefly to cool down. Once that has happened, the task-related issues should be discussed as a group.

This approach to managing emotions is useful when the emotional issues are related to tasks. Team norms that encourage open communication of emotions increase the performance benefits of task-related conflict (Jehn, 1995). However, norms that encourage open communication about relationship-oriented conflict have a negative impact on teams. When emotions are about personal or relationship issues, it is not a benefit to process them with the team.

LEADING VIRTUAL TEAMS: RUNNING VIRTUAL MEETINGS TO ENSURE EVERYONE IS FOLLOWING THE AGENDA AND PEOPLE ARRIVE AT THE SAME UNDERSTANDING

Problem*:* It is more difficult for the leader of a virtual meeting to set and manage an agenda of activities. It is more difficult for participants of a virtual meeting to follow and keep focused on the agenda and activities of a virtual meeting.

Solution: Several solutions can be employed by a virtual meeting leader to address these issues.

1. Publish the agenda ahead of time. Prior access to the agenda permits meeting participants to adequately prepare materials and resources for effective participation. With virtual meetings, it is more likely the meeting leader may not be aware of potential available resources and information or scheduling conflicts that could impact meeting effectiveness. Prior access to the agenda may mitigate these issues.

2. Break the meeting into short chunks. While any well-organized meeting is broken into agenda items, focus and activity at a virtual meeting is improved by breaking the meeting into shorter agenda segments. This is because distributed participants will have trouble maintaining focus during long segments; will cognitively check out during segments of little interest to them (and then have trouble reengaging); and will have fewer cognitive cues to integrate large chunks of complex material generated during long segments. Shorter segments mitigate these issues and provide more opportunity to reengage participants.

3. Script the virtual meeting more tightly than a face-to-face meeting. The advantages of tight scripting are that without nonverbal cues, verbal instructions must be unambiguous and clear; tangential discussions, which contribute to distributed participants losing focus on the agenda, are less likely to occur; and distributed participants who have lost focus are more likely to be able to refocus their attention by linking the activity to the agenda.

4. Create a common visual focus during meetings. The existence of a shared visual focus reinforces a shared understanding among meeting participants. In a face-to-face meeting, shared focus may be on the face of the speaker, on a public display, or on an object of shared exploration (e.g., a photo, a model, a device). In a virtual meeting, the leader must be careful in selecting communication and collaboration tools to ensure that shared focus is present.

5. Create a team display of the meeting process. The common metaphors for this are "dashboard" or "scoreboard." This information might include any of the following information:

   • list of meeting participants, perhaps with access to profiles about each;
   • access to team databases or support information;
   • view of meeting agenda with indication of the current place on the agenda; and
   • relevant statistics describing meeting or project progress.

6. Provide separate communication channels for task and process issues. In a face-to-face meeting, participants who have questions about the meeting process or need personal support can find a moment to engage the leader in a side conversation. In a virtual meeting, a leader must provide a channel for process questions and technical support. If no secondary channel is provided, participants will use the primary channel, interrupting the meeting in order to acquire process support. By choosing tools so that two channels are available, each clearly indicated

for specific purposes, process support can occur with minimal disruption to the meeting activities. For example, most web conferencing products (e.g., WebEx, GoToMeeting) not only provide a primary channel for audio conversation and visual data presentation, but also contain a text chat channel that can be employed for process support by the leader or facilitator.

Summary

Communication is one of the central activities of a team—it is an ongoing process in which members are continuously influencing and are influenced by other team members. By understanding how your verbal and nonverbal communication impacts the team, you can employ communication choices that are more effective and appropriate for the functioning of the team. The meaning of words and nonverbal gestures are often ambiguous and subjective, particularly in teams with diverse members. This requires that members clarify definitions and confirm interpretations to avoid misunderstandings. The team's ability to effectively process information depends on members who actively question their assumptions, seek disconfirming information, and do not speak in false dichotomies. Mutual respect for masculine and feminine communication styles provides insights as to the needs of team members and fosters a more fulfilling environment. Trust is needed for members to fully participate in teams, which necessities developing psychological safety and supportive communication climates. This strongly impacts the willingness of members to pool knowledge in order to make better decisions.

Recognizing and managing emotions is an important aspect of a team's communications. Emotional intelligence is both an individual skill and a set of team norms that encourage effective ways to handle emotions in teams. Emotionally intelligent teams have more supportive communications and higher levels of trust, and team members handle conflict in a collaborative fashion.

Team meetings operate more effectively if a facilitator structures the communication before, during, and after the meeting. Providing an agenda in advance allows both that members are adequately prepared and that they are held accountable for coming to the meeting prepared. During meetings, the facilitator should maintain an open and collaborative climate, manage disruptive behaviors, manage differences, summarize important decisions, and evaluate the group process. After meetings, provide the team with minutes summarizing the decisions and remind members of actions expected before the next meeting.

A number of important communication skills are useful for team members to learn and perform. Asking open-ended, nonthreatening questions fosters better team interactions. Active listening helps clarify the communicator's meaning and acknowledges the importance of the message. Giving constructive feedback is a technique that helps team members learn to improve their performance. Teams can be disrupted by emotions; learning how to process emotions in a group is an important skill.

Team Leader's Challenge 6

You are the leader of a customer service improvement team that meets weekly at the end of the workday. Early in the team's life, the team had some communication skills training. You closely follow the analysis and decision-making structures from the company's *Customer Service Improvement Manual.* Over time, as the team has become more comfortable with analyzing quality problems and creating solutions, you have been using less structure in facilitating the team meetings.

However, you begin to notice problems with the meetings. Not everyone is participating, and the discussions are becoming dominated by several of the older male team members. You notice that their critical personal remarks have silenced some of the women team members. An argument that took place several meetings ago has caused other team members to stop participating during the meetings. Also, discussions tend to drift off topic and seem like repeats of previous conversations.

What should the team leader do to get the team's communications back on track?

What is the best way to handle problem team members during the meetings?

Does the team need more skills training, more communication structure, or outside facilitation? Justify your answer.

SURVEY: TEAM EMOTIONAL INTELLIGENCE

Purpose: To make you aware of your level of emotional intelligence. The survey shows how an emotional intelligence perspective affects communication in a team. You may know what the most emotionally intelligent response is to a situation, yet recognize that you do not always act in this manner.

Directions: Imagine you are a team member facing the following difficult situations. Select the response that best indicates what you think someone *should* do and what you *would* most likely do in that situation.

1. You are a relatively new member to the project team. The team leader has given you an important assignment. This is your chance to show the team leader your value to the team, but only if you are successful. If you fail at this task, it could damage your career.

   a. Thinking about the assignment makes you feel anxious, so you put off working on it for awhile.

   b. Try to relax, think about some alternative approaches to the assignment, and then talk with some other team members about which alternative is best to try.

   c. Work on the assignment for several weeks before telling the other team members about it.

   d. Explain to the other team members how worried you are and ask them to support your ideas.

   People should do: _____ I would do: _____

2. You are a member of a manufacturing team and a friend of yours on the team has borrowed one of your tools. Although you asked him to return the tool to you, he has not done it so far.

   a. Ignore it. Maintaining a friendship is more important than getting the tool back.

   b. Act coolly toward him until he returns the tool.

   c. Explain to your friend that you need the tool and ask him politely to return it.

   d. Friends don't act this way, so you should think about ending the friendship.

   People should do: _____ I would do: _____

3. During the last few team meetings, you notice that one of the team members seems nervous when talking with you.

   a. Decide that the team member isn't interested in working with you, so you focus your communications toward other team members.

   b. Try to interact with the team member in more informal situations so that you can get to know him better.

c. Communicate more formally with this team member since he is not being friendly.

d. Be very careful around the team member because you suspect that you have done something to offend him.

   People should do: _____ **I would do:** _____

4. A team member who works near you has the annoying habit of singing to himself while working on a computer. This is really starting to bother you.

   a. Tell the team leader that it is his responsibility to fix the situation by getting the person to stop or moving him to another work area.

   b. Make jokes about this habit to the team member and hope that he gets the hint.

   c. Explain to the team member that this habit annoys you and ask that he stop doing it.

   d. Ignore the problem because you don't want to disrupt team relations.

   People should do: _____ **I would do:** _____

5. While making lunch in the break room, you accidently knock over a cup of coffee that falls on the floor.

   a. Get angry at yourself because you are a clumsy person.

   b. Clean up the mess and laugh about how accidents always seem to happen to you.

   c. Become embarrassed and leave the break room before anyone sees you.

   d. Glare at the other people in the break room so they won't say anything.

   People should do: _____ **I would do:** _____

6. You have been working on an important part of the team project for the last several months. When you present your work at a team meeting, the team leader criticizes your work.

   a. Ignore the criticism and convince yourself that the team leader was just having a bad day.

   b. Focus on trying to improve your work based on the criticisms you received.

c. Feel so emotionally upset that you go home for the day.

d. Think about how unfair the criticisms are and how the team does not appreciate your hard work.

People should do: _____ I would do: _____

7. There is a heated disagreement at the team meeting about how to handle a problem. Another team member forcefully attacks your position.

a. Hold firm to your position and make new arguments to support it.

b. Get angry with the critical team member and attack his position.

c. Try to develop alternative solutions to the problem in a calm fashion.

d. Shift the discussion at the meeting to a new topic.

People should do: _____ I would do: _____

8. At a social gathering of the team, a male team member criticizes a female team member who is not present. You like and respect the female team member.

a. To get along with the group, agree and add a few other negative comments about the female team member.

b. Don't say anything during the event, but later in private tell the male team member how you really feel about his comments.

c. Tell the male team member that his criticisms are inappropriate and then shift to another topic of conversation.

d. Don't say anything, but then later feel bad about not intervening in the conversation.

People should do: _____ I would do: _____

Scoring:

Scoring is based on demonstrating empathy and showing respect. The most emotionally intelligent responses are the following: 1 = b, 2 = c, 3 = b, 4 = c, 5 = b, 6 = b, 7 = c, 8 = c.

Discussion:

1. How well did you do on the survey? How does your score compare to others?

2. Is there a difference between your "should" and "would" answers? How do you explain the difference? Is this a problem?

3. Focus on question #8. Why is the best answer *c* instead of *b*? When and how should you stand up for others?

SOURCE: Adapted from Greenberg, J. (2011). *Behavior in Organizations* (10th ed.). Boston, MA: Prentice Hall.

ACTIVITY: OBSERVING COMMUNICATION PATTERNS IN A TEAM

Objective: Communication within a team often develops into patterns. Team members can either speak to the entire team or speak to individual team members. Some team members talk a lot, while others remain relatively silent. Observing communication patterns reveals whether the team is working collaboratively, developing subgroups, or being dominated by certain individuals.

Activity: During a team meeting or group discussion of the Team Leader's Challenge, note when a team member speaks and to whom. The member can either speak to another individual or to the team as a whole. Using Activity Worksheet 6.1, record the team's communication pattern by drawing arrows connecting the various communicators. Use slash marks on the arrows to note additional communications.

Analysis: Was most of the team's communication to the team as a whole? Did you notice any patterns of communication? Were certain team members more likely to dominate the team's discussion? Can you determine who the team leader is by observing this communication pattern? How equal were the team's communications?

Discussion: What should the team leader do to facilitate more equal participation in team discussions?

ACTIVITY WORKSHEET 6.1
Communication Patterns in a Team

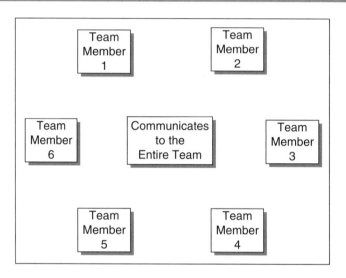

PART III

Issues Teams Face

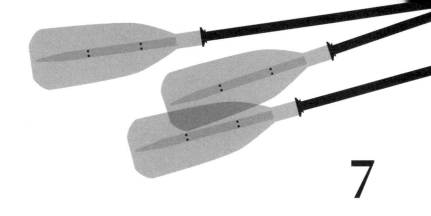

7

Managing Conflict

Conflicts of various types are a natural part of the team process. Although we often view conflict as negative, there are benefits to conflict if it is managed appropriately. People handle conflict in their teams in a variety of ways, depending on the importance of their desire to maintain good social relations and to develop high-quality solutions.

Teams can use a variety of approaches for managing conflicts. Developing a healthy solution to a conflict requires open communication, respect for the other side, and a creative search for mutually satisfying alternatives.

Learning Objectives

1. Why is lack of conflict a sign of a problem in a team?

2. What are healthy and unhealthy sources of conflict?

3. When is conflict good for a team? When is it bad for a team?

4. How does the impact of conflict vary depending on the type of conflict?

5. What are the different approaches to conflict resolution?

6. Which approach to conflict resolution is best? Why?

7. What can teams do to prepare for conflicts?

8. How can a mediator help facilitate management of a team conflict?

9. What should a team do to create an integrative solution to a conflict?

7.1 Conflict Is Normal

Conflict is the process by which people or teams perceive that others have taken some action that has a negative effect on their interest. Conflict is a normal part of a team's life. Unfortunately, people have misconceptions about conflict that interfere with how they deal with it. These misconceptions include the following:

- Conflict is bad and should be avoided.
- Misunderstandings by team members cause conflict.
- All conflicts can be resolved to everyone's satisfaction.

In a dynamic team, conflict is a normal part of the team's activity and is a healthy sign. If a team has no conflict, it might be a sign of a problem. A team without conflict might be suffering from unhealthy agreement, have a domineering leader who suppresses all conflict and debate, or perform its task in a routine manner not trying to improve.

Teams often do not handle their conflicts very well. Sometimes rather than trying to manage their conflicts, they try to ignore or avoid them. This is called "defensive avoidance." To avoid a conflict, everyone becomes quiet when a controversy occurs. Decision-making problems, such as the Abilene paradox, are in part caused by the desire to avoid controversy. Team members accept what the leader says in order to avoid conflict. The consequences are poor decision making and more problems later in the team's life.

The causes of team conflict change during the team's development (Kivlighan & Jauquet, 1990). During the initial stage, there is little conflict because team members are being polite and trying to understand everyone's positions. This gives way to team conflicts about operating rules and status issues as the team sorts out its roles and rules. Once the team becomes task oriented, conflicts arise about how tasks should be performed. Often, the final stages of a project have little conflict because team members are focused on implementing their earlier decisions.

The impacts of conflict on a team depend on its stage of development. Many team development theories propose that teams must overcome conflict in the early stages of team development before becoming a cohesive and productive team (Tekleab, Quigley, & Tesluk, 2009). Learning how to successfully manage conflict is an important developmental process for a team. In addition, task conflict is more valuable during the planning stages of a team project than during the implementation stages (O'Neill, Allen, & Hastings, 2013). Conflict during the implementation stage may interfere with the coordination of the team's activities.

It is more appropriate to talk about conflict management than about conflict resolution. Conflict is a normal part of a team's operation, and some conflicts cannot be fully resolved. The resolution of a conflict depends on the type of conflict. If it is about task issues, the solution is an agreement. Typically, once the agreement is made, it continues to operate. If the conflict is about relationship issues, then an agreement, periodic checks on how well the agreement is working, and opportunities to redefine the agreement are needed. This is true because agreements about relationship issues can change as the relationship changes.

7.2 Sources of Conflict

Conflict may arise from many sources, including confusion about people's positions, personality differences, legitimate differences of opinion, hidden agendas, poor norms, competitive reward systems, and poorly managed meetings. The difficulty is to determine the source in order to identify whether this is a healthy conflict for the team or a symptom of a hidden problem that needs to be uncovered. If the conflict is about legitimate differences of opinion about the team's task, then it is a healthy conflict. The team needs to acknowledge the source of conflict and work on resolving it. However, sometimes a conflict only appears to be about the team's task and in reality is a symptom of an underlying problem. Finding the root cause of the conflict is important; the team should not waste time dealing with only the symptoms of the conflict. Table 7.1 presents a list of healthy and unhealthy sources of conflict.

Legitimate or healthy conflicts are caused by a variety of factors. Differences in values and objectives of team members, differing beliefs about the motives and actions of others, and different expectations about the results of decisions can all lead to conflicts about what the team should do. These differences create conflicts, but these conflicts have a positive effect on team problem solving and decision-making (Tjosvold, Wong, & Chen, 2014). Through conflict, opposing views are heard, challenges and problems are identified, and new, more creative solutions are developed.

Hidden conflicts that are not really about the team's task may spring from organizational, social, and personal sources. Organizational causes of conflict

Table 7.1   Sources of Conflict

Healthy
- Focus on task issues
- Legitimate differences of opinion about the task
- Differences in values and perspectives
- Different expectations about the impact of decisions

Unhealthy
- Competition over power, rewards, and resources
- Conflict between individual and team goals
- Poorly run team meetings
- Personal grudges from the past
- Faulty communications

include competition over scarce resources, ambiguity over responsibilities, status differences among team members, and competitive reward systems. One common type of organizational conflict is the conflict between the team's goals and the goals of individual team members. This is especially true for a cross-functional project team made up of representatives from different parts of an organization (Franz & Jin, 1995). Hidden agendas (i.e., the hidden personal goals of team members) may lead to conflict in the team that can be difficult to identify and resolve. Gaining agreement about the overall goals of the team and renegotiating team roles can help deal with this type of conflict.

Conflict may be due to social factors within the team. A team with a leader who has poor facilitation skills can have poorly run meetings with a lot of conflict. Poor team norms often show up in poorly managed meetings. When meetings are unproductive, conflict may arise because team members are dissatisfied with the team process. Spending time evaluating and developing appropriate norms helps deal with this type of conflict.

Conflicts may arise from personality differences or poor social relations among team members. These may be due to grudges stemming from past losses, misinterpretations about another person's behavior, or faulty communication, such as inappropriate criticism or distrust. These are often called "personality differences," but typically their source is interpersonal. Although team members are disagreeing about issues, the root cause of the conflicts is an unwillingness to agree. However, it can be difficult to determine whether someone has a legitimate disagreement about an issue or is opposed to agreeing for personal reasons. To deal with these sources of conflict, team building and other approaches to improving social relations are important.

Another source of conflict emerges from intergroup dynamics (Tajfel & Turner, 1979), which is grounded in theories of social identity (Tajfel, 1982b) and self-categorization (Turner, Hogg, Oakes, Reicher, & Wetherell, 1987). There is a tendency for members of teams and organizations to have conceptions of "us" and "them," which can be based on various social categories (e.g., gender, race, ethnicity, college major, etc.), organizational departments (e.g., sales, administration, accounting, etc.), and/or cross-functional team roles (e.g., researchers, designers, engineers, artists, writers, etc.). We view members of our own category (us) as "ingroup" members and those who are not in our category (them) as "outgroup" members, which contributes to intergroup bias (Hewstone, Rubin, & Willis, 2002). One consequence of intergroup bias is in-group favoritism, whereby people automatically and without awareness assign more trust, cooperation, resources, positive evaluations, and empathy to ingroup members compared to outgroup members. By contrast, outgroup derogation can result in discrimination, poor evaluations, and negative attitudes toward outgroup members. In teams, these tendencies can marginalize some members while privileging others, causing intergroup conflict over incompatible goals, competition for resources, cultural differences, and power discrepancies (Cox, 1994).

7.3 Impact of Conflict

Conflict may have both positive and negative effects on a team. It can help the team operate better by exploring issues more fully, but it can lead to emotional problems that damage communication. Studies on conflict in work teams show that the impact of conflict depends on the type of conflict, the characteristics of the team, and how the conflict is managed (Jehn, 1995).

Benefits of and Problems With Conflict

Although people often view conflict as a negative event, conflict in teams is both inevitable and a sign of health. Healthy teams are organized to gain the benefits of multiple perspectives. Team members with these multiple perspectives view issues differently and learn from one another in the process of resolving their differences. Conflict is an integral part of the team process; it becomes unhealthy for the team when it is avoided or viewed as an opportunity to dominate an opponent.

The benefits of conflict are that it encourages the team to explore new approaches, motivates people to understand issues better, and encourages new ideas (O'Neill et al., 2013). Controversies bring out problems that have been ignored, encourage debate, and foster new ideas. When opposing views are brought into the open and discussed, the team makes better decisions and organizational commitment is enhanced (Cosier & Dalton, 1990). When conflict is dealt with constructively, it stimulates greater team creativity. For this to happen, team members must be willing to participate in the conflict resolution process.

Conflict can have negative effects on a team by creating strong negative emotions and stress, interfering with communication and coordination, and diverting attention from task and goals. Conflicts can destroy team cohesion, damage social relations, and create winners and losers, inevitably becoming a source of conflict in the future. One factor that determines whether a conflict will have a positive or negative effect is the emotional intensity of the conflict (Todorova, Bear, & Weingart, 2014). Mild task conflict occurs when teams debate, express differences of opinions and are willing to disagree with each other, while intense task conflict occurs when team members clash or argue about differences of opinion and criticize each other. Intense task conflicts sometimes lead to relationship conflicts. Intense conflicts can have negative effects on the team even when the conflicts remain task oriented because they discourage further communication within the team.

Whether conflicts are productive or unproductive also depends on how the team tries to resolve its conflicts (Witeman, 1991). Productive conflicts are about issues, ideas, and tasks. The team typically tries to resolve productive conflicts in a cooperative manner. The team takes a learning approach to the conflict. Unproductive conflicts are about emotions and personalities. The team typically tries to resolve these conflicts with one side trying to dominate the other. In productive conflicts, team members focus cooperatively on solving the problems.

Conflict in Work Teams

Whether conflict has a beneficial or detrimental effect on a team depends on the type of conflict and the team's task (DeWit, Greer, & Jehn, 2012). Meta-analysis studies on the impacts of conflict on teams find negative impacts for relationship and process conflict, but generally positive impacts for task conflicts.

Relationship conflict has a negative impact on team performance and cohesion because it distracts members from the task and consumes the emotional resources of the team (Tekleab et al., 2009). Process conflict occurs when people performing routine tasks have differences over how the team is managing the tasks or coordinating the role assignments of the members (Behfar, Mannix, Peterson, & Trochim, 2011). Process-related conflict is detrimental to a team's performance because is it often related to feelings of inequity about the distribution of resources and responsibilities among team members (O'Neill et al., 2013). Task conflict occurs when people performing nonroutine tasks differ about what is the best approach. This type of conflict usually has a positive effect on team performance.

Professional project teams are examples of teams performing nonroutine tasks. For this type of decision-making or creative team, conflict is a sign that diverse opinions are presented. The team benefits from this diversity, and conflict helps improve the quality and creativity of decisions. However, when a conflict becomes intense, it can be detrimental to the team. Conflict may reduce the team's ability to reach consensus, hurt social relations in the team, and reduce acceptance of its decisions (Amason, 1996).

For a production or service team, the impact of task-related conflict depends on the type of task the team is performing (Cohen & Bailey, 1997). Task conflict disrupts performance on a routine task, but can improve performance on a nonroutine task. When the team is performing a routine task, process conflict is a sign that its jobs are poorly defined or that team members are unwilling to cooperate and work together. Conflict among team members in this situation usually is not productive. However, when the team is performing a nonroutine task, such as evaluating how to improve quality, conflict is a natural part of the problem-solving process.

Relationship conflict is detrimental regardless of the type of task a team is performing (Jehn, 1995). Although relationship conflict creates dissatisfaction for the team, it often does not overly disrupt the team's performance. In many cases, team members try to avoid working with members with whom they have issues on a personal level. Consequently, relationship conflict hurts performance only when the task requires interdependent actions.

This distinction between the effects of task and relationship conflict does not always hold (DeDreu & Weingart, 2003). Conflict disrupts performance and reduces satisfaction because it creates stress and negative feelings and distracts members from performing the task. Low levels of conflict in decision-making tasks may improve the quality and creativity of decision making, but this effect vanishes when the conflict intensifies. A little conflict may stimulate thinking, but more intense conflict distracts people because of their emotions.

The reality is that task and relationship conflict are often correlated (Choi & Cho, 2011). Disagreement on a task issue can lead to personal attacks. It is difficult to say, "I don't like your ideas" and not have it heard as, "I think you are stupid." Relationship conflicts often lead to increased task conflicts because of the negative emotions that are created. One factor that affects the relationship between task conflict and performance is trust. When team members have a high degree of trust in each other, task-related conflict is less likely to lead to relationship conflict. Teams with high levels of trust can tolerate task-related conflict and use the conflict productively.

Conflict Management

The way a team manages the conflict process determines whether the conflict is constructive or destructive to the team (DeChurch, Mesmer-Magus, & Doty, 2013). The conflict management style a team uses can be either cooperative or competitive (Somech, Desivilya, & Lidogoster, 2009). The cooperative style focuses on developing collaborative solutions that are good for the individual and the team, while the competitive style focuses on what is good for the individual. The cooperative style encourages communication and the exploration of alternative approaches to solving problems, while a competitive style discourages communication.

Constructively managing conflicts requires team members to openly express their views, listen and understand the positions of other team members, and then try to integrate the opposing opinions into an agreement (Tjosvold et al., 2014). An open and supportive communication environment allows the team to resolve their differences without disrupting the relationships within the team (Tekleab et al., 2009). Even resolving relationship conflicts can help the team to better understand and appreciate each other. The development of trust among team members helps to prevent task-related conflict from leading to relationship conflict.

The primary precondition for constructive controversy to operate is that team members believe that they are in a cooperative relationship where team members are committed to helping each other satisfy their goals. Teams can benefit from task conflict when they have a high degree of trust and psychological safety (DeDreu & Weingart, 2003). To use conflict constructively, teams need to cultivate an environment that is open and tolerant of diverse viewpoints, where team members feel free to express their opinions and have the ability to resist pressure to conform to the team (Ilgen, Hollenbeck, Johnson, & Jundt, 2005). They need to develop cooperative work relationships so that disagreements are not misinterpreted as personal attacks. A "constructive controversy" uses communication styles that focus on issues and ideas and not on personal criticism (Tjosvold, 1995).

7.4 Conflict Resolution Approaches

The conflict resolution approaches available to teams vary, depending on the team members' desire to be assertive and cooperative. Because team members have long-term relationships with one another, they should try to use a collaborative approach to conflicts whenever possible.

Two Dimensions of Conflict

There are several ways people and teams can try to resolve conflicts. The approaches they take depend on their personalities, their social relations, and the particular situation. The types of conflict resolution approaches can be analyzed using the following two dimensions: distribution (concern about one's own outcomes) and integration (concern about the outcomes of others) (Rahim, 1983; Thomas, 1976; Walton & McKersie, 1965). In other words, people in a conflict can be assertive and try to get the most for themselves, or they can be cooperative and concerned with how everyone fares. These two dimensions are independent and lead to the creation of five different approaches to conflict resolution (Figure 7.1):

1. *Avoidance.* This approach tries to ignore the issues or denies that there is a problem. By not confronting the conflict, team members hope it will go away by itself.

2. *Accommodation.* Some team members may decide to give up their position in order to be agreeable. They are being cooperative, but it costs the team the value of their opinions and ideas.

Figure 7.1   Conflict Resolution Approaches

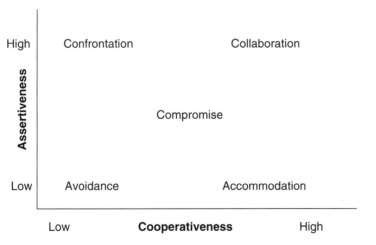

SOURCE: Thomas, K. (1976). Conflict and conflict management. In M. Dunnette (Ed.), *Handbook of industrial and organizational psychology.* Chicago, IL: Rand McNally. Copyright © 1976 Marvin Dunnette.

3. *Confrontation.* Acting aggressively and trying to win is one way to deal with a conflict. However, winning can become more important than making a good decision.

4. *Compromise.* One way to balance the goals of each participant and the relations among the teams is for everyone to "give in" a little.

5. *Collaboration.* When both sides of a conflict have important concerns, the team needs to search for solutions that satisfy everyone. This requires both cooperativeness and respect for others' positions.

Comparing Different Approaches to Conflict Resolution

Although all these approaches can be used to resolve conflict, each approach has problems. Avoidance, accommodation, and confrontation may work to resolve the conflict, but all of these approaches create winners and losers. Teams using these styles often have trouble implementing decisions and find themselves addressing the same issues later. Compromise works somewhat better because everyone wins a little and loses a little. A compromise promotes equity or fairness, but usually does not result in optimal decisions.

When possible, teams should use a collaborative approach to conflict resolution. In collaboration, team members search for the alternative solution that allows everyone to win. Although finding a collaborative solution may be time consuming and difficult, it has many benefits. Collaboration encourages creativity, leads to greater commitment to decisions, and improves relationships among team members (Pruitt, 1986).

Members of work teams have long-term concerns about their relationships that go beyond specific situations or conflicts. Teams with shared goals and long-term commitments are likely to show more concern for other team members when conflicts arise. Conflicts arise from different perspectives and interests, but the shared goals encourage concern for the perspectives of others. This is why work teams tend to use collaboration and accommodation when resolving internal conflicts (Farmer & Roth, 1998).

Although collaboration may be the best approach in theory, it cannot always be achieved in practice. Occasions arise when different approaches to conflict resolution are best (Tjosvold et al., 2014). For example, in a conflict with an emotionally upset boss, a good short-term strategy is to be accommodating. In an emergency situation, people are more likely to accept a confrontational style because they value a quick resolution. There are times when avoiding a conflict because its intensity would hurt team relationships or letting the team leader make the decision for political reasons may be valuable. Collaboration is the best approach when team members have relatively equal status and there is time to work through a solution. Other approaches may be better when there are large differences in power and a quick resolution is needed.

7.5 Managing Team Conflicts

Teams can prepare for conflicts by creating an environment that allows for dealing with conflicts without creating emotional and relationship problems. Mediators or facilitators can help teams to manage their conflicts by controlling communications and building trust. Virtual teams often require facilitators and face-to-face meetings to manage conflicts. Managing conflicts requires using negotiating tactics to find solutions acceptable to all sides of the issue.

Preparing for Conflicts

Teams often try to ignore or avoid conflicts rather than addressing them. This strategy allows the conflict to grow, and sometimes task conflicts become relationship conflicts because they have not been resolved. The negative emotions from these unresolved conflicts disrupt trust, hurt communications, and make the conflicts harder to resolve.

Teams should take a more proactive approach to conflict management by preparing for conflicts. Preparing for conflicts means developing approaches to identify conflicts in early stages and creating an environment that supports constructive controversy so that disagreements can be expressed.

Because people try to avoid conflict, problems within a team often go unspoken and unaddressed. Teams need to create a communication climate where members feel safe to raise issues and voice disagreement (Kayser, 1990). Leaders need to facilitate team meetings in a manner that encourages participation from all members. In addition, teams should regularly conduct group process evaluations to help identify problems and periodically set aside time for task and social reflexivity sessions to identify unresolved issues and team process problems (West, 2004).

The most important aspect of preparing for conflicts is to create a psychologically safe communication environment that allows for constructive controversy to occur (Edmondson & Roloff, 2009). The goal is to make it safe for team members to address task conflicts without creating unwanted emotional problems within the team. This requires a sense of trust among team members that dealing with a conflict will not damage their relationship within the team. Psychological safety encourages teams to address conflicts in a collaborative fashion rather than to avoid them (Bradley, Postlethwaite, Klotz, Hamdani, & Brown, 2011). It allows dealing with task conflicts to have a positive impact on team performance without creating relationship conflicts that hurt performance.

Teams can engage in other preemptive conflict management strategies to help avoid conflicts (Marks, Mathieu, & Zaccaro, 2001). Preemptive conflict management strategies include the development of cooperation and trust-building among members, team contracts that identify how to handle difficult situations, and the development of norms for managing communications within a team. These actions help the team effectively address conflicts and reduce the destructive impact of conflicts when they occur.

Facilitating Conflicts

Successful conflict management requires developing trust among participants (Ross & Ward, 1995). If members on one side trust members on the other side and believe everyone wants a fair solution, they are better able to negotiate a solution. Many conflict reduction approaches are designed to build trust among the parties in a conflict. For example, in a study of bargaining through email, allowing participants to engage in a "get acquainted" telephone call before the bargaining session increased chances of reaching an agreement by 50% (Nadler, Thompson, & Morris, 1999).

Outside mediators or facilitators can sometimes help manage team conflicts when the issues have become too emotional. Mediators operate by gaining trust among participants, managing hostilities, developing solutions to conflicts, and gaining commitment to the solutions from participants (Carnevale, 1986). They use a variety of tactics to do this. Some tactics focus on the emotional or relationship aspects of situations, whereas others are oriented more toward problem-solving aspects.

In highly emotionally charged situations, direct communication can lead to threats and aggressive language. Mediators help control the communications between people on both sides of the conflict to ensure courtesy and respectful communication. They create controlled opportunities for each side to express their views and listen to and acknowledge the other side's perspective. This helps reduce the impact of miscommunication and confusion about the other side's position. Mediators search for small areas of agreement in order to build trust and demonstrate that there is common ground.

Virtual Team Conflicts

Virtual teams, or teams that interact primarily through communications technology, may have more conflicts and more problems resolving conflicts

(Hertel, Geister, & Konradt, 2005). Conflicts are more likely to occur in virtual teams because miscommunication is more likely to occur. This is especially true for emotional issues because people are not very good at communicating emotions in writing and the increased anonymity of communications technology may encourage more uninhibited emotional communications. Once conflicts start in virtual teams, they have a tendency to escalate (sometimes called "email wars") because the miscommunications build with each message.

Not only are conflicts due to miscommunication more likely to occur in virtual teams, but they are also harder to resolve. Virtual teams often have less developed social relations and group cohesion, which makes resolving social issues more difficult. Also, there is less pressure toward agreement in virtual teams, so team members are less willing to accommodate the views of other team members. The ability to send messages to all team members and others increases the number of participants in the conflict.

When conflicts escalate in virtual teams, the first step in managing the conflict is to stop sending electronic messages advocating your position or expressing your emotions. These messages are often misinterpreted, so they do not help to resolve the conflict. In many cases, the team leader needs to intervene and facilitate the resolution of virtual conflicts to prevent them from continuing. Since the core of the problem is often miscommunication, a face-to-face meeting is often necessary to resolve the misunderstandings.

Negotiating Conflicts

Negotiation or bargaining is a process where two sides that are engaged in a conflict exchange offers and counteroffers in an effort to find a mutually acceptable agreement. One of the most important dimensions in understanding how negotiation works in conflict resolution is whether participants have a win-win or a win-lose perspective (Walton & McKersie, 1965). A win-lose perspective is based on the belief that what is good for one side is incompatible with what is good for the other (Thompson & Hastie, 1990). With a win-win perspective, participants believe a solution that satisfies both sides is possible.

The goal of managing team conflicts is to develop integrative, win-win agreements that are beneficial to both sides. Integrative agreements are more rewarding than compromises and improve ongoing relationships among parties (Pruitt, 1986). The keys to developing integrative agreements are focusing attention on interests rather than positions and developing trust and rapport between the conflicted parties.

When a team becomes involved in a conflict, members often form coalitions on the basis of their position on the conflict. Rather than focusing on issues of interest, they focus on whether others are for or against their position. Thompson and Hrebec (1996) found that 50% of people in a conflict failed to realize when they had interests completely compatible with each other, and 20% failed to reach agreement even when their interests were compatible. One reason for this failure is that they did not exchange information about their interests and overlooked areas of common interest (Thompson & Hastie, 1990).

Imagine being on a committee whose goal is to reduce violence in local high schools. As the committee begins to search for solutions, a conflict arises over whether the schools should use electronic surveillance technology. Committee members divide over this issue, and all future ideas are evaluated on the basis of support for or opposition to this position. Over time, the debate becomes increasingly hostile, and new ideas are rejected according to whoever expressed them rather than being evaluated for their quality.

The solution to this conflict is to find an integrative agreement that addresses the committee's goal (i.e., to improve safety in the schools), but does not depend on either position. The participants need to step back from their emotional involvement in supporting their positions and understand what is really important to them. There are alternative approaches to reducing violence without decreasing privacy in the schools. Some examples include training students in conflict management, using students to monitor compliance with safety rules, and providing teachers with training to help them deal with aggressive incidents.

The search for an integrative solution can be difficult. It is often useful for a team to either use an outside facilitator for a difficult conflict or receive training in facilitating conflicts. Adapted from Fisher, Ury, and Patton (1991), the following is the structure for negotiation of a conflict:

1. Separate the people from the problem.
   - Negotiations must deal with both the issues and the relationship, but these two factors should be separated.
   - Diagnose the cause of the conflict. What goals are in conflict? Identify what each side in a conflict wants; make sure each side clearly understands the issues.
   - Encourage both sides to recognize and understand their emotions. Ask them to view the conflict from the perspective of the other side and practice active listening.

2. Focus on the shared interests of all parties.
   - Focus on the issues, not on positions.
   - Identify how each side can get what it wants. Determine the issues that are incompatible between the two sides. Recognize that both sides have legitimate multiple interests.

- Have each side identify and rank its goals in the conflict. This often shows that the important goals of each side are different, thereby helping each side see how to trade off unimportant goals to get what it really wants.

3. Develop many options that can be used to solve the problem.
   - Creatively try to generate alternatives that provide mutual gains for both sides. Separate generation of ideas from selection of alternatives.
   - Look for areas of shared interest. Invent multiple solutions as well as solutions to parts of the problem.
   - Practice viewing the problem from alternative perspectives.

4. Evaluate the options using objective criteria.
   - Develop objective criteria to use as a basis for decisions. Define what fair standards and fair procedures to use to resolve the conflict. Agree on these principles before agreeing on a solution.
   - Talk through the issues in order to eliminate unimportant issues. Discuss important differences, searching for the common points on each side.
   - Focus on solutions to which both sides can agree. Do not give in to pressure.

5. Try again.
   - Creative solutions are difficult to develop. Practice brings about success.
   - Teams do not always resolve their conflicts, but they do try to manage conflicts while working through their various tasks.
   - Establish monitoring criteria to ensure that agreements are kept.
   - Discuss ways in which the team can deal with similar issues in the future. How can the team improve its ability to manage conflicts?

SOURCE: Adapted from Fisher, R., Ury, W., & Patton, B. (1991). *Getting to yes: Negotiating agreement without giving in* (2nd ed.). Boston: Houghton Mifflin.

 ## LEADING VIRTUAL TEAMS: REDUCING CONFLICT AND DEVELOPING COLLABORATION

Problem: Because trust, social relations, and miscommunication are problems for virtual teams, it is harder to create a psychologically safe environment that encourages collaboration rather than conflict.

Solution: Many approaches discussed in Chapter 5 (Cooperation) can be used to help create an environment to support collaboration. In addition, a meeting leader might employ a structured process that identifies competing assumptions and objectives of different subgroups represented in a meeting or project. These processes can be used in face-to-face meetings, but they provide additional value in virtual meetings.

Many structured analysis processes exist to help facilitate a collaborative discussion of a conflict, and some of these are available as virtual collaboration tools. These processes commonly identify the key subgroups, the objectives of each group, and what underlying assumptions or values guide the decisions of each group. Exercises that explicitly identify and communicate this information can help members of each subgroup better understand the rationale for the behaviors and messages made by members of other groups during the meeting. This information provides context for hearing and understanding messages and therefore can contribute to trust along the lines of "I may not agree with you, but I understand where you are coming from when you say this."

Summary

Conflict is a normal part of a team's existence. It is a sign of healthy team interactions. However, teams often do not handle conflict well. Sometimes they make bad decisions in order to avoid conflict rather than learning how to manage it effectively.

Conflict may be analyzed in terms of its sources and types. Conflicts that are healthy for a team come from disagreements on how to address task issues; conflicts that are unhealthy originate from organizational, social, or personal sources. The type of conflict determines the way it should be managed. When conflicts are about misunderstandings and task issues, they can be managed using negotiation to develop acceptable agreements. When conflicts arise from social or personal sources, they often require team building to develop social skills and improve social relations.

Conflict brings both benefits and problems to a team. Conflict helps the team perform its task by fostering debate over issues and stimulating creativity. Conflict hurts the team when it creates strong negative emotions, damages group cohesion, and disrupts the team's ability to operate.

Approaches to resolving conflicts vary, depending on how assertive participants are about getting their way and how cooperative they want to be. Although team members use different conflict resolution approaches depending on the situation, collaboration typically is the most effective approach. Collaboration attempts to identify an alternative solution that satisfies both parties. Although they may be more difficult and time-consuming to achieve, collaborative solutions encourage acceptance and support for the results.

Improvement of a team's ability to manage conflict can be achieved in several ways. Creating a psychologically safe environment helps teams collaboratively deal with conflicts rather than trying to avoid them. Mediators can be used to help manage communications during a conflict and develop trust among the participants. Integrative solutions to conflicts can be developed through the use of structured negotiation practices that focus on the interests of all parties involved.

Team Leader's Challenge 7

The high school in your town has been having problems. Recently, the number of gangs at school has increased. Acts of vandalism and juvenile delinquency are also increasing. Although there have not been any major outbreaks of violence, stories in the media of violence in other communities have raised concerns among parents. The school board created a committee of teachers, administrators, students, and concerned parents to develop proposals for dealing with problems at the local high school. You are the leader of this committee.

The meetings started with polite sharing of ideas, but tensions soon became apparent. The four groups had very different ideas about the degree of seriousness of the problem and appropriate solutions. Polite criticism of ideas shifted into cynical asides and finally into heated attacks. As people became more emotional, the negative comments became more personal. You are aware that some of the participants have fought over other school issues in the past.

How can you (the leader of the committee) reduce the negative emotions in this situation?

How do you build trust among the groups?

What can be done to negotiate agreement among the four groups?

SURVEY: CONFLICT RESOLUTION STYLES

Purpose: Understand your preferred style for dealing with conflicts. There are five basic approaches for dealing with conflicts: avoidance, accommodation, confrontation, compromise, and collaboration. The style that you prefer depends on how assertive you are about getting what you want and how much you value your relationship with the other participants.

Directions: Use the following scale to indicate the amount of your agreement with each of the following statements about how you deal with conflict.

1	2	3	4	5
Strongly Disagree				Strongly Agree

_____ 1. I try to avoid stating my opinion in order not to create disagreements.

_____ 2. When there is a disagreement, I try to satisfy the needs of the other people involved.

_____ 3. I use my influence to get my position accepted by others.

_____ 4. I try to find the middle course to resolve differences.

_____ 5. I try to discuss an issue with others to find a solution acceptable to all of us.

_____ 6. I keep my opinions to myself if they disagree with others' opinions.

_____ 7. I usually go along with the desires of others in a conflict situation.

_____ 8. I am usually firm about advocating my side of an issue.

_____ 9. When I negotiate, I usually win some and lose some.

_____ 10. I like to work with others to find solutions to a problem that satisfy everyone.

_____ 11. I try to avoid disagreements with others.

_____ 12. I often go along with the recommendations of others in a conflict.

_____ 13. I stick to my position during a conflict.

_____ 14. I negotiate openly with others so that a compromise can be reached.

_____ 15. To resolve a conflict, I try to blend the ideas of all of the people involved.

Scoring:

Add questions 1, 6, and 11 to obtain your Avoidance score.

Add questions 2, 7, and 12 to obtain your Accommodation score.

Add questions 3, 8, and 13 to obtain your Confrontation score.

Add questions 4, 9, and 14 to obtain your Compromise score.

Add questions 5, 10, and 15 to obtain your Collaboration score.

Discussion: Did you have a preferred conflict resolution style? What would encourage you to be more collaborative? How do you deal with people who use a different style of conflict resolution?

SOURCE: Adapted from Rahim, M. (1983). A measure of styles of handling interpersonal conflict. *Academy of Management Journal, 26,* 368–376.

ACTIVITY: OBSERVING CONFLICT RESOLUTION STYLES

Objective: Team members use one of the following five styles to handle conflicts and disagreements:

- Avoidance: trying to ignore the issue or deny that there is a problem

- Accommodation: giving up one's position in order to be agreeable

- Confrontation: acting aggressively and trying to get one's way

- Compromise: seeking a balance so that everyone gets at least a part of what they want

- Collaboration: searching for a solution that satisfies everyone

Activity: Observe a team or group discussion and note what happens when there is conflict or disagreement. As an alternative, divide a group and assign them positions on a debate topic. As another alternative, see the Team Leader's Challenge, which presents a conflict with multiple roles (teachers, administrators, students, and parents) that could be assigned and used to create a conflict. Using Activity Worksheet 7.1, note the types of communications that occur during the conflict.

Analysis: How well did the group members handle the conflict? Which conflict resolution styles did the team members use? How effective were the conflict styles in persuading others? Did the team handle its conflicts in a constructive manner?

Discussion: How can the team better handle conflicts? What can be done to encourage more use of collaboration as a conflict resolution style? Would an outside facilitator be helpful? What would the facilitator do?

ACTIVITY WORKSHEET 7.1
Observing Conflict Resolution Styles

	Group Members					
	1	2	3	4	5	6
Gives ideas and suggestions						
Clarifies or organizes the discussion						
Criticizes or attacks others' ideas						
Agrees with or supports others' ideas						

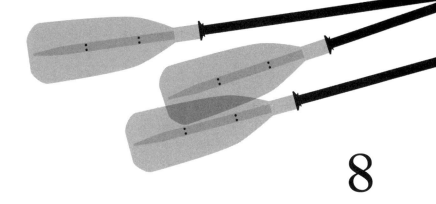

8

Power and Social Influence

Teams use their power to influence behaviors by providing information on how to behave and by exerting pressure to encourage compliance. Team members gain power from personal characteristics and their positions within the team and organization and use a variety of power tactics to influence other members. The dynamics of power in teams is a major influence on the leader's behavior, how team members interact, the impact of minorities, and the amount of influence members have on one another.

Empowerment is at the core of teamwork where members have been given power and authority over a team's operations. Within the team, members need to learn how to use their own power to work together effectively. Learning how to act assertively, rather than passively or aggressively, encourages open communication and effective problem solving.

Learning Objectives

1. How do conformity and obedience influence people's behaviors?

2. What are the different bases of power?

3. How does one decide which influence tactics to use?

4. How does having power change the power holder?

5. How does unequal power affect team interactions?

6. How does a group minority become influential?

7. What is empowerment?

8. What problems does an organization encounter when trying to empower teams?

9. How do passive, aggressive, and assertive power styles affect a team and its members?

8.1 Definitions of Power and Social Influence

Social influence refers to attempts to affect or change other people. Power is the capacity or ability to change the beliefs, attitudes, or behaviors of others. We often think about power in terms of how individuals try to influence one another, but a team has collective power. Conformity occurs through influence from the group, either by providing information about appropriate behavior or through implied or actual group pressure. In addition, obedience occurs through influence from the leader of the group.

There is an important distinction between compliance and acceptance. Compliance is a change in behaviors due to social pressure, but it is not a change in beliefs or attitudes. Acceptance is a change in both behaviors and attitudes due to social pressure. However, if individuals are repeatedly influenced to change their behaviors, they often internally justify the new way of behaving. Therefore, changes in behavior often lead to changes in attitudes.

Why do people change because of social influence? Social psychologists provide two main reasons for the effects of social influence: normative influence and informational influence (Deutsch & Gerard, 1955). Normative influence refers to change that is based on the desire to meet the expectations of others and to be accepted by others. Informational influence is change that is based on accepting information from others about a situation.

Social psychologists conducted several classic studies on power to demonstrate the basic characteristics of social influence. These studies show how a team influences the behaviors of its members and the power that team leaders have over the members.

Conformity

Asch's (1955) conformity studies show that even when group pressure is merely implied, people are willing to make bad judgments. The participants in these experiments were asked to select which line was the same length as a target line. Participants who worked alone rarely made mistakes. However, when participants were in a room with people giving the wrong answers, the participants gave the wrong answers 37% of the time. Only 20% of participants remained independent and did not give in to group pressure. The others conformed to group pressure even though there was no obvious pressure to conform (i.e., no rewards or punishments).

Follow-up studies using this approach to study conformity helped explain why people gave in to the group even when there was no direct pressure. For many of the participants, the influence was informational. They reasoned that if the majority were giving answers that were obviously wrong, then the participants must have misunderstood the instructions. Other participants went along with the majority for normative reasons. They feared that group members would disapprove of them if their answers were different. Later studies showed that nonconformists were rated as undesirable group members.

The level of conformity is affected by the group size and unanimity. A group of about five people shows most of the conformity effects. There is not much difference in conformity when using larger groups (Rosenberg, 1961). Unanimity is very important. Many of the conformity effects are greatly reduced when there is even limited social support for acting independently (Allen & Levine, 1969).

These studies show the power a team has over its members. In these experiments, temporary groups set up in psychology laboratories were able to change what people believed and how they behaved. The impact on a team where members have ongoing relationships with one another is much stronger. This is especially true when the team has a high degree of group cohesion: Cohesive teams have more power to influence members (Sakuri, 1975).

Obedience

The Milgram (1974) obedience studies show that people are obedient to authority figures even when the requested behaviors are inappropriate. In these obedience studies, participants believed they were part of a learning experiment. They were asked to give an electric shock to a learner whenever the learner made a mistake. They also were asked to increase the level of shock with each mistake. Nearly all participants were willing to administer mild shocks. Most (65%) continued to administer shocks even after the learner had stopped responding and they believed that the shocks being administered had increased to dangerous levels.

The level of obedience in these studies was influenced by several factors. The more legitimate the authority figure, the more likely people were to be obedient. They were more likely to obey when the authority figure was in the room monitoring their performance. Whenever possible, participants did not administer a shock to the learner and then lied to the authority figure about their actions. The closer the participants were to the victim (the more they could see or hear the victim's pain), the less obedience there was. Finally, when there was a group of people running the shock device, participants were less obedient if one other person refused to obey.

The important finding in the Milgram studies is that obedience occurs even when the authority figure does not have power to reward or punish participants. In most teams, the leaders are given limited power by their organizations. For example, team leaders usually do not conduct performance evaluations of members. Instead, evaluations usually are done by outside managers. Even without this source of power, the tendency of team members to obey authority figures gives leaders considerable power over team operations.

8.2 Types of Power

Team members use various types of power to influence one another and the team. The types of power that members possess can be examined in several ways. The study of bases of power is concerned with the sources of power, whereas the study of influence tactics examines how various power tactics are used.

Bases of Power

There are two types of power that an individual can have in a team or organization: personal or soft power and positional or harsh power (French & Raven, 1959; Raven, Schwarzwald, & Koslowsky, 1998). Personal or soft power derives from an individual's characteristics or personality and includes expert, referent, and information power. Positional or harsh power is based on an individual's formal position in an organization. It includes legitimate, reward, and coercive power. Definitions for these bases of power are provided in Table 8.1.

The types of power are related to each other and are often used together (Podsakoff & Schriesheim, 1985). For example, the more one uses coercive power, the less one is liked, so the less one has personal or soft power. The more legitimate power one has, the more reward and coercive power one typically has. Because team leaders have less legitimate power than traditional managers, they often rely on expert and referent power to influence the team (Druskat & Wheeler, 2003).

Table 8.1 Types of Power

Personal or Soft Power	
Expert	Power based on one's credibility or perceived expertise in an area
Referent	Power based on another's liking and admiration
Information	Power based on the knowledge or information one has about a topic
Positional or Harsh Power	
Legitimate	Power based on the recognition and acceptance of a person's authority
Reward	Power based on the ability to reward (reinforce) a desired behavior
Coercive	Power based on the ability to threaten or punish undesirable behavior

SOURCE: Adapted from French, J., & Raven, B. (1959). The bases of power. In D. Cartwright (Ed.), *Studies in social power* (pp. 150–167). Ann Arbor: University of Michigan Press.

The use of personal sources of power is often more effective than the use of positional sources (Kipnis, Schmidt, Swaffin-Smith, & Wilkinson, 1984). One reason is that the people under influence are more likely to resist the use of positional power and are less satisfied with its use. Because of this, leaders typically prefer using expert power most often and coercive power least often. However, the use of expert power is limited. The fact that someone is an expert in one area does not make him or her an expert in another area.

Reward and coercive power can be used to influence people to do what is desired. In that case, though, people do what is desired only because they desire the reward or fear the punishment. The result is compliance, but not acceptance. These two strategies are useful for changing overt behaviors, but not for changing attitudes and beliefs. The influencer has to monitor the behaviors to ensure results are forthcoming (Zander, 1994).

Teamwork should rely on the personal power of team members. Team decision making is better when people who are most expert or have relevant information to add dominate the discussion rather than when people who have the authority to make decisions dominate. Cooperation is more likely to be encouraged when team leaders use personal power sources than when they use threats of punishment. When team leaders rely on positional power to get their teams to comply with their requests, members are likely to feel manipulated and so may resist.

Influence Tactics

Team members can use a variety of social influence tactics to change one another. Descriptions of these tactics are presented in Table 8.2. Their use depends on the target for influence (e.g., subordinate, peer, superior) and the objective of the influence (e.g., assign task, get support, gain personal benefit) (Yukl & Guinan, 1995).

These power tactics vary by directness, cooperativeness, and rationality. Direct tactics are explicit, overt methods of influence (e.g., personal appeals and pressure), whereas indirect tactics are covert attempts at manipulation (e.g., ingratiation and coalition tactics). Cooperative tactics encourage support through rational argument or consultation; competitive tactics attempt to deal with resistance through pressure or ingratiation (Kipnis & Schmidt, 1982).

Table 8.2   Social Influence Tactics

Rational argument	Use logical arguments and factual information to persuade
Consultation	Seek a person's participation in the decision
Inspirational appeals	Attempt to arouse enthusiasm by appealing to a person's ideals
Personal appeals	Appeal to a person's sense of loyalty or friendship
Ingratiation	Use flattery or friendly behavior to get a person to think favorably of you
Exchange	Offer to exchange favors later for compliance now
Pressure	Use demands, threats, or persistent reminders
Legitimizing tactics	Make claims that one has the authority to make the request
Coalition tactics	Seek the aid and support of others to increase power of request

SOURCE: Adapted from Yukl, G. (1989). Managerial leadership: A review of theory and research. *Journal of Management, 15*, 251–289.

Finally, some tactics are based on rational argument or the exchange of support, whereas inspirational and personal appeals rely on emotion.

People prefer direct and cooperative strategies. The most effective tactics are rational argument, consultation, and inspirational appeals (Falbe & Yukl, 1992). These are the more socially acceptable tactics and are useful in most situations. However, status differences in a team determine which tactics are used. Traditional leaders often use pressure and legitimizing tactics to influence subordinates, while subordinates often use rational argument, personal appeals, and ingratiation to influence leaders. Team leaders have less positional power than managers, so they are more likely to use cooperative influence strategies (Druskat & Wheeler, 2003).

8.3 Power Dynamics

The use of power changes the dynamics of the group process. Unequal power changes the way the leader treats other team members and the way members communicate with one another. Subgroups that disagree with the majority can have substantial influence on how the team operates. The level of interdependence among team members changes the power they have over one another.

Status and the Corrupting Effect of Power

Power is rewarding, so people with power often want more of it (Kipnis, 1976). It has a corrupting influence: People with more power often give themselves a higher share of rewards. It is easy for someone with power to give commands rather than make requests. Because powerful people get mostly positive feedback from subordinates, they begin to care less about what subordinates say and have an inflated view of their own worth.

Kipnis (1976) demonstrates the corrupting nature of power in studies on teams in business organizations and families. He documents a cycle of power where power leads to a desire to increase one's power. Table 8.3 shows how the cycle operates.

One of the problems with this effect is that its impact is often unconscious. Over time, powerful leaders come to believe their subordinates are externally controlled and therefore must be monitored and commanded by their leaders to get them to do anything. It is a self-reinforcing cycle. A team may try to deal with this problem by rotating team leaders. When leaders know that they will eventually become just another team member, they are less likely to use controlling power tactics.

Table 8.3   Cycle of Power

- Access to power increases the probability that it will be used.
- The more power is used, the more power holders believe they are in control.
- As power holders take more credit, they view the target as less worthy.
- As the target's worth is decreased, social distance increases.
- Use of power elevates the self-esteem of the powerful.

SOURCE: Adapted from Kipnis, D. (1976). *The powerholders*. Chicago, IL: University of Chicago Press.

Unequal Power in a Team

Teams vary in the ways power is distributed. When teams have unequal power levels among members, there tends to be more mistrust, less communication, and more social problems than in more egalitarian groups. Teams with powerful leaders tend to have less communication and more autocratic decision making, thereby reducing the quality of team decisions.

Unequal power is often caused by status differences, which have an impact on team communication (Tost, Gino, & Larrick, 2013). High-status members talk more and are more likely to address the entire team. High-status leaders have lower opinions of other team members' communications, are less willing to view issues from the perspective of others, and are less likely to listen to others. Team members communicate more with high-status people and pay more attention to what they say. Low-status members often talk less because they recognize that their contributions are not valued. They are unwilling to state their true opinions if they differ from those of high-status people. Consequently, when high-status people speak, people either agree or say nothing. As a result, high-status people have more influence in team discussions. This communication pattern does not lead to good decision making or to satisfied and motivated team members.

Women tend to experience a 'backlash effect' from engaging in high-status displays (e.g., speaking for longer, taking charge, etc.), which—according to established gender hierarchies—are reserved for men (Rudman, Moss-Racusin, Phelan, & Nauts, 2012). Because of the backlash effect, when women display status cues they are perceived by both men and women as less likeable, less competent, and less suitable for leadership. Moreover, women may purposely speak less than men in order to prevent the backlash effect, which can threaten their ability to attain positions of power and status in organizations and teams. For example, while high-power men tend to speak more, high-power women speak just as much as low-power women and low-power men (Brescoll, 2012).

Unequal status within a team can have positive and negative effects on the ability of the team to manage conflicts (Greer & van Kleef, 2010). In some cases, for example factory teams, unequal status can help resolve conflicts because powerful leaders are better able to manage the process and coordinate a decision to resolve the conflict. However, unequal status in professional teams may lead to more team conflicts because of feelings of inequality and increased internal competition. These teams are more resistant to solutions dictated by the team leader.

In theory, a team should have only equal-status communication, but this is not always the case. The team leader may assume a higher status than the other team members. A team is sometimes composed of members with different levels of status within the organization. Team members should leave their external status positions at the door so that everyone on the team has equal status. However, it is difficult to interact as an equal with someone in one situation and be deferential with the same person in other situations. This is why teachers sometimes have difficulty interacting in student teams, for example.

When power is unequal because of status or other factors, a team can try to improve the situation by using team norms to equalize power and control communication. Norms level the playing field in a team. They equalize power by putting constraints on the behaviors of powerful members. For example, the norm of consensus in decision making limits the power of the leader. The team may have norms that encourage open and shared communication, prevent the use of intimidation or threats, and value independent thinking. An alternative approach is to train the team leader in facilitation skills so that he or she is better prepared to promote safe and equal communications within the team (Tost et al., 2013).

Various cultures have a different degree of acceptance for unequal power in teams and organizations. Power distance reflects the extent to which those who are less powerful accept and expect power to be unequally distributed in teams, organizations, and institutions (Hofstede, 2011). People from societies with a large degree of power distance—such as those in Eastern Europe, East Asia, and Africa—tend to accept authority without justification, are obedient to those with power, and may expect to be told what to do. By contrast, people from societies with a low degree of power distance—like the United States and Western Europe—tend to expect equal treatment, may not show deference to managers, and expect to be consulted by superiors. How team members respond to power imbalances and status display can be greatly influenced by cultural expectations of power distribution.

Minority Influence

Most of this discussion of power focused on the impact of powerful people or the pressure from the group majority. However, a team may have individuals or minorities that resist group pressure. The term "minority" here has a statistical meaning; a minority is a person or subgroup within a larger group that has fewer members than the majority. A minority may resist the leader and group pressure and eventually be influential in changing the group (Moscovici, 1985). The ability of minorities to influence the majority group depends on their consistency, self-confidence, belief in their autonomy, and relationship to the group overall.

Minorities become influential by sticking to their positions (Nemeth, 1979). When minorities are consistent, their determination makes the majority think about its position. A team can put quite a bit of pressure on minorities to change; it takes self-confidence to resist this pressure. If minorities are going to be influential, they must appear to be autonomous and able to make their own choices. If the minorities are viewed as supported or influenced by an outside group, their impact is reduced. Finally, minorities must appear to be part of the team. They are less effective if they reject the team or are always seen as dissenters (Levine, 1989).

It can be difficult to be a minority team member who disagrees with the majority. Because of the desire to be accepted by the team, individuals are often unwilling to disagree or even present an alternative view. When minority opinions have some support within the team, they are more likely to be expressed and accepted by the team (Ilgen, Hollenbeck, Johnson, & Jundt, 2005). Teams that create a climate of trust and psychological safety encourage members to express their unique opinions.

An important value of a minority is its ability to stimulate team members to view an issue from more than one perspective (Peterson & Nemeth, 1996). When a minority disagrees with the team's view of a situation, the team is encouraged to rethink its position and to consider the issue from multiple perspectives (Park & DeShon, 2010). The overall effect on the team is to encourage more flexible thinking, which increases creativity and innovation. The minority may not get its way, but over time it can have a substantial impact on how the team thinks and acts.

Impact of Interdependence

Task interdependence is the degree to which completing a task requires the interaction of team members. Teams with high levels of interdependence are more likely to be effective if they have autonomy, or the power and authority to control how they operate (Langfred, 2000). In highly interdependent teams, autonomy allows team members to work together more efficiently, control their own interactions, and increase internal coordination. These actions help improve performance when the team faces task uncertainty (Cordery, Morrison, Wright, & Wall, 2010). Autonomous teams are better able to respond to changing situations and to deal with an unpredictable environment.

Interdependence may help a team perform better by changing the amount of power team members have over one another (Franz, 1998). Dependence in a relationship is one of the bases of power. Heightened levels of overall task interdependence are associated with increased personal power. The more team members need one another to complete a task, the more power each team member has over the team.

8.4 Empowerment

Empowerment in a workplace refers to the process of giving employees more power and control over their work. It is the shifting of power and authority from managers to employees. In one sense, empowerment is the core notion of teamwork. A team must have the power to control how it operates; this element is what makes a team different from a work group. A team cannot operate successfully if a manager controls its internal operation.

The success of empowerment programs depends on an organization's willingness to share information and power with its employees (Hollander & Offerman, 1990). Leaders love the idea of empowerment in theory, but they primarily engage in command and control actions because that is what they are comfortable doing (Argyris, 1998). Delegating authority is stressful for managers because organizations typically hold them responsible for the outcome of the team's work. Although they may feel discomfort delegating authority to a team, supporting empowerment leads to more effective team performance.

Empowerment can be viewed at the team or individual level (Mathieu, Gilson, & Ruddy, 2006). Team empowerment is the delegation of authority or responsibility to the team, while individual empowerment is when team members accept responsibility and are given the ability to make decisions and solve their own problems. The team leader has an important role in encouraging both team empowerment and individual empowerment (Chen, Kirkman, Kanfer, Allen, & Rosen, 2007). Mutual trust and respect encourages individual team member empowerment, while delegating authority and responsibility to the team and involving the team in decision making encourages team empowerment.

Empowerment is a benefit both to the individuals and teams that are empowered and to their organizations (Seibert, Wang, & Courtright, 2011). Employees who work in empowered jobs have increased motivation because of a sense of control over their work. Empowerment increases employees' sense of responsibility for their work and confidence in their ability to perform a task. Empowerment helps to increase employee engagement, which is one's commitment and dedication to one's work (Mills, Fleck & Kozikowski, 2013). The ability to change how the team works encourages continuous improvements and innovative solutions to problems (Burpitt & Bigoness, 1997). Empowered teams provide better customer service because they are more willing to accept responsibility for handling customer problems (Kirkman & Rosen, 1999). Organizations benefit by having teams that function more effectively, have greater organizational commitment, and show increased acceptance of change.

The level of empowerment for teams in organizations is increasing, and teams are now using shared leadership more often to operate (Tannenbaum, Mathieu, Salas, & Cohen, 2012). This change is driven by the recognition that self-management and empowerment are motivating for teams. However, economic pressure and organizational downsizing also are encouraging this trend. Team members are being asked to do more and take on more responsibility because of reductions in middle management. These business changes are requiring teams to take more responsibility for developing the team, regulating the team's operations, and improving the team.

Degrees of Empowerment Programs

The amount of empowerment a team possesses depends on the actions of external leaders, the responsibilities given to the team, the organization's human resources practices, and the social structure of the team (Kirkman & Rosen, 1999). External leaders encourage team empowerment by allowing the team to set its own performance goals and letting the team decide how to accomplish those goals. When teams are given more responsibilities for production, customer service, or quality improvements, they experience more empowerment. Human resources policies may give the team more control over staffing, performance evaluation, and training to promote empowerment. Increased participation in team decision making promotes empowerment.

Organizations use a variety of approaches to promote empowerment, ranging from simple changes (e.g., suggestion boxes for employee input), to work teams, to fully empowered self-managing teams (Lawler, 1986). Although these programs have features in common, they differ in what is shared and the breadth of involvement activities.

Sharing information is the minimum requirement for empowerment. However, for a team to be fully empowered, it is necessary for it to have the power to make and implement decisions. Without some power to act, employees have little incentive to continue to improve the way their team operates.

A second dimension of analyzing empowerment programs is the breadth of empowerment activities. Most empowerment programs give team members control over job content (i.e., the task and work procedure they perform), but not over job context (i.e., goals, reward systems, and personnel issues) (Ford & Fottler, 1995). For example, quality programs may allow employees to make changes to improve the quality of their work operations, but may not allow them to influence personnel decisions. By contrast, at the original Saturn automobile plant, which used empowered work teams, team members controlled their work processes, dealt with external customers, hired new team members, and conducted performance evaluations.

Successful Empowerment Programs

Although research shows that empowerment is effective, empowerment programs are limited by managerial beliefs about power. If power is viewed as a limited commodity, increasing team power reduces managerial power. This ambivalence about power makes managers reluctant to empower teams (Herrenkohl, Judson, & Heffner, 1999). However, when teamwork programs are successful, everyone in the organization gains in power.

One of the main problems with empowerment programs is resistance from managers and supervisors (Mathieu, Gilson, & Ruddy, 2006). Managers are often told to empower work teams under their supervision, but they are held responsible for how the team performs. This is why surveys show that although 72% of supervisors believe that empowerment is good for the organization, only 31% believe that it is good for supervisors (Klein, 1984). Although some supervisors support empowerment, many are concerned about loss of status and lack of support from upper management.

Resistance from supervisors and managers may be handled in a number of ways (Klein, 1984). Supervisors need to be involved in the design of the empowerment programs. The roles of supervisors should be evaluated, and their new responsibilities and authority should be clearly defined. Often supervisors need additional training in teamwork skills to prepare them for their new roles as team leaders.

The success of team empowerment programs relates to the organization's structure and culture (Hempel, Zhang, & Han, 2012). Organizational decentralization enhances team empowerment because decision-making authority is delegated downward to the team. Organizational formalization at higher levels can enhance team empowerment if it reduces uncertainty within the organization. Managers should allow team members to make their own decisions and have control over their work, but organizations should create formal goals and values for the teams. This provides guidance to the team and reduces uncertainty but at the same time gives the team the flexibility to decide the best ways to operate.

8.5 Application: Acting Assertively

People express power through their behaviors. They may act passively, aggressively, or assertively (Alberti & Emmons, 1978). Their emotional tone and the ways they confront problems define these power styles. Assertiveness is both a skill and an attitude (Jentsch & Smith-Jentsch, 2001). When team members act assertively, they show their willingness to be independent and accept responsibility for their actions.

Power Styles

The use of these power styles has important impacts on communication in teams. For example, teamwork problems are one of the chief causes of major airline accidents. Accidents happen when crewmembers are unwilling to communicate problems to their superiors. This lack of assertiveness in a team is a major problem—for airline crews, medical teams, police teams, and firefighting teams, among others—which is why assertiveness training is a standard element in training for action teams (Cannon-Bowers & Salas, 1998). Table 8.4 presents an overview of power styles, their impacts on teams, and situations where they often are used.

Table 8.4   Power Styles

	Style	Impact	Use
Passive	• Polite and deferential • Avoids problems	• Resentment and confusion	• Dangerous situations • Unequal status
Aggressive	• Forceful and critical • Focuses on winning	• Satisfaction and withdrawal	• Emergencies • Unequal status
Assertive	• Clear and confident • Problem solving	• Satisfaction and trust	• Most situations • Equal status

Passive

The passive style is polite and deferential. A sweet, pleasant, or ingratiating emotional tone is added to one's communication. A person using the passive approach tries to avoid problems by not taking a stand or by being unclear about his or her position. By being evasive, the person using this approach is trying not to upset or anger anyone by disagreeing. The person's desire to be liked by others is based on personal insecurity or fear of the situation.

The goal of the passive approach is to win approval and acceptance. Unfortunately, this style does not work well. Passive people often feel stressed and resentful, in part because problems never seem to go away. The receivers of passive communication often have mixed responses. They often get their way, but they are uncertain what the passive communicator really believes, so tend to lack respect for a person using this approach.

The passive approach is appropriate in some situations. When a conflict becomes highly emotional, a passive response may defuse the situation. When interacting with a person of higher status, a passive response may be expected from a subordinate. There are situations where being assertive is risky. For instance, acting aggressively toward the boss may be an inappropriate or dangerous tactic.

Aggressive

The aggressive style is forceful, critical, and negative. A negative emotional tone is added to the communication so that it appears more powerful. A person using the aggressive approach deals with problems and conflicts by trying to win and refusing to compromise. The underlying emotions of the aggressive style are anger, insecurity, and lack of trust. In some ways, this is similar to the passive style, which is why people sometimes swing back and forth between passiveness and aggressiveness without ever reaching an assertive position.

Use of the aggressive style is often rewarded. In many situations, people give in to people who are acting forcefully, in part because of a misapplication of the rule of reciprocity. People may defer and agree to someone's position because it is important to them, simply because they then expect to get their way in things that are important to them. What the aggressive person does is act forcefully in all situations. There is a cost to the aggressive style. People on the receiving end of the aggressive style feel resentment, act defensively, and try to withdraw from the situation.

The aggressive style can be appropriate, as in problem or emergency situations requiring forceful action. It can be a valuable approach for dealing with blocked situations where progress is stalled. If there is resistance and change is vital to the team's goals then aggressiveness can be the appropriate response.

Assertive

The assertive style uses clear and confident communication. No emotions are added to messages. Assertiveness is communicating openly with concern for both others and oneself. It is taking responsibility for one's own communication. The assertive person takes a direct problem-solving approach to conflicts and problems. The goal is to find the best solution, so the person is willing to listen and compromise.

Although they are not always successful, assertive communicators are generally satisfied with their performance. The assertive style shows respect, encourages trust in others, and inspires open communication in a team. High self-esteem and trust in the team underlie the assertive style.

The assertive approach is appropriate in most situations in which people are interacting on an equal basis and should be the most typical type of communication within a team. The absence of the assertive approach is a sign of unequal status differences that are disrupting communication within the team, or unresolved conflicts that are creating a defensive communication environment in the team.

Use of Power Styles

Teams are more productive when their communication is primarily assertive (Lumsden & Lumsden, 1997). Both passive and aggressive styles create resentment and inhibit open communication. Teams may adopt unproductive power styles for several reasons. An aggressive style triggers a passive response, whereas an assertive style triggers an assertive response. Assertiveness is a power style used among people with relatively equal power; passiveness and aggressiveness are power styles used among people with differing levels of power.

Although the most appropriate power style to use depends on the situation, there is a tendency for people to have preferred power styles they enact regardless of the situation (Ames, 2008). They may focus primarily on the task or social aspects of situations. A task orientation leads to the use of more forceful power styles, while a social focus leads to less assertive styles.

Differences in power styles are often attributed to personality, gender, or racial differences. This explanation is rarely true and gets in the way of improving team communication. For example, women often act more passively than men in business teams, causing some men to assume that women are passive. Kipnis (1976) shows that this stems from organizational power, not gender. When men and women have equal power in a situation, women are not more likely than men to act passively.

Assertiveness is primarily a reflection of the distribution of power in a team. To encourage assertive communication, the team needs to reduce power differences among its members. In an organization, people work in a hierarchy that gives everyone different amounts of power. However, when people are working in a team, they need to treat fellow team members as if everyone has the same amount of power.

Encouraging Assertiveness

Assertiveness is the power style most appropriate for teamwork. The primary key to encouraging assertiveness is to equalize power among team members. However, equalizing power might not be enough. People develop habits in communicating, so it may be necessary to provide team members with training in assertive communication (Alberti & Emmons, 1978). Assertiveness training programs use a number of techniques to encourage better communication in teams:

1. *Active listening.* Active listening is summarizing and repeating a speaker's message to ensure it has been understood. This technique clarifies the message, shows respect and attention, and encourages more communication.

2. *Positive recognition.* Learning how to give others positive recognition reduces the need for manipulative power tactics. Too often, high-status people criticize what they do not like, but do not acknowledge what they like.

3. *Clear expectations.* Learning to state expectations clearly is another communication technique that encourages assertiveness. People often misinterpret behaviors as inappropriate or resistant when in reality they are caused by not understanding what is desired. Clarifying expectations lets everyone know the actual issues.

4. *Assertive withdrawal.* Being assertive is not always the right response, so people need to know when not to participate. When situations become either too emotionally heated or threatening, people need to learn how to send a clear message of their desire to postpone or terminate conversations.

Assertiveness is a situation-specific behavior (Jentsch & Smith-Jentsch, 2001). The willingness to be assertive depends on the situation and the individual's relationship to the other people involved. People may be assertive in social or personal situations, but not in work situations. They may be assertive with friends, but not with strangers or business associates. This is why it is important to conduct assertiveness training in environments where team members need to apply assertive behavior.

LEADING VIRTUAL TEAMS: ENSURING DISSENTING VOICES ARE HEARD AND EMPOWERING THE TEAM

Problem: Meetings may suffer from power or status imbalances among meeting participants that disrupt communications.

Solution: Meetings, both virtual and face-to-face, that make use of Group Support Systems (GSS) tools can address power imbalances through careful design of meeting processes using those tools. GSS are collaboration technologies that support virtual team meetings and processes, such as decision making and problem solving. GSS tools can help mitigate power imbalances through their ability to allow anonymous meeting contributions. Anonymity is more easily implemented in virtual than in face-to-face meetings.

The meeting leader, by channeling discussion through text channels rather than voice channels, can provide for varying levels of anonymity in most commercial GSS products (e.g., ThinkTank, MeetingSphere). These products support anonymity by removing author information from discussion contributions.

Anonymous discussion contributions minimize the status impacts of the contributor, which encourages team members to evaluate the message based on the information and logic of the content only. Further, using this anonymity empowers participants in unequal power positions to make riskier contributions and submit ideas that might otherwise have been unstated.

If the meeting leader values the expert power of particular team members, the leader can either request those participants to identify their contributions or assign every subgroup a label indicating their area and level of expertise (e.g., professional area, years of experience) that is attached to each contribution while still preserving sufficient anonymity. If a meeting leader values identification of the subgroup of the participants, a subgroup label can be assigned to their contributions.

Summary

Power is the ability to change the attitudes, beliefs, and behaviors of others. Teams have power because they can influence members by suggesting how people should behave. Teams also exert social pressure to get members to conform to team norms. One way team leaders have power is through obedience to authority.

Power can be analyzed by examining where it comes from and the types of techniques that are used to exert power. Team members gain power through personal bases (e.g., being an expert) and positional bases (e.g., having authority delegated by the organization). Influence tactics can be based on encouraging others or trying to control others. People prefer to use personal power bases and cooperative tactics because these approaches are less likely to create resistance.

The use of power by teams has several important dynamics. Power tends to corrupt its users. People with power tend to use it and take personal credit for the success of their teams, which encourages them to continue to use this power approach. Unequal power in teams caused by status differences among members disrupts team communication—High-status people talk more, and people tend to agree with them more often. As a result, low-status people become reluctant to state their true opinions. Minorities in teams may be influential if they are consistent, self-confident, and autonomous. By resisting the influence of the majority, minorities focus their team's discussion on their positions. Interdependence among team members increases their power to influence one another.

One of the core notions of teamwork is empowerment. To be effective, teams need power, authority, and responsibility to control their own behaviors. Unfortunately, organizations often have trouble sharing managerial power with teams. Empowerment programs may range from simple information sharing with team members to development of self-managing teams. Successful empowerment programs must deal with the perceived loss of power by supervisors and managers by incorporating them into the teams' activities.

Team members may act in a passive, aggressive, or assertive manner. These are personal power styles. Although there are situations in which acting passively or aggressively is appropriate, in most team situations assertiveness is the best approach. Assertiveness encourages clear communication and a rational approach to problems, but is disrupted by unequal status in the team. There are several techniques for training group members to act more assertively.

Team Leader's Challenge 8

You are the manager of a technical services team that provides support services for other organizations. Over the past year, you have been trying to make the transition to a more self-managing team. For instance, you now call yourself the "team leader" rather than the manager. As part of the transition, the team now makes decisions about scheduling, partnering, and other task assignments. Team meetings where employees passively listen to instructions have been replaced by team discussions and group decision making. You have worked hard to encourage team members to speak up at meetings, and they are now contributing more.

At today's meeting, a team member suggested a new way to organize work practices. You told the team you didn't like the idea because you had tried a similar plan in the past and it did not work well. Another team member ignored your explanation and complained that you were stifling innovation and were unwilling to share power with the team.

How can you (the team leader) respond to a "bad" idea without discouraging team participation?

What is the best way to handle team members who challenge the leader's authority?

What norms could be adopted to help the team communicate more effectively?

How much power sharing (or empowerment) is appropriate for a work team?

ACTIVITY: USING POWER STYLES—PASSIVE, AGGRESSIVE, AND ASSERTIVE

Objective: Team members may use one of three different power styles. The passive style is polite and deferential. This approach tries to avoid problems by not taking a stand or by being unclear about one's position. The aggressive style is forceful, critical, and negative. This approach deals with problems and conflicts by trying to win. The assertive style uses clear and confident communication. The assertive person takes a direct problem-solving approach to conflicts and problems.

Activity: Observe the interactions in a team discussion of the Team Leader's Challenge. Write down examples of passive, aggressive, and assertive behaviors you observed. Using Activity Worksheet 8.1, note the frequency of team members acting passively, aggressively, or assertively. An alternative activity is to break into groups and have individuals take turns using one of the three power styles during a group discussion. Participants should analyze their own and others' performances according to their perception and reactions to each style.

Passive behavior: _____

Aggressive behavior: _____

Assertive behavior: _____

ACTIVITY WORKSHEET 8.1
Observing Passive, Aggressive, and Assertive Power Styles

	Team Members					
	1	*2*	*3*	*4*	*5*	*6*
Passive						
Aggressive						
Assertive						

Analysis: Which power style did the team use most often? Did certain team members adopt a similar power style for most communication? Was the team's communication dominated by assertive, passive, or aggressive communication? Did the leader primarily use the assertive style?

Discussion: What triggers the use of a power style? Is it personality or team characteristics? How would you encourage the team to engage more in equal-status assertive communication?

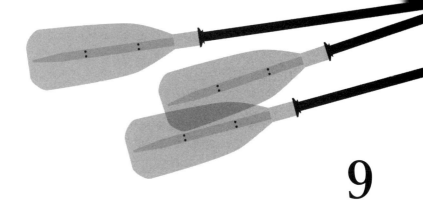

9

Decision Making

Decision making is a central activity of teams. One of the benefits of teams is their ability to bring together multiple skills and perspectives in making decisions. Teams use different approaches to make decisions, from consultation to consensus. These approaches vary in quality, speed, and acceptance by team members.

Teams encounter a number of problems when trying to make good team decisions: Group polarization and groupthink are two examples of these problems. There are structured decision-making approaches that help improve the decision-making process. Although it may be difficult at first, learning how to make consensus decisions is an important skill for teams to develop.

1. What are the main advantages and disadvantages in using groups to make decisions?

2. What factors produce team decisions that are superior to individual decisions?

3. How are consultative, democratic, and consensus decision making different?

4. What factors are useful for evaluating a decision-making approach?

5. How does the normative decision-making theory help teams make decisions?

6. What factors disrupt the ability of teams to make good decisions?

7. How do group polarization and groupthink affect a team's decision-making process?

8. What are the benefits of and problems with structured decision-making techniques, such as the nominal group technique?

9. How can teams improve their ability to achieve consensus decision making?

9.1 Value of Group Decision Making

Using groups to make decisions creates both advantages and disadvantages. Depending on the situation, group decisions may or may not be superior to individual decisions.

Advantages and Disadvantages of Group Decision Making

A team brings more resources to a problem than are available to one person. Team members pool their knowledge through group discussion. Their interaction leads to new ideas that no single member would have developed. (This is called "process gain.") Also, incorrect information is more likely to be identified and rejected by a team rather than by an individual (Rajaram, 2011). A team has a better memory for past facts and events, so it is less likely to repeat mistakes. Overall, team members combine different skills and knowledge to make higher quality decisions.

Group decision making has motivational effects on team members (Zander, 1994). Being part of a team encourages members to try to make good decisions and to perform better. Members become more committed to a decision in which they participated so they are more likely to support its implementation.

Group decision making affects the skills of team members and the team as a whole. Members benefit by gaining a better understanding of the issues involved by participating in the discussion. The team benefits by learning to make decisions. Over time, a team can become more efficient at decision making, thereby reducing many of the problems inherent in group decision making.

The main disadvantage with group decision making is that teams are less efficient in making decisions because they suffer from process loss

(Steiner, 1972). When teams enter into discussions, some of the discussions are about coordination and social issues. This "wasted" discussion time (called "process loss") prevents teams from focusing solely on their tasks.

Teams encounter many communication problems when trying to make decisions (DiSalvo, Nikkel, & Monroe, 1989). To be efficient, group decision making requires skillful facilitation. Decisions can get bogged down in emotional conflicts that waste time and damage the morale of teams. Powerful team members or people who like to talk too much can dominate discussions and disrupt a group's ability to make decisions. Finally, discussions in a team can get sidetracked or become disorganized.

One of the benefits of group discussions is the availability of information available from the diverse team members. However, group discussions are not necessarily good at eliciting this information. Analyses of team interactions show that information known by most of the team members is more likely to be discussed than information held by specific individuals (Stasser & Titus, 1985). In other words, teams do not pool all the knowledge available. Instead, they focus on the knowledge that is common to all members.

Finally, sometimes a team can work hard to make a decision when it is not really important (Zander, 1994). The team may be asked to make a decision, but it is really only a recommendation, and the decision is left to individuals higher in the organization. This creates a sense of wasted time and effort and may discourage future participation in the team.

When Are Group Decisions Superior to Individual Decisions?

Group decisions are better than individual decisions when teams successfully pool resources to solve problems or make decisions. Successful pooling is affected by several factors. One factor is team composition. Teams with heterogeneous members with complementary skills make superior group decisions. Diversity of opinion is a major advantage of using teams (Wanous & Youtz, 1986). If a team is composed of similar members with identical skills and knowledge, there is little benefit to be derived from making group decisions.

Another factor is good communication. Group decisions are better only if the discussion process successfully pools the knowledge and ideas of the team members. However, group discussions typically focus on shared information rather than on the unique information held by members. Poor communication skills and problems managing group discussions can prevent teams from using their resources (DiSalvo et al., 1989).

A third factor relates to the need for teams to make decisions. Teams are needed for tasks that are too complex for one individual to perform or problems that are too difficult for one individual to solve. For a simple problem, the issue is whether anyone has the correct answer and whether the team accepts the correct answer. A simple problem does not require that the team spend time making a decision.

From these considerations, one can outline the types of situations in which individual decision making is better than group decision making. Individual decision making is preferable when the issue does not require action from most team members; the decision is so simple that one person has enough information to make a good decision; or the decision has to be made quickly.

9.2 Approaches to Group Decision Making

When thinking about how to make decisions, teams often decide to vote. However, this approach can lead to problems. There are several methods teams can use to make decisions, and it is important to use the type of decision-making process best suited to the problem. Not all problems need full participation; voting can sometimes create problems rather than solve them. For important decisions, teams might need to reach consensus.

The options that teams can use to make decisions may be viewed as lying along a continuum, from leader-based decisions to decisions made with full participation (Johnson & Johnson, 1997). These options are shown in Table 9.1. Although there are many approaches a team can employ, teams typically use either consultative, democratic, or consensus decision making.

In consultative decision making, one person has authority to make the decision, but he or she may ask for advice and comments from team members

Table 9.1   Approaches to Group Decision Making

Leader Oriented
- Leader decides.
- Leader assigns expert to make the decision.
- Consultative: Leader consults with team and then decides.

Group Technique
- Team uses mathematical techniques (averaging).
- Team uses structured decision techniques (e.g., nominal group technique).
- Democratic: Team votes, and majority rules.

Full Participation
- Consensus: All team members participate and agree to accept the decision.

before deciding (Kerr & Tindale, 2004). Although this advice has an impact, the leader typically gives more weight to his or her own opinion and the opinions of members with similar views.

The consultative approach is often used in a work team when the leader has management authority and responsibility for the team decision. Teams also use consultative decision making when a project is divided into parts and one person is responsible for a part. That person may ask for advice and may need to coordinate with others, but if it primarily affects the person's part of the project, he or she makes the final decision.

The consultative approach uses only some of the team's resources. Its disadvantages are that it does not fully develop commitment to a decision, does not resolve conflicts among team members, and may encourage competition among team members to influence the leader. However, it is a very efficient decision-making approach, taking little time to complete, and it may provide the leader with crucial information to help make a decision.

In democratic decision making, the team votes on a decision. One of the major advantages of the democratic approach is that it is a quick way of including all team members' opinions. Majority decisions often work better than stricter criteria (such as two-thirds or unanimity) (Kerr & Tindale, 2004). Simple majorities produce high-quality decisions with little cognitive effort.

Although voting is a popular decision-making style, it can create problems for a team. Voting can prematurely close discussion on an issue that has not been fully resolved. This can lead to a lack of commitment from the losing minority. Because there are winners and losers, voting may create resentment among team members. Those who disagree with the vote may be unwilling to support and implement the decision after it has been made (Castore & Murnighan, 1978).

The consensus approach to decision making requires discussion of an issue until all members have agreed to accept it. Acceptance does not mean that the decision is a member's favorite alternative: It means that the member is willing to accept and support the decision.

Consensus decision making might be time consuming, but it is the best way to fully use team resources. When it is successful, it also improves the team operation. The consensus approach should be used for important decisions requiring the full support of the team for implementation. It takes time, energy, and skill to reach consensus, but consensus decisions have a greater likelihood of being implemented by the team.

In a sample of work teams in more than 100 companies, Devine, Clayton, Philips, Dunford, and Melner (1999) found that most (62%) of the teams used consensus decision making. In the other teams, decisions were made by the leaders or managers (25%) or by voting (13%). The use of consensus decision making was positively related to team effectiveness for all types of teams.

Evaluating Group Decision-Making Approaches

The primary criteria for evaluating a decision-making approach are quality, speed, and acceptance or support (Johnson & Johnson, 1997). A good decision-making approach should use the resources of the team to make a high-quality decision. The decision-making process should reflect efficient time management. Once a decision has been made, the members of the team should be willing to accept it and support its implementation. The importance of these three criteria varies depending on the situation. For example, in an emergency situation, time is essential and acceptance is less important because people are often willing to support any decision.

The first criterion is quality. In general, decision-making techniques that include group discussion and participation lead to higher quality decisions. This is especially true if the problems are complex or unstructured or if leaders do not have enough information to make good decisions. However, for some issues, leaders can make high-quality decisions alone. In other examples, the importance of quality as a decision criterion varies because some issues are relatively trivial, so high-quality decisions are not necessary. In those cases, having leaders make the decisions saves time for teams.

The second criterion is speed. Group decision making is slower than individual decision making, but the importance of speed as a criterion varies. In many cases, the issue is not speed, but priority. It is important to prioritize the decisions a team needs to make. Some decisions are important and must be made quickly, whereas other decisions can be put off until the team gathers more information. Teams often spend too much time on unimportant decisions and not enough time on the important ones.

The third criterion is acceptance. To the extent that a decision requires the support and acceptance of team members to be implemented, the decision should include input from team members (Murnighan, 1981). Teams often use decision-making techniques (e.g., voting) to speed up the decision-making process, but these techniques can limit the level of acceptance of the decisions. When acceptance is important, teams should use consensus decision making.

These three evaluation criteria are interrelated. The relationship between quality and speed is fairly obvious. When more time is available for making a decision, there is also more time for gathering and analyzing information, which improves the quality of the decision. Speed and acceptance are also related. Comparisons of Japanese and U.S. decision making found that

U.S. organizations make decisions faster. However, the U.S. organizations are both slower and more likely to fail at implementation. In Japanese organizations, final decisions are not made until commitment has been gained to implement the decisions from all relevant participants. Once they make decisions, they are quickly able to implement them.

Normative Decision-Making Theory

How should a team leader choose to make a decision? There are both advantages and disadvantages with the consultative, democratic, and consensus approaches. It is difficult to sort out these factors and determine the best approach for a team. Normative decision-making theory addresses this problem (Vroom & Jago, 1988; Vroom & Yetton, 1973). It is a leadership theory that can be used by teams to help select the best decision-making approach.

Normative decision-making theory is based on the assumption that the best type of decision-making approach depends on the nature of the problem. The problem determines how important quality, speed, and acceptance are in reaching a decision. Once the nature of the problem is understood, the best decision-making approach can be selected. This practice is typically used by the leader to analyze a problem to determine the best decision-making approach.

The analysis of the problem focuses on two issues: whether a quality decision is important and whether acceptance of the decision by subordinates is important. Seven questions are used to analyze a problem (see Table 9.2). Once a leader analyzes the nature of the problem, a decision tree is used to

---

Table 9.2   Questions for Analyzing a Problem

1. Is a high-quality decision required?
2. Do I have enough information to make such a decision?
3. Is the problem structured?
4. Is it crucial for implementation that subordinates accept the decision?
5. If I make the decision alone, is it likely my subordinates will accept it?
6. Do subordinates share the goals that will be reached through the solution of this problem?
7. Do subordinates disagree about the appropriate method for attaining goals so that conflict will result from the decision?

SOURCE: Adapted from Vroom, V., & Yetton, P. (1973). *Leadership and decision making.* Pittsburgh, PA: University of Pittsburgh Press.

tell the leader what type of decision-making approach to use. In general, the leader should use more group-oriented approaches (e.g., democratic, consensus) when a high-quality decision is needed or when team acceptance is needed to implement the decision. Research testing of the theory has been fairly supportive, although the results depend on the decision-making skills of the leader. (It does not work for a team leader to use consensus decision making if the leader does not have the skills to facilitate the decision-making process.)

The normative decision-making theory makes some important points about group decision making. When the decision is important and requires support to implement, the decision-making process should be group oriented. However, when the decision is trivial and just needs to be made, it is a waste of the team's time to discuss it. Often people believe that democratic or consensus decision making is best for value reasons, but this can lead to a team wasting too much time on trivial issues. One important function of the team leader is to manage the situation. The leader handles the minor and administrative decisions so the team has the time to focus on the important issues.

9.3 Decision-Making Problems

There are many different types of problems that can disrupt a team's ability to make a good decision. Disagreements, negative emotions, time pressure, and external stress can cause these problems. Group polarization can affect a group decision by making the result more extreme because of interpersonal processes. The term *groupthink* describes a number of group decision-making flaws caused by the group's desire to maintain good relations rather than to make the best decision.

Causes of Group Decision-Making Problems

Disagreements

Probably the most common group decision-making problem is premature closure—that is, trying to avoid disagreement by voting to make a quick decision. This technique works for making the decision, but often leads to implementation problems later. Politics, a domineering leader, hidden agendas, poor norms, and other factors can cause disagreements. Because of the disagreements, there is social pressure for people to agree with each other in a meeting, so misinformation is often not corrected and may be amplified (Sunstein & Hastie, 2014). The group discussion focuses on common information because members are less willing to express their unique perspective because it is at odds with the group. These problems relate to the group process rather than to the topic of the decision. When these problems disrupt the discussion of the decision, the group needs to focus on improving its internal communication.

Too little disagreement can also be a problem. Disagreement helps stimulate thinking and leads to better decisions. Group discussions with some disagreement lead to better decisions than conflict-free group discussions (Schwenk, 1990). However, these constructive conflicts come at a cost. Group discussions with substantial disagreement are rated as less satisfying experiences by team members and reduce interest in continuing to interact with the team.

Impact of Emotions

Emotions have both positive and negative effects on group decision making. Positive emotions can help to improve group discussions and decision making (Emich, 2014). When team members feel positive, they are more likely to share their unique perspective with the team, and they are more likely to ask questions and try to understand other team members' perspectives. Positive emotions encourage team members to feel more confident interacting in the team. This increases the information available to a team when making a decision, which improves the quality of those decisions.

However, negative emotions can create problems for group decision making. When teams face a lot of pressure, they tend to become risk averse and head toward safe, generic solutions that have worked in the past (Gardner, 2012). There is a drive toward consensus that prevents the stating of alternative views, ideas, and perspectives. Team members tend to defer to the team leader. Communications focus on shared knowledge rather than unique perspectives. These factors reduce the amount of team creativity and the quality of decisions.

Negative pressure on a team may be due to time constraints or outside influences. Teams respond to time pressure by trying to make quick decisions. To do this, they often use decision-making approaches that are simple and inadequate (Zander, 1994). For example, a team may support the first useful suggestion and prevent further discussion of alternatives. A team may select a plan that has worked in the past without fully examining whether it is applicable to the current situation. Finally, a team may delegate the decision to the leader or a team member, thereby forgoing the benefits of team analysis.

Stress from forces outside a team may also lead to poor decision making. When teams experience stress, they have a stronger desire for uniformity of opinion among members (Kerr & Tindale, 2004). This desire for unanimity means that the team exerts stronger pressure on deviant opinions. This can lead to groupthink or allowing the leader to make the decision. Stress disrupts the decision-making process by reducing the number of ideas generated and the analysis of issues. It can cause a desire to make decisions more quickly in order to reduce uncertainty, thereby rushing the decision-making process. All this leads to poor quality decisions.

Group Polarization

Although it might be expected that the outcome of group discussions would be a decision that corresponds to the average of the team's initial position, this is not always the case. The effect of a group discussion can lead to a final decision that is more extreme than the average position of its members, which can be either a riskier or more cautious decision, depending on the initial inclination of the team. This phenomenon is called *group polarization.*

Original research by Stoner (1961) showed that groups made riskier decisions than individuals. This was called the "risky shift phenomenon." However, subsequent research showed that this actually was an intensification effect. Groups tend to move toward an extreme and become either more risk oriented or more conservative (Myers & Lamm, 1976). The group polarization effect occurs only when the group has an initial tendency, not when there are major differences of opinion among the members. There are several explanations for group polarization that examine the role of normative and informational influences.

Normative influence describes how the existing team norm affects the decision-making process. Team members want to create a favorable impression, so they compare their answers to the team norm and then shift their positions to try to attain more consistency with the norm (Myers & Lamm, 1976). The team norm shifts as members change their positions in an attempt more typically represent the team's position. The combined effect of these shifts is to move the team decision more to the extreme. This is especially important when the decision is primarily a matter of values or preferences.

Information influence is caused by the amount of exposure to information during a group discussion. When a team discusses an issue, most of the discussion is from the dominant position (Kerr & Tindale, 2004). People prefer to hear information they agree with, so other team members reward the sharing of common information. Because team members are more exposed to arguments supporting the dominant position, they shift their opinions in that direction (Burnstein & Vinokur, 1977).

Groupthink

The most famous type of group decision-making problems is groupthink, a term coined by Janis (1972). Janis used the analysis of historical decisions to show how decision-making processes can go wrong. The U.S. invasion of Iraq in 2002, based on the belief that Iraq possessed WMDs (weapons of mass destruction), is an example of groupthink. Groupthink occurs when group members' desire to maintain good relations becomes more important than reaching a good decision. Instead of searching for a good answer, they search for an outcome that preserves group harmony. This leads to a bad decision that is then accompanied by other actions designed to insulate the group from corrective feedback. Since the initial identification of groupthink, researchers have expanded on the causes and implications of this phenomenon (Table 9.3).

Table 9.3   Model of Groupthink

Antecedent Conditions

Structural: Group has a domineering leader and limited input from outside the group.

Cohesiveness: The desire to maintain good relations is dominant.

Stress: Outside forces put stress on the group to make a decision.

Decision Symptoms

Illusion of invulnerability: Group believes that its decision will work.

Direct pressure on dissenters: Group suppresses negative comments in group discussion.

Self-censorship: Group members do not state their opinions if they differ from the group.

Illusion of unanimity: Group members believe that everyone agrees with the decision.

Mind guards: Group members protect the leader and group from negative information about the decision.

Decision Defects

Group considers only a few alternatives when making a decision.

Group fails to examine the adverse consequences of its decision or consider what to do if the decision does not work.

Group does not seek the advice of outside experts.

SOURCE: Adapted from Janis, I. (1972). *Victims of groupthink*. Boston, MA: Houghton Mifflin.

Three main factors contribute to groupthink: structural decision-making flaws, group cohesiveness, and external pressure (Parks & Sanna, 1999). Structural decision-making flaws create bad decisions because they impair the group decision-making process. These flaws include ignoring input from outside sources, a lack of diversity in viewpoints within the group, acceptance of decisions without critical analysis, and a history of accepting decisions made by the leader. Group cohesiveness encourages groupthink by creating an environment that limits internal dissension and criticism. This is similar to the Abilene paradox discussed in the Cooperation section of Chapter 5. External pressure for a decision limits discussion time and encourages the group to support the first plausible option presented to the members.

The external pressure experienced by the group leads to a set of symptoms of groupthink. These symptoms convince the group that it has made a good decision and that everyone in the group agrees with it. Consequently, there is internal pressure on members not to voice their concerns and objections. The collective effect of these symptoms is a poor decision, made without considering alternative options or long-term consequences of the decision.

There are a variety of tactics that groups can use to help overcome the groupthink effect and other decision-making problems (Sunstein & Hastie, 2014). Because the leader has more influence than other members, leaders should reserve expressing their opinion at the beginning of the group's discussion. The group should establish a norm that encourages critical thinking during decision-making. Members should acknowledge each other's areas of expertise and roles, and the leader should request that members present the unique perspective from their roles. Finally, after a decision has been made, the group should schedule another meeting to identify the benefits and problems with decisions before finalizing them.

9.4 Decision-Making Techniques

There are several decision-making techniques developed to manage group decision-making problems. These techniques structure the decision-making process with a set of process rules. They are technically good approaches, but they sometimes appear like magic to the users. An answer appears that represents the group's opinion even though the group has never discussed the issues.

Nominal Group Technique

The nominal group technique is a decision-making technique that allows a group of people to focus on the task of making a decision without developing any social relations. It is called "nominal" because it does not require a true group. This technique can be used by a collection of people who are brought together to make a decision.

When using this technique, the leader states the problem to the group. People write down their solutions to the problem privately. Each person then publicly states his or her answer, and the answers are recorded so everyone can see them. Group members may ask questions to clarify the others' positions, but they cannot criticize the ideas. The participants then use a rank-ordering procedure to rate the value of the solutions. This rank ordering is used to select the group's preferred solution.

The advantage of the nominal group technique is that it is relatively quick, discourages pressure to conform, and does not require group members to get to know one another before the decision-making process (Delbecq, Van de Ven, & Gustafson, 1975). However, this technique requires a trained facilitator to conduct the session, and only one narrowly defined problem can be addressed at a time.

Delphi Technique

The Delphi technique uses a series of written surveys to make a decision (Dalkey, 1969). A group of experts is given a survey containing several open-ended questions about the problem to be solved. The results of this survey are summarized and organized into a set of proposed solutions. These solutions are sent to the participants, who are then asked to comment on the solutions, which are based on the first survey. The process is repeated until the participants start to reach agreement on a solution to the problem.

The Delphi approach is useful when it is necessary to include a specific set of people in a decision who are distributed geographically and cannot meet in person (Delbeq et al., 1975). The number of people involved makes no difference, so a large group of people could participate at the same time. This approach is also useful when there is great disagreement on an issue that requires subjective judgments to resolve. However, the process is time-consuming (more than a month for a typical decision) and requires skills in developing and analyzing surveys.

Ringi Technique

The Ringi technique is a Japanese decision-making technique used for dealing with controversial topics (Rohlen, 1975). It allows a group to deal with conflict while avoiding a face-to-face confrontation. (Face-to-face confrontations are considered inappropriate in Japanese culture.) In this approach, a written document presenting the issue and its proposed resolution is developed anonymously. This document is circulated among group members, who individually write comments, edit the document, and forward it to other group members. After completing a cycle, the comments are used to rewrite the document, and it is recirculated through the group. This process continues until group members stop writing comments on the draft.

The Ringi approach can be a slow process, and there is no guarantee that the group will come to agreement. However, anonymous comments allow everyone to state their true convictions, while avoiding any embarrassment that might arise in a confrontation.

Evaluation of Decision-Making Techniques

The group decision-making process is structured by these techniques to eliminate all but task-oriented communication among group members. The Delphi and Ringi techniques use only written communication. The nominal group technique requires each group member to generate ideas independently and then to interact only to choose among alternative ideas. This structuring of the decision-making process allows decisions to be made by larger groups of people who do not have to meet. These approaches can produce decisions that are as good as or better than decisions produced from group discussions, and they can do so more efficiently. In addition, people are satisfied with their levels of participation using these approaches (Van de Ven & Delbecq, 1974).

However, these techniques are based on the assumption that socializing, unequal participation, and other aspects of group discussions are problems. Not all group researchers agree on this point (McGrath, 1984). The social aspects of the group process may have significant benefits. The detached and impersonal atmosphere of these decision-making techniques reduces people's acceptance and commitment to a decision. In addition, the political acceptability of the solution may not be as great as a solution produced by a group discussion, which typically is dominated by the higher status participants.

9.5 Application: Consensus Decision Making

Consensus decision making uses all of a team's resources fully, encourages support for implementation of decisions, and helps build team skills. Consensus decision making is a slow process because people typically are not good at it. A team should practice consensus decision making to improve its decision-making skills so that when important problems arise the team has the ability to handle the problems effectively.

Reaching consensus does not mean every team member believes the solution is best (Hackett & Martin, 1993). Consensus is achieved when each team member can answer "yes" to the following questions:

- Are you willing to agree that this is what the team should do next?
- Can you go along with this position?
- Can you support this alternative?

In other words, a team can support the decision 100% even though not all members completely agree with it. Consensus is the voluntary giving of consent.

The goal of consensus decision making is to develop a collaborative solution that allows all participants to win. Rather than voting, where one side wins and another side loses, consensus decision making attempts to create win-win solutions. Teams using consensus decision making not only make better decisions, but the process helps improve their decision-making skills and social relations among team members.

A team leader or facilitator can help gain consensus through a number of techniques. The team needs to be given adequate time to work through an issue. Conflict should be viewed as valuable, so team members need to be encouraged not to give in just to avoid conflict. Flipping coins or voting when differences emerge is not an acceptable alternative. Team members need to recognize that giving in on a point is not losing and that agreeing is not winning. The goal is to negotiate a collaborative solution, not beat the other side in a debate. Table 9.4 presents some guidelines to help team members reach consensus.

Table 9.4   Guidelines to Help Reach Consensus

1. Avoid arguing for your own position without listening to the position of others.
2. Do not change your position just to avoid conflict.
3. Do not try to reach a quick agreement by using conflict-reduction approaches, such as voting or tossing a coin.
4. Encourage others to explain their position so that you better understand any differences.
5. Do not assume that someone must win and someone must lose when there is a disagreement.
6. Discuss the underlying assumptions, listen carefully to one another, and encourage the participation of all members.
7. Look for creative and collaborative solutions that allow both sides to win rather than compromises where each side only gets some of what it wants.

SOURCE: From Johnson, D. W., & Johnson, F. P. (1997). *Joining Together: Group Theory and Group Skills* (6th ed.). Boston, MA: Allyn & Bacon.

These guidelines show the techniques people can use to help obtain consensus on an issue, but they can be difficult to apply. When people disagree, the emotions generated by the disagreement work against these guidelines. Conflict is uncomfortable, and people want to end it quickly. It is psychologically easier to adopt a quick solution strategy rather than to be patient, listen, and search for collaborative solutions.

If a team gets stuck trying to reach consensus, it can use several options to break the impasse. The team can agree to not agree, and then move on to a related issue. Changing topics and returning to an issue later reduces the emotional tension created during a conflict. If a decision must be made quickly, the team can decide that it must use an alternative, such as voting, or it may decide to develop a compromise solution wherein each side gives in on one or more of its demands. When time is available, the team may ask for outside help or bring in a trained facilitator to manage the decision process.

LEADING VIRTUAL TEAMS: ENCOURAGING AGREEMENT ON A DECISION

Problem: It is harder to obtain agreement on a decision in a virtual meeting than in a face-to-face meeting.

Solution: The difficulty of obtaining agreement to decisions in virtual meetings is probably due to the difficulty of completing the communication feedback loop, as discussed in Chapter 5 (Cooperation). The techniques presented there are relevant here as well. In addition, the virtual meeting leader might consider some additional decision-making approaches:

1. Selecting in rather than selecting out. Team members don't want to accept that their contribution has been voted out of consideration; they want to feel as though their idea has at least been heard and understood by all other participants. This requires that each participant complete the feedback loop for each contribution, a difficult and time-consuming outcome to achieve in a virtual meeting.

   However, if decisions are made by including ideas in rather than voting them out, this requirement for trust is minimized. Consider a process where a set of ideas is brainstormed using a brainstorming or list-building tool. Instead of employing a traditional process where participants are asked to vote to select a subset of the ideas for further consideration, the leader can place the set of generated ideas in front of the team. Then, the leader can ask, "Please look at the list and select one idea not already selected that you think should be included on our shared list for further consideration." When members select an idea, the leader then has the opportunity to clean up the wording of the idea, and to engage the team verbally to increase the likelihood of shared understanding of the idea, before adding the reformed idea to the shared list. The leader then asks every member for a new idea not already on the list; they may pass if they don't have a new contribution.

This process quickly ensures a list of unique well-formed ideas is created and any favorite idea of an individual team member is not left out of consideration. From this point, the team can discuss and evaluate the shorter list of ideas.

2. Applying anonymity to the decision-making process. It is possible to apply anonymity to a virtual evaluation or voting process, similar to the way anonymity can support discussion processes. Ask team members to anonymously evaluate a list of ideas and provide a rationale for each evaluation point. A GSS (Group Support System) software application can support the evaluation process and report on the accumulated rationale of all evaluators, organized by topic.

A meeting leader can then employ this anonymous data set to focus the discussion. The team can discuss the different evaluations using the anonymous rationales without risking public support for any particular evaluation or triggering emotional arguments that might be present because people are defending their positions.

In practice, what often occurs in this sort of evaluation activity are differences of terminology due to misunderstanding, different understanding of facts, or different subgroup values and assumptions. All these outcomes are useful to a successful decision-making process. If the leader employs a meeting technique that permits anonymous polling during the discussion, the group can visually watch how support for ideas changes as a result of their successful deliberation. This use of a GSS for anonymous voting with vote explanation is an example of how a virtual meeting can be more effective than a face-to-face meeting without such technology.

Summary

The largest advantage of group decision making is the ability to bring more resources to solving a problem. It also helps motivate team members and develop their skills. However, group decision making takes time and does not always succeed. Group decisions are better than individual decisions when the team has a diversity of perspectives, the discussion is open, and the problem is suitable for a group.

The main approaches to group decision making are consultative, democratic, and consensus. These approaches vary in time required, quality of the decisions, and support for implementation. The decision-making approach used depends on the nature of the problem. The normative decision-making theory provides a way to analyze problems to help determine the best decision-making approach.

A team's ability to make a decision can be disrupted by too much or too little conflict, pressure to decide quickly, and outside stress. Group decisions tend to be more extreme than individual decisions because of the group polarization effect. The desire to maintain good relations within a team may disrupt the group decision-making process and cause groupthink. Groupthink leads to inadequate decisions that are strongly defended by the group members.

Several structured techniques for decision making have been developed to manage certain problem situations. The nominal group technique may be used in large groups with limited social interaction. The Delphi technique uses a series of surveys for decision making and can be used with large groups that never meet in person. The Ringi technique is a Japanese approach that helps avoid confrontations in the decision-making process. These techniques gain efficiency by structuring the decision-making process, but they may reduce support for the decision because of a decreased sense of participation.

Consensus decision making is the approach that best uses the resources of a team. A number of techniques can be learned to help improve the team's ability to make consensus decisions.

Team Leader's Challenge 9

You are the head of a university department with 10 faculty members. Although you try to organize meetings using an agenda, things do not always work out as planned. Faculty members often spend too much time talking about minor issues and do not get around to dealing with important issues. Most of the time, you try to get the group to reach consensus on issues. This is because voting often fails to resolve the conflict over the issue, so you have to discuss and redecide the issue in the future.

The dean is pressuring you to make a decision about an admissions policy for new students. You have brought the topic up several times in department meetings, but the faculty cannot reach an agreement about the details of the policy. The dean wants an answer soon or he will elect to impose a policy on the department.

How can you (the head of the department) improve decision making at department meetings?

What type of decision style should you use for the admissions policy?

If the department is unable or unwilling to make a decision, how should you handle the situation?

ACTIVITY: MAKING CONSENSUS DECISIONS

Objective: Consensus decision making requires discussing an issue until all agree to accept it. Acceptance does not mean that the decision is the member's favorite alternative: It means the member is willing to accept and support the decision. Learning consensus decision making is an important skill for a team.

Activity: Form a group and have it develop consensus answers to the following questions:

- What is the most important skill for a team member to possess?
- What is the most important characteristic of a good team leader?
- What is the greatest benefit of using teamwork?
- What is the greatest problem with using teamwork?

While the group is trying to reach consensus, have an observer use Activity Worksheet 9.1 to note whether the group follows the Guidelines to Help Reach Consensus.

ACTIVITY WORKSHEET 9.1
Observing the Guidelines to Help Reach Consensus

Did the team follow the guidelines presented below?	Yes	No
1. Avoid arguing for your own position without listening to the position of others.		
2. Do not change your position just to avoid conflict.		
3. Do not try to reach a quick agreement by using conflict-reduction approaches, such as voting or tossing a coin.		

4. Encourage others to explain their position so that you better understand any differences.		
5. Do not assume that someone must win and someone must lose when there is a disagreement.		
6. Discuss the underlying assumptions, listen carefully to one another, and encourage the participation of all members.		
7. Look for creative and collaborative solutions that allow both sides to win rather than compromises where each side only gets some of what it wants.		

Analysis: Was the group successful in reaching consensus for its decisions? Did the group follow the guidelines for consensus decision making?

Discussion: What advice could you give a team to improve its ability to make consensus decisions?

ACTIVITY: GROUP VERSUS INDIVIDUAL DECISION MAKING

Objective: There are benefits and problems with group decision making. Although groups should make superior decisions because they can combine information from multiple members, aspects of the group decision-making process may prevent the group from fully using its resources.

Activity: Create a list of about 15 items that can be ranked and compared to a correct answer. This could be a commercially available "survival" task, the populations of a set of states, or the rankings by historians of U.S. presidents. Have the participants rank the items individually and then as a group through group discussion. You may want to have an observer record the number of communications from each group member during the discussion.

Analysis: Present the correct rankings and calculate the difference between the individual and group rankings versus the correct answers. Is the group score better than the average of the individual scores? Is the group score better than the best individual score? If you used an observer, what is the relationship between knowledge of the topic and amount of communication?

Discussion: What are the advantages and disadvantages of group decision making? What factors prevent the group from fully using the knowledge of its members?

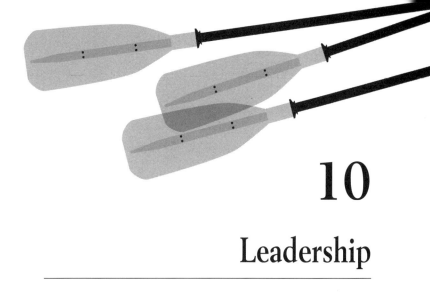

10

Leadership

A team has many ways of selecting a leader and assigning leadership roles. The leader may be assigned by the organization, the team may be self-managing, or leadership roles may be distributed among team members. What is the best style of leadership? There is no definitive answer to this question, but a number of approaches have been suggested. Situational leadership theory is one approach to helping the leader decide the best way to act, depending on the characteristics of the team members.

Organizations are experimenting with new forms of team leadership. In self-managing teams, many leadership functions are turned over to the teams. Self-managing teams provide a variety of benefits, but they require the development of group process skills to operate effectively. It is apparent that team leadership requires skills and responsibilities that are different from traditional leadership approaches. Team leaders do not manage the team: They help the team solve problems in order to be more effective.

Learning Objectives

1. How do leadership characteristics vary by the roles that leaders perform and the amount of power they possess?

2. What factors influence who becomes a team's leader?

3. What are the main approaches to studying leadership, and what are their implications?

4. What are some of factors that reduce the importance of leadership?

5. What are the key elements of situational leadership theory? How does a leader's behavior relate to the readiness level of the group?

6. What are the benefits of and problems with self-managing teams?

7. What are the functional roles and responsibilities of team leaders?

8. How does coaching improve the operation of teams?

10.1 Alternative Designs of Leadership for Teams

Team leadership is a process whereby an individual influences the progress of team members toward attainment of a goal. Types of leaders vary by method of selection and the roles they are expected to perform. Often, the person who emerges as the leader of a team may not be the one best suited for the role.

Characteristics of Team Leadership

Although we normally think of a single individual in the position of leader, this is not always the case. Instead of talking about leadership as pertaining to any one person, we need to recognize that leadership is a process or set of functions that may be performed by many of a team's members (Day, Gronn, & Salas, 2004). Teams vary in their types of leaders, the distribution of leadership roles, and the power imbued in their leaders.

There are leaderless groups, teams with leaders assigned by their organizations, teams that select their own leaders, and self-managing teams. Most teams have one person assigned to the role of leader. The leader may be selected by the organization and assigned to the team, the team may elect the leader, or the position of leader may be rotated among the team members. A team may start out sharing and rotating the leadership functions until a leader emerges from the team's interactions.

Leaders vary in the power or authority they possess. When a leader is assigned by an organization, the leader may have the authority to make the team's decisions. It is then up to the leader to decide how team decisions should be made. When the leader is elected or rotated, he or she typically has limited power and serves primarily as facilitator of the group process. A designated leader with organizational power is useful when the task is very complex and structure is needed, when there is significant conflict among team members, or when someone is needed to manage the relationship between the team and other parts of the organization (Lumsden & Lumsden, 1997).

A team leader is not the same as a manager. A manager is given power and authority by the organization over subordinates, whereas a team leader typically does not have this type of power. A manager is responsible for the actions of his or her subordinates, whereas it is the team (and not the leader) that is responsible for the actions of its members. A manager has the authority to make decisions, whereas a team leader facilitates decision making. Finally, a manager is responsible for handling personnel issues (e.g., employee hiring, evaluation, reward), whereas team leaders usually do not have the authority to perform these personnel functions.

Shared Leadership

Rather than centralizing the role of leadership, a team's leadership roles may be shared on the basis of different tasks performed by the team (Wellins, Byham, & Wilson, 1991). Shared leadership is the notion that leadership functions can be shared or performed by various members of a team (Drescher, Korsgaard, Welpe, Picot, & Wigand, 2014). Leaders perform a variety of functions in a team, and these functions do not have to be performed by the same person. The team's task can be divided into specific functions, and the responsibilities for each function assigned to a team member to perform. Team members may be rotated through the different roles to develop the skills within the team. For example, a factory team may divide its task into quality, safety, maintenance, supplies, and administration. Rather than having the team leader assigned responsibility for all of these functions, one team member may be in charge of each function.

Shared leadership focuses on participative decision making, developing social relations and support, and empowerment (Day, 2013). Leadership is located in the connections and relationships among team members rather than the actions of one particular person. Leadership becomes a dynamic, ongoing process of mutual influence that can be performed by any member of the team. The development of shared leadership capacity is an important resource for the team when it faces challenges that no single individual is capable of managing.

Research shows that shared leadership has overall positive impacts on a team (Wang, Waldman, & Zhang, 2014) and helps to improve both the task and social aspects of team performance. Shared leadership has a stronger effect on performance when the team's task is more complex, knowledge based, and requires interdependent coordinated activity. Shared leadership emphasizes the social relations among team members and the collective enactment of leadership. Because it promotes communication and support among team members, shared leadership promotes trust, team cohesion, and satisfaction.

Leader Emergence

When no leader is assigned to a group, a leader usually emerges from the group to coordinate its actions (Hemphill, 1961). The person who becomes the leader may not be an effective leader. Leaders tend to be taller and older than their followers, but these characteristics are unrelated to effectiveness (Stogdill, 1974). Men are five times more likely than women to be group leaders (Walker, Ilardi, McMahon, & Fennell, 1996), but gender is unrelated to leader effectiveness (Eagly, Karau, & Makhijani, 1995). Studies of military teams show that leaders have more physical ability and better task performance skills (Rice, Instone, & Adams, 1984). Although task skills relate somewhat to leader effectiveness, physical ability has little relationship to effectiveness.

Personality variables like extroversion have been shown to effect who becomes a team leader (Bendersky & Shah, 2013). Extroverts express confidence, dominance, and enthusiasm so they are often initially selected as leaders. However, over time personality becomes less important than task and teamwork related skills. As teams work together, these skills become more important than having certain personality characteristics.

The most important predictor of group selection of a leader is the participation rate (sometimes called the "babble effect"). Group members are more likely to select the most frequent communicator as the leader (Mullen, Salas, & Driskell, 1989). Unfortunately, the quantity of communication is more important than quality for leadership selection. It appears that people who communicate frequently demonstrate active involvement and interest in the group, and this implies a willingness to work with the group members.

Leader prototype theory provides another way to explain the emergence of leaders with characteristics unrelated to effectiveness (Lord, 1985). This theory examines the relationship between the leader and the perceptions of team members. Members have certain implicit notions about what constitutes a good leader. To the extent that the leader meets these expectations, the leader is more influential. Although the specific traits of good leadership vary in the minds of followers, it is usually assumed that effective leaders are intelligent, dedicated, and possess good communication skills.

Leadership prototype theory explains some of the problems with the way team members select leaders. Members rely on their prototypes to decide who should be their leaders, but these prototypes of good leaders are not necessarily accurate. For example, gender differences in leadership may be due to the way gender stereotypes relate to prototypes about leaders. The typical female stereotype emphasizes expressive qualities, such as emotion and warmth, whereas the typical male stereotype emphasizes instrumental qualities, such as productivity and power (Williams & Best, 1990). Although both expressive and instrumental qualities are needed in leaders, members tend to emphasize the importance of instrumental qualities (Nye & Forsyth, 1991). This causes team members to view males as more likely candidates for leadership and to see male behaviors as more important in leaders.

10.2 Approaches to Leadership

Leadership is a topic most people believe is very important and is the subject of an immense amount of research. However, we do not understand leadership very well, and inherent problems in studying leadership cause this dilemma. The fact that people believe leadership is important does not make it true (Meindl & Ehrlich, 1987). Instead of an optimal leadership style, different types of leaders are useful in different situations, and leaders are more important in some situations than in others.

The four historical approaches to research on leadership have different implications for organizations and teams (Table 10.1). The trait or personality approach is based on the belief that good leaders have certain characteristics. If this is true, then psychological tests could be used to identify and select good leaders. An alternative is the behavioral approach, which defines leadership by the ways leaders act. This approach attempts to determine what good leaders actually do in order to identify those actions and train people to be good leaders. The situational approach questions the necessity of leadership. It attempts to determine when leaders are needed and what factors can substitute for leadership. The final approach is the contingency approach, which attempts to combine personality or behavioral characteristics of leaders with situational characteristics. For example, it may be impossible to say what a good leader does, but possible to define good leadership in an emergency situation.

Table 10.1   Models of Leadership

Model	Implication
Trait or personality	Use tests to select good leaders
Behavioral	Train people to be good leaders
Situational	Understand substitutes for leadership
Contingency	Link traits or behaviors to situations

Trait or Personality Approach

The trait approach is the oldest model of leadership, with hundreds of studies conducted during the 1930s and 1940s (Yukl, 1989). It assumes that good leaders have a certain set of characteristics. If these characteristics are identified and measured, subsequently, it should be possible to know how to select good leaders.

Many leadership traits have been examined, but research has failed to confirm a strong relationship between traits and leadership (Kirkpatrick & Locke, 1991). More recent research suggests that sets of traits are associated with good leadership. For example, effective leaders have more drive, honesty, leadership motivation, self-confidence, intelligence, knowledge of business, creativity, and flexibility. No single trait can predict good leadership, but effective leaders do differ from typical followers in exhibiting higher levels of these characteristics overall. The basic problem with the trait approach is that people who are successful leaders in one situation (e.g., business) are not necessarily successful in others (e.g., politics, religion).

A good example of the problem with the trait approach is the value of intelligence. "Good leaders should be intelligent." This seems like an obvious statement, but is it true? Are the most intelligent people the best leaders? Are the smartest U.S. presidents the most effective? Would most college professors make great business leaders? It is true that good leaders tend to be more intelligent than average, but leaders are not necessarily the most intelligent people in their organizations. In addition, the importance of intelligence varies. In a dictatorship (e.g., the military), intelligence is an important characteristic of good leaders. In a democracy (e.g., local politics), good leaders must be able to easily relate to others and have good communication skills. These communication skills are more important than intelligence.

Motivation is another example of the problem with the trait approach. Successful leaders are motivated, but what type of motivation is important? The difference between successful entrepreneurs of small businesses and managers of large companies is not a difference in the level of motivation: It is a difference in the type of motivation. Successful managers in large organizations have a strong need for power and a moderately strong need for achievement (McClelland & Boyatzis, 1982). The power motivation of such managers is focused on building their organizations and empowering their subordinates rather than on gaining personal power and control. By contrast, successful entrepreneurs have a strong need for achievement and independence without an overwhelming need for power.

Flexibility, or the ability to adapt to a situation, is considered an important characteristic of good leaders. Obviously, not all situations require the same approach, particularly since people also like consistency and leaders who stand for things. We malign politicians who are too influenced by public opinion polls, but that is a flexible approach to leadership. Clearly, we do not want too much flexibility in our leaders.

Behavioral Approach

The behavioral approach defines leadership as a set of appropriate behaviors. The goal of this approach is to define how good leaders act in order to train people to be good leaders. Rather than focusing on issues, such as intelligence and creativity, most of the research on leader behavior focuses on two issues: decision-making style and task versus social focus.

The decision-making approach primarily examined the benefits of authoritarian leadership in comparison with democratic leadership. As was noted in Chapter 9, there is no one best way to make a decision. The best type of decision-making approach depends on the situation or problem (Vroom & Jago, 1988).

Research in this area demonstrates some of the problems and benefits of different decision-making approaches. Democratic leaders tend to encourage higher morale, job satisfaction, and commitment in their followers. However, democratic decision making can be slow, and leaders may be viewed as weak. Autocratic leaders tend to be more efficient decision makers, but this style can create dissatisfaction and implementation problems among followers.

Behavioral research also examines whether leaders should focus on the tasks or on the social relations among the team members (Likert, 1961). Is a leader's primary role to organize and manage the task or is it to ensure that social relations are good, team members feel satisfied and motivated, and the team can maintain itself? Research in this area has been contradictory and inconclusive, except for the finding that team members like leaders who show social consideration (Yukl, 1989).

Similar to the issue with the various styles of decision making, the most effective behavioral approach to leadership depends on the situation. If a team is performing a routine task, the leader should focus on social relations, because the team does not need help with the task. If a project team is working on a difficult problem, a good leader helps the team better understand and work on the task. If a team is capable of self-management, the leader should ignore both task and social issues and focus instead on concerns outside the team.

One new example of the behavioral approach to leadership is the leader-member exchange model. This approach looks inside a team to see how the leader and subordinates interact (Graen & Uhl-Bien, 1995). Leaders form different types of relationships with subordinates, which creates in-groups and out-groups. In-group members get more attention from leaders and more resources for performing their jobs. Consequently, they are more productive and more satisfied than out-group members. The distinction is made by leaders early in the relationship and is based on little information about the subordinates. Sometimes it is influenced by irrelevant factors, such as similarity, personality, and attraction rather than by actual performance. The importance of this perspective is the recognition that a team comprises a variety of individuals. A leader does not treat everyone alike, and a leader may be performing effectively with some team members, but ineffectively with others.

Situational Approach

Are leaders really important to the success of teams? When are leaders important? These questions are the basis of the situational approach to leadership. The value of this approach is in understanding the situational factors that affect leadership and its alternatives.

When historians study great leaders, they note the relationship between leaders and situations. Charismatic leaders require situations where people have important needs and are searching for others to help resolve those needs (Bass, 1985). This same statement is true for other historically important leaders: They led during dramatic times.

People often overrate the importance of leaders (Meindl & Ehrlich, 1987). Although leaders may have a strong impact on the success of organizations, in most day-to-day operations their impact is considerably less. However, leaders are cognitively important for followers. It is difficult to explain the success or failure of organizations, so leadership becomes a simplified explanation for what has happened and why.

One of the chief values of the situational approach is in examining alternatives to leadership or factors that can substitute for leadership. These factors relate to the characteristics of employees, jobs, and organizations (Yukl, 1994). Competent, well-trained, and responsible employees need leaders to a lesser degree. Routine jobs that are highly structured do not require leader supervision. Organizing into teams and developing a cohesive team spirit reduce the need for leaders.

Contingency Approach

The contingency approach is the researcher's answer to the problems with leadership research. If one cannot define the traits or behaviors of good leaders separate from the situation, then leadership theories should combine these factors. However, a good research theory may be difficult to use in practice. Contingency theories are complex and more difficult to understand and apply than are other theories.

Contingency theories start by focusing on some characteristic of a situation. Various theories examine the type of task, level of structure, or favorableness of the situation for the leader. The theories then examine some aspect of the leader's personality or behavior, such as interpersonal skills or task orientation. These two sets of factors are linked to show either how the leader should behave depending on the situation or what type of leader would function the best given the situation. For example, because of preference or training, some people tend to be autocratic leaders. Autocratic leaders work well in situations where they have considerable power and followers are motivated to comply. This is why the military trains leaders to handle emergency situations forcefully and selects leaders who can act in this way.

Yukl's (1989) multiple linkage model is a contingency theory that relates to leading teams. The theory states that successful performance of a team depends on the following six intervening variables: member effort, member ability, organization of the task, teamwork and cooperativeness, availability of resources, and external coordination. Situational factors both directly influence these variables and determine which variables are most important. The role of the leader is to manage and improve these intervening variables. In the short run, most leader actions are intended to correct problems in these six variables. In the long run, the leader tries to make the situation more favorable by implementing improvement programs, developing new goals and directions, improving relations with the organization, and improving the team's climate.

10.3 Situational Leadership Theory

From a teamwork perspective, one of the most important leadership theories is situational leadership theory (Hersey & Blanchard, 1993). This theory links the leader's behavior to characteristics of the team. The value of this theory goes beyond simply telling the leader how to behave. Situational leadership theory is a developmental theory that assumes that one of the goals of leadership is to develop the team. As such, it is one of the most team-oriented of the leadership theories.

Situational leadership theory starts with the assumption that there are four basic styles of leadership, based on a combination of task and relationship orientation. Leaders can be directing (high task and low relationship), coaching (high task and high relationship), supporting (low task and high relationship), or delegating (low task and low relationship). The appropriate style depends on the maturity or readiness level of the team. Team readiness is based on the skills of team members, their experience with the task, their capacity to set goals, and their ability to assume responsibility. As the team's readiness level increases, the leader's behavior shifts from directing to coaching, supporting, and then delegating.

To see how this theory works, imagine you are the leader of a team of adolescents in a summer work program. On your first day as leader, your team has little experience with the task and little experience working together. As the leader, you need to take control of the situation and get the team to start working together. A task-oriented (directing) approach is needed. As the team gains some experience over time, your leadership style should soften (coaching) to reward the team's accomplishments. Once the team learns how to perform the job and act responsibly, you need to further reward members by allowing them to participate in the decision-making process (supporting). This both helps increase their commitment to the team and helps develop their leadership skills. When the team can take full responsibility for performing its task, your job shifts to addressing issues outside the team since you are no longer needed to guide the team. As the leader, you delegate most of the internal leadership functions and let the team manage itself (delegating).

As may be seen from this example, situational leadership theory makes two important points. First, the leader needs to adjust his style of acting relative to the readiness of the team. Second, leadership is a developmental process, and the leader's behavior should promote team maturity or readiness.

Situational leadership theory advocates matching the leadership style to the maturity or readiness of the team (Lorinkova, Pearsall, & Sims, 2013). This may be appropriate in the short run; however, a directive style of leadership where the leader makes the decisions about the team's operations does not promote development of the team. An empowering or supportive approach to leadership (which is advocated for more developed or mature teams) may slow performance at first, but this approach helps to develop the team over time. In the long run, this supportive approach leads to better team performance.

A team that is unprepared for teamwork may need a directive leader in order to perform well, but directive leadership does not develop the team and make it more able to function in the future (Lorinkova et al., 2013). The directive leader encourages dependence on the leader for performance rather than team learning and development. Leaders need to focus on empowering the team, which requires a nondirective approach to leadership. An empowering approach to leadership enhances performance by encouraging participation and collaboration and by having team members take responsibility for team performance. Its focus is on team learning and positive team member interactions. The goal is to develop a team's ability to perform without the need of a leader.

An empowerment approach to leadership focuses on developing the team through active participation in decision making, collaboration in developing work roles and processes, and learning how to improve performance (Lorinkova et al., 2013). This education stage takes time away from the task, so it reduces short-term performance. However, it improves long-term team performance because the team develops collective competence, confidence, and commitment to the team. In the long run, this approach encourages team learning, performance, and resilience.

10.4 Self-Managing Teams

As organizations become more team oriented, they sometimes shift to the use of self-managing teams (Wellins & George, 1991). Self-managing teams provide a number of benefits beyond the use of standard work teams. However, developing self-managing teams can be a difficult process, and this type of team is not necessarily suited for all situations.

Self-managing teams shift responsibility for performance to team members (Hackman, 1986). This reduces the need for managers and allows the remaining managers to focus on tasks outside the team. When they are successful, self-managing teams encourage the empowerment of employees and the development of team member skills. The shift to self-managing teams is not an all-or-nothing process. Rather, there are many levels of self-management depending on how willing the organization is to give the team new responsibilities.

Although the idea of self-managing teams has been around since the 1960s (as part of sociotechnical systems theory, or STS), the use of self-managing teams was not common until the 1980s, when they were used primarily with factory and service teams (Manz, 1992). By the 1990s, more than 40% of large companies in the United States were using self-managing teams with at least some employees (Cohen, Ledford, & Spreitzer, 1996). The most important reasons for companies to introduce self-managing teams in manufacturing were to improve performance and quality (de Leede & Stoker, 1999).

Leading Self-Managing Teams

Leading self-managing teams requires new approaches to leadership (Druskat & Wheeler, 2003). Even though self-managing teams control their internal operations, external leaders do have important roles: They provide valuable coaching, support, and motivation for teams. However, many self-managing service and production teams perform relatively routine tasks. Under normal conditions, they do not require assistance from external leaders. It is when the teams encounter problems that external leaders may be needed.

For self-managing teams, the external leader may either provide support or directly intervene in the team's operations (Morgeson, 2005). When leaders intervene by preparing teams for change or providing supportive coaching, they are viewed as effective leaders and increase satisfaction with leadership. When they directly intervene into the team's operations, they decrease satisfaction with leadership. Active involvement by the leader is viewed as negative by the team, since it takes away the team's autonomy. Active interventions are only related to team effectiveness and satisfaction when the team cannot manage on its own.

Motivating Self-Managing Teams

In self-managing teams, motivation is based on the actions of team members rather than external leaders (Stewart, Courtright, & Barrick, 2012). It is the team members who become responsible for monitoring, coordinating, and motivating work performance. They have two approaches to influence team motivation: normative and rational. In normative influence, the sense of belonging and attachment to the team creates social pressure on members to perform. Group cohesion becomes the motivating force for the team. In rational influence, the ability of team members to evaluate and reward each other's performance provides motivation to achieve. The rational approach deals with the problem of social loafing because team members are aware they are being evaluated by their peers.

Normative and rational motivation strategies overlap or substitute for each other to motivate teams, although the combination of the two may be more effective for motivating individual performance (Stewart et al., 2012). In highly cohesive teams where there is social pressure for all team members to work well together, normative motivation works well for both individual and team performance. However, in low-cohesion teams, individual motivation is more dependent on peer evaluations and the reward system. The rational approach also supports team empowerment, since allowing team members to have control over the performance evaluation and rewards system is one way to empower teams. Therefore, the rational approach has other benefits for self-managing teams, such as strengthening team members' belief that they can influence the strategic and operational activities of the team.

Success of Self-Managing Teams

The benefits of self-management for production and service teams do not necessarily apply to professional teams. Cohen and Bailey's (1997) review of the factors that relate to team success in different types of work teams found that self-management did not improve the performance of project teams.

The highest performing project teams had leaders who were highly involved in managing the task. Because members of project teams already have substantial autonomy, they may not view self-management as a personal benefit. In addition, their projects are nonroutine and difficult, so leaders who help provide structure are viewed as a benefit.

There is a number of reasons why production or service teams are better suited than professional teams for self-management. In production teams, team members can be cross-trained, which allows them to understand the issues involved in each other's work. In professional teams, team members have different types of expertise, thereby limiting members' understanding of each other's perspectives (Uhl-Bien & Graen, 1992). Production teams have clear performance measurements and can use quantitative feedback to evaluate and improve performance. In most cases, it is difficult to analyze and measure the performance of professional teams (Orsburn, Moran, Musselwhite, Zenger, & Perrin, 1990). Finally, production workers place more importance on their social relations and are less competitive when compared to professionals and managers (Lea & Brostrom, 1988).

In their study of professional teams, Levi and Slem (1996) found little evidence that self-managing teams performed better, or that employees preferred to work on that type of team. The idea of self-management is attractive to many employees in theory, but so is having a good leader to manage, teach, and reward efforts. The lack of a single best approach to leadership should not be too surprising. When the task is complex and the team's goals are unclear, a strong leader is needed to provide clear direction. When the task is relatively routine, the need for a leader is greatly diminished. The more experience people have in performing the task and working as a team, the better able they are to become self-managing.

10.5 Application: The Functional Approach to Leading Teams

Although there is a substantial amount of research on both leadership and team development, there is limited research on the most effective types of leadership for teams (Zaccaro & Klimoski, 2002). Traditional leadership theories do not adequately explain team leadership. Team leaders can adopt various roles, ranging from being an active participant in the team to being an external leader who sets the team's overall direction and allows the team to manage its internal processes.

From a functional leadership perspective, the goal of the team leader is to help the team operate more effectively (Zaccaro & Marks, 1999). Team leadership is a form of social problem solving where the leader helps to identify what team functions need improvement and then develops actions to correct the situation (Day, 2013). This includes helping the team interpret and diagnose problems, generate and evaluate solutions, and implement those solutions. Functional leadership is not defined by a specific set of leader behaviors, because the appropriate behavior depends on the characteristics of the team, its task, the environmental context, and the problems it is facing. It is not a specific style of leadership behavior, but rather a problem-solving approach to dealing with the problems that teams face.

There are three core leadership functions: setting the direction for the team, managing the team's operations, and developing the team's leadership abilities (Zaccaro, Heinen, & Shuffler, 2009). The focus of the team leader depends on the situation the team faces and the maturity of the team. Leaders help the team solve problems in order to meet its goals, while developing the skills and abilities of the team members so they have the collective capacity for leadership. They promote team learning by giving performance feedback to the team and using this information to help the team develop performance strategies that are more effective.

Functional team leaders do not micromanage teams, but support and empower them (Garvin, 2013). Research on project team leaders at Google shows that effective leaders give the team freedom, while being available to provide advice and support when needed. Leaders are good coaches who make it clear that they trust the team, while also serving as a strong advocate for the team within the larger organization.

There are several approaches that team leaders can take to support the team (Hackman, 2012). Leaders can focus on the structure and context of the team to ensure it has the capabilities to succeed. Alternatively, team leaders can be actively involved in the internal operations of the team to facilitate performance. Finally, leaders can assume the role of coach to provide guidance to the team when they encounter challenges to performance. From a leadership perspective, establishing the context for the team is the most important factor.

Providing a Context for Teams

Team leaders provide a supportive context for teams by focusing on the team's direction, structure, and external relations (Hackman & Walton, 1986; Wageman, Hackman, & Lehman, 2005). One of the primary roles of the team leader is to set the direction for the team. Establishing a clear and engaging direction for the team is a crucial part of motivating team performance.

The leader has to create a situation that enables successful performance. This includes a facilitative group structure and a supportive organizational context. A facilitative group structure includes tasks that are engaging, a team whose members have the skills to complete the task, and team norms that encourage effective performance. A supportive context provides the team with necessary information and resources and rewards team excellence.

The third leader role is oriented toward the team's external relations. The leader links the team to the organization and buffers the team from any interference from the organization. The leader has a public relations job to perform, making sure the team has the resources and support it needs from the organization.

Facilitating Internal Operations

Team leaders who are actively involved impact the team's cognitive, motivational, emotional, and coordination processes (Zaccaro, Rittman, & Marks, 2001). From a cognitive perspective, team leaders help identify the issues that the team needs to manage, facilitate problem solving by the team, and help form the team's performance strategies. They do not solve the team's problems, but facilitate the team's ability to engage in effective problem solving.

Another major role of the leader is to motivate team members to work hard for the team. Leaders do this by facilitating team cohesion and a sense of collective efficacy. They develop challenging task assignments that require interdependence in order to encourage commitment. Leaders acknowledge good performance and celebrate team successes to reward team performance.

From an emotional perspective, the leader helps manage the team's stress and promote a positive mood among team members. The leader impacts the team's mood by modeling positive states, providing counseling and support to team members, and managing conflict in a constructive manner. This means creating a safe environment where team members feel free to participate without fear of punishment.

Finally, the leader improves coordination in the team by identifying the individual roles of team members, matching team members' capabilities to their roles, developing performance strategies, and monitoring and providing feedback about performance. The leader is also responsible for creating times for the team to reflect on its performance and reevaluate its goals and processes.

Team Coaching

Team coaching is a team leader intervention designed to improve coordination and performance by providing guidance to the team (Hackman & Wageman, 2005). There are three types of team coaching: motivational, consultative, and educational. Motivational coaching is designed to minimize social loafing and increase team commitment. Consultative coaching focuses on strategies to improve team performance and increase coordination among team roles and tasks. Educational coaching helps build the knowledge, skills, and abilities of team members and the team as a whole.

How the leader coaches a team depends on its stage of development. These stages affect the readiness of the team to accept and use different types of coaching. At the beginning of a project, team members need to become oriented toward each other and prepare to work on the task. A coaching intervention that motivates the team by enhancing commitment to both the team and task is appropriate. During the midpoint transition period, strategy-oriented coaching that helps the team analyze and improve operations is valuable. When most of the team's work has been completed, educational coaching helps the team learn from the experience and enables members to use these lessons in future team activities.

Coaching is about building the team, not about directing the team how to do its work. Unfortunately, too often team leaders focus on managing the team's activities rather than on building the capabilities of the team. Research shows that leaders who actively listen to team members and incorporate their ideas into the team's decisions help improve both members' evaluations of their teams and the quality of team decisions (Cohen & Bailey, 1997). Problem leaders tend to micromanage their teams, engage in autocratic decision making, and be overconfident of their own skills (McIntyre & Salas, 1995). This pattern of leadership reduces respect for such leaders and prevents constructive feedback in order to improve their behavior.

LEADING VIRTUAL TEAMS: NEW APPROACHES TO LEADERSHIP IN VIRTUAL TEAMS

Problem: Leading virtual teams requires different approaches because of the inability to monitor team members' activities and difficulties communicating via technology.

Solution: While many factors influence the style of virtual team leaders, there are several approaches to leading virtual teams that should be considered.

1. Manage by outcomes, not by process. In most virtual settings, a leader should provide explicit measurable objectives and context, but delegate internal operations and processes to individuals or subteams. Leaders should recognize that long distance supervision of work hours, processes, and norms is often difficult and counterproductive. Team members need clear and measurable performance expectations and then should be left to their own process and schedule as long as they are able to produce the expected results.

2. Support the development and maintenance of distributed environments. Virtual team members depend on technology to do their work and communicate with team members. The virtual leader should focus on ensuring that team members have adequate and appropriate technical tools to complete their assignments. Part of the leader's role is to ensure that team members have the tools and technical skills required to succeed.

3. Manage by problem solving. Virtual leaders should use a coaching style of leadership by providing tools and support for team members as needed and by removing barriers that impede team member performance. The ability to work independently under a coaching style of leadership might be one consideration when selecting members for a virtual team.

4. Remain sensitive to time differences. The virtual leader of a global team must be sensitive to daily time differences. Setting a regular meeting time inconvenient to the same subset of the team creates a power and performance difference among team members. Synchronous meetings should be scheduled with sensitivity to the clock of all team members with any necessary inconvenience rotated among different team sites.

5. Stay more explicit in your communication. The virtual leader must communicate more clearly and more explicitly than she or he would in a face-to-face setting. Because nonverbal cues are less available, nuance of tone and meaning (for example, urgency) must be conveyed through words alone.

Summary

Leadership can be centralized in one person or distributed among various roles. Teams vary in types of leadership, selection of leaders, and delegation of leader powers. Teams rarely exist without leaders, since leaders emerge through a team's interactions. Leaders may be designated by their organizations, or teams may select their own leaders and be self-managing.

There are four main approaches to studying leadership:

1. The trait or personality approach defines the personality characteristics of successful leaders.

2. The behavioral approach examines the value of different behavioral styles, such as task orientation and social orientation.

3. The situational approach identifies the factors that make leaders important (change) or less important (mature teams).

4. The contingency approach links traits and behaviors to the situations to which they best apply.

Each of these approaches has different implications for the way leaders should be selected and trained.

One of the most important leadership theories for teams is situational leadership theory, which defines four styles of leadership: directing, coaching, supporting, and delegating. The leader should select the style to use based on the readiness level of the team. In addition, the leader should use an appropriate style to promote team development.

Self-managing teams shift responsibility for teams from management to the team members. The chief examples of self-managing teams at work are factory and service workers, where employees are cross-trained and taught teamwork skills. Developing self-managing teams among professionals can be difficult because of the nature of their tasks and the relationships among team members. The use of self-managing teams requires new roles for team leaders.

The functional approach to team leadership provides advice about what factors a leader should focus on to improve the team's functioning. Team leadership is viewed as a form of problem solving designed to help the team succeed. Leaders can focus on providing a supportive context, facilitating internal operations, or coaching to provide guidance. These actions are designed to help the team operate more effectively and to develop the team's leadership abilities.

Team Leader's Challenge 10

You are an attorney in a law office with several other attorneys, paralegal assistants, clerical staff, and an office technician. Leadership is shared among the attorneys, and you are the leader for the staff meetings and for office management issues. Decisions about how the office operates are made in weekly meetings with the entire staff. The office technician has informed you that problems are increasing with the office computer system and it is time to make a major change. This technological decision will affect the work of everyone in the office.

The office functions well and people have good working relationships. Although they do not welcome learning a new computer system, many people in the office recognize that a change in technology is needed. For most office decisions, the staff discusses issues and makes a group decision. However, there are many technical aspects to the computer system decision, and you are uncertain whether everyone should be involved in this decision.

How should you (the leader for office management issues) make the decision about the new computer system?

Are the team members capable of making this decision, or is this a time when more authoritative leadership is important?

What leadership style is best here? Why?

SURVEY: LEADERSHIP STYLES

Purpose: To help you understand your preferred leadership styles. Situational leadership theory says that the best style of leadership depends on the characteristics of the situation. However, people often have preferred leadership styles that they use frequently, regardless of the situation.

Directions: Imagine that you are the leader of a team facing the eight situations that are listed below. How should you as the team leader make the decisions to resolve the situations? Review these four decision options and select which approach is best for each situation:

Option A: Make the decision yourself and tell the team what to do.

Option B: Ask the team members for advice, but make the decision yourself.

Option C: Facilitate the team's decision-making process.

Option D: Let the members of the team decide by themselves what to do.

_____ 1. The team's performance has been dropping, and personality clashes are increasing. You have tried to be friendly and sympathetic to their problems, but this does not seem to be working. What should you do to improve the team's performance?

_____ 2. Because of financial problems in the organization, you have been ordered to make budget cuts for the team. There are a variety of options, including reducing the number of team members or work hours. How should you make the budget cuts?

_____ 3. You are considering a major change—replacing the office computer system. The team works well together and has been consistently successful. They respect the need for change, but they are not computer experts. How should you make the decision and manage the change program?

_____ 4. It is the beginning of the sports season and your team needs to reduce the number of players on the roster from 27 to 25. How should you decide who will be removed from the team?

_____ 5. You have received information that indicates some recent quality problems in the team's work. The team has a good record of accomplishment. You are not sure what is causing the performance problems. What should you do to improve the situation?

_____ 6. The team has just completed a major project deadline and it is time to celebrate. You think a party or social activity is an appropriate reward. What kind of celebration should you have?

_____ 7. The team has been performing fairly well. The previous team leader was very controlling. You want the team to continue to be successful, but you would also like to improve the social relations among team members. How should you try to improve the situation?

_____ 8. The team's office is being redecorated and there are many decisions to be made. These decisions relate to furniture, carpeting, wall colors, and so on. The budget for the project has already been established. How should these decisions be made?

Scoring:
The number of situations you marked A is your Directing score.
The number of situations you marked B is your Coaching score.
The number of situations you marked C is your Supporting score.
The number of situations you marked D is your Delegating score.

Discussion: Did you have a preferred leadership style? In which situations is this leadership style most appropriate? How flexible are you with your leadership style?

SOURCE: Adapted from Greenberg, J., & Baron, R. (1997). *Behavior in organizations: Understanding the human side of work* (6th ed.). Upper Saddle River, NJ: Prentice Hall.

ACTIVITY: OBSERVING THE LEADER'S BEHAVIOR

Objective: Situational leadership theory defines four types of leader behavior: directing, coaching, supporting, and delegating. The most useful behavior depends on the readiness level of the team. Team readiness relates to the skills, experience, and responsibility level of the team.

Activity: Select a variety of situations to observe and analyze the behavior of leaders. These situations can come from teams or organizations you belong to, videos of leaders interacting with teams, business case studies, or the Team Leader's Challenges in this book. Use Activity Worksheet 10.1 to classify the leader's behavior using the types from situational leadership theory, rate the readiness level of the team, and analyze the match between these factors.

Analysis: According to situational leadership theory, does the style of behavior used by the leader match the readiness level of the team? Was the style of leadership used effective? How should the leader behave to be more effective?

Discussion: What are the implications of using a leadership style that is too controlling or task oriented? What are the implications of using a leadership style that gives subordinates too much freedom and responsibility? How will team members respond to these styles of leadership?

ACTIVITY WORKSHEET 10.1
Rating the Leader's Behavior

Which of the following styles best describes the leader's behavior?

_____Directing (high task and low relationship)

_____Coaching (high task and high relationship)

_____Supporting (low task and high relationship)

_____Delegating (low task and low relationship)

Overall, how would you rate the readiness level of the team?

_____ Low _____ Medium _____ High _____

How well did the leader's behavior match with the group's readiness level?

Leadership Style			
Directing	*Coaching*	*Supporting*	*Delegating*
Low	Medium		High
Group Readiness			

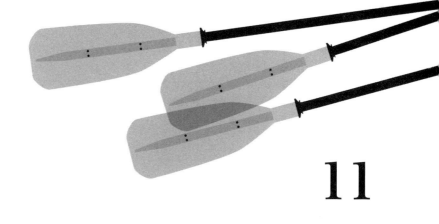

11

Problem Solving

Team problem solving is studied using three different approaches: the methods that teams use to solve their problems, the types of behavior that contribute to effective problem solving, and the techniques used by teams to improve team problem solving. Team problem-solving approaches are based on a rational model of the process that includes six stages: problem definition, evaluation of the problem, generating alternatives, selecting a solution, implementation, and evaluation of the results. In practice, however, this rational approach is rarely followed, and teams often find themselves developing solutions before they understand the problems.

At each stage of the problem-solving process, teams can use a number of techniques to improve their problem-solving abilities. Using these techniques helps teams become more effective as problem solvers.

Learning Objectives

1. How do teams typically solve problems?

2. What factors help improve a team's ability to solve problems?

3. What factors disrupt a team's ability to solve problems?

4. What are the main steps in the rational approach to problem solving?

5. How do the characteristics of the problem, team, and environment affect the way a team analyzes a problem?

6. What is the value of using a structured approach to generating and evaluating alternatives?

7. What factors affect the implementation of a solution?

8. Why should problem-solving teams use structured techniques to analyze and solve problems?

9. What are some of the techniques that teams can use to help in their problem-solving efforts?

11.1 Approaches to Problem Solving

A problem is a dilemma with no apparent solution, an undesirable situation without a way out, a question that cannot currently be answered, the difference between the current situation and a desired state, or a situation team members must manage effectively (Pokras, 1995). The problem can come from the environment or arise from the team. Problems often first surface for a team as symptoms that cause undesirable effects.

In a work environment, a problem for many teams is simply how to complete their tasks or assignments. A team's assignment contains two primary problems: (1) determining the nature of the assignments and how to complete them and (2) managing problems and obstacles encountered when performing them. These obstacles may be technical issues, conflicting viewpoints, or interpersonal conflicts.

The perfect way to solve a problem is to define it and then decide how to solve it. This may seem obvious, but the biggest problem teams have is generating solutions without first understanding the problem. Defining and evaluating the problem is the most difficult step for teams to perform.

The first step in problem solving is to discuss and document individual views until everyone agrees on the nature of the problem (Pokras, 1995). Teams are often given ill-defined problems and undeveloped criteria for evaluating them. Teams need to challenge the definitions of the problems, searching for their root causes. They also need to define what successful resolutions would look like in order to evaluate alternative solutions. The result should be agreement on the issues that need resolution and clear statements of the problem.

Teams may rush through the problem definition stage, only to find that they have to return to it during the solution or implementation stage. This is a time-consuming approach to problem solving. Understanding as much as possible about a problem at the beginning can reduce the overall time spent solving the problem.

Another common flaw is ignoring the final stage: evaluating the solution. Often teams are created to solve problems, but are not responsible for implementation or evaluation. Evaluation is ignored because no one wants to present negative information to superiors. Rather than learning from mistakes made, the mistakes are hidden from the team and organization. As a result, they are often repeated because of lack of feedback.

There are three approaches to team problem solving: descriptive, which examines how teams solve problems; functional, which identifies the behaviors of effective problem solving; and prescriptive, which recommends techniques and approaches to improve team problem solving (Beebe & Masterson, 1994).

11.2 Descriptive Approach: How Teams Solve Problems

The descriptive approach examines how teams typically solve problems. Researchers focus on different aspects of the group system in order to understand the problem-solving process. These different perspectives offer alternative ways of understanding the methodology.

One perspective using the descriptive approach is to identify the stages a team goes through during problem solving (Beebe & Masterson, 1994). This approach is similar to the stages of team development discussed in Chapter 3. The four stages a team uses when solving a problem are forming, storming, norming, and performing.

In the forming stage, the team examines the problem and tries to better understand the issues related to it. The storming stage is a time of conflict, when different definitions of the problem and preliminary solutions are discussed. Often, the team jumps ahead to arguing about solutions before it has reached agreement on the problem, so it must return to the problem definition stage to resolve this conflict. In the norming stage, the team develops methods for analyzing the problem, generating alternatives, and selecting a solution. The establishment of these methods and other norms about how to operate helps the team members work together effectively. In the performing stage, these methods are used to solve the problem and develop plans to implement the solution.

Rather than going through problem-solving stages, many teams start the problem-solving process by generating solutions. Teams generate alternatives and select solutions in a variety of ways. Strategies include selecting a solution at random, voting for the best solution, taking turns suggesting each member's favorite solution, trying to demonstrate that a solution is correct, or inventing novel solutions (Laughlin & Hollingshead, 1995). Once a solution becomes the focus, the team analyzes it to determine whether it is correct or at least better than the proposed alternatives. If the majority of members believe that it is, the solution is accepted. If that majority does not, a new solution is generated by one of the preceding techniques.

11.3 Functional Approach: Advice on Improving Team Problem Solving

The functional approach tries to improve a team's ability to solve problems by understanding the factors related to effective problem solving and the factors that disrupt team problem solving.

Factors That Improve Team Problem Solving

An effective team should include intelligent problem solvers or vigilant critical thinkers. The team should analyze the problem, develop alternatives, and select the best solution. The problem-solving process should be relatively free of social, emotional, and political factors that disrupt a rational analysis. The following are characteristics of effective team problem solvers (Beebe & Masterson, 1994; Janis & Mann, 1977):

- Skilled problem solvers view problems from a variety of viewpoints to better understand the problem.
- Rather than relying on its own opinions, an effective team gathers data and researches a problem before making a decision.
- A successful team considers a variety of options or alternatives before selecting a particular solution.
- An effective team manages both the task and relational aspects of problem solving. It does not let a problem damage the team's ability to function effectively in other areas.
- A successful team's discussion is focused on the problem. Teams that have difficulty staying focused on the issues, especially when there are conflicts, are usually not successful.
- An effective team listens to minority opinions. Often the solution to a problem lies in the knowledge of a team member, but is ignored because the team focuses on the opinions of the majority.
- Skilled problem solvers test alternative solutions relative to established criteria. The team defines what criteria a good solution must meet and uses those criteria when examining alternatives.

Factors That Hurt Team Problem Solving

Project teams often jump quickly to the solution stage without adequately defining the problem (Hackman & Morris, 1975). The teams do not discuss their problem-solving strategies or develop plans to research possibilities. Typically, they try to apply solutions that have worked in the past. When teams rush to solve problems, their decision-making process is often based on intuitive, automatic, emotional thinking rather than on rational, conscious, logical thinking (Milkman, Chugh, & Bazerman, 2009). In many cases, problem solving is improved by slowing down the decision-making process in order to promote rational rather than intuitive thinking. Teams that spend time following a structured approach to problem solving make better decisions and members are more satisfied with the problem-solving process.

A team may not follow a structured approach to problem solving because of constraints on the process, such as limited time, money, and information. Because of these constraints, teams often seek "satisficing" solutions rather than optimal solutions (Simon, 1979). Perfection is expensive and time consuming. Collecting all relevant information needed to solve problems may take longer than the time or resources available to teams. In most cases, teams try to find acceptable solutions (those that meet their basic needs), given the constraints of the situation.

It often is difficult to determine the best solution. There are trade-offs, such as cost versus effectiveness of the solution. Solutions differ according to their probabilities of success, the amount of resources needed for their implementation, and the politics of implementing them. These trade-offs do not have correct answers: They rely on the judgment of the team. This difficulty determining the best solution limits a team's ability to objectively select the best solution.

As discussed in Chapters 6 and 9, communication problems may interfere with a team's ability to analyze and solve problems. During a team discussion, more time is spent on reviewing shared information than on discussing specialized information that might be pertinent to a solution (Stasser, 1992). Although the team's discussion should be focused on the problem, team discussions can get sidetracked and disrupted in many ways (DiSalvo, Nikkel, & Monroe, 1989). Ideally, a team should spend more of its time sharing information, planning, and critically evaluating ideas than on discussing non-task-related issues. Teams often fail to follow these steps (Jehn & Shaw, 1997), although the team's ability to solve problems would be increased.

A team's problem-solving process can be disrupted by a number of non-task-related factors. Team members may support a position because of their desire to reduce uncertainty or avoid social conflict. Politics may encourage members to support alternative solutions out of loyalty to their creators or as payback for past political support. Competition in the team may encourage political advocacy rather than a search for the best alternative (Johnson & Johnson, 1997). Teams are better able to solve problems when power is relatively equal among team members because this encourages more open communication and critical evaluation of alternatives.

11.4 Prescriptive Approach: Rational Problem-Solving Model

The functional approach illustrates what can go right (and wrong) with the team problem-solving process. The prescriptive approach presents a strategy that encourages teams to solve problems more effectively. This approach is based on the assumptions that (a) team members should use rational problem-solving strategies, and (b) using a structured approach will lead to a better solution. The value of formal structured approaches to problem solving varies depending on the type of problem. The more unstructured and complex the problem, the more helpful it is if the team uses a structured approach to solve it (Van Gundy, 1981).

An outline of the prescriptive approach is presented in Figure 11.1, which shows the main steps in a formal, rational, problem-solving model.

Figure 11.1   Rational Problem-Solving Approach

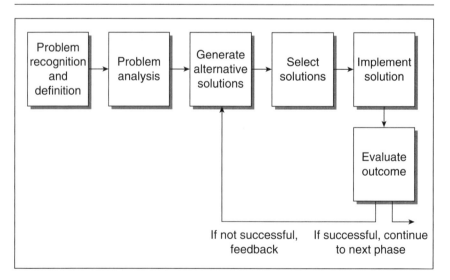

SOURCE: Adapted from Dewey, J. (1910). *How we think.* New York, NY: Heath and Van Gundy, A. (1981). *Techniques of structured problem solving.* New York: Van Nostrand Reinhold.

Problem Recognition, Definition, and Analysis

Problem recognition, definition, and analysis are key progressions in effective problem solving. However, teams often rush through these stages of the problem-solving process. In their desire to develop solutions quickly, they focus on the symptoms of the problem rather than trying to understand the real causes of the problem (Pokras, 1995).

Unfortunately, even when a team takes the time to identify and analyze a problem, the problem and its causes may be misinterpreted. Many things can go wrong in the problem analysis process. The ability to successfully identify and analyze a problem depends on the characteristics of the problem, the team, and the environment (Moreland & Levine, 1992).

Problems vary in their levels of severity, familiarity, and complexity. The more severe a problem is, the more likely it is to be identified as a hindrance. Acute problems with identifiable onsets and impacts are often recognized, whereas chronic problems that are less visible are often ignored. Problems that are familiar are more easily recognized. Novel problems are more difficult to interpret, and teams may assume they are unique, one-time events that will go away by themselves. Complex problems are difficult to analyze and interpret. It is common for a team to select only part of a complex problem to analyze and solve, as a way to simplify the situation (although this might not be an effective way to resolve the entire problem).

Teams vary in their levels of desire and ability to identify problems. Team norms have a strong effect on problem identification. Teams with norms supporting communication and positive attitudes toward conflict are more likely to identify and discuss problems. Teams vary in how open they are to the environment. Closed teams that are internally focused are less likely to be aware of problems in the environment. Open teams monitor what is happening in the environment. Also, they are better able to prepare for problems in the future because they identified the issues beforehand.

Team performance affects the problem identification process. A team that is performing successfully will sometimes ignore problems. From their perspective, the problems cannot be very important, given that the team is currently successful. Unsuccessful teams also have a tendency to ignore problems. These teams must focus on their main performance problems and as a result are less likely to see other problems. The notion of continuous improvement is a teamwork concept designed to help deal with this issue. In continuous improvement, teams assume that part of their function is to improve operations. In essence, all teams—both successful and unsuccessful—are required to identify problems and work to solve them on an ongoing basis.

Characteristics of the environment also affect a team's ability to identify and analyze problems. Many modern environments (e.g., political, business, technological) have substantial levels of change and uncertainty. The rapidity of change creates a need to stay alert and prepare for future problems, while the level of uncertainty makes it more difficult to do so. Teams vary in their relations to the outside environment. For example, some work teams are required to accept the definitions of problems given by their organizations, while other teams are open to information about potential problems from outside sources (e.g., customers, suppliers, and the public).

Once a team identifies a problem, it may decide not to solve it (Moreland & Levine, 1992). There are other alternatives. The team may decide to deny or distort the problem, thus justifying their choice to ignore it. The team may decide to hide from the problem, given that problems sometimes go away by themselves. If the problem is difficult for the team to understand (because of novelty or complexity), it may decide just to monitor the problem for the time being. Working collaboratively to solve a problem requires identification, the belief that the problem is solvable, and the motivation to solve it. These are the necessary conditions for the first two stages of the rational problem-solving process.

Generating Alternatives and Selecting a Solution

Finding an effective solution depends on developing high-quality alternatives (Zander, 1994). The ability of a team to accomplish this is related to the knowledge and skills of team members. However, it also depends on the team's climate and built-in constructs. The climate of an effective team encourages open discussion of ideas, where minority ideas are heard and taken seriously by the majority.

Teams sometimes use creativity and other structured techniques to generate alternative solutions to problems. Techniques such as brainstorming and the nominal group technique (discussed in Chapter 12) are used to generate alternatives. An important value of these techniques is that participation by all team members is encouraged. However, these participation techniques are useful only if the team is willing to give divergent ideas a fair evaluation. Too often, conformity pressure leads teams to adopt solutions used in the past.

After generating alternatives, teams must consider how to determine the best solution. Teams should consider the positive and negative effects of each alternative. The ability to implement the solutions must be considered. This involves the ability of teams to enact the solutions and an understanding of how outside groups will respond to the solutions.

Any good solution meets three criteria: (1) It is a prudent agreement that balances the needs of various team members, (2) it is an efficient problem-solving approach that does not consume too much time and resources, and

(3) it is a process that fosters group harmony (Fisher, Ury, & Patton, 1991). Once a set of alternatives is developed, the team should not argue about the merits of each solution. To do so encourages a conflict based on positions. Instead, the team should develop ways of evaluating the benefits and costs of the alternatives. The focus should be on analyzing the alternatives to aid selection rather than on the politics of getting an individual position adopted. This often leads to a final solution containing elements from multiple alternatives.

Sometimes none of the available alternative solutions is appealing, in which case the team selects the least objectionable proposal. This leads to rationalizing among team members to bolster their belief that the decision is acceptable. Teams may overemphasize the positive attributes of a selected solution and deny its negative aspects in order to justify their choice (Janis & Mann, 1977).

After the team has made its decision, it may want to hold a "second chance" meeting to review the decision. Even when the team decides by consensus, it is useful to have a second-chance meeting to air concerns about the decision. The meeting helps prevent factors such as groupthink and the pressure to conform from inappropriately influencing the decision.

Implementation and Evaluation

A solution is not a good one unless it is implemented. This requires commitment from a team to support and enact its solution. As mentioned in Chapters 8 and 9, one of the benefits of team decision making is that participating in the decision process creates a sense of commitment to it.

A problem-solving team is obliged to think about implementation issues when making a decision (Zander, 1994). It is not useful to agree on a solution that cannot be implemented. This means that the team should plan how the solution is to be implemented, including consideration of the people, time, and resources needed for implementation. It may be useful to bring the people affected by the planned solution into the decision-making process to encourage their acceptance of the solution.

Evaluation is one of the most overlooked steps of the problem-solving process. Even when teams do a good job of analyzing the problem and developing solutions, there are unforeseen factors that may lead to failure. Lewin's action research model (Lewin, 1951) is a research-based approach to problem solving that emphasizes the importance of the evaluation stage. In this approach, solutions are considered hypotheses that need to be tested. When solutions are implemented, their impacts are evaluated and used to determine their effectiveness and to identify further actions that need to be taken (and later evaluated).

Evaluation requires examining how the solution was implemented and what the effects were. (These two evaluations are sometimes called "process evaluation" and "outcome evaluation.") These evaluations require that the team provide a definition of a successful outcome, something it should have done during the problem identification stage.

Sometimes, even when the solution resolves the problem, the undesirable situation does not change significantly. This happens when a team solves only part of a larger problem and the rest of the problem comes to the foreground. By taking a larger perspective on the problem, the team may be able to determine the more critical parts of the problem that should be solved. The evaluation stage provides information for future problem identification and solving.

11.5 Problem-Solving Teams

Problem-solving teams are typically established for brief periods to solve specific organizational problems or to encourage organizational improvements (Fiore & Schooler, 2004). These teams work on a variety of issues, such as quality, process improvement, reengineering, and organizational development. Problem-solving teams may be composed of people from different organizational levels, from production and service employees to professionals and managers, and from different parts of an organization. Consequently, team members often do not know one another's areas of expertise and may have communication problems because of professional language and background differences. Because of these characteristics, problem-solving teams often rely on facilitators and the use of structured problem-solving techniques.

Teams must have a shared conceptualization of a problem in order to solve it. A team cannot coordinate its problem-solving efforts without this shared mental model. In problem solving, the mental model includes the nature of the problem, roles and skills of team members, and the mutual awareness of team members. A shared understanding of a problem ensures that all team members are solving the same problem.

A problem-solving team may use an engineering problem-solving technique called "process mapping" (Fiore & Schooler, 2004). Process mapping works as a problem-solving tool because it leads to the construction of a shared mental model for the team. The team develops a process map of how the situation currently operates (an "as is" map) that defines the parts of a process and the linkages among the parts. The team then develops a "should be" map that describes how the process should operate. These maps are then used to analyze the organization's operations and develop recommendations for improvement.

The value of process mapping is that it facilitates team communication regarding the problem definition, which improves later problem solving. In jointly developing the process map, the team arrives at a shared understanding of the problem. This overcomes the tendency of teams to skip to the solution stages of a problem. It also creates an environment where diverse team members can share their knowledge about the problem.

As team members engage in process mapping, the unique knowledge of each team member is made explicit. The team becomes aware of both the unique and common knowledge it shares. It is forced to negotiate its understanding of the issues related to the problem. Process mapping creates an external representation of a shared problem that facilitates the team's ability to work together to solve the problem. It forces the team to acknowledge deficiencies (the problems in the "as is" map) before attempting to develop solutions.

Process mapping is one of many problem-solving techniques used by teams (Katzenbach & Smith, 2001). The value of such techniques is that they provide a structure for communications and focus the team on clearly defining the problem before it develops solutions. This type of structure is especially important for temporary problem-solving teams because of the sometimes limited English language skills of production and service workers and the communication jargon of diverse professional teams.

Research demonstrates that structured approaches help teams make better decisions, increase members' satisfaction with solutions, and increase commitment to implementation (Pavit, 1993). These problem-solving approaches are effective because they promote more equitable participation in decisions, reduce the negative impact of unequal status, and increase the likelihood that the ideas of low-status employees are considered.

11.6 Application: Problem-Solving Techniques for Teams

Teams can choose several useful techniques to help them at each stage of the problem-solving process. These techniques structure the group process and better enable the team to focus on the problem. Four of these problem-solving techniques are discussed here and used in the activity at the end of the chapter. *Problem analysis* is a technique to help in the problem analysis stage. The *criteria matrix* is used to assist in selecting a solution. *Action plans* improve the implementation of a solution. *Force field analysis* can be used in many stages of the problem-solving process. The following sections examine these techniques in more detail.

Problem Analysis

Problem solving begins by recognizing that a problem exists, and that most of the real problem lies hidden. Typically, the first encounter with a problem is only with its symptoms. The team must then find the problem itself and agree on its fundamental sources. It should separate the symptoms (which are effects) from the causes. Before using the tools in this approach, team members investigate the problem by gathering more information about it. With this new information, the team can analyze the cause of the problem.

There are several tools that may be useful at this stage (Pokras, 1995). Symptom identification is a technique that has the team tabulate all aspects or symptoms of a problem. In force field analysis, the team analyzes the driving and restraining forces that affect a problem. In charting unknowns, team members discuss what they do not know about the problem, which generates hidden facts, questions, and new places to look for information. In repetitive "why" analysis, the team leader states the problem and then continues with the statement, " . . . which was caused by what?" This question is repeated several times to examine underlying causes of a problem.

Criteria Matrix

Techniques to generate alternatives are presented in Chapter 12. Once the team has generated alternative solutions, a selection process is required to review and evaluate them. If the team did a good job generating alternatives, they should have a number of options from which to choose. If the team used creativity techniques like brainstorming, there should be many unworkable ideas. Because some approaches obviously are not going to work, they should be eliminated from further analysis. Then the team should review the options and look for ways of combining solutions. After this, the team can develop a criteria matrix to evaluate the alternatives objectively.

A criteria matrix is a system used to rate alternatives (Pokras, 1995). The first step is to decide what criteria to use to rate the alternatives. There are many criteria possible to evaluate alternative solutions, including cost, effectiveness, acceptability, and ease of implementation. A team may want to use a rating scale for its analysis (e.g., 0 = not acceptable, 1 = somewhat acceptable, 2 = acceptable). Since all evaluation criteria are not of equal importance, it is important to remember to not merely select the alternative with the highest score. For example, one alternative solution may be less expensive to implement, but not as effective. If the team is highly concerned about cost, this may be the preferred alternative. The criteria matrix allows the team to analyze and discuss the relative merits of the alternatives in a structured manner.

Action Plans

The implementation stage focuses on generating action plans, considering contingency plans, and managing the project on the basis of these plans. An action plan is a practical guide to translating the solution into reality—a step-by-step road map, if possible (Pokras, 1995). It emphasizes the timing of various parts and assigning responsibility for actions. The plan also should establish standards to evaluate successful performance.

Events rarely go as planned. The team should establish a monitoring and feedback system to ensure that team members are aware of the progress made. Larger action items should be broken down into stages and monitored. Feedback to the team on progress with individual assignments should be a regular part of team meetings.

Force Field Analysis

Force field analysis is an approach to understanding the factors that affect any change program (Lewin, 1951). It examines the relation between the driving and restraining forces for change. The driving forces are what the team wants to achieve and the factors that minimize the problem. The restraining forces are the obstacles that prevent success and the factors that contribute to the problem. This approach can be used at many stages of the problem-solving process, but it is especially valuable in examining implementation issues.

When implementing a solution to a problem, teams want to increase the driving forces that encourage the change and reduce the restraining forces that prevent the change from occurring. Teams often focus on the driving forces that are promoting the change. However, most unsuccessful change efforts are due to the restraining forces (Levi & Lawn, 1993). Reducing the power of the restraining forces is a necessary precondition for change.

Force field analysis provides a method for teams to study their problem-solving activities. Using Lewin's action research model (1951), teams use group discussions to identify the driving and restraining forces affecting any proposed solution. The team uses this information to decide on strategies for implementation. A cycle of generation, analysis, and application of results may be repeated during the implementation process.

Levi and Lawn (1993) used this approach to analyze the driving and restraining forces that affected project teams developing new products. The project teams were driven by interest in new technology and an organizational culture that encouraged innovation. However, the success of producing and marketing new products was restrained by technical problems in manufacturing and by financial issues. Understanding these forces encouraged the project teams to include members from manufacturing and marketing in the design teams to address these problems.

Summary

Problem solving requires that a team analyze the nature of the problem, then develop and implement a solution. Unfortunately, many things can go wrong during these two steps. The study of team problem solving uses descriptive, functional, and prescriptive approaches to understand and improve the problem-solving process.

The descriptive approach looks at how a team solves a problem. The problem-solving process goes through developmental stages similar to stages of team development. Solutions are often generated in a rather haphazard fashion that sometimes seems more political than logical.

The functional approach provides advice on how to improve the team problem-solving process. An effective team views problems from multiple perspectives, analyzes a variety of alternatives using established criteria, and manages the group process to ensure that all members may participate. The team's ability to solve problems may be hurt by rushing to the solution stage, constraints limiting the amount of analysis, confusion about evaluation criteria, and social factors that disrupt the group process.

The prescriptive approach to problem solving includes a series of structured stages. The problem identification and analysis stage is affected by the severity and complexity of the problem, team norms about discussing problems, and the amount of uncertainty in the environment. The process of developing and selecting alternative solutions is improved by creativity techniques to generate alternatives and by analysis techniques to examine alternatives in a systematic manner. Implementing solutions requires planning and an evaluation system to provide feedback on the process.

Organizations use temporary problem-solving teams to deal with a variety of issues and to encourage improvement. These teams function more effectively if they use structured techniques, such as process mapping.

The team may use a variety of techniques to improve its problem-solving skills. Problem analysis techniques help clarify what is known about a problem. A criteria matrix is used to evaluate alternative solutions. Action plans create a map to guide implementation. Force field analysis may be used at several stages to evaluate alternatives and implementation programs.

Team Leader's Challenge 11

Your organization uses improvement teams composed of professionals and managers throughout the organization to solve important organizational problems. Team membership is highly valued because participation provides good visibility to upper management. Consequently, team members are highly motivated to perform. You have been selected to lead the next team. To prepare for the role, you have been discussing problems with former team leaders.

The last improvement team got off to a fast start. At the first meeting, the team diagnosed the problem and started generating solutions. Members quickly focused on a preferred alternative and began developing an implementation program. After several months of work, the team presented its proposal to top management. However, when it started implementing the proposal, serious problems became apparent and the project was scrapped.

How can the new team leader avoid the problems of the previous project team?

What problem-solving approaches should you use?

How can you prevent the team from wasting time on a proposal that does not really solve the problem?

ACTIVITY: USING PROBLEM-SOLVING TECHNIQUES

Objective: Problem solving is improved when a team follows a structured approach. The team should analyze the problem thoroughly before developing alternatives. It should develop a set of alternatives and then use evaluation criteria to help select a solution. Force field analysis can be used to understand the issues related to implementing a solution.

Activity: Have the team follow a structured approach to problem solving. The team can be given either an organizational problem or a social problem to solve. For example, develop a program to improve graduation rates at a university or encourage the use of condoms. After a problem has been selected, the team should use a repetitive "why" analysis to understand the causes of the problem, develop several alternative solutions, use the criteria matrix to analyze the alternatives, select an alternative solution, and use force field analysis to understand the issues that can affect implementation of the solution.

Step 1: Analyze the problem using a repetitive "why" analysis (Activity Worksheet 11.1). State a clear definition of the problem. Then, complete the following analysis of the causes of the problem by asking what caused the problem. Repeat to identify underlying causes. This analysis helps the team understand the different causes of the problem.

ACTIVITY WORKSHEET 11.1
Repetitive Why Analysis

Problem Definition:		
Why? Causes of the problem	Why? Underlying causes	Why? Underlying causes

SOURCE: From Pokras, S. (1995). *Team problem solving.* Menlo Park, CA: CRISP.

Step 2: Generate alternative solutions to the problem. Make sure that each alternative relates to at least one of the causes identified in Step 1.

Step 3: Analyze the alternative solutions using a criteria matrix (Activity Worksheet 11.2). For this activity use cost, effectiveness, and acceptability as criteria for evaluating the alternatives. Rate each alternative solution as high, medium, or low on these three criteria and then combine these into an overall rating. Use this analysis to select a preferred solution.

ACTIVITY WORKSHEET 11.2
Criteria Matrix

	Evaluation Criteria			
Alternative Solutions	*Cost*	*Effective*	*Acceptable*	*Overall*

SOURCE: From Pokras, S. (1995). *Team problem solving.* Menlo Park, CA: CRISP.

Step 4: Good ideas often do not get implemented because the advocates focus on the benefits of the proposals and ignore the problems. Evaluate the benefits and problems of your solution using force field analysis (Activity Worksheet 11.3).

ACTIVITY WORKSHEET 11.3
Force Field Analysis

Driving Forces: What are the benefits of our approach? Who will support it? Why?	*Restraining Forces: What problems does our approach have? Who may resist it? Why?*

SOURCE: From Pokras, S. (1995). *Team problem solving.* Menlo Park, CA: CRISP.

Step 5: Develop a plan to implement your proposal based on the results of the force field analysis.

Analysis: Did the team members find the use of the structured problem-solving approach helpful? What aspects of it did they like or dislike? Did it improve the quality of the solution?

Discussion: What are the advantages and disadvantages of using a structured approach to problem solving?

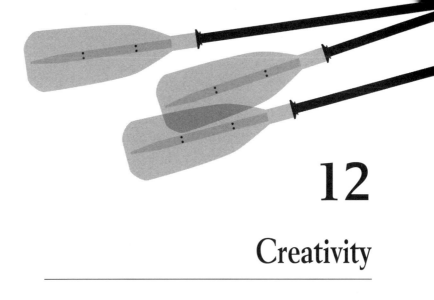

12

Creativity

Developing creative solutions to problems is an important concern for teams; teams can use a number of techniques to stimulate group creativity. However, the dynamics of teams tend to limit creativity because of cognitive, social, and organizational problems. The solution to promoting creativity in teams requires approaches that combine the benefits of individual creativity and team creativity. Organizations can help encourage creativity by providing supportive organizational climates.

Learning Objectives

1. What are the different ways of defining creativity?

2. What are the psychological factors that help and hurt individual creativity?

3. Why do teams have problems in developing creative ideas?

4. What factors improve teams' abilities to be creative?

5. How can teams encourage creativity as an ongoing team process?

6. What are some of the organizational factors that affect creativity?

7. What are some ways to use brainstorming, the nominal group technique, and brain writing to improve team creativity?

8. What are the advantages of using multiple team sessions to encourage creativity?

12.1 Creativity and Its Characteristics

Creativity can be defined from the standpoint of a person, a product, or a process (Amabile, 1996): Creativity describes the inventiveness of a creative person; describes some products, things, or ideas that are innovative and creative; and describes the process that produces creative things or ideas.

Most research examines creativity from the individual perspective, trying to find out who is creative by using personality tests or other psychological measures. However, there are problems with this person-oriented approach. Creativity varies in degree and is not simply a personality trait that some people have and others do not. Creativity skills can be enhanced through training for both individuals and teams. Creativity relates to the match between the person and the application. In other words, people are not creative in all areas. Talent, learned skills, and situational factors affect creativity. Creative talent alone is insufficient for solving problems creatively.

From a teamwork perspective, it is more useful to define creativity in terms of its products and processes than in terms of personality, because this shifts the focus from the individual to the team. What is a creative product or idea? How should a team act to be creative? The answers to both questions show the dual nature of creativity (Table 12.1). Creativity is the search for novel and useful ideas as well as the balancing of divergent and convergent thinking. In the generation stage, people or teams use divergent thinking to develop novel ideas. In the application stage, they use convergent thinking to make those ideas useful.

Something is creative if it is novel or unique and is appropriate, acceptable, and useful. Novelty is not sufficient: A creative solution also must effectively solve a problem. Because of this, creativity requires a combination of divergent and convergent thinking processes (Van Gundy, 1987). Divergent thinking generates potential ideas, and convergent thinking analyzes and focuses solutions. These two types of thinking relate to the novelty and usefulness aspects of the definition of creativity.

To encourage their own divergent thinking, people must suspend judgment of ideas. Participants in a creative activity should try to generate as

Table 12.1 Aspects of Creativity

	Generation	*Application*
Process	Divergent	Convergent
Product	Novel	Useful

many ideas as possible and remain receptive to new ideas. Creativity requires time for incubation, given that creative solutions often occur to people when they are not thinking about the problem. Ideas need to be combined, modified, and played with to encourage creative alternatives.

Taking a systematic approach to selecting a creative solution requires convergent thinking. Evaluation criteria are developed and then used to sort out the many ideas generated. All the alternatives are analyzed to avoid premature acceptance. People need to be realistic and not too critical of the ideas. The overall goal is to analyze and select the best available alternative.

Creative thinking is important and serious work for teams, but it should also be an opportunity for fun. IDEO is a famous industrial design firm that is noted for its creative approaches to design that solves problems, such as the design of Apple's first computer mouse. They believe that creative design best comes from the creative friction within diverse teams (Druskat & Wolff, 2001). However, they use a variety of approaches to help manage the emotional dynamics of team creativity. They make sure to find out why people become upset or quiet during team meetings. When they have brainstorming sessions, they do not tolerate criticism of new ideas and playfully "attack" (with foam toys) violators. They create opportunities for fun and play to help deal with the stress of being creative when working under deadlines.

The creativity of teams relates to individual, group, and organizational factors. Managing the relationships among these factors is the key to promoting creativity within teams. Teams need to have creative members who work together effectively in a supportive organizational context.

12.2 Individual Creativity

Individual creativity develops from an interaction of personal and situational factors (Amabile, 1996). People are creative when they have domain-relevant skills, creativity-relevant skills, and appropriate task motivation.

Domain-relevant skills are the skills, knowledge, and talent people have in a particular application area. People are not creative in all areas—they are creative in areas where they are most skilled. For example, artists might not be creative bridge designers, and a creative bridge designer might not be artistic.

Creativity-relevant skills are the appropriate cognitive styles that encourage creativity and knowledge about creativity techniques. Cognitive styles include the ability to break out of established mental sets, appreciate complexity, suspend judgment, and use broad categories to view issues. Creativity techniques are approaches to help people play with ideas and view problems from alternative perspectives.

Task motivation includes intrinsic motivation and attitude toward the task. Intrinsic motivation is motivation from personal interest rather than from external reward. It relates to the qualities of the task itself. When people are intrinsically motivated, they engage in an activity for its own sake, not to achieve a reward for performing the task. Motivation is needed to encourage people to apply their creative skills.

Individual creativity can be disrupted by several psychological factors, which operate by shifting focus away from the task and toward external issues. Individual creativity may be limited by the use of extrinsic rewards, communication issues, evaluation apprehension, and restriction of paradigms.

Extrinsic rewards can hurt creativity in several ways. Being rewarded to perform a task may sometimes reduce the intrinsic motivation for the task (Deci, 1975). A person may enjoy the creativity of painting, but being paid to paint all day may reduce his or her desire to paint. The use of rewards focuses the creator on satisfying the person or organization providing the rewards. Rather than trying to be creative, individuals try to satisfy someone else, which may cause conservative or altered production instead of creative production.

When someone talks in a team, the listeners are often thinking about what is wrong with what is being said rather than actually listening to the ideas. This evaluation process discourages creativity (Amabile, 1996). When team members are concerned about appearing stupid, outrageous, or inappropriate, their anxiety limits their creativity.

Evaluation apprehension hurts creativity—especially the ability to generate novel ideas. It has a more detrimental impact on people with low skills and low self-confidence. An exception to this negative impact is found in work environments where evaluations focus on providing feedback on ideas and the organizational climate uses positive recognition to reward competence. In that case, evaluation may have a positive impact on creativity.

Our internal mental sets or paradigms limit creativity. It is difficult to view a situation from a new perspective. Many famous creative ideas have come from looking at something commonplace from a different perspective. For example, Post-it Notes were developed by scientists wondering how to use a "low-tack" glue that had been discovered by accident. Many creative ideas in science come from younger scientists who are not fully indoctrinated into the existing paradigm or from interdisciplinary scientists who are changing fields. It is common to become locked in old ways of thinking or routine ways of working, so we do not see creative alternatives to our situation.

12.3 Group Creativity

Creativity is an important skill to cultivate for both individuals and groups. Groups have been shown to be less creative than individuals in some circumstances. Brainstorming, the best-known technique for encouraging group creativity, is criticized as being ineffective. However, creative teams are sometimes able to overcome these problems. Teams can develop practices that encourage creativity as an ongoing process.

Problems With Group Creativity

When it comes to creativity, groups face many of the same problems as individuals. When people try to creatively solve a problem as a group, they typically produce fewer ideas than the sum of individuals working alone (Amabile, 1996). Even working alone in the presence of others reduces an individual's creativity. This is especially true if the others observe and evaluate what individuals are doing.

Several group dynamic factors limit creativity (Van Gundy, 1987). Groups may develop negative or critical communication climates that discourage creativity. Interpersonal conflicts in groups may discourage creativity. Groups consume more time than when individuals work alone, making the process of group creativity slower and less efficient. Finally, conformity pressure and domineering members can hurt creativity in the group process.

Cognitive interference and social inhibitors are the main reasons group interaction leads to less creativity than when individuals work alone (Paulus, 2000). Cognitive interference is the disruption of thinking that occurs while one is waiting to speak in a group (also called "production blocking"). During the wait, creative ideas are forgotten, time runs out before the member has a chance to present the idea, and group discussion may drift to irrelevant topics. Social inhibitors relate to anxiety about how others evaluate members' ideas and to social loafing, which is the reduction in motivation caused by when a member's performance is hidden in the group's output.

Brainstorming

The best-known and most widely used group creativity technique is brainstorming (Osborn, 1957). Brainstorming is designed to deal with the problem of using group discussions for creativity. In group discussions, groups spend too much time evaluating and criticizing ideas and not enough time generating ideas. The four basic rules of brainstorming are (1) criticisms are strictly forbidden, (2) free thinking and wild notions are encouraged,

(3) numerous ideas are sought, and (4) combining and building on the ideas of others is good. (How to conduct a brainstorming session is presented below under "Application: Group Creativity Techniques.")

Brainstorming improves creativity relative to unstructured group discussions (Stein, 1975). It can be improved by asking participants to think of ideas alone before the brainstorming session, by facilitating the group discussion to make participation more equal, and by ensuring that people do not criticize presented ideas. The primary benefit of brainstorming is separating the generation of ideas from the evaluation of ideas. This reduces criticisms during the discussion of new ideas and encourages the participation of those who would otherwise remain silent.

Research on the effectiveness of brainstorming often shows that it is not superior to individuals working alone (Mullen, Johnson, & Salas, 1991). Brainstorming does not increase the number or quality of creative ideas when compared with the sum of individuals working separately. The chief problem with brainstorming is that group discussions force people to wait their turn (Diehl & Stroebe, 1987). Members in a brainstorming session must take turns speaking rather than stating ideas when they first pop up. People waiting their turns are not using their time effectively by developing other creative ideas.

Despite the negative research on brainstorming, it remains a popular technique, especially in businesses. There are several reasons for this (Parks & Sanna, 1999). First, people in business believe that group interaction stimulates others. This is such a compelling idea that people are unwilling to reject it on the basis of research. Second, people involved in brainstorming sessions believe that brainstorming works; their personal experience supports its benefits. Finally, participating in a brainstorming session may encourage commitment to implementing the final solution.

Research on virtual or electronic brainstorming shows that computer-based forms of brainstorming are more effective than traditional brainstorming in improving group creativity (Dennis & Valacich, 1993). Using collaboration technology minimizes problems of production blocking and evaluation apprehension. In virtual brainstorming, people are able to review others' ideas and develop and modify their own ideas at their leisure.

Research on virtual brainstorming has shown a number of interesting effects. In virtual groups, instead of reducing creativity, group size increases the number of creative ideas. The number of ideas increases when group members receive feedback on their performance instead of evaluations, which tends to discourage ideas. The anonymity of the communication medium seems to encourage people to make more comments on the elicited ideas. (Techniques for conducting a virtual brainstorming session are presented at the end of this chapter.)

Strengths of Team Creativity

Using teams to develop creative solutions to problems has its benefits: Compared to single individuals, teams are able to develop more ideas. The social interaction of working in teams can be rewarding. Teams can create supportive environments that encourage creativity. Diverse teams are more likely than homogeneous teams to develop creative solutions. Teams provide support for the implementation of creative ideas.

One of the problems with brainstorming for creativity is that it discourages criticism (Lehrer, 2012). Criticism, feedback on ideas, and debate are activities that encourage team creativity. Teams working on creative tasks need to have the conflict that arises from differences of opinions and ideas (Yong, Sauer, & Mannix, 2014). They need to share, select, and combine these different perspectives. However, this criticism must be done in a constructive manner, which implies an environment where team members feel safe to criticize each other.

A team with creative conflicts produces ideas that are more creative (Nemeth, 1979). When the team is exposed to contradictory ideas from some members, the thinking of the majority is stimulated, producing ideas that are more creative. Dissent stimulates divergent thinking and encourages the team to view an issue from multiple perspectives. It encourages more original and less conventional thoughts about the issue.

A study of Chinese information technology (IT) teams shows how conflict relates to team creativity (Farh, Lee, & Farh, 2010). Both too little and too much task conflict can inhibit team creativity. The most creative teams had moderate levels of task conflict that occurred during the early stages of the team's project. Novel ideas, which arise from task-related conflict during early team discussions, were more likely to be valued and used to develop creative solutions. To encourage creativity, team leaders need to recognize that some conflict is good and give team members time early in the project to voice their opinions. In addition, team leaders need to create a climate of psychological safety so team members feel safe bringing up new ideas.

Team composition is an important factor in team creativity (Lehrer, 2012). Highly creative teams are composed of members who are somewhat familiar with each other. Creativity problems can arise with long-term teams who are too familiar with each other and teams composed of total strangers. One way to negate this type of problem is to add a few new members to an established team when engaging in creative activities.

Teams that learn by doing or have direct experience working in an area are more creative than teams with little or indirect experience (Gino, Argote, Miron-Spektore, & Todorova, 2010). Creativity requires team members to exchange and build on each other's ideas. Prior experience is necessary to understand the existing situation and to recognize opportunities for creativity. However, experience has a mixed effect on creativity. Experienced teams tend to generate more creative ideas in a brainstorming session, but the ideas tend to be more incremental improvements rather than radical innovations.

Diversity is another team composition factor that relates to creativity. Diverse teams are more creative because they generate more ideas, try out more novel ideas, and view issues from multiple perspectives (Jackson, 1992). However, diversity does not always make a team more creative (Hoever, Knippenberg, Ginkel, & Barkema, 2012). Creative teams constructively discuss each other's ideas and integrate the inputs from different members. This requires perspective taking, which is trying to appreciate the different perspectives given by other team members. When team members are instructed to engage in perspective taking during team discussions, teams become more creative.

How teams operate can have a positive effect on team creativity. To enhance creativity, brainstorming is better than unstructured group discussion. When trained facilitators run brainstorming sessions, teams generate more ideas that are creative (Offner, Kramer, & Winter, 1996). This creativity enhancement continues to affect the team after the facilitator leaves because the team has learned how to brainstorm more effectively.

Several methods can improve the brainstorming process to further promote creativity (Paulus, 2000). First, facilitators should structure the team interaction to avoid disruptive communications and premature evaluations. Team sessions should be followed by individual sessions. Teams should use organizing techniques to reduce the number of alternatives to evaluate after the idea generation stage. Finally, teams should be diverse. This diversity must be managed to reduce potential conflict, make members aware of the expertise of others, and focus the discussion on the unique contributions of individual members.

One of the values of team brainstorming is the stimulation of ideas (Paulus, 2000). There is a cognitive benefit to being exposed to other people's ideas because creative ideas often occur through unique associations with other ideas. Exposure to other ideas can help a member break out of limiting cognitive categories. This effect is increased if the team has a diversity of knowledge, experience, and perspectives.

Although team brainstorming may stimulate creative ideas, it may be difficult to demonstrate the benefits of the team interaction (Paulus, 2002).

Team interactions limit the ability of individuals to verbalize ideas. It takes time for people to fully process and develop new ideas. The stimulating benefits of team interaction may occur later, when team members have a chance to think about what has occurred. An incubation period is important for both individual and team creativity; this shows the importance of taking breaks during the creativity process and having multiple creativity sessions. Team brainstorming sessions should be followed by individual idea generation to incorporate the benefits of both individual and team creativity (Paulus, 1998).

Team creativity relates to the individual, the team, and the organization. Are teams more or less creative than individuals? It depends on how the process is managed. The question is really not relevant in many organizational situations. Important problems often require individual and team creativity because the problems are too complex to rely solely on individual creativity.

Creativity as an Ongoing Team Process

Team creativity is often characterized by a diverse group of people generating many ideas through interaction with each other (Harvey, 2014). However, this model of team creativity does not explain how some teams are consistently creative like the animation studio Pixar. Instead of viewing creativity as simply an idea generation activity, highly creative teams view creativity as an ongoing process.

Creativity is more than just generating ideas; it includes the analysis of ideas and the constructive development of ideas into creative processes and products (Fairchild & Hunter, 2013). The creative process takes time and requires a nurturing and encouraging environment. It takes time for teams to develop the open and supportive communication climate that supports the types of constructive controversy that lead to ongoing creativity.

Ongoing team creativity is an interactive process that focuses on the conflict between different perspectives (Harvey, 2014). It starts during the initial idea generation stage, but continues throughout the implementation of the idea. Pixar provides a good example of the ongoing team creative process. When animators and technologists start the development process for a new film, they do not plan the entire film at the beginning. Through group discussion, they identify creative ideas and the teams develop prototypes based on these ideas. These creative ideas come from the integration of art and technology. The teams meet regularly to analyze the prototypes and creatively develop ways to improve on them. Creativity is emphasized throughout the process of developing the film through these feedback interactions.

For this creative synergy to happen, teams require both constructive controversy and psychological safety (Fairchild & Hunter, 2013; Somech & Drach-Zahavy, 2013). Constructive controversy supports creativity because it results in team members sharing a wider range of ideas, more closely analyzing ideas, and developing more original solutions. However, this only occurs when the team has sufficient psychological safety that creates an open learning climate for discussion and innovative thinking. In order for creativity to flourish, team members need to feel comfortable expressing their opinions as well as giving and receiving feedback from others.

12.4 Organizational Environment and Creativity

Organizations benefit from creativity. Businesses want to be innovative to create new products and services to expand their operations. Companies get stuck in old patterns of behavior and look for new ideas to help them break out of the rut. The world is a dynamic place with a fast rate of change, and organizations must change creatively to survive. To be more creative, they need to hire creative people, use team creativity effectively, and establish organizational climates that promote creativity.

Organizations must rely on team creativity because the problems they face are too complex for individual solution. Often, creative solutions for problems require a multidisciplinary perspective. The development of the first Macintosh computer is a good example. How can one creatively redesign the personal computer, considering all the electronic, manufacturing, artistic, psychological, and human factors involved? It is not a job for an individual—it is a job for a design team. In order to combine the talents of a variety of fields, team creativity is essential.

Organizations also must develop creative solutions for problems that cut across organizational boundaries. Additionally, this requires a team perspective to fully understand and integrate the issues involved. The use of a team to develop creative solutions for cross-departmental problems encourages support for the implementation of solutions.

Individual and team creativity can survive only in organizational environments that support creativity. Although organizations say that they want to encourage creativity, their actions may not support it. Organizations want both stability and change; this contradiction creates problems. Team creativity requires cooperation, but many organizations encourage competition. There are many things that organizations could do to promote creativity, but there are probably just as many obstacles within organizations that prevent creativity from happening.

Organizations say that creativity is a valuable goal, but they often reject creative ideas (Mueller, Melwani, & Goncalo, 2012). This negative bias toward creativity is due to uncertainty. When people are uncertain, they tend to favor well-known and practical ideas rather than creative ones. Uncertainty also interferes with people's ability to recognize creative ideas.

Creativity implies risk. Organizations focus on providing consistency, minimizing error, and reducing risk. This is the inherent conflict with organizational creativity. The problem is not that there are no creative individuals and teams in organizations, but rather that their creativity is not rewarded.

To foster creativity, organizations must develop climates that support creative people and teams. Organizational climates should promote both the task and social aspects of creativity (Van Gundy, 1987). Climates that support the task aspects of creativity provide the freedom to do things differently, empower people to act on their ideas, encourage active participation, and provide support to those involved in creative tasks. Climates that support the social aspects of creativity allow the open expression of ideas, encourage risk taking, promote acceptance of novel ideas, and reflect confidence in their employees.

When teams are developing creative solutions to problems, they need to interact with the surrounding organization (Lehrer, 2012). This can be done informally outside of the team meetings or by bringing outsiders into the team's creativity sessions. While working on creative projects, teams should publicize their working ideas to other members of the organization in order to get ideas, comments, and feedback. It is useful to get outsiders' views to encourage creativity.

Gaining feedback from the organization requires an organizational climate that supports creativity. IDEO, a company whose business is to develop creative solutions, provides a good example of this type of organizational climate (Amabile, Fisher, & Pillemer, 2014). Their organizational culture promotes "collaborative generosity"—people throughout the company provide help, new perspectives, experience, and ideas to promote the development of creative ideas. Promoting collaboration helps teams to become more creative. Collaboration requires creating psychological safety, so team members feel safe to discuss their problems with each other. Unfortunately, many organizations discourage helping because they promote competition among peers.

Performance teams, such as athletes or musical groups, show how providing the appropriate context can encourage creativity (Sawyer, 2012). Highly creative teams work on tasks that challenge their skills, have clear goals, receive immediate feedback on their work, and have the freedom to concentrate on the tasks. They are able to successfully manage the tensions inherent in the creative process. These tensions include convention versus novelty, structure versus improvisation, critical analysis versus freewheeling thinking, listening to the team versus speaking out with your own opinion. The key problem for team creativity is finding the right amount of structure to support improvisation, without providing so much structure that creativity is smothered.

Work environments can either stimulate or provide barriers to creativity. Table 12.2 presents a list of environmental factors that research has shown affects creativity in the workplace (Amabile, 1996).

Table 12.2 Environmental Stimulants and Obstacles to Creativity

Factor	Stimulant to Creativity	Obstacle to Creativity
Freedom	Employees need the freedom to decide what tasks to perform and how to perform them, and they need control over their work process.	A lack of freedom in the way employees select projects and perform tasks discourages creativity.
Management	Managers need to be good role models, have good technical and communication skills, provide clear directions, but use limited controls and protect teams from negative organizational influences.	Management styles that discourage creativity include unclear direction, poor technical and communication skills, and too much control.
Encouragement	New ideas need to be encouraged. There should be no threat of evaluation.	A lack of support or apathy toward new approaches reduces the motivation for creativity.
Recognition	Employees should believe that creativity will receive appropriate feedback, recognition, and reward from the organization.	Inappropriate, unfair, and critical evaluations and the use of unrealistic goals limit creativity.
Cooperation	The organizational climate should support cooperation and collaboration, acceptance of new ideas, rewards for innovation, and the allowance of risk taking.	Interpersonal and intergroup competition within an organization or work group disrupts the creative process.

Table 12.2   (Continued)

Factor	Stimulant to Creativity	Obstacle to Creativity
Time	Creativity requires time to explore new ideas and requires less rigid schedules.	Too great a workload, or day-to-day crises that redirect focus away from long-term projects, reduce creativity.
Challenge	Tasks that are interesting, important, and not routine encourage creativity.	Organizations that emphasize consistency and do not support risk taking discourage creativity.
Motivation	There should be the desire to do something important, or a sense of urgency to create and complete the task because of competition from outside the organization.	Organizational factors, such as bad reward systems, excessive bureaucracy, and a lack of regard for innovation reduce creativity.

SOURCE: Copyright © 1996 Teresa M Amabile. Reprinted by permission of Westview Press, a member of the Perseus Books Group.

12.5 Application: Team Creativity Techniques

Developing creative ideas is an important part of a team's work. The tools a team uses to promote creativity can be applied in a variety of ways. Creativity techniques, for example, are useful in all stages of problem solving (Van Gundy, 1987). The techniques help clarify objectives, define and analyze problems, generate alternative solutions, and prepare for implementation.

Premature evaluation is the biggest problem limiting team creativity. Team members may want to try out new ideas, but critical comments from other members prevent their consideration. Team members often are not good at supporting one another's ideas, making designated noncritical times vital to creativity. A team should develop rules for openness and safety in presenting ideas; members should practice the technique of building on rather than criticizing an idea. If they do not like an idea, team members should try going with it by suggesting other related ideas to which they do not object. Learning this skill of cooperation is very helpful.

A team often need not decide on a solution the minute it is proposed. It is better to run a brainstorming session and then wait until another meeting before selecting a solution. Waiting allows members to come up with fresh ideas on their own. Such an approach to team creativity captures both individual creativity (often done alone) and synergistic creativity (arising from group interaction).

Developing creative ideas requires more than just a group session (Figure 12.1). The process begins by developing an open climate that encourages participation. Team members are more likely to develop creative ideas if they have time to prepare for and research the topic. After generating creative ideas, the team selects the best ideas and refines them. Multiple sessions may be necessary to fully develop useful creative ideas.

Brainstorming

Brainstorming includes a variety of methods for structuring team creativity sessions. Besides classic brainstorming, alternatives include procedures that force team members to combine the ideas of others, use of pictures to "comment" on ideas, and role-playing alternative perspectives such as viewing the problem from the perspective of historic or fictional characters. (How would Einstein try to solve this problem?) Team facilitators who use brainstorming often have techniques to equalize the level of participation from team members.

To start a brainstorming session, the team leader clearly states the purpose or issues to be discussed and reviews the guidelines for brainstorming (Table 12.3). A distinct period of time (perhaps 20 to 30 minutes) should be set aside for the brainstorming session. During the session, the leader acts primarily as facilitator and recorder. After ideas are generated, the leader helps the group prioritize the list into a manageable size for further consideration.

At the beginning of the brainstorming session, it is useful to have team members silently think about creative ideas related to the topic and to write these ideas down. This individual reflection period before the team discussion helps to generate more ideas and energizes the start of the team discussion.

During the brainstorming session, all team members should try to suggest as many ideas as possible. Every idea is accepted by the team and

Figure 12.1 Creativity Flowchart

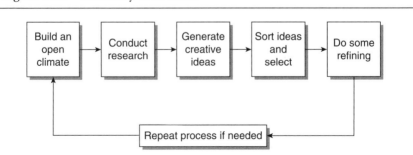

Table 12.3   Guidelines for Brainstorming

Question	Announce the question or issue to be addressed.
Reflect	Silently think and write down ideas.
Toss out	All team members toss out as many ideas as they can.
Accept	All ideas are accepted, regardless of how practical or impractical they are.
Record	All the ideas are listed for everyone to see.
Prompt	The facilitator asks the main question again to help keep people on track.
No editing	The facilitator reminds the team that no one is allowed to criticize or evaluate until the process is done.
Build	Everyone should build on one another's ideas, using the ideas as a springboard to new directions.

SOURCE: From Pokras, S. (1995). *Team problem solving*. Menlo Park, CA: CRISP.

written down by the recorder. The leader's job is to keep team members on track by refocusing them on the issue. No one is allowed to criticize ideas. Instead, members are encouraged to build on suggestions made by others. It is up to the leader to ensure that no criticisms occur during the brainstorming session.

One of the key problems in brainstorming sessions is that people often spend their time looking for the faults in new ideas (West, 2012). This reduces enthusiasm and participation in creativity activities like brainstorming. Rather than saying "no" or "yes, but," team members are encouraged to say "yes, and." Try saying "yes" and then build on the idea being presented before deciding it will not work. This simple technique changes the climate of a team meeting and encourages everyone to try out new ideas.

Nominal Group Technique and Brainwriting

The nominal group technique and brainwriting are similar approaches that combine the benefits of individual and group creativity. As with brainstorming, they separate the idea generation stage from the evaluation stage. However, in these approaches, individuals generate their ideas in writing rather than in team discussion.

Both techniques start with the same general approach as brainstorming. A team is brought together, and the facilitator announces the question. In the nominal group technique, each participant spends 20 to 30 minutes writing down ideas. After this stage is complete, the ideas are listed for all participants to see, and the group is able to ask clarifying questions about the ideas.

Brainwriting has several variations. One approach is to ask members to write down an idea on a sheet of paper and then pass the paper to the person on the right. The next person is required to write a new idea that builds on the previous idea(s). This cycle is repeated until either time is up or the team has exhausted all their ideas. An alternative is for each team member to write down several ideas on a sheet of paper, throw the papers into a central pool, and pull out another member's paper to write on. Again, team members are to build on the ideas presented in the papers they choose. When the team is finished generating ideas, all the lists are combined for team review. A third approach uses idea generation on Post-it Notes. The team's ideas are written on Post-it Notes, then posted on a wall; this encourages playful combination of ideas. Brainwriting can also be conducted using a virtual team approach (see Leading Virtual Teams at the end of the chapter).

These approaches are effective alternatives to brainstorming. Because individuals are writing down their ideas, no one needs to wait a turn to contribute. The techniques are structured to encourage participation from all team members. Typically, they include team discussions at the end so that members have the opportunity to build on one another's ideas.

Selecting a Solution

One problem with creativity activities like brainstorming is that they can generate many possible options with no easy way to select the best one. However, after a brainstorming session, it is often easy to prioritize the suggestions and focus on a limited number of options.

One way to narrow the focus is by multiple voting (Scholtes, 1994). A team reviews the alternatives generated by the brainstorming session and combines items that seem similar. Each team member then selects two to five alternatives that he or she would like to support. When all team members have completed their selections, the votes are tallied and items that received zero to one vote are removed. The alternatives that were selected are discussed, and the team considers new ways of combining or synthesizing alternatives. These steps are repeated until only a few options remain. At this stage, the team can use consensus to select the final alternative.

Multiple-Stage Creativity Approaches

To gain the benefits of group and individual creativity, teams may use a multiple-stage process (Paulus, 1998). This approach uses time as a buffer between team creativity activities. People are often creative at odd moments when they are not thinking about the problem, such as while walking or taking a shower. It is difficult to be creative on command, especially in front of others. Creativity is hard to rush, given that stress and time pressure tend to make individuals and teams more conservative and less creative.

Group creativity research unfortunately assumes that teams must be creative on demand. In most organizational contexts, a team works on problems over time. The team meets and discusses the problem, then tries to be creative. Sometime later the team reconvenes to make its selection process. By separating activities in time and allowing team members to enter new ideas over time, the benefits of both individual and team creativity are realized.

 ## LEADING VIRTUAL TEAMS: VIRTUAL CREATIVITY

Problem: Virtual teams are potentially more creative than face-to-face teams or individuals working independently because of less cognitive interference and social inhibitors. This inspiration can occur if the leader appropriately captures the benefits of virtual creativity.

Solution: There are several guidelines and techniques a virtual leader can follow to gain the advantages of virtual creativity.

1. Involve participants from varied knowledge areas and cultural backgrounds. The geographical distribution of virtual teams may enable the participation of individuals representing different experiences and backgrounds. The broader the base of participants engaging in a shared idea generation process, the more it should broaden the base of ideas contributed.

2. Take multiple parallel approaches to the same problem. When idea generation occurs in one location, any idea heard by the rest of the group influences their thinking. When an initial idea takes the group in a particular direction, other directions of creative thought may be completely abandoned. The solution to this is to introduce multiple initial ideas simultaneously without cross influence and then build on each. Brainwriting is the most established technique to do this. While brainwriting can be used face-to-face, brainwriting is readily used in a virtual setting. Most commercial GSS (Group Support Systems) products support brainwriting (often called electronic brainstorming); brainwriting can be implemented in a wiki or even Google Docs. Using brainwriting tools, a leader can break the group into subgroups and have each subgroup generate ideas separately. When this virtual approach is used, ideas from one subgroup do not influence other subgroup discussions.

3. Anonymity is more easily accomplished in a virtual setting. Anonymity may benefit the creativity process by removing social inhibitors. Reduction of these inhibitors may lead to the contribution of riskier and more novel ideas. Anonymity also enables the leader to seed risky or provocative ideas into the discussion in order to encourage more out-of-the box thinking by other participants.

4. Role play techniques during idea generation may contribute to a broader set of ideas and perhaps more novel ideas. Role play may be easier to manage in a virtual setting because of the reduced level of social inhibitors. A simple role play technique is to assign a celebrity identity (historical or popular culture) to each participant and ask everyone to generate ideas that the celebrity might produce. Imagine the broad base of ideas that might be contributed if participants are asked to imagine themselves as the Dalai Lama, Lady Gaga, Abraham Lincoln, Martin Luther King, or Batman. Some GSS and creativity products permit users to contribute ideas with the signature of a celebrity.

Summary

From a group dynamics perspective, creativity typically is defined as a product or process. Creativity leads to the development of what is both novel and useful. The creative process uses divergent and convergent thinking to develop these creative ideas.

Individuals and groups have difficulty being creative on demand. Creativity requires skills in the topic area, inventiveness skills, and motivation. Extrinsic rewards, communication issues, evaluation apprehension, and rigid paradigms reduce individual creativity.

Groups are often not more creative than individuals working alone. Cognitive and social factors related to the group process limit creativity.

Brainstorming is better than unstructured discussions, but has a limited effect on improving group creativity. However, teams can encourage creativity by effectively managing the group process, acknowledging the value of constructive conflict, creating a psychologically safe environment, embodying a diverse membership, and holding multiple sessions.

Although organizational leaders claim they want to encourage creativity, their actions often do not match their words. Creativity is required for organizations to adapt to the changing environment, but organizations tend to encourage consistency and stability rather than innovation. Organizations can either encourage or discourage creativity through factors, such as management orientation, availability of resources, recognition for risk taking, and a cooperative climate.

Certain techniques can improve group creativity. Brainstorming structures team discussions to reduce the negative effects of evaluation. The nominal group technique and brainwriting combine individual and group creativity techniques. Selection techniques can be used to reduce the number of alternatives. It is important for teams to use creativity techniques, but it also is important to use multiple team sessions so that creative ideas have time to incubate. When these techniques are used, team creativity is improved.

Team Leader's Challenge 12

You are the leader of a team of writers and artists at an animation studio. This is a great group of highly talented and creative people, but not an easy team to lead. Team members are individualistic, idiosyncratic, and temperamental, to mention just a few of their personality traits. You have managed to organize them into a project team, facilitated their interpersonal issues, and the team has succeeded in producing a successful short film.

You feel lucky that your team was successful in the last project. It is now time to start over with a newly composed team. Whether you organize a new team or use the previous team, it is difficult to get a team to work together creatively. What you really want to do is to set up a mechanism to encourage continuous creativity. It is more than just hiring creative people—you want to use teamwork as a way to make creative projects a regular occurrence in the organization.

What are the benefits of and problems with using a team approach to creative work?

How can teamwork be used to encourage creative work?

How can you (a team leader) use teams to ensure creative projects keep flowing from the organization?

ACTIVITY: COMPARING DIFFERENT CREATIVITY TECHNIQUES

Objective: Creativity may be improved by using one of the creativity techniques presented in this chapter. Teams can try out these techniques to see how well they work.

Activity: Divide members into three teams and have each team use a different creativity technique—group discussion, brainstorming, or brainwriting. Each of these is useful for generating alternative solutions. Spend about 20 minutes using the creativity technique, then use multiple voting to select the preferred alternative. For a creative challenge, try developing a new advertising slogan for your organization, or write a creative caption for a cartoon in *The New Yorker* magazine.

Group Discussion. Have the group discuss creative solutions to the problem.

Brainstorming. To start a brainstorming session, the team leader must clearly state the issues to be discussed and review the guidelines for brainstorming. During the brainstorming session, all team members should try to suggest as many ideas as possible. Every idea is accepted by the team and noted on the recorder's sheet. The leader's job is to keep team members on track by keeping them focused on the issue. No one is allowed to criticize ideas. Instead, members are encouraged to build on the suggestions made by others. It is up to the leader to make sure no criticisms occur during the brainstorming session.

Brainwriting. Brainwriting starts with the same general approach as brainstorming. Teams are brought together, the leader announces the issue, and team members are told to be open and build on each other's ideas. The difference is that the team's interaction is in writing. Have each person write down several alternative ideas, throw his or her paper into a central pool, and pull out someone else's paper to add to. Team members are to build on the ideas presented in the lists they receive. When the team is finished generating ideas, combine all lists for the team to review.

Selecting a solution using multiple voting. The team reviews the alternatives generated by the creativity session and combines items that seem similar. Each team member selects two to five alternatives that he or she would like to support. After all team members have completed their selections, tally the votes and discard items that received zero or one vote. Discuss the alternatives selected and look for ways to combine or synthesize them. Repeat these steps until only a few options remain for the team to use to arrive at a consensus.

Analysis: Which technique generated the most creative solution? What did team members like and dislike about the creativity technique they used? Would they want to use the technique in the future?

Discussion: What are the advantages of and problems with using group discussion and these two creativity techniques? How can you encourage a team to be more creative?

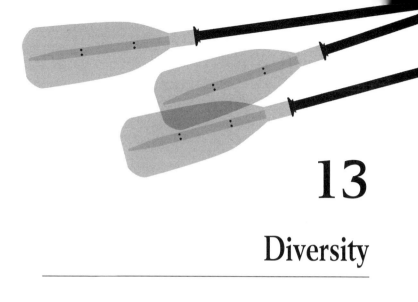

13

Diversity

Diversity in a team stems from differences in demographic, psychological, and organizational characteristics. Research reveals that the various effects of this diversity on teams is dependent on how the research is conducted, the type of diversity examined, and the type of tasks performed. In most cases, diversity is a benefit once a team learns how to create a context that supports diversity. A team with diverse members performs better on decision making, problem solving, and creativity tasks.

Diversity in a team can lead to problems caused by misperceptions about others and competition among subgroups. These problems disrupt team communication and reduce the ability of the team to fully use its resources. Diversity problems are unlikely to go away by themselves, but actions can be taken to help teams improve relations among their members in order to gain the benefits of team diversity.

Learning Objectives

1. Why is the importance of dealing with diversity issues increasing for teams?

2. What are different types of diversity?

3. What are the trait approach and the expectation approach to explaining diversity?

4. How do cognitive processes, leader behavior, and social processes explain the causes of diversity problems?

5. What are the main problems that diversity can cause for teams?

6. What are the differences between the performances of homogeneous versus diverse teams?

7. What are the challenges of using cross-functional teams?

8. What are some of the approaches organizations can use to create a context that supports diversity?

13.1 The Nature of Diversity

Diversity is at the core of teamwork. If people have identical knowledge, skills, or perspectives, then there is little reason to organize them into teams, and it is simpler to just have a supervisor tell the individuals what to do. It is the integration of differences that is the core value of teamwork. But, diversity is also a central challenge for teamwork. How do you get different people to work together smoothly and effectively as a team? From sociological and organizational perspectives, the topic of diversity is increasing in importance. Diversity has many meanings, all of which have different impacts on how teams function.

Why Diversity Is Important Now

Understanding diversity in work teams is important because of the increasing numbers of women and ethnic minorities entering the workforce (Jackson & Ruderman, 1995). Women and ethnic minorities are now in all levels of the organizational hierarchy and no longer primarily work only in certain types of jobs (Jackson, 1992). In today's organizational environment, diversity occurs in jobs in all areas of organizations.

Age or generational diversity is also increasing in organizations. People are living longer and retirement ages are being extended (Carnevale & Stone, 1995). The relationship between younger and older workers is changing as generations are more likely to work together because organizational hierarchies are flatter. New technology has reversed some of the differences between younger and older workers. For instance, younger workers may be more skilled with technology and may serve as mentors for older workers.

Diversity is increasing by design as well. Organizations are recruiting a more diverse workforce to improve relationships with customers. A design team does not create a car for male buyers only; products must be sensitive to all potential customers. Increasing workforce diversity enables organizations to be more sensitive to the diverse markets in society. In addition, globalization is increasing diversity. As organizations become more global, their workforce must be able to interact in culturally diverse teams.

Correspondingly, the more pronounced the use of teams in the workplace, the greater the importance of diversity issues because people must interact with one another to perform their jobs. Teams must deal with the diversity that comes from differences in occupations, departments, and organizational statuses. Work is more interdependent, making it vital for different types of people to be able to communicate with others in new ways.

Types of Diversity

Although we often think of diversity in terms of gender or ethnicity, three types of diversity affect teams in organizations: demographic (e.g., gender, ethnicity, age), psychological (e.g., values, personality, knowledge), and organizational (e.g., tenure, occupation, status). Table 13.1 presents an overview of these types of diversity. Demographic diversity relates to the social categories people use to classify others (McGrath, Berdahl, & Arrow, 1995). In our society, distinctions of gender, race, ethnicity, nationality, age, religion, and sexual orientation are considered important in many situations, but that is not true in all societies or eras. For example, religion is a more important demographic variable in the Middle East than in the United States. Differences among European immigrants were considered very important in the United States during the early 1900s, but these are not viewed as culturally important differences today.

Table 13.1 Types of Diversity

Demographic	Psychological	Organizational
• Gender • Race and ethnicity • Nationality • Age or generational • Religion • Sexual orientation	• Values, beliefs, and attitudes • Personality and cognitive and behavioral styles • Knowledge, skills, and abilities	• Status • Occupation • Department or division • Tenure

SOURCE: Adapted from McGrath, J., Berdahl, J., & Arrow, H. (1995). Traits, expectations, culture, and clout: The dynamics of diversity in work groups. In S. Jackson & M. Ruderman (Eds.), *Diversity in work teams: Research paradigms for a changing workplace* (pp. 17–45). Washington, DC: American Psychological Association.

Psychological diversity relates to differences in people's cognitions and behavior. People vary in their values, beliefs, and attitudes. They may be conservative or liberal, religious or not religious, risk oriented or risk averse. People differ in personality and behavioral styles. As discussed in earlier chapters, people may be competitive or cooperative, assertive or aggressive. Finally, people differ in task-related knowledge, skills, and abilities. Team members may be technical experts, have artistic skills, or communicate well.

Organizational diversity is caused by differences in a person's relationship to an organization. Factors, such as organizational rank, occupational specialty, department affiliation, and tenure are examples of organizational variables. These variables primarily affect an individual's status in the organization, which has important consequences for how people interact in teams. Occupational differences relate to differences in language or terminology that may lead to miscommunication, while power differences may disrupt the team's communication process.

The different types of diversity are not easily isolated from each other. Teams often comprise all three types of diversity, but research is often unclear how to categorize these types of diversity (Cox, 1995). On the one hand, it makes sense to view demographic factors (e.g., gender) as different from organizational factors (e.g., status). On the other hand, one of the main effects of demographic differences is that we give more power and status to certain team members than to others.

The types of diversity vary in how easily they can be observed. Diversity based on age, sex, or race can be considered surface-level factors, as opposed to deep-level factors like psychological variables (Harrison, Price, Gavin, & Florey, 2002). Surface-level factors affect people immediately. People who are similar in surface-level factors are more likely to be initially attracted to each other and form stronger social attachments. Deep-level diversity takes time to recognize. Consequently, the effects of these deep-level differences on teams take time to develop. Although when people think about diversity they often only consider surface-level factors, it is deep-level diversity that has the strongest positive impacts on team performance (Harrison & Humphrey, 2010).

How Diversity Affects a Team

There are two ways to view how diversity affects a team (McGrath et al., 1995). The trait approach assumes that diversity affects how people act. In other words, people with different backgrounds have different values, skills, and personalities; these differences affect how they interact in a team. The expectations approach focuses on the beliefs that people have about what other people are like. These expectations change how they interact with people from different backgrounds.

As people work together in a team, they develop a sense of identity with the team, which becomes stronger as the team becomes more cohesive. Over time, members develop emotional bonds, create a common language for communicating, and share experiences. This leads to a convergence of attitudes, beliefs, and values that reduces the importance of background differences among team members (Harrison et al., 2002).

Although continued interaction affects some types of diversity, it does not affect all types. Interaction does not change people's personalities, their specialized skills, their races, or their ages. However, it does not have to change these characteristics to reduce the impact of diversity. People identify with a team to the extent that membership is emotionally important to them and they care about its collective goals (Brewer, 1995). One implication of team formation is that team members shift their social categories and create a new social identity. Members working together in a team develop the category of *teammate*. This category can become emotionally more important than the other ways that members previously categorized the people on the team.

13.2 Problems of Diversity

In diverse teams, members have different approaches to problems and access to different sources of information. This should help improve team performance, but only if the team uses these task-relevant differences. Unfortunately, diversity may lead to misperceptions that reduce communication by minority members and increase emotional tension and conflict within the team. This prevents the team from fully using its resources.

Misperception

False stereotypes and prejudices of team members cause diversity problems. People from different backgrounds hold different values and respond to situations differently. These differences in values and behavior can be threatening to a member's sense of what is appropriate. To deal with the psychological anxiety, people may either ignore or misinterpret the contributions of minority members. (Minority in this case means people with different backgrounds from those of most group members.) Over time, minority members respond to this by contributing less to team communication. The lack of power these members experience causes them to have less impact on the team's decisions (Tolbert, Albert, & Simons, 1995).

Teams members often use gender as an irrelevant cue for expertise (Cohen & Zhou, 1991). Those who are perceived to have expertise generally have greater influence in decision making and are assigned leadership roles in teams. However, teams members tend to value the expertise of a man above that of a women, regardless of actual expertise (Ridgeway, 1997). This is particularly salient today in historically male-dominated contexts, such as science and engineering teams. A recent study showed that the male tendency is to evaluate less educated female teammates more favorably when compared to highly educated female teammates (Joshi, 2014). Additionally, the team gender composition also impacted the extent to which the expertise of highly educated women was used—teams dominated by men used women's expertise less when compared to teams with a higher proportion of women. These results indicate that gender inequality remains present in teams. One way of combating this is to reach a 20% team membership of minorities and/ or women, which research indicates is the point at which discrimination against these members tends to drop (Pettigrew & Martin, 1987).

One benefit of diversity is to increase the types of information and variety of perspectives used to analyze and solve problems in a team (Van der Vegt & Bunderson, 2005). This benefit is lost if the team ignores the input of minority members, or if the minority members do not provide input. The problem of diversity in teams occurs when the team overlooks the right answer because the "wrong" person came up with it.

Emotional Distrust

The dividing of a team into in-group and out-group members creates social friction. Power conflicts create a climate of distrust and defensive communication. Rather than forming a social unit, the team may become subdivided into cliques or divided along fault lines (Mannix & Neale, 2005).

These emotional issues create several group process problems. Diversity may lead to an increase in conflict because people are more distrustful. Not only are there more conflicts, but the conflicts are more difficult to resolve. Emotional distrust prevents the team from forming the social bonds necessary to create a cohesive team. Diversity may prevent the benefits of team cohesion from being realized.

Failure to Use Team Resources

The way the team treats minority members not only reduces their input in the team, but may reduce their desire to contribute. Over time, minority members become less committed to the team's goals and less motivated to perform for the team (Ancona & Caldwell, 1992). This in turn is used to justify not rewarding minorities or failing to provide them with opportunities and support to achieve more.

Additionally, diversity affects turnover and socialization in work teams (McGrath et al., 1995). Minority members are more likely to have higher turnover in a team. It is easier for a team to socialize new members into the team if their characteristics are similar to those of the majority. However, a team that starts with a high level of diversity is more likely to have lower minority turnover and a less difficult time socializing diverse new members.

13.3 Causes of Diversity Problems

There are several ways of viewing the causes of diversity problems. One view sees diversity as arising from our cognitive processes and is an artifact of our need for social classification. This misperception creates interpersonal problems in the team. A special case of this is misperceptions by the team leader. An alternative view sees diversity as due to power conflicts arising from intergroup competition. Another view believes that diversity problems rather than being caused by psychological issues reflect power struggles between groups.

Diversity as a Cognitive Process

Diversity is a social construction based on our cognitive processes. People categorize their social world into groups and treat the members of those groups differently based on their categories (Wilder, 1986). These categories are relatively arbitrary. For example, we are more likely to categorize people in ways that are easily observable (e.g., race rather than religion). Once these categories are formed, they have important implications for how people perceive and interact with others.

Social perception is the process of collecting and interpreting information about others. The primary reason people categorize others is to simplify the world (Srull & Wyer, 1988). Dividing people into categories makes it possible to predict what other people are like. It is a simplification, often not very accurate, but an unavoidable component of human cognition. The problem with social perception is that it leads to premature judgments about what others are really like.

Stereotypes are cognitive categorizations that describe people in preconceived groups. Stereotypes may be positive, negative, or both. For instance, people may believe that engineers are very analytical, and this may be a good or bad attribute depending on the context. Stereotypes make people in a category seem similar to one another, yet different from us (Wilder, 1986).

This social perception and categorization process, by itself, is not bad. It helps people interact with others. The problem is that the process creates inaccuracies and biases that lead to misperceptions. Table 13.2 shows a set of common perceptual biases that negatively affect how we perceive others. From these biases, it is easy to see how our social perceptions can err.

The problem of diversity is more than just categorization and perceptual biases. When people classify others, they divide their social worlds into in-groups and out-groups. This cognitive distinction has an emotional component (Tajfel, 1982a). We view the group we belong to (our in-group) more positively, and we like, trust, and act friendlier toward in-group members. The addition of an emotional component to our categories shows how stereotypes become prejudices and discrimination. Prejudice is an unjustified negative attitude toward a group and its members. Prejudices typically are based on stereotypes. Prejudices may lead to discrimination if there is social support for negative behavior toward the out-group.

From this cognitive perspective, the problem of diversity is that we misperceive people. People prejudge others on the basis of their categories rather than on how others actually behave. This causes people to treat others inappropriately, to have poorer communications, and to dislike and distrust others without getting to know them (Mannix & Neale, 2005).

Generational Differences: Traits or Stereotypes?

Research identifies many generational differences among people working today. Successive generations tend to be more neurotic, extroverted, conscientious, and have higher self-esteem (Lyons & Kuron, 2014). From a work attitude perspective, the newer generation of workers has less overall job commitment and satisfaction. Regarding teamwork, there are mixed results, with some studies showing no generational differences, while other studies find older workers are more comfortable with working in teams. Overall, there is an increase in individualism, and a decrease in the desire to work in teams.

These generational differences are statistically significant, but how should a team leader or member use this information? "Statistically significant" does not mean that every 20-year-old is less of a team player or more conscientious than every 50-year-old. Regardless of generational trends, each team member is a person, not a category, and should be treated as an individual. Be careful about turning information about group traits into stereotypes that affect how you treat your teammates.

Team Leader

Diversity also affects a team through the relationship between a team member and a leader (Tsui, Xin, & Egan, 1995). As was noted in Chapter 10, leader-member exchange theory describes the dynamics of this relationship. According to the model, the team leader decides early in the relationship whether the team member is part of the in-group or the out-group. If part of the in-group, the team member receives more resources, mentoring, and assistance; has better performance evaluations; and is more satisfied with being part of the team than are members of the out-group.

There are two important insights from the leader-member exchange theory. First, the in-group/out-group evaluation occurs very early in the relationship, before the leader actually knows much about the performance of the team member. Second, the impact of this early impression has long-lasting effects on the relationship between the member, the leader, and the team.

A leader's quick decision that a team member is either in-group or out-group often stems from the perceptual biases listed in Table 13.2. During the

Table 13.2   Perceptual Biases: The Common Ways People Misperceive Others

First impression error	The tendency to base judgments on our first impressions and ignore later information that contradicts these judgments. Once we form a positive first impression, we create the circumstances to justify that first impression.
Fundamental attribution error	The tendency to explain why someone is acting in a particular way by using personal rather than situational explanations. We tend to explain other people's behavior using personality traits and demographic variables rather than looking at situational causes.
Similar-to-me effect	The tendency to view people who are similar to us in a positive light.
Halo effect	Once we have an overall positive or negative impression of someone, we assume that they are good (or bad) at everything. For example, if we like someone, we often assume they are competent and dependable.
Selective perception	The tendency to focus on and remember only information that confirms our beliefs and to ignore information that contradicts them.

SOURCE: Adapted from Greenberg, J., & Baron, R. (1997). *Behavior in organizations: Understanding the human side of work* (6th ed.). Upper Saddle River, NJ: Prentice Hall.

initial interaction with the leader, the team member is categorized (first impression error). The leader assumes that the behavior of the team member is caused by his or her personality rather than by the situation of interacting with a new leader (fundamental attribution error). The leader is more likely to rate favorably a team member who is similar to the leader (similar-to-me effect). The leader is more likely to rate a team member favorably on many issues if the member's overall stereotype is positive (halo effect). Subsequent interactions rarely alter this first impression because information that supports the impression is remembered, while conflicting information is ignored (selective perception).

Diversity as a Social Process

An alternative view is that diversity problems arise from social competition and conflict. Why are gender and ethnicity important ways of classifying people? To a sociologist, it is because women and minorities are challenging the power position of white males in our organizations and society. Women and minorities are competing for scarce resources (e.g., jobs, office space, project resources) that the majority group wants to control.

When groups compete, their members form prejudices about each other. As noted in Chapter 5, when competing groups are united by common goals, these prejudices are reduced. A person can classify his or her social world in a variety of ways, but prejudices arise when the out-group is perceived as a threat to an individual's resources or power.

Diversity affects team interaction by creating power differentials within the team (McGrath et al., 1995). Many of the negative effects of diversity are a direct result of the impacts of unequal power within the team. As discussed in Chapter 8, unequal power in a team disrupts its communication process. In teams with unequal power among members, the level of communication is reduced and the powerful members control the communication process. Power differences affect team cohesion because individuals with similar status are more likely to interact with one another and form friendships (Tolbert et al., 1995). Power differences may also lead diverse teams to have more internal conflicts because of conflicting goals and increased miscommunication.

Conflicts in a diverse team can lead to the formation of "faultlines" (Mannix & Neale, 2005). A faultline occurs when the team becomes divided into opposing sides of an issue due to the formation of subgroups rather than reflecting the actual opinions of team members. For example, a team may become divided by gender and then team members support their gender's position instead of stating their actual opinion. Faultlines encourage conflict rather than the merging of diverse perspectives to solve problems.

13.4 Effects of Diversity

The results of research on the effects of diversity on teams depend on how the research is conducted, the type of diversity examined, and the tasks the teams are performing. Functional diversity has positive effects on team performance, while personal diversity may decrease cohesion and increase conflict in teams. Sometimes organizations create diversity in teams on purpose to achieve a particular goal. Cross-functional teams are a type of diverse team used to deal with complex issues requiring a variety of skills.

Research on the Effects of Diversity on Teams

The large numbers of studies on the effects of diversity on teams produced inconsistent results. Part of the problem is the difference between short-term laboratory research on teams and the study of actual working teams. Homogeneous teams function better in the short run. However, many of the problems with diversity are related to miscommunication that reduces or disappears over time (Northcraft, Polzer, Neale, & Kramer, 1995). Another problem issue relates to the tasks the team is performing. Diversity is a benefit for some types of tasks, but may be a problem for others. The type of diversity studied also causes confusion. Is diversity in demographic variables (e.g., gender, ethnicity) the same as diversity in personal variables (e.g., values, personality, skills)? Does it make sense to combine all types of diversity studies?

Finally, it must be asked whether these are even the right questions. Does it make sense to study the effects of diversity separate from an organizational context? The impact of diversity on a work team depends on the organizational climate and on how the team deals with diversity (Adler, 1986). Diversity is a fact of life for most organizations. The important question is not whether diverse teams are better or worse than homogeneous teams, but rather how to make diverse teams operate more effectively.

To clarify the research on the effects of team diversity, several meta-analyses have been conducted that examine more than a hundred studies (Bell, Villado, Lukasik, Belau, & Briggs, 2010; Jackson, 1992; Mannix & Neale, 2005; Van Knippenberg & Schippers, 2007). Two main theoretical perspectives are used to help explain the inconsistent effects of diversity on teams. The information/decision-making perspective states that differences in knowledge, skills, and perspectives may lead to higher quality and more creative decisions and improved performance. The social categorization perspective states that differences among team members may lead to in-group/out-group divisions within the team that decrease team member friendships, trust, and cooperation, and disrupt the group process.

These different theoretical perspectives led to separating the research studies on the effects of diversity in teams by the types of diversity and the types of tasks the team is performing. One of the most basic divisions of diversity is by personal attributes (surface-level diversity) versus functional attributes (deep-level diversity). Personal attributes include differences in personality, values, and various demographic variables (e.g., age, gender, and race). Functional attributes concern knowledge, abilities, and skills relating to the work environment and differences in perspectives about task issues. Surface-level diversity may lead to problems with communication and team cohesion, and increases in conflict, but often has mixed or limited effects on overall team performance. Deep-level diversity has positive effects on team decision making, creativity, and performance. The positive effects of diversity are more likely to occur in some types of tasks: Diversity improves problem solving and decision making, tasks that require creativity, complex tasks, and less routine work.

There are several moderating variables that impact how diversity affects teamwork. Teams that work cooperatively on interdependent tasks generally benefit from diversity. Teams with a learning orientation that engage in team reflexivity activities are more likely to benefit from diversity. Time working together reduces the negative social impacts of surface-level diversity, while increasing the value of deep-level diversity. As expected, teams in diverse organizations that value and support diversity are more effective at deriving the benefits of diversity.

The challenge of diversity is to get the benefits of functional diversity and differences in perspectives, while managing the communication and conflict problems created by diverse people working together. Positive benefits accrue when a team learns how to overcome the challenges created by diversity (Mannix & Neale, 2005). Diversity can improve problem solving by increasing the number of perspectives. A diverse team is likely to have a greater variety of interpersonal relationships that provide avenues for more information gathering and assistance. Diversity in top management teams is related to innovativeness and willingness to make strategic changes in the way the organization operates.

Harrison and Klein (2007) developed an alternative approach to understanding the effects of diversity on teams by classifying the types of diversity as separation, variety, and disparity. Separation is differences on a particular attribute along a horizontal dimension, such as beliefs, attitudes, and values; variety is categorical differences, such as professional background or expertise; and disparity is differences along a vertical dimension, such as status or power. Separation negatively affects teams by reducing cohesiveness and increasing conflict, but it improves decision making. Variety has positive effects on teams by improving creativity, innovation, and decision making, although it may increase task conflict. Disparity has the most negative impacts on teamwork because it creates more competition, reduces communication, and promotes social withdrawal.

Diversity of multiple types can occur at the same time. For example, ethnic differences can be variety (type of ethnic background), separation (linked to differences in values), and disparity (differences in status among ethnic groups). The impact of diversity is context dependent—it depends on the team's purpose, members' beliefs, and how diversity is managed. For example, ethnic differences may lead to disagreements on some issues but not be relevant to other team activities.

Cross-Functional Teams

In most cases, diversity in a team is something that doesn't happen on purpose. The team members who come together to complete a task may or may not be a diverse set of individuals. However, there are cases in which diversity is created for a purpose. Cross-functional teams are a good example of diversity by design.

The complexity of organizations and the tasks they perform often require cross-functional teams (Northcraft et al., 1995). For example, when an organization designs a new product, the design team often includes members with different technical skills (e.g., electronics, materials, and programming) because of the complexity of the product. The design team may include members from different departments (e.g., marketing, engineering, manufacturing) to ensure that the innovation is supported by the entire organization. The diversity in cross-functional teams relates to both functional and organizational diversity.

Cross-functional teams are highly valuable because they bring together knowledge and expertise that exists throughout an organization. The integration of information in these teams promotes new product development and encourages organizational learning. However, cross-functional teams are often difficult to operate because the competing viewpoints that are necessary for creativity create conflicts that hurt team relationships. The diversity of viewpoints in these teams is crucial for their success, but success only happens if team members are willing to share their knowledge and learn from each other (Edmondson & Nembhard, 2009).

A successful cross-functional team is like a successful negotiation: The participants retain their individual values and differences while forming an agreement that uses these differences in a synergistic way (Uhl-Bien & Graen, 1992). The challenge of cross-functional teams is learning to manage conflict constructively. Some conflicts arise from legitimate organizational or professional differences (Pelled, Eisenhardt, & Xin, 1999). Resolution of these conflicts is part of the value of cross-functional teams. However, other conflicts are related to stereotyping, distrust, and biases that limit communication among team members. Such biases prevent teams from negotiating agreements even when the agreements are in everyone's best interest.

13.5 Application: Creating a Context to Support Diversity

Diversity is both a strength and a problem for teams (Dyer, Dyer, & Dyer, 2007). When diversity is not handled effectively, it can increase conflict, create emotional problems, and reduce team effectiveness. The key to gaining the value of diversity is to create an environment that supports constructive controversy so that members are able to express their differences in a safe and useful manner. Diversity programs focus on increasing awareness to eliminate misperceptions, improving group process skills, creating a safe environment for communication, and dealing with team and organizational issues.

Increasing Awareness

Organizations try to deal with diversity issues through training programs to increase multicultural awareness. Awareness programs are designed to make people more aware of their assumptions and biases about other groups. The goal is to increase knowledge and awareness of diversity issues, challenge existing assumptions about minority groups, and eliminate stereotypes (Battaglia, 1992).

Diversity practices that acknowledge differences among cultures (multiculturalism) have a more positive impact on social interaction than practices that focus on ignoring differences and avoiding inappropriate behavior (color blindness) (Vorauer, Gagnon, & Sasaki, 2009). Multicultural approaches lead to an outward focus and encourage more interaction with other team members. In contrast, color blindness encourages a prevention focus where team members are concerned about not offending others. Anxiety over saying the wrong thing reduces communication, which can lead to increased misunderstandings among team members.

Although emphasizing similarities among team members may increase group harmony, it discourages viewing issues from multiple perspectives (Todd, Hanko, Galinsky, & Mussweiler, 2011). Acknowledging differences among team members encourages viewing issues from multiple perspectives, which improves decision making. Multicultural teams are more likely to be creative when team members recognize and respect the differences among the team (Crotty & Brett, 2012). This encourages team members to feel more comfortable to state ideas from their unique perspective. Team members acknowledge their cultural differences and try to combine these different perspectives in unique ways to support the development of creative ideas.

Awareness training needs to go beyond just teaching about cultural differences (Triandis, 1994). Increased understanding should lead to the development of social contacts and friendships that cut across demographic boundaries. It is these informal social contacts that develop into relationships that reduce misperceptions, lead to improved understanding of differences, and promote trust. To build this bridge among team members, the team should develop a team culture that spans the differences (Mannix & Neale, 2005). Actions as simple as discussing what members have in common and their unique contributions are a way to start the bridging process.

Improving Group Process Skills

Many conflicts in diverse teams are due to miscommunication caused by stereotypes and distrust. To deal with them, team members can be trained to communicate better with one another and to appreciate the unique contributions of other members (Northcraft et al., 1995). Skill-based diversity programs improve people's interpersonal skills to better manage diversity issues (Battaglia, 1992).

One approach to managing diversity is to break down the social boundaries between people. This does not happen by just having members interact in a team. There must be approaches that equalize power in the team for communication to break boundaries (Nkomo, 1995). When individuals feel the threat of negative stereotypes related to cultural identity, they often limit their participation in the team (Curseu, Schruijer, & Boros, 2007). Without an active attempt to reduce power differences within a team, ethnic diversity is likely to reduce collaboration and communication from less powerful team members. One way to achieve this is to structure and facilitate the team's communications to equalize participation among members.

A team leader can use a variety of group process facilitation techniques to improve diversity relations in the team (Armstrong & Cole, 1995). Developing agreement on the team's purpose, norms, and roles improves communication among members. Team leaders can minimize the impacts of status differences by encouraging participation from all team members and showing appreciation of their views. If the team is having trouble with open discussions, procedures to structure the team's communication can help improve this situation.

It can be especially difficult for a "minority" team member to speak up in a team if that individual is alone (Mannix & Neale, 2005). The influence of minority opinions is increased with even limited support. This prevents the team from ignoring the information because of the member presenting. The leader should make sure the team hears the minority view by creating appropriate communication norms and climate.

Creating a Safe Environment

Although diversity can benefit team performance, it does create challenges of collaborating across differences (Edmondson & Roloff, 2009). People often prefer working in homogeneous teams, but the positive conflict that arises from disagreements among diverse team members stimulates team learning, problem solving, and creativity. This positive impact of diversity only occurs if team members are able to disagree with each other in a safe environment.

One of the disappointing findings about team decision making is that teams tend to focus on shared information during discussions rather than on the unique information held by individuals (Mannix & Neale, 2005). Although diverse teams have the potential to perform better than homogeneous teams, this only occurs if the team can gain access to members' unique contributions. The more successful the team is at creating an open communication climate that promotes trust and provides support to members, the more willing members are to risk stating their unique information on a topic.

The key is to create a psychologically safe team environment that encourages communication and collaboration from all team members (Edmondson & Roloff, 2009). Sharing individual perspectives and developing a climate that values cultural differences can encourage this type of collaborative environment. Safe team climates allow differences to be brought to the surface and discussed without fear of retribution. When the team climate encourages safety, the differences within a diverse team can be used to increase team effectiveness. When a safe climate does not exist, diversity is likely to lead to communication difficulties and problems with collaboration.

Improving Organizational Issues

Developing superordinate goals or strong collective team identities can help diverse teams work more effectively together (Van der Vegt & Bunderson,

2005). When the team has a strong sense of team identity, members are more willing to share ideas and pay attention to the ideas of other team members. Team identification helps members move beyond individual differences and focus on the needs of the team. Culturally diverse teams outperform culturally homogenous teams in later phases of a team's life (Gibson, Huang, Kirkman, & Shapiro, 2014). It takes time to develop shared team values and a team identity that helps the team overcome the challenges of cultural differences.

The benefits of team diversity occur because of the ability to share diverse information, knowledge, and perspectives, thereby bringing together a larger pool of information for problem solving (Pieterse, Knippenberg, & Dierendonck, 2013). This benefit may be hidden from the team if team members are not motivated to discuss and explore the different perspectives within the team. Differences among people may discourage open communication, and perceptual biases may limit learning from others. Teams need to develop a learning orientation to obtain the benefits of diversity.

Diversity should not be linked to task assignments (Rico, Sanchez-Manzarares, Antino, & Lau, 2012). For instance, a team should not assign Asian members the technical issues, women the communication functions, and younger members the computer tasks. When tasks and stereotypes are linked, stereotypes and prejudices become a rational way of explaining what happens in the team.

In some cases, the problems created by diversity are related to the performance evaluation and reward system. When members of a team are not working together cooperatively, the evaluation and reward system is one of the first places to look for a cause for the problem (Northcraft et al., 1995). Members of the leader's in-group are more likely to receive better performance appraisals and rewards, and in-group membership may be related to the leader's stereotypes. In a cross-functional team, members are often evaluated and rewarded by the departments they represent rather than by the team. Given this situation, their commitment to the team's goals is limited. Such conflicts are primarily about the organization's reward system rather than about diversity.

Summary

Diversity is increasingly relevant for organizations because of the increased numbers of women and minorities in the workplace, the desire for workforces to reflect the diversity in society, and changes in how people work together. Although we often think of diversity in terms of demographic differences (e.g., gender, ethnicity, age), diversity also includes psychological (e.g., values, personality, knowledge) and organizational (e.g., tenure, occupation, status) differences among people. The impact of diversity on teams can be caused by differences among types of people or expectations about differences that cause people to treat each other differently.

The problems created by diversity have several causes. People categorize others and use stereotypes to explain differences between groups. The categorization process can lead to misperceptions and cognitive biases. Team leaders are affected by these biases and may treat team members differently because of their backgrounds. Diversity may be due to competition and conflict between groups.

The biases created by diversity may cause members of a team to misperceive and discount the contributions of minority members. This reduces minority members' ability to contribute to the team's efforts. Emotional distrust leads to defensive communication and power conflicts. These factors disrupt the operation of the team and reduce minority members' motivation to participate.

The effects of diversity on teams are complex. The performance differences between homogeneous and heterogeneous teams depend on the types of diversity and tasks. Personal or surface-level diversity may increase conflict in teams, while functional or deep-level diversity improves team performance on a variety of tasks. Cross-functional teams are an example of diversity purposely created by organizations.

Organizations can develop programs to help teams better manage diversity issues. Diversity programs are designed to increase awareness of the differences among types of people, to improve a team's ability to communicate, to create a psychologically safe work environment, and to create goals and reward systems that encourage working together.

Team Leader's Challenge 13

You are the professor in an undergraduate engineering design class. The year-long class uses student teams to complete a complex design project. Your goal is to simulate a real-world professional experience in the class, but you also need to ensure that it is a safe and productive learning experience for the students.

Like many engineering classes, there are few women students. In the past, you have not been concerned about gender issues when assigning students to project teams. However, last year you received several complaints from women students about feeling bullied and unsupported in their teams. These students were the only women in their design teams.

How should you (the professor) distribute the few women engineering students among the project teams?

Are there actions you could take to provide support for the women students in the class?

How do you handle complaints from women students about team relations?

SURVEY: ATTITUDES TOWARD DIVERSITY

Purpose: Increase your awareness of how well you enjoy working in a diverse team. Attitudes toward diversity have behavioral, cognitive, and affective components. *Diversity of contact* is the behavioral component that relates to an interest in participating in diverse activities, *relativistic appreciation* is the cognitive appreciation of similarities and differences in people, and *sense of connectedness* refers to the affective component or the degree of comfort interacting with others.

Directions: Using the scale below, indicate the amount of agreement with each of the following statements about yourself.

1	2	3	4	5
Strongly Disagree				Strongly Agree

_____ 1. I like to go to dances that have music from other cultures.

_____ 2. Interacting with people with disabilities gives me a different perspective on the world.

_____ 3. It is hard for me to feel close to someone from another race.

_____ 4. I enjoy attending events where I can meet people from different ethnic backgrounds.

_____ 5. Knowing how a person is different from me can enhance our friendship.

_____ 6. I find it difficult to interact with someone from another culture.

_____ 7. I am interested in learning about how different cultures live.

_____ 8. Knowing people from different ethnic groups helps me understand myself better.

_____ 9. I do not feel at ease when I am around people from another culture.

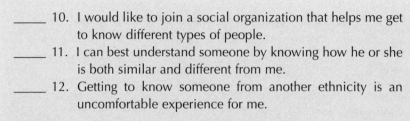

_____ 10. I would like to join a social organization that helps me get to know different types of people.

_____ 11. I can best understand someone by knowing how he or she is both similar and different from me.

_____ 12. Getting to know someone from another ethnicity is an uncomfortable experience for me.

Scoring:

Add questions 1, 4, 7, and 10 to obtain your Diversity of Contact score.

Add questions 2, 5, 8, and 11 to obtain your Relativistic Appreciation score.

Add questions 3, 6, 9, and 12 to obtain your Sense of Connectedness score.

Discussion: How do your attitudes toward diversity compare to other team members? What can you do to help improve your attitudes toward working in diverse teams? How are the behavioral, cognitive, and affective aspects of diversity related?

SOURCE: Adapted from Miville, M., Gelso, C., Pannu, R., Liu, W., Touradji, P., Holloway, P., & Fuertes, J. (1999). Appreciating similarities and valuing differences: The Miville-Guzman Universality-Diversity Scale. *Journal of Counseling Psychology, 46*(3), 291–307.

ACTIVITY: UNDERSTANDING GENDER AND STATUS DIFFERENCES IN A TEAM

Objective: Diversity can be caused by demographic (e.g., gender), psychological (e.g., personality), or organizational (e.g., status) differences. The more powerful group is more likely to communicate, speak forcefully, and contradict others. It is sometimes assumed that women's communication is more polite and deferential than men's communication, but this may have more to do with status than gender or personality differences. This activity helps explore this question.

Activity: Use the observation form (Activity Worksheet 13.1) to record the communication in a team meeting that comprises male and female members. Alternatively, organize a small group discussion on the Team Leader's

Challenge with a mixed gender group. You may also want to create all-male and all-female groups for comparison purposes.

Analysis: Women and low-status team members use the first two communication styles more often, while men and high-status team members use the last two communication styles more often. Compare the various communications of women with that of men in the group, and compare the communication level and style of high-status (e.g., leader) with that of low-status members. Also, note which type does most of the communicating in the group.

Discussion: How do you explain the differences among communication styles of team members? Are these differences because of status, personality, or gender differences? What should a team do to make sure diversity differences do not interfere with full participation and acceptance in the team?

ACTIVITY WORKSHEET 13.1
Observing Team Communication Differences

	Team Members					
	1	2	3	4	5	6
Phrases ideas tentatively and politely						
Shows agreement and support for others						
Confronts issues using direct and forceful language						
Contradicts and disagrees with others						
Total number of communications:						

PART IV

Organizational Context of Teams

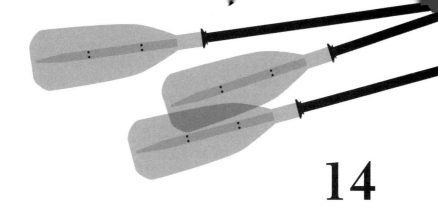

14

Team, Organizational, and International Culture

The shared values, beliefs, and norms of a team, organization, or nation are known as its culture. A team's culture affects how team members communicate and coordinate work. Organizational and international cultures affect the ways that individuality, status, and risk taking are accepted and used. These organizational cultural differences affect how teams operate within organizations.

The success of work teams depends on the level of support they receive from their organization, which in turn depends on the organization's culture. At the same time, the use of teams changes an organization's culture.

International differences in culture impact how teams are used and operate. Transnational teams are composed of members from different cultures who are linked by communication technology. These teams must manage their cultural differences in order to operate effectively.

Learning Objectives

1. What is a team's culture and how is it created?

2. How does a team's culture affect its performance?

3. What is organizational culture, and what are the effects it has on people in organizations?

4. What are the two main types of organizational cultures that affect the use of teams?

5. How do the different dimensions of international culture affect teamwork?

6. How do United States and Japanese teams differ?

7. How do differences in international culture affect teamwork?

8. What strategies can transnational teams use to manage cultural differences?

14.1 Team Culture

A team's culture is the shared perception of how the team should operate to accomplish its goals. Team norms, member roles, and patterns of interaction are included in the team culture. Teams do not develop their culture from scratch—they incorporate cultural norms and values from their organization and society (Wheelan, 2005). Agreement about norms, values, and roles (about the team's culture) reduces anxiety and improves communication in a team.

A team's culture and its norms often develop through precedent (Thompson, 2004). Behavior patterns that emerge early in a team's life define how the team operates in the future. The leader also plays a key role in the development of a team's culture (Schein, 1992). Leaders should try to establish an appropriate culture early in the team's life, because it is easier to begin to establish a culture than it is to change an existing one.

A benefit of teamwork is the sharing of information among team members to coordinate work activities (Zarraga & Bonache, 2005). This knowledge sharing requires a collaborative team culture. Team members may be reluctant to share information, given that information is a valuable individual commodity in work organizations. A collaborative team culture includes mutual trust, leniency in judging others, courage to state opinions, and willingness to help. When a collaborative culture exists, the team is better able to use the resources of its members.

Team culture relates to team support or the availability of helping behaviors within a team (Drach-Zahavy, 2004). Support includes both emotional support and help or assistance in performing the task. The level of team support relates to the leader's behavior and the team culture. Role modeling by the leader and other team members encourages team members to provide one another with support. Teams that are group oriented (rather than individualistic) and are less status oriented provide more team support. Studies on high-stress action teams like nursing teams show that supportive team cultures reduce the negative impacts of work stress (Drach-Zahavy, 2004).

Team culture has an impact on whether training is used by a team (Smith-Jentsch, Salas, & Brannick, 2001). Team culture relates to the degree to which the team expects and supports attempts to try newly learned skills. Culture does not affect what is learned in training, but does affect whether the newly learned skills are applied. For example, acting assertively is highly dependent on the team culture established by the leader. If the team leader rewards assertiveness, team members are more likely to act assertively after receiving communications training.

For many work teams, the team's culture is a reflection of the organization's culture (Thompson, 2004). Companies that are successful using teams often have norms that foster participation and innovation. However, culture is more a property of the team than it is of the entire organization. Teams may have cultures and norms different from those of their larger organization. For example, the Hawthorne studies (Mayo, 1933) showed that work teams in the same area of the factory could have different team cultures leading to different performance levels (Sundstrom, McIntyre, Halfhill, & Richards, 2000). Developing a strong team identity and culture is especially important for teams that span organizational and international boundaries. The team's culture provides a way to unite team members who have different views of teamwork and teamwork practices.

14.2 Defining Organizational Culture

The concept of organizational culture arose during the 1980s as a way to explain why some organizations were consistently successful. Peters and Waterman (1982) used the concept of organizational culture as a way of describing the practices of the best U.S. companies. Schein (1992) was influential in arguing that the principles for examining national cultures could be used to describe organizational cultures.

Organizational culture refers to the shared values, beliefs, and norms of an organization. Researchers studying organizational culture emphasize various aspects as key to understanding how organizations operate. For Deal and Kennedy (1982), an organization's customs, rituals, and traditions help reveal the underlying values that guide organizational decision making. Davis (1984) focuses on the shared meanings and beliefs of organizations because they affect an organization's strategies and operating procedures.

Kilmann and Saxton (1983) view culture as determining the team norms and behavioral patterns of employees.

Regardless of which characteristic of organizational culture is selected, there are features of cultures that are common to all perspectives (Schein, 1992). All members of an organization share its organizational culture. Culture provides structural stability for the organization because its influence is pervasive and slow to change. The varied aspects of culture are integrated and form a consistent pattern within the organization. Culture reflects the shared learning by organization members that contains cognitive, behavioral, and emotional elements. Finally, organizational culture affects both the internal operations of the organization and how it relates to its external environment.

Teams and organizational culture have a mutually influencing relationship. Teamwork occurs more easily in some types of organizational cultures than in others. For example, cultural norms about power and control affect the way communication flows in an organization (Zuboff, 1988). Team-based work practices like total quality management may be unsuccessful because they contradict cultural norms about communication and power (Bushe, 1988). The use of teams changes the ways people work with and relate to one another, which changes the organizational culture. Over time, an organization's work systems tend to become congruent with its organizational culture.

Organizations are not uniform and do not necessarily have uniform cultures. Rather than viewing organizations as having single cultures, organizations may be viewed as containing networks of groups that develop their own styles of operating and interacting. These are organizational subcultures. Such subcultures arise from mergers and acquisitions, geographic differences in facility locations, or occupational areas in an organization.

Organizations may be characterized by assessing the integration of their separate subcultures (Van Maanen & Barley, 1985). When the shared beliefs and assumptions held by working groups are similar across organizations, the organizations have strong cultures. For example, in the 1980s and 1990s, Hewlett-Packard had a strong organizational culture that defined how managers should treat employees: encouraging an open-door policy, fostering independence, and promoting equal-status relations. These practices operated throughout all divisions of the company.

One important cause of subcultures is related to an employee's occupational community. An occupational community refers to the shared knowledge, language, and identity formed by those working in a particular area of specialization (Schein, 1992). For example, engineers and sales representatives have different occupational communities, and therefore occupy different subcultures within an organization. Even in strong organizational cultures like Hewlett-Packard, people from engineering and sales use different professional languages and have different styles of interacting with others. This can make working together on cross-functional teams difficult (Adler, 1991).

14.3 Organizational Culture and Teamwork

An organizational culture that encourages employee involvement and participation is a necessary support for teamwork. In a supportive organizational culture, managers are less likely to resist using teams, and there are better relations between teams and other parts of the organization. Self-managing teams are much more likely to be successful in organizations whose culture supports empowerment and teamwork. Overall, organizational culture is one of the largest predictors of the successful use of teams by companies (Levi & Slem, 1995).

Organizational culture defines the norms that regulate acceptable behaviors in an organization. When these cultural norms conflict with the use of teams, organizations have a difficult time using teams successfully. For example, norms about communication that are part of an organization's culture may limit the organization's ability to use teams. Many organizations do not have open communication from workers to managers, across departments, or from top management to the rest of the organization. This limits the amount of communication that occurs in a team and the team's ability to relate to other parts of the organization.

Walton and Hackman (1986) identify two distinct types of organizational cultures that affect the use of teams: control cultures and commitment cultures. Status and power drive the control strategy. It is hierarchical and tightly controlling. The relations among people are adversarial and untrusting. It is difficult to operate teams in this context. The commitment strategy reduces the number of organizational levels of authority, focuses on quality, and adopts methods to encourage open communication and participation. It uses teams and gives them the authority to operate successfully. This type of culture empowers both individuals and teams to increase commitment to their organization's goals.

Obviously, most organizations fall somewhere between these two approaches. Although managers may want to shift to a commitment strategy, if the existing culture is control oriented, it will be difficult to change. Developing teams is a struggle when their use is not compatible with the existing cultural practices. Teams operate better in a commitment-oriented culture because they are given the resources, training, and power they need to succeed.

It is critical for the organizational culture to support collaborative work for teams to operate successfully (Dyer, Dyer, & Dyer, 2007). It is an arduous task for a traditional control-oriented culture to change enough to promote good teamwork. Organizations may want to promote teamwork and create commitment-oriented organizational cultures; however, they may resist changing the existing system of power, authority, and rewards. Employees are often cynical of announcements by management that it will simply create teams when the culture does not support the use of teams.

The importance of organizational culture as a primary support for teamwork is both a problem and a benefit (Levi & Slem, 1995). Organizational culture is not easy to change. Developing an organizational culture that supports teamwork is a long-term process. It is not something that can be dictated by top management or announced as a new organizational program. Changing an organizational culture requires a consistent effort on the part of management to show that employee involvement and teamwork will be valued and rewarded. This must be done through both communication and action. If what an organization says it believes does not match its actual behavior, a credibility gap is created, and trust between the organization and its employees drops.

In organizations without uniform cultures, cultural change may occur within subcultures (Dyer et al., 2007). However, even successful subcultures do not necessarily spread to other parts of an organization. For example, General Motors (GM) created a new organizational culture at its Saturn facility to support teamwork. Although this team-based approach to manufacturing was successful, the approach was not adopted by other GM facilities. Although there are many successful examples of production teams and even self-managing teams, these approaches reveal limited impact on manufacturing companies (Vallas, 2003). Production teams are often islands of innovation surrounded by traditional work systems because management has not allowed a culture of teamwork to spread throughout the organization.

There is a benefit to this relationship between organizational culture and teamwork. Once an organization begins to create an organizational culture that supports teamwork, the culture can support a wide variety of teams. The organizational culture provides the foundation, and from that foundation an organization is able to experiment with developing the types of teams that can successfully fulfill its mission.

14.4 Dimensions of International Culture

Dimensions allow the establishment of frameworks that to use to compare different cultures. Several approaches have been used to determine the dimensions of international culture. Triandis (1994) reviewed the approaches used by anthropologists. Hofstede (1980) studied employees in international companies to compare national differences. Both of these approaches identified a similar set of key dimensions.

Organizational cultures can be compared on three dimensions: individualism versus collectivism, power and status, and uncertainty and risk avoidance (Table 14.1). The following subsections examine these three dimensions and show how they can be used to compare teams in the United States and Japan.

Individualism Versus Collectivism

The individualism-collectivism dimension is a predominate component of national cultures that has a strong influence on teamwork. The interactions of individualistic members tend to embody autonomy, privacy, individual recognition, immediate family and self-orientation, openness and candor, task-oriented group activities, and I-language (Hofstede, 2011). Given these traits, people high in individualism are associated with greater comfort engaging in conflict, general resistance to working in teams and/or self-management teams (Kirkman & Shapiro, 1997), and performing worse in groups when instructed to "do your best" compared to having specific group or individual goals (Erez & Somech, 1996). Still, other research shows that individualistic groups tend to be more creative then collectivist groups (Goncalo & Staw, 2006). People from the United States, Australia, Great Britain, Canada, the Netherlands, and New Zealand tend to score the highest on individualism (Hofstede, Hofstede, & Minkov, 2010).

By contrast, collectivism is associated with loyalty to the group, opposition to other groups, belongingness, cooperation, we-language, relationship-oriented group activities, harmony, disapproving of self-promotion, and following group opinions. People value the ties between people and are expected to look after one another. Self-interest is subordinate to the interests of the social group or team, making conformity expected and discouraging open conflict. Indeed, a popular Japanese proverb is "the nail that sticks out will be hammered down," emphasizing the desire for conformity in collectivist cultures. Collectivist members are less likely to resist team membership and more likely to accept self-management, which enhances team

Table 14.1 Dimensions of Organizational Culture

Individualism	↔	Collectivism
Low power distance	↔	High power distance
Risk taking	↔	Risk avoidance

effectiveness (Kirkman & Shapiro, 1997). Most of the world is composed of people living in collectivist cultures; for example in collectivist countries like Guatemala, Ecuador, and Panama (Hofstede et al., 2010). Also, many countries in South East Asia, such as India, South Korea, Thailand, and Japan are comparatively more collectivist than the United States.

Power and Status

The power dimension of culture is the degree to which people in a culture accept unequal power. High-power cultures are status oriented, while low-power cultures are more egalitarian. In high-power cultures, large power and status differences are acceptable. In such cultures, great respect and deference are shown to higher-status people; as a result, on teams, challenging their authority is uncomfortable and members are more willing to accept the leader's decisions.

In low-power cultures, people are less willing to accept the authority of others on the basis of the positions they hold in an organization. Their viewpoint is more egalitarian. Team members take initiative and do not automatically accept management directives.

A high-power culture can be a problem for teams because team members are more willing to accept the team leader's view, which indicates a lack of independence by the members that can reduce team creativity. Participation is not easy for people in high-power cultures because they believe communication from above is more important than their own ideas. In an unequal status situation, the higher-status person does most of the communicating, and most communication is directed at the person with highest status.

Conversely, a team in a low-power culture can be difficult to manage. Members' more open communication styles can create more conflicts. Their sense of independence from the organization's authority may lead the team into decisions that are not sensitive to the politics of the organization. Egalitarian communication in decision making may improve the quality of the decisions, but reduce the team's ability to implement them because of lack of deference to the concerns of the surrounding organization.

Uncertainty and Risk Avoidance

Cultures vary in willingness to accept uncertainty and the desire to avoid taking risks. Uncertainty is the degree to which people feel threatened by ambiguous situations or change. In risk-avoidance cultures, social harmony and stability are valued. People want to have rules and norms that define appropriate behavior, and they prefer things to stay the same so they know what is expected of them.

Risk-avoidance cultures value social harmony more than change. Open conflict is considered inappropriate; people avoid controversies or become compliant during controversies. People in risk-avoidance cultures try to maintain the security of the status quo, in part because they fear the potential for failure during change.

Risk-taking cultures value change. They tend to be action oriented and do not plan changes in advance. People in these cultures are open and willing to try out new ideas. Conflict is more likely to be viewed as positive because it encourages new ideas and change.

Comparing the United States and Japan

The United States and Japan present a valuable comparison of the effects of culture on teamwork. Applying the dimensions discussed above, U.S. organizations tend to display individualism, low power, and risk taking, whereas Japanese organizations tend to display collectivism, high power, and risk avoidance. These differences significantly affect the use of teams and how teams operate.

The focus of U.S. management practice is on controlling, motivating, and rewarding individual performance. The individual remains independent of the organization and is expected to remain committed to the organization only as long as it is in his or her best interest. There is less use of teamwork in the United States than in other industrialized countries (Cole, 1989). The focus on competition and individualism in U.S. culture limits teamwork, especially among professional and managerial staff.

In the Japanese approach to management, the individual does not have a job, but rather is part of the organization (Ouchi, 1981). Japanese organizations stress the interdependence of all employees. Their participative style is marked by mutual respect and common interests (Pascale & Athos, 1981), and consensus decision making is practiced at all levels of their organizations.

Teamwork programs, such as quality circles and production teams, are more common in Japanese companies. Management creates these teams to serve as mechanisms for employee participation. The focus of teamwork is on improving the productivity of the work system. Participation allows employees to make suggestions, but management retains control over all decisions (Cole, 1989). Unlike teamwork programs in the United States, participation does not imply power sharing with the workers in hierarchical Japanese corporations.

The Japanese have a more cautious view of change because their culture is more attuned to the value of promoting social harmony. Japanese companies tend to implement incremental changes because of their concern for social relations and job security (Prochaska, 1980). On teams, there is less conflict and more conformity. Consequently, Japanese teams are viewed as less creative and less willing to take risks than U.S. teams.

Japanese teams use consensus decision making. Consensus is easier to reach in Japanese teams because people are less independent and try to avoid conflict. They are confident that compromise solutions can be found, so they do not rush to decisions. This makes Japanese decision making slower, but the implementation of decisions faster. Once a Japanese team has made a consensus decision, it knows that everyone supports the implementation of the decision.

This comparison between U.S. and Japanese cultures demonstrates several points about organizational culture. First, cultures affect how teams operate. Second, national cultures affect organizational cultures. Third, cultures do not prevent the use of teams, but they do affect the way teams operate.

14.5 International Differences in Teamwork

International cultural differences have a variety of impacts on the meaning of teams and how they operate. Globalization and virtual teamwork have increased the use of teams that incorporate members from different cultures. Becoming aware of cultural differences and one's own cultural biases is important for effective teamwork.

Cultures have different views about the meaning of teams at work (Gibson & McDaniel, 2010). The individualism-collectivism dimension influences the expectations and understanding of teamwork, resulting in different metaphors that contribute to various expectations of team roles, values, scope, membership, and objectives (Gibson & Zellmer-Bruhn, 2001). Those from individualistic cultures tend to assess teams and teamwork using metaphors of *sports* (e.g., clear objectives, coach, players, competitions, etc.), *associates* (e.g., cliques, clans, crews, etc.), or *military* (e.g., engaging in campaigns, battles, survival, etc.), while those from collectivist cultures observe teams and teamwork using metaphors of *family* (e.g., parental roles like father, mother, brother, etc.) and *community* (e.g., teammates are buddies, friends, neighbors, etc.). Psychological safety can be influenced by the metaphors used by teams—a family provides a safer climate than the military. This also suggests team members from different nations likely have different expectations for how a team will be managed—for example, a member of a team expecting a familial teamwork environment will not have their expectations of guidance and support met if they are involved with a team managed as associates.

Cultures also have different interpretations of team success (Gibson & McDaniel, 2010). Mexicans emphasize socioemotional relations as an important criterion for team success, while Anglos emphasize primarily task performance. For example, forging business relationships in Mexico may begin with more informal interactions during dinner where business topics are initially avoided in favor of fostering interpersonal relationships. Trust operates differently in different cultures. In Japan, trust within a team is based on personal ties with team members, while trust in U.S. teams is based more on a common team identity and on performance. These different meanings for teamwork imply differences in team norms and in the importance of building relationships among team members.

Differences among cultures are likely to cause communications errors (Vignovic & Thompson, 2010). People communicating in a second language are more likely to make spelling and grammar errors. In addition, cultures have different communications norms that can lead to misinterpretation. For example, when Americans email, they often use a conversational style in the message. However, Chinese business professionals tend to write brief, direct email messages that are solely task oriented. This can lead to the misinterpretation by Americans that Chinese people lack social skills, are unfriendly, or are untrustworthy.

Communication problems can also occur because of differences about the expression of emotions (Adam, Shirako, & Maddux, 2010). When team members are negotiating, expressing anger may lead to greater concessions from American negotiators, but to fewer concessions from Asian and Asian American negotiators. The reason for this difference is that displaying negative emotions is less acceptable in Asian cultures. Cultural rules for displaying emotions make it acceptable for Western individualistic cultures to amplify emotional expressions, while Eastern collectivist cultures tend to limit or suppress the expression of emotions, especially negative emotions. However, in other cultures like Israel, the display of negative emotions is a useful conflict technique that can help the parties better understand the nature of the conflict and encourage a quicker resolution.

Team decision-making practices are impacted by culture (Gibson & McDaniel, 2010). In collectivist, high-power cultures like Japan, team members are more cooperative, more likely to support the opinion of the leader, and more likely to use equal allocation approaches to resolve dilemmas. However, individualist cultures like the United States may make higher quality decisions because they are more willing to tolerate and be influenced by minority opinions during a group discussion.

When trying to resolve conflicts, cultures have different preferences about approaches (Gibson & McDaniel, 2010). U.S. teams prefer integrative solutions that maximize mutual interests, while Germans prefer using existing rules and practices, and Japanese prefer to defer to higher status individuals. Americans focus on synthesizing the conflicting interests of the parties involved in a conflict, while Chinese try to avoid conflict, focus on the collective interest, and defer to authority decisions. Chinese prefer a cooperative approach to conflict because of their increased concerns about preserving social relations and obedience to authority figures.

Attitudes toward team empowerment affect how different cultures use teams at work (Hempel, Zhang, & Han, 2012). In high-power cultures like China, empowerment practices and self-managing teams are less likely to be used. In Chinese companies, managers often control the behaviors of team members. However, in a study of high technology teams in China, when teams were given more empowerment, team performance improved. Although cultures may encourage certain practices, team members may respond well to alternative approaches to managing teams.

14.6 Transnational Teams

Transnational teams are composed of individuals from different cultures working on activities that span national borders (Snell, Snow, Davison, & Hambrick, 1998). This type of team is formed in a global company or through alliances among companies in different geographic areas. Transnational teams use representatives from two or more countries to ensure that the perspectives of local organizations, cultures, and markets are represented in the team. The main challenge for such teams is to learn how to integrate this cultural diversity into a functioning unit.

Transnational teams deal with three important concerns for global companies: local responsiveness, global efficiency, and organizational learning (Snow, Snell, Davison, & Hambrick, 1996). Their work serves to customize products and services to different cultures and coordinate local activities and markets for global companies. At the same time, transnational teams help integrate operations across parts of a multinational organization to improve efficiency. Transnational teams encourage innovation by bringing together ideas from various parts of an organization.

Characteristics of Transnational Teams

While the multiple perspectives of transnational teams can be a benefit, the diversity within a team can create communication, trust, and conflict problems that limit team effectiveness (Burke, Priest, Wooten, Diaz Granados, & Salas, 2009). The ability of members of multicultural teams to understand or make sense of other team members' behavior relates to cultural distance. High cultural distance creates problems because team members have difficulty interpreting the meaning of other team members' behaviors, so the team has difficulty communicating and interacting.

The importance of people's cultural identity can vary within a team (Burke et al., 2009). People have multiple identities; the identity that is most salient depends on the situation. People can identify with their national, organizational, or team culture when interacting within a team. A team leader can promote a sense of similarity among team members to encourage a common social identity. This helps improve social relations among team members. Alternatively, a team leader can encourage members to view each other as unique individuals in order to foster personal identities. This may encourage members to present their unique perspective during group decision making.

To be successful, transnational teams must deal with differences in culture that affect how people work and communicate in teams (Earley & Gibson, 2002). The two main cultural dimensions that affect these teams are individualism/collectivism, and status or power distance. Teams from Asian, collectivist cultures are slower to develop team cohesion and performance than multicultural and individualistic culture teams (Takeuchi, Kass, Schneider, & Van Wormer, 2013). These differences are difficult to resolve because these teams rely on technology for their communications.

Many of the difficulties transnational teams experience stem from communication problems (Earley & Gibson, 2002). Cultures vary in how they communicate information. For example, in collectivist cultures like some Asian countries, communication is often indirect with a positive tone. Communication frequently uses qualifiers and ambiguous words to avoid confrontation and preserve group harmony. In individualist cultures, communication is more direct, even when it is conveying negative information. Communication is about facts and is viewed as distinct from the relationship with the listeners.

Rewarding transnational team members may pose problems because of cultural ideas about how rewards should be given (Snell et al., 1998). A focus on individual rewards may be considered inappropriate for teamwork in collectivist cultures. Although team rewards are valuable, team members are often more responsive to the rewards they receive from their home organization.

Cultures vary in how status oriented they are (Earley & Gibson, 2002). In high-power cultures, communication is more formal, with most coming from higher status members. In those cultures, lower status members tend to be polite and deferential in their communications. In low-power cultures, communication is more information oriented and participation is more equal.

Miscommunication in transnational teams is made worse by a teams' reliance on communications technology. Virtual teams can be a problem when spanning cultures because of the difficulty communicating gestures, nonverbal cues, symbolic content, and contextual information (Gibson & McDaniel, 2010). In addition, individualists have more favorable attitudes toward virtual teams than collectivists. This makes it more difficult for transnational teams to develop trust and mutual understanding in their communications (Earley & Gibson, 2002). Culture-based communication problems are more difficult to manage in these virtual teams.

Some of the technological characteristics of virtual teams help to improve the performance of culturally diverse teams (Gibson, Huang, Kirkman, & Shapiro, 2014). Communication technologies, such as email, social media, and computer conferencing, help teams overcome the constraint of being physically separated. Decision-aid technologies, such as knowledge databases and decision support software, help teams overcome problems created by cultural difference. The ability with today's technology to document communications allows team members to review past communications and encourages individual accountability. Relying on technologies like email reduces stereotyping, biases caused by accents, and in-group/out-group distinctions that can hurt team performance.

Creating Effective Transnational Teams

The main challenges of transnational teams are to understand the meaning of the behaviors of other team members and to develop a mental model of how to operate as a team (Burke et al., 2009). Team members need to learn perspective taking, which is the ability to see the world from the vantage point of another. It helps reduce anxiety about interacting with others, facilitates social coordination, and develops social bonds in a team. In addition, cultural differences about how to operate need to be negotiated in order to develop common understandings. Teams that are good at negotiating differences of opinion and values are better able to manage their cultural differences. Strategies to develop effective transnational teams include spending more time initially starting the team, training the team, and using strong leadership. The goal of these actions is to develop a hybrid team culture that can unify the team.

Transnational teams should schedule face-to-face meetings early in their existence to develop personal relationships and a shared understanding among team members (Earley & Gibson, 2002). Clearly, shared goals, norms, member roles, and agreement about performance criteria should be established (Snow et al., 1996). These are part of a formal team contract that needs to be developed at the onset of teamwork to reduce any later misunderstandings. Transnational teams should spend more effort developing project plans and other types of project management structures. Face-to-face meetings need to be scheduled at key points in the plan to clarify any misunderstandings about the team's progress.

Training programs that explain the organization's strategy and culture encourage a common perspective (Snell et al., 1998). This type of training is especially useful at the onset of teamwork. Cross-cultural team building that increases awareness of cultural differences in work practices and communication improves team operations. Teamwork skills that should be the focus of training include conflict resolution, negotiation skills, project management, and interpersonal communication. In addition, training in the use of communications technology can decrease misunderstandings caused by differences in the use of technology.

Strong leaders are valuable for coordinating actions and managing conflicts in the team (Katzenbach & Smith, 2001). Strong team leaders are more acceptable in some cultures like Japan, so it may be hard to avoid using them. Virtual teams often need leaders who are more powerful to help coordinate communications and work assignments. Multicultural teams perform better when they have strong designated leaders (Earley & Gibson, 2002). Leaders provide direction, motivate team members, and ensure the team stays on course. Leaders help develop the hybrid culture that unites a diverse team.

When multicultural teams encounter internal problems, it is important for team leaders to try to understand if the root problem is cultural misunderstandings (Dibble & Gibson, 2013). It is impossible to eliminate cultural differences, but teams can increase their understanding of the cultural differences in norms, expectations, and attitudes. Increased awareness and appreciation of cultural differences encourages collaboration because team members are better able to interpret communications and adjust their behavior to allow better coordination of efforts. Without this awareness, team members often "retreat" and do not communicate when encountering culture-based conflicts.

Effective transnational teams often develop a strong hybrid culture that provides a common sense of identity for team members and facilitates their interactions. A hybrid culture is both a set of rules about how to act and a set of expectations about how the team operates (Earley & Mosakowski, 2000). It creates a shared understanding that allows members to better interpret communication from other team members. This is more likely to occur when team leaders acknowledge cultural differences rather than trying to ignore or suppress dissimilarities (Gibson & McDonald, 2010). Cultural diversity is a benefit to teams because of the variety of perspectives their members contribute, but teams need to develop their own hybrid culture to encourage collective effort. Because developing a hybrid culture takes time, team performance in transnational teams typically improves over time.

LEADING VIRTUAL TEAMS:
DEALING WITH CULTURAL ISSUES

Problem: Virtual teams are more likely to be cross-cultural, which makes communications problems in virtual teams more important to address.

Solution: Some of the recommendations for improving cross-cultural communication in virtual teams have been discussed in Chapter 5 (Cooperation) and Chapter 10 (Leadership). The following are other factors to consider.

1. Understanding cultural differences in both behavioral norms and language is vital to building trust. A better understanding of the dimensions of international culture enables any leader to more effectively address communication and behavioral differences that arise in virtual teams.

2. Stay sensitive to local cultures. The virtual leader must be sensitive to the norms of the different national and ethnic cultures of team members. Cultures vary by the way they relate to time, including the daily calendar (some cultures start early in the morning, some start later; some cultures take siestas; some cultures have midday prayer), religious and ethnic holidays, willingness to work during family time, and the importance of being on time. Team members from high power distance cultures are less likely to speak up when there are status differences in the team. Members from risk or conflict avoidant cultures may be less likely to participate, especially during a conflict. Collectivists are more motivated by team rewards, while individualists prefer individual recognition and rewards.

3. Remain aware of your communication practices. Identify and communicate to the team which members are participating in their second or third language. The virtual leader should limit jargon, metaphor, cultural reference, and colloquial terminology because these may not translate to other English-speaking cultures and may be lost on participants for whom English is a second language. Also, it is important to note that English words and phrases take on subtly different meanings in different national cultures. For example, if a virtual leader asks a team member from India whether his work will be finished by Friday and he answers "yes" (which is what he most likely will answer), he does not mean that it will be finished on Friday. What he means is that he heard you and understood the question. The experienced virtual leader would will not ask him a yes/no question, but ask instead, "When will your work be completed?"

Summary

A team's culture is defined by its norms, roles, and values. Team culture develops over time, but is strongly influenced by its organizational context. Culture has many influences on how a team operates because it affects commitment to the team, styles of communication and collaboration, and the support members provide for one another.

Organizational culture relates to the shared values, beliefs, and norms of an organization. It provides a sense of identity to its members and defines acceptable behaviors. Organizations may have unified cultures or may be composed of networks of subcultures based on occupation or background.

The use of teams in an organization depends on its organizational culture. Cultural norms can either support teamwork or limit a team's ability to operate effectively. Two distinct types of organizational cultures are those based on power and control and those based on participation and commitment. The two types provide very distinct contexts for teamwork. The importance of organizational culture for teamwork is both a benefit and a problem. Once an organizational culture supports teamwork, it is usually able to support a wide variety of types of teams. However, it is difficult to change organizational cultures that do not support teamwork.

International culture may be viewed as varying along three dimensions: individualism, power, and uncertainty. The individualist-collectivist dimension defines the group orientation and cooperation of people. The power dimension examines whether people accept power differences or strive for egalitarian relations. The uncertainty dimension concerns whether people value rules and stability or are willing to take risks to change how they operate. United States and Japanese companies differ on these three dimensions of teamwork.

Differences in international culture affect the meaning of teams and many teamwork processes. Multicultural teams are more likely to have communication problems because of language differences and differences in communication norms. Decision-making practices, conflict resolution approaches, and support for empowerment are impacted by cultural differences.

Transnational teams are composed of members from different national cultures who deal with problems of global connectivity and local responsiveness for multinational companies. These teams must deal with cultural differences that affect communication and power dynamics while relying on technology for communication. Successful transnational teams tend to spend more time initially developing social relations and team practices in order to create a unifying hybrid team culture.

Team Leader's Challenge 14

You are the manager of the sales staff at a consumer products store that is part of a national chain. The company is very hierarchical and operates following strict, bureaucratic procedures. It is a classic "command and control" organizational culture.

You are concerned that the strict focus on rules and procedures is hurting customer service and relations. Employees seem more concerned about following the rules than they are about pleasing the customers. You believe that shifting to teamwork, with you as team leader rather than manager, would encourage more customer service orientation among the staff. However, you are uncertain whether teamwork is compatible with the organization's culture.

How can you (the manager) create teamwork in an organizational culture that is not team oriented?

What kinds of problems do you expect to encounter using teams in this organizational environment?

How do you handle relations between the team and the larger organization?

SURVEY: INDIVIDUALISM-COLLECTIVISM

Purpose: Understand your position along this important cultural dimension. Individualism-collectivism is considered by many to be the most important dimension for explaining differences among cultures. It also has a direct relationship to teamwork, since it concerns how people view and relate to others. Individualism-collectivism can be analyzed as a perception of oneself or as norms about how to relate to others.

Directions: The following is a list of opposing beliefs. Circle the number that reflects your personal position along the continuum between these opposing beliefs.

1. I enjoy being different from others.   1   2   3   4   5   I enjoy being similar to others.

2. I see myself as independent from others.   1   2   3   4   5   I see myself as part of a social group.

3. I present my personal accomplishments when meeting new people.   1   2   3   4   5   I present my group's accomplishments when meeting new people.

4. It is important for me to act as an independent person.   1   2   3   4   5   It is important for me to be a member of a group.

5. When I have a need, I rely on myself.   1   2   3   4   5   When I have a need, I turn to others for help.

6. If there is a conflict between personal and group values, I follow my personal values.   1   2   3   4   5   If there is a conflict between personal and group values, I follow the values of the group.

7. I do what is enjoyable to me personally.   1   2   3   4   5   I do what the people around me feel is most enjoyable to do.

8. I follow my personal attitudes.   1   2   3   4   5   I follow the group's norms and rules.

9. When making decisions, I am not overly sensitive to the feelings of other people around me.   1   2   3   4   5   I take the feelings of people around me into account when making decisions.

10. I do not hesitate to change my relationships even if it is not in my best interest at the moment to do so.   1   2   3   4   5   I maintain established relationships even if they are not in my best interest anymore.

Scoring:

Add questions 1, 2, 3, 4, and 5 to obtain your score for self-perception of collectivism.

Add questions 6, 7, 8, 9, and 10 to obtain your score for following collectivist social norms.

Discussion: What are the benefits and problems with individualists and collectivists on teams? How similar are members of your team on this dimension? What are the problems with working on teams with people from a strongly collectivist culture?

SOURCE: Adapted from Fisher, R., Ferreira, M., Assmar, E., Redford, P., & Harb, C. (2009). Individualism-collectivism as descriptive norms: Development of a subjective norm approach to culture measurement. *Journal of Cross-Cultural Psychology, 40*(2), 187–213.

ACTIVITY: EVALUATING A TEAM'S CULTURE AND CULTURAL CONTEXT

Objective: Teams have cultures that are similar to and different from the cultures of their organizations and countries. It is essential to understand these cultural differences because teams encounter difficulties when their team cultures are at variance with the cultural context of their organizations or countries. Organizational and international cultures vary on the following four dimensions:

- In control-oriented cultures, leaders attempt to monitor and control the behavior of subordinates, whereas leaders in commitment-oriented cultures are facilitators who guide and motivate subordinates.

- In individualist cultures, people seek individual achievement and recognition, whereas in collectivist cultures people value the ties between themselves and others, and self-interest is subordinate to that of the team.

- In high-power cultures, people show great respect to higher-status people and feel uncomfortable challenging authority. In low-power cultures, people take a more egalitarian view and are less willing to accept authority.

- In risk-avoidance cultures, people value stability and group harmony, whereas people in risk-taking cultures value action and are willing to take risks.

Activity: Discuss with members of an existing team their team's culture and the cultural context for the team. The existing teams can be either work teams or student teams at a university. Use the rating form (Activity Worksheet 14.1) to note the team's culture and its cultural context on the four dimensions.

Analysis: How similar is the team's culture to its cultural context? On which dimensions are there culture gaps? What problems can occur when there are differences between the team's culture and its cultural context?

Discussion: Why is it important for a team's culture to be compatible with its cultural context?

ACTIVITY WORKSHEET 14.1
Evaluating a Team's Culture and Its Cultural Context

Rate the team by placing a "T" on the scale below; rate the cultural context by placing a "C" on the scale.

Commitment Oriented————————————————————Control Oriented

Individualism————————————————————————Collectivism

Low Power————————————————————————————High Power

Risk Taking————————————————————————Risk Avoidance

ACTIVITY: COMPARING UNITED STATES AND JAPANESE TEAMS

Objective: Culture has a major impact on how people act in teams. Cultures do not prevent the use of teams, but they do effect how the teams operate. The impacts of culture create opportunities and problems for teamwork.

United States and Japanese team members differ on the major dimension of international culture. The United States is an individualistic, low-power distance, risk-taking culture; while Japan is a collectivistic, high-power distance, risk avoidance culture.

Activity: Form a group and discuss the benefits and problems with leading a United States versus Japanese team. You could also select other international cultures, such as Mexico or Israel, for comparison.

Analysis: Would you prefer being a team leader of a United States or Japanese team? Why? In what situations or tasks are the different cultures' teams better? How would your management of these cultural teams differ?

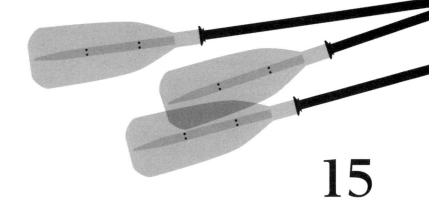

15

Virtual Teamwork

Most of our experience with teams is through face-to-face interactions. However, increasingly we are engaging in virtual teamwork where technology is used for communication and team processes. There are various technologies available for virtual teams. The use of technologies by teams changes how people interact and the dynamics of the group process. Virtual teams offer both benefits and challenges. The available technologies are still evolving, and teams are learning how to select, use, and adapt them to meet their needs. Changes in technology and how it is used may improve the effectiveness of virtual teams in the future.

Learning Objectives

1. What is the difference between the direct effects and secondary effects of a technology?

2. How do communication and collaboration technologies support teamwork?

3. What are the main characteristics used to analyze communication technologies?

4. How do communication technologies affect status, anonymity, and miscommunication?

5. How can communication norms help deal with the communication problems in virtual teams?

6. How are task performance, decision making, and social relations affected by using communication technologies?

7. What factors should be considered when selecting the right technologies for teams?

8. What can be done to improve the performance of virtual teams?

9. How will the performance of virtual teams change in the future? Why?

15.1 Use of Communication Technologies

The availability of communication and collaboration technology has directly led to the creation of virtual teams. A virtual team is any team whose member interactions are mediated by time, distance, and technology (Driskell, Radtke, & Salas, 2003). Communication technologies, such as email and videoconferencing, help teams share information, while collaboration technologies like group support systems help teams solve problems, make decisions, and work together. The use of technology by teams relates to the availability of technology and the operational skills required, the tasks the team needs to perform, and the norms for the use of the technology (Duarte & Snyder, 2006). Although we talk about virtual teams as technology dependent with a lack of collocation, many teams that are collocated rely heavily on technology for communications and still use face-to-face meetings for team interactions (Gibson, Huang, Kirkman, & Shapiro, 2014). Most large companies use virtual teams to some degree, and many teams use technology to support their activities (Hertel, Geister, & Konradt, 2005). International surveys reveal that 46% of all organizations use virtual teams, and in a subset of that sample, 66% of multinational organizations use virtual teams in the workplace (Minton-Eversole, 2012).

Virtuality refers to the degree of electronic communication dependence among team members (Gibson et al., 2014). Various information communication technologies (ICTs) enable different kinds of interactions for teams depending on media richness and synchronicity. Media richness varies from low to high depending on the amount of information that can be transferred through the median (Daft & Lengel, 1986). For example, face-to-face interactions provide rich transfer of social cues, gestures, and non-verbal communication, which ideally suits it to more emotional, complex, and personal conversations. On the other end of the media spectrum, text messages are limited in how well information can be transferred, which led to the development of emojis and emoticons in an attempt to provide additional social context to a message. Somewhere in the middle of this communication range are media-like phone conversations and videoconferences (e.g., Google Hangout, Skype, etc.), which provide more, but not all, of this relevant social information.

Media synchronicity is another aspect of ICTs that influences interactions of team members (Dennis & Valacich, 1999). While synchronous media (e.g., face-to-face communication, teleconference, videoconference, etc.) allow for real time and concurrent participation by all team members and allow for immediate feedback, asynchronous media (e.g., emails, chat messages, etc.) involve temporal gaps in responses, less immediate feedback, and lack of concurrent participation.

Virtuality is a continuum from face-to-face to fully virtual teams, but a three-part classification is useful (Mesmer-Magnus, DeChurch, Jimenez-Rodriguez, Wildman, & Shuffler, 2011). There are face-to-face teams that meet personally. There are low virtuality teams that use synchronous, media-rich technologies like videoconferencing for meetings. Third, there are high virtuality teams that use asynchronous, media-poor technologies like email to communicate. Understanding the degree of a team's virtuality allows skillful members to match the team's needs with the capacities of the various media available for interaction. For example, rich synchronous media are more appropriate for managing conflict and sharing complex information sharing.

Communication technologies have widespread effects on organizations (Axley, 1996). Technology directly affects work design, organizational design, and communication patterns as well as secondary social effects caused by the reduced social cues in the messages (Sproull & Kiesler, 1991). The primary goals of virtual teams are to improve task performance, overcome the constraints of time and space, and increase the range and speed of access to information (McGrath & Hollingshead, 1994). These goals are related to the direct effects of technology.

As with other types of technology, the largest effects of communication and collaboration technology are often the secondary effects, which are the unanticipated social and organizational effects. Because communication plays an important role in maintaining social relations and organizational culture, the lack of social information when using communication technology may limit the development of social relations in a team and organization (Duarte & Snyder, 2006). Although communication technologies structure how people and teams communicate, people do not passively accept the constraints of technology. Instead, they adapt and modify technologies to suit their needs (McGrath & Hollingshead, 1994).

The impact of technology on teams varies with culture and age differences (Tannenbaum, Mathieu, Salas, & Cohen, 2012). Younger team members may prefer using texting and social media, while older team members may prefer face-to-face or telephone communications. Communicating via technology may add to cultural miscommunications because of the lack of nonverbal cues in an email or videoconference.

Communication Technologies and Teams

Communication and collaboration technologies can be used to support teamwork in four different ways (McGrath & Hollingshead, 1994; Mittleman & Briggs, 1999). First, technologies can gather and present information for a team, such as collaborative document management systems and electronic whiteboards. Second, technologies can help team members communicate both internally and externally. Third, collaboration technologies like group support systems can help teams process information by providing systems to structure brainstorming, problem solving, and decision making. Fourth, technologies like electronic meeting systems can be used to structure the group process through meeting agendas, assignment charts, and project management tools.

The use of technology creates new ways for teams to meet and interact. The options for virtual teams are presented in Table 15.1.

Same-time, same-place (STSP) meetings are traditional face-to-face team meetings. Even when a team primarily interacts via technology, there is a value to face-to-face meetings. These are especially important when the team is formed to help establish social relations. Technology does have an impact on team meetings. Group decision support systems help structure meetings, especially for activities, such as brainstorming and voting.

Table 15.1 Types of Meetings Created by Communication Technology

Type of Meeting	Example
STSP—Same-time, same-place meetings	Face-to-face meeting
STDP—Same-time, different-place meetings	Videoconferencing
DTSP—Different-time, same-place meetings	Computer databases
DTDP—Different-time, different-place meetings	Intranet bulletin board/websites

SOURCE: Adapted from Mittleman, D., & Briggs, R. (1999). Communication technologies for traditional and virtual teams. In E. Sundstrom (Ed.), *Supporting work team effectiveness* (pp. 246–270). San Francisco, CA: Jossey-Bass.

Same-time, different-place (STDP) meetings are distributed meetings in which team members interact through a combination of audio, video, or text. Although videoconferencing is the most popular image of STDP technology, it is not necessarily the most useful technology. Electronic meeting systems provide audio with shared data. Participants often prefer being able to manipulate data and images related to the task rather than focusing on images of the other participants.

Different-time, same-place (DTSP) meetings are useful for work teams that exist across different shifts or for teams whose members travel frequently or telecommute. The information technology serves as a storage system so members can pass on information as needed. Project management and other software systems can create a framework for noting the status of a project.

Different-time, different-place (DTDP) meetings are those in which team members share the same virtual space on a website. Technologies, such as online bulletin boards, chat rooms, and databases help support a team's operations. This allows team members to participate in the team process whenever and wherever the opportunity arises.

Characteristics of Communication Technologies

The characteristics of communication methods can be used to analyze the differences among communication technologies (Table 15.2). Axley (1996) uses the following four criteria for evaluating communication methods: speed, reach (number of employees receiving the communication), interactivity, and cue variety (or richness). Reichwald and Goecke (1994) believe that social presence and media richness are the main variables for analyzing communication technologies. Richness relates to the speed of feedback, the number and type of sensory channels, and the degree to which the source seems personal. Social presence refers to the degree to which using the technology resembles the experience of communicating with another person. This factor often relates to the richness of the communication media.

Another characteristic of many communication technologies is the ability to document the message. These electronic records have important task and social impacts (Sproull & Kiesler, 1991). For example, the capability of communication technologies to document a message may inhibit managers from using them for fear of recording errors. It makes email messages sent to team members valuable task reminders, since the messages can be printed or stored.

An essential factor in analyzing the effectiveness of team communication is the richness of the communication (Daft & Lengel, 1986). The effectiveness of a communication technology depends on the fit between the task requirements and the richness of the technology. A task requiring the team to generate ideas requires only the transmission of the ideas,

Table 15.2   Analysis of Communication Methods

Method	Speed	Interactive	Richness	Social Presence	Document Message
Face-to-face	Slow	High	High	High	No
Group meeting	Slow	Moderate	High	High	No
Instant messaging	Fast	High	Low	Low	Yes
Email	Fast	Moderate	Low	Low	Yes
Team website	Moderate	Low	Low	Low	Yes
Print	Moderate	Low	Low	Low	Yes
Group support system	Moderate	Moderate	Low	Low	Yes
Computer databases	Moderate	Low	Low	Low	Yes
Videoconference	Fast	Moderate	High	Moderate	No

SOURCE: Adapted from Levi, D., & Rinzel, L. (1998). Employee attitudes toward various communications technologies when used for communicating about organizational change. In P. Vink, E. Koningsveld, & S. Dhondt (Eds.), *Human factors in organizational design and management* (Vol. 6, pp. 483–488). Amsterdam: Elsevier Science.

whereas negotiating a conflict requires processing the emotional contexts of the messages. The messages need to include the facts as well as the emotions of the participants.

Information richness has both positive and negative effects (Duarte & Snyder, 2006). One reason that face-to-face groups are not as good as virtual teams for brainstorming is that the richness of the communication media gets in the way. In brainstorming, the presence of others is a distraction from the task. It is inefficient to use a medium that is too rich. However, it is ineffective to use a medium that is not rich enough. The level of uncertainty in the communication increases the importance of information richness; this is why technologies like email are not good for tasks like negotiation.

15.2 Communication Impacts

When people communicate via technology, their communication is altered. Communication technologies change how status is perceived, the level of anonymity of the communicators, and the amount of miscommunication. Some of these changes are due to a lack of norms for managing the communication process rather than to the technology.

Status Differences

One of the main differences between face-to-face teams and virtual teams is status differences. Research on student groups shows that status differences are reduced in virtual teams (Parks & Sanna, 1999). The reduction in status equalizes participation in virtual team discussions. In face-to-face team discussions, a few dominant people with higher status talk the most; many team members limit their discussion and primarily support the main positions that emerge. In virtual decision making, the interaction is more democratic. Social cues are reduced, and people communicate on the basis of their knowledge or opinions rather than on their social status.

Not all research on virtual teams had this equalization effect. In a typical work team, higher-status members assume leadership positions, direct team activities, and are more likely to express their opinion (Driskell et al., 2003). They demonstrate status by their responsiveness to messages, with subordinates responding more quickly to messages from superiors. Virtual teams may limit the effects of status because status cues are not as prevalent as they are in face-to-face communications. However, in actual work settings, team members are aware of the status of the other communicators regardless of the technology. Field studies on existing teams with established status hierarchies (such as the military or medical teams) show no communication change related to the use of technology.

Status differences have a mixed effect on performance (Driskell & Salas, 2006). When status differences reflect actual differences in ability or competence, then it is desirable for higher status individuals to be more influential. However, when status is based on irrelevant factors like cultural stereotypes, then status disrupts the ability of teams to make good decisions. Over time, the effects of status on a team's communications tend to decrease as members get to know one another better and communication becomes linked more to knowledge than to status.

Anonymity

The members of virtual groups are more anonymous. This leads to what psychologists call deindividuation, which is the loss of self-awareness and evaluation apprehension caused by feeling anonymous. It has a number of negative social effects (Parks & Sanna, 1999). For example, people are more likely to engage in social loafing in teams when they feel anonymous.

One of the impacts of anonymity on virtual teams is that people are more willing to say things they would not say in face-to-face interactions. This is why "flaming" (uninhibited negative remarks) occurs in electronic bulletin boards and emails. Although flaming or other types of disinhibited emotional communication occur in laboratory studies, it is not a typical problem with work teams that are less anonymous (Hertel et al., 2005). Most virtual teams develop communication norms that regulate emotional communications.

Anonymity creates less pressure to conform in virtual teams (Mesmer-Magnus et al., 2011). Lack of social pressure affects how teams manage conflict and make decisions. Virtual teams often have higher levels of conflict and are less able to resolve conflicts and reach consensus in decision-making situations. These effects are partially due to the lack of social pressure that would normally increase people's willingness to agree and seek compromises during disagreements.

There are also positive impacts on virtual teams because of increased anonymity (Duarte & Snyder, 2006). When anonymous group support systems are used to generate ideas for problem solving and decision making, team members are more willing to participate and generate more ideas. Electronic brainstorming generates more creative ideas than face-to-face brainstorming.

Miscommunication

Virtual teams often have increased conflict because of misunderstandings and reduced communication (Hertel et al., 2005). These communication problems increase the emotional frustration of people working in virtual teams. This is one reason why the effectiveness and member satisfaction of virtual teams is positively related to the level of personal communications among team members. Many of these problems go away as teams learn how to interpret communications from other team members.

Virtual teams have difficulty establishing and maintaining mutual knowledge (Driskell et al., 2003). They lack contextual cues during communications: This leaves members less certain about the people with whom they are interacting, unsure how the message is being conveyed, and unclear as to whether the communication is successful. It is more difficult to know whether fellow members of virtual teams have adequately understood a communication. Facial cues and nonverbal feedback reduce the uncertainty one feels with a communication. Without this information, inaccuracies and confusion can occur that reduce team performance.

For example, the reduced social cues in email messages make it difficult to communicate emotions, but people are often unaware of this problem and believe they are communicating effectively. Email readers often cannot tell whether the writer is attempting to be sarcastic or funny (Kruger, Epley, Parker, & Ng, 2005). A writer's overconfidence in his or her ability to communicate via email is a cause of miscommunication in virtual teams.

Miscommunications using technology can cause people to make faulty assumptions about the characteristics of the communicator (Vignovic & Thompson, 2010). This misinterpretation can be especially important when the teams communicate across cultures. In a laboratory study, email messages were sent that either contained technical language errors (spelling or grammar) or etiquette errors (short messages without conversational tone). Grammar and spelling errors led recipients to believe the sender lacked intelligence and conscientiousness, while etiquette errors caused the recipients to believe the sender lacked extroversion, agreeableness, and trustworthiness. When told that the sender was from another culture, recipients forgave the technical errors (they assumed the errors were due to culture and not personality), but did not forgive the etiquette errors.

The problems of miscommunication also occur in videoconferencing. When people are videoconferencing, they can also be multitasking outside of the other person's view (Turkle, 2011). It does not require the full attention of face-to-face interaction. Although you can see each other, you cannot make eye contact. It does not have the interactive quality of a face-to-face communication because of limited nonverbal cues. Although there are some advantages of videoconferencing over the telephone, it mainly just matches the face to a name and is not the best medium for reading nonverbal cues (Hambley, O'Neill, & Kline, 2007).

Communication through some media can also distort or attenuate some patterns of communication. For example, poorer audio quality over phone or videoconferencing may distort accents and make communication more difficult for other members to understand, while these distortions may be alleviated through nonverbal channels like email or text (Gibson et al., 2014). Indeed, those who are socially anxious or are nonnative speakers of a language may prefer to express themselves nonverbally through text-based email or forums.

Communication Norms

With experience, many virtual teams overcome their communication problems and operate as effectively as face-to-face teams. This is due to the development of social relations that help interpret the communications from other team members and the use of communication norms that improve team communications (Vignovic & Thompson, 2010).

The use of email, videoconferencing, and other communication technologies have led to a number of etiquette errors caused by lack of established communication norms. Senders of email messages often treat them like telephone calls (e.g., informal, private, no record), whereas receivers may treat them as letters (e.g., formal and public messages that can be copied and redistributed). Senders are often shocked and sometimes embarrassed when their private email messages are distributed to others. New users often show bad form by distributing "junk" news to people who do not care about it, writing overlong messages, or trying to be funny. Emotions are difficult for many people to put in writing (Kruger et al., 2005). In email messages, emotions seem to get out of control easily, and interpersonal conflicts may arise that are primarily due to miscommunication. The solution is the development of communication norms for the technologies.

Communication norms can help both high and low virtual teams (Duarte & Snyder, 2006). Email norms identify when email should be used to communicate, how the message should be constructed (use of capital letters, abbreviations), timeliness of responses, and who should receive messages. For example, a team may have a rule limiting the size of email messages or a rule controlling the use of distribution lists. Norms also identify when not to use email. To limit conflicts, one important norm is to never send an email when you are upset or in an emotional state. Email should not be used to resolve interpersonal issues or to avoid personal interactions.

Norms can help improve communications in videoconferences. When participants start a videoconference, they should announce their presence. Team members need to identify themselves when speaking. Side conversations during a videoconference are to be avoided. If you are having a problem hearing or understanding someone, you should notify the speaker.

15.3 Team Impacts

When teams depend on technology for communication, it changes how they perform. The impacts on team performance depend on the type of task. Decision making and the development of social relations are impacted. Many of these performance differences are reduced as people become more experienced working in virtual teams.

Task Performance in Virtual Teams

From an individual's perspective, the advantages of virtual teams include flexibility, control over time, and empowerment of team members

(Hertel et al., 2005). However, there are disadvantages, such as isolation, decreased interpersonal contact, and increased miscommunication and conflict. Overall, the performance of face-to-face and virtual teams is fairly similar (Parks & Sanna, 1999). This is especially true if experienced users are being studied. Many of the disadvantages of virtual teams diminish when teams have time to adjust to using the technology.

Although there are few overall differences in performance, some tasks are better suited to virtual teams (Hertel et al., 2005). Virtual teams are more successful on idea generation and problem-solving tasks in which the team must organize information to find the correct answers. However, virtual teams perform poorly on decision-making and negotiation tasks where the goal is to reach consensus. For decision-making tasks, virtual teams take more time, exchange less information, and have lower member satisfaction than face-to-face teams. Most organizations prefer to use face-to-face communication for negotiation tasks because of the difficulty in reaching consensus in virtual teams.

Again, brainstorming is the chief example of improved performance from virtual groups (Parks & Sanna, 1999). Virtual brainstorming groups achieve better ratings on all criteria. More ideas are generated, and the ideas tend to be of higher quality. In addition, people prefer to brainstorm using computers. Unlike face-to-face groups, the virtual brainstorming process is not disrupted by larger group size. The anonymity of virtual groups is a benefit in brainstorming because people are less concerned about criticism of their ideas. The only problem with virtual brainstorming in large groups is social loafing, but this occurs in large face-to-face groups as well.

Virtual teams have several problems that are greater than face-to-face teams (Duarte & Snyder, 2006). Trust is more important in the operation of virtual teams and more difficult to create. Building social relations among team members is more difficult. Conflicts are more difficult to detect and harder to resolve in virtual teams.

To see some of the positive and negative impacts of communication technology on teams, the next sections examine decision making and social relations in virtual teams.

Decision Making

One of the most consistent findings regarding the differences in decision making between virtual and face-to-face teams is that less information is communicated in virtual teams (Roch & Ayman, 2005). There are trade-offs in the value of face-to-face versus virtual team communications (Mesmer-Magnus et al., 2011). Virtual teams are better than face-to-face teams at sharing unique information, even though they have overall lower levels of information sharing. Virtual teams also outperform face-to-face teams in idea generation and decision making (Rains, 2005). Face-to-face communication offers easier coordination, allows reading of nonverbal cues, and helps build trust and social relations. Face-to-face communication is also associated with greater levels of consensus, efficiency, and communication (Rains, 2005). Virtual team communications are less inhibited by social norms and group pressure, allow multiple communications to occur (no waiting), may be more convenient (no scheduling problems for meetings), and provide a record of the communication.

During team decisions, members of virtual teams are more focused on the logic and factual basis of the arguments than on the social characteristics of the people making the arguments (Roch & Ayman, 2005). They are less likely to be distracted by irrelevant social information, such as gender, age, and race, that may lead to biased interpretations of the communication. This allows virtual team members to better judge the abilities of other members. Virtual teams are better at weighing the quality of the opinions of individual members and using this information in a group decision.

The asynchronous aspect of high virtual teams has some communication advantages (Mesmer-Magnus et al., 2011). Because members have time to think about their response, they are more likely to research what they want to communicate. More people are able to participate in the communication process because they do not have to wait their turn in a team discussion. There are fewer status cues in the communication environment, and team members are less influenced by social pressure. These aspects encourage the sharing of unique information among team members.

The effects of more open communication of information—that is, how overtly information is shared with all members—and the sharing of unique information have differential impacts on team performance (Mesmer-Magnus et al., 2011). The sharing of unique information in virtual teams strongly relates to creativity, problem solving, and overall team performance. Unique information sharing is more important than overall information sharing in predicting team performance. However, the openness of communication in face-to-face teams relates to both team performance and team satisfaction and cohesion.

Social Relations

People are less likely to be satisfied working in a virtual group than in a face-to-face group (Parks & Sanna, 1999). They may feel a lack of social support and experience increased stress working in a virtual team. Some of these negative effects are likely to disappear over time (McGrath & Hollingshead, 1994). Virtual work teams improve as they become more accustomed to using the technology, develop group norms for working together, and develop social relations that improve communication.

Virtual teams have a difficult time developing social relations and team cohesion (Driskell et al., 2003). Members of virtual teams are more anonymous, which leads to weaker relational ties and less team identification. Because of the limited ability to convey emotions via technology, it is more difficult for virtual teams to develop trust among members (Penarroja, Orengo, Zornoza, & Hernandez, 2013). Even in videoconferencing, the reduced emotional and social information impedes understanding the meaning of other team members' communications, which limits the development of trust. Virtual teams tend to be task focused, and often do not spend enough time on the social communications that are necessary for the development of trust and team cohesion.

Teams that have already developed good social relations may be more effective working in virtual teams. Occasional face-to-face meetings are needed to develop and support the social relations among members. When team members have never met personally, they are less effective using communication technology for difficult problems, because they have not developed the ability to "read" the emotional meanings of member communications.

It is essential to take a life-cycle approach to understanding the social impacts of using virtual teams (Hertel et al., 2005). The impact of technology varies depending on stage of the team. When new teams are created, a face-to-face meeting is important for team members to get acquainted with one another, clarify the team goals and member roles, and develop norms for operation. Virtual teams encounter a number of team maintenance problems. For instance, it may be more difficult to motivate virtual teams and control social loafing, create trust among members, and develop team cohesion and identification. Because of this, member satisfaction in virtual teams depends on the opportunities to meet face-to-face and exchange non-work-related personal information.

15.4 Selecting the Right Technology

Virtual teams have a variety of available technologies to use. Teams may have problems if they fail to consider whether the technology matches the requirements of a given task. However, some tasks like negotiating conflicts are difficult for virtual teams, regardless of the technology used.

Factors to Consider When Selecting Technology

Although there are many technologies available to support virtual teams, team members rarely use the sophisticated collaboration technologies (Zigurs & Khazanchi, 2008), and still rely primarily on email. There is no one best technology for virtual teams. The best technology depends on characteristics of the task, the team, team members, and the group process.

The acceptance of a communication technology depends on the characteristics of the team members and the social relations within the team. Team members' willingness to use technologies like teleconferencing systems is dependent on many personal factors: anxiety about using the systems, self-confidence about system knowledge and applications, and institutional supports, such as training and technical assistance (Park, Rhoads, Hou, & Lee, 2014). Preferences in communication technology also depend on attitudes toward the communicator (Levi & Rinzel, 1998). When the source of the communication is seen as trustworthy, almost any communication medium is acceptable to the team; however, when it is not viewed as trustworthy then face-to-face or other information-rich communication is required to evaluate the truthfulness of the message.

There are several theories that propose preferred technologies for virtual teams (Zigurs & Khazanchi, 2008). The media richness theory supports richer technologies (those with feedback, multiple cues, and personal focus) in order to better process equivocal information and facilitate understanding. Adaptive structure theory notes that team members develop new structures and processes to facilitate use of the available technology. Task-technology fit theory advocates that teams use different types of technology depending on the tasks performed. The issue is not whether a particular technology is good or bad for teamwork, but what pattern of technology use is best for the tasks a team is performing (Tannenbaum et al., 2012).

Powerful (or rich) multimedia communication technologies might not be the best for all tasks (Dertouzos, 1997). For example, because contracts require specific wording and the ability to store and study documents, print may always be the preferred communication medium. Videoconferencing can be distracting to users. Adding audio to a virtual team may improve communications by better conveying the social and emotional aspects of communication (Driskell et al., 2003). However, there seems to be limited benefit to videoconferencing compared to electronic meeting systems that provide audioconferencing and the ability to work on shared documents. In some cases, team members turn off the pictures during videoconferences in order to avoid distractions and to concentrate on the documents under discussion.

Virtual teams adapt and modify communication technologies to fit their needs. Teams need to be aware of the impacts of using communications technology and need to develop guidelines to operate effectively with the technology (Tannenbaum et al., 2012). Team members need to know when to be connected and how quickly to respond to communications. The negative impacts of technology on teams are decreasing because of the increase of rich forms of technology like videoconferencing; increased experience using communication technology in teams; and increased use of technology in other aspects of people's professional and personal lives. Because of the increased number of technology options and the more personal and professional member experience, teams are better at adapting the technology to fit their requirements.

Virtual teams select different technologies for different types of team tasks (Parks & Sanna, 1999). Email or texting is used to keep team members informed and share information, but rarely for negotiation and decision making. Videoconferencing is useful for discussing issues and listening to presentations. Shared databases are used to coordinate working on the technical aspects of projects, while social media may be used to develop and maintain social relations. Project management software is used so team members can monitor one another's performances and manage projects as teams. Group support systems are collaboration technologies designed to support virtual meetings and teamwork. The types of team tasks that collaboration technologies deal with include idea generation, alternative selection, clarification and organization of ideas, evaluation of alternatives, and building consensus (Briggs, Kolfschoten, Vreede, & Dean, 2006).

Matching Technology to the Team and Task

Different types of teams have different communication needs, so the right technology to use depends on the type of team (Bikson, Cohen, & Mankin, 1999; Mittleman & Briggs, 1999). Production teams use information technology to coordinate activities, track work progress, and analyze production information. Service teams are dependent on communication technologies and shared databases to coordinate their activities and access information about customers and products. Communications technology allows project teams to form without regard to place, offering the ability to include members with crucial skills who in the past simply by virtue of their location could not otherwise be on the team. Group support systems help project teams perform a variety of team processes. Management teams tend to rely on videoconferencing because of their preference for face-to-face rather than written communication.

Table 15.3 shows the match between technology and some team processes (Duarte & Snyder, 2006). There are several important points to consider. First, all the technologies are at least somewhat useful for the tasks. Even when there is not a perfect fit, experienced virtual team members can adapt the technology for the task. Second, group support systems have specialized functions for some tasks, such as electronic brainstorming and structured decision making. This specialization makes them very useful when the team's task is one of these functions. Third, no technology is very useful for negotiating conflicts, especially when the conflicts are highly emotional. Although conflict can be managed using technology, unproductive interpersonal conflict is harder to detect and manage in virtual teams.

There may be limits to the ability of virtual teams to fully adapt (Hambley, O'Neill, & Kline, 2007). Virtual teams are highly task focused, which is useful in the short run. However, virtual teams have difficulty establishing trust and developing social relations. This lack of social development creates communication problems. Virtual team members do not learn how to "read" the emotions in each other's communication and do not develop a sense of mutual trust. Without social development, virtual teams may become mired in conflict and failed negotiations because of miscommunication. Additionally, team members who use computer-mediated communication for over

Table 15.3   Match Between Technology and Team Processes

Technology	Generating Ideas and Sharing Information	Routine Problems and Decisions	Complex Problems and Decisions	Negotiating Conflicts
Instant messaging and email	Useful	Useful	Somewhat useful	Somewhat useful
Team website	Useful	Useful	Somewhat useful	Somewhat useful
Group support systems	Very useful	Very useful	Useful	Somewhat useful
Video-conferencing	Somewhat useful	Useful	Useful	Somewhat useful

SOURCE: Adapted from Duarte, D., & Snyder, N. (2006). *Mastering Virtual Teams* (3rd ed.). San Francisco: Jossey-Bass.

90% of their interactions reported significantly lower levels of effectiveness, commitment, and harmony (Johnson, Bettenhausen, & Gibbons, 2009).

15.5 Challenge of Virtual Teams

The two main challenges facing virtual teams are dealing with communications problems and creating effective interpersonal relationships (Thompson & Coovert, 2006). Miscommunications are more common in virtual teams; they create more problems because virtual teams have a difficult time identifying and correcting communication problems. Virtual team members typically communicate less frequently with each other and are more likely to suffer from diminished social relations (Priest, Stagl, Klein, & Salas, 2006).

Although researchers once believed that increased use of videoconferencing would reduce communication problems, videoconferencing has had only a limited impact on improving communication in virtual teams (Thompson & Coovert, 2006). Even though videoconferencing is a highly rich communication medium, it cannot compensate for the lack of informal social encounters that occur when teams are located together. Addressing the challenges of virtual teams requires new approaches to team building. Changes in technology, people, and interaction styles may help virtual teams function more effectively in the future.

Team Building in Virtual Teams

There are a number of strategies for improving the operation of virtual teams, including more time to deal with problems, face-to-face initial meetings, the use of instant communication channels, development of operating structures and communication norms, better training, and appropriate leadership (Thompson & Coovert, 2006). These strategies deal with communication problems by better managing the task and creating alternative communication opportunities to improve social relations. Developing trust among team members is the foundation for both task and social communication in virtual teams.

Virtual teams follow a developmental process similar to other types of teams (Haines, 2014). In the early stages of virtual team development, the objective is to develop a structure that allows the team to operate effectively later. This includes clarifying roles and responsibilities and establishing trust among team members. The developmental sequence in virtual teams is to create a sense of belonging to the team, which encourages commitment to the team's goals, which helps to develop trust among team members. This sequence sets the stage for later team performance.

The effects of leadership on virtual teams is important because these teams have challenges that make leading them more difficult than face-to-face teams (Huang, Kahai, & Jestice, 2010). Virtual teams start with lower levels of cohesion and trust among members. They often do not have a shared set of norms and work procedures. Since they are located in different places, it is more difficult for team members to view themselves as part of a team. Technology constraints on communication create confusion about taskwork and limit development of social relations.

The standard approaches to team leadership may not be effective in overcoming these barriers to team performance (Hoch & Kozlowski, 2014). Leaders do not have the option to easily monitor and supervise team members. Consequently, virtual teams need to focus on empowering individual team members to perform. Higher performing virtual teams have members that display more leadership behaviors, especially behaviors related to keeping track of the team's work and performance (Carte, Chidambaram, & Becker, 2006). Leaders of virtual teams also need to take a more active role in developing the social aspects of teamwork.

Virtual teams need to have periodic face-to-face meetings in order to function effectively (Dube & Robey, 2008). They require kick-off meetings at the beginning of a project and then periodic meetings during project milestones. Virtual teams need more structure, such as clear objectives and detailed plans, so that team members can monitor their own behavior and more easily coordinate with others. They need norms that regulate communications and define appropriate netiquette; a well-defined structure and periodic meetings are needed to ensure coordination and collaboration because most of the work is done individually.

One of the problems with virtual teams is developing and maintaining social relations (Dube & Robey, 2008). Often, virtual team meetings are entirely focused on communicating task-related information. Periodic face-to-face meetings that include social activities are helpful for building social relations. In addition, team members can be encouraged to informally communicate with each other on a regular basis using technology. Maintaining social ties using information technology is an appropriate business use of the technology.

Cross-cultural communication problems are more likely in virtual teams because virtual teams are often used to connect team members in different countries (Vignovic & Thompson, 2010). Culturally heterogeneous virtual teams tend to experience more conflict and lower levels of cohesion and satisfaction compared to culturally homogenous groups (Staples & Zhao, 2006). However, the negative effects of culture were attenuated when teams only had short-term projects. This suggests that the negative effects of culturally diverse teams may not be present at the beginning of a team, but emerge later on. Additionally, norms of emotion display can differ between culturally heterogeneous and homogenous teams—one study shows that culturally diverse teams tend to display more positive emotions and suppress negative emotions compared to culturally homogenous teams (Glikson & Erez, 2013).

One approach for dealing with these communication problems is to help team members recognize the cultural differences that may be causing the problems. For example, IBM has a social networking site for employees (called "BluePages") so that employees can recognize professional, language, and cultural differences. Other approaches to cross-cultural issues include explicit development of communication norms and training in communication methods for virtual teams.

It is a challenge to develop trust in a virtual team (Priest et al., 2006). Trust is often developed through social relations, but this is difficult to do in a virtual team. Additionally, virtual teams may be particularly prone to sub-grouping, leading to in-group favoritism and out-group discrimination in the form of biased information sharing and conflict between subgroups (Yilmaz & Peña, 2014). Trust in virtual teams is often based on meeting performance expectations, primarily from early team experiences. Team leaders can encourage trust by dividing the project into defined tasks, establishing clear performance expectations, and monitoring their completion. Periodic meetings that review performance help ensure that team members remain trustworthy. Additionally, encouraging a supportive communication climate and fostering psychological safety have been shown to overcome many of the barriers to virtual interaction (Gibson & Gibbs, 2006).

Future of Virtual Teams

Most virtual teams rely on email and occasional videoconferences to coordinate their work (Dube & Robey, 2008). Although virtual teams have unique challenges, over time these teams often develop effective ways to perform. Virtual teams will evolve in the future because of changes in technology, the characteristics of new employees, and the development of new types of social interactions.

New technologies, such as project management software and discussion forums, could help improve coordination of tasks in teams. Most of the research on groupware (the software and technology that supports teams) examines email and videoconferencing (Driskell & Salas, 2006). Unfortunately, up to now groupware development focuses on technological issues rather than group dynamics. As a result, it is primarily individual communication technology that has been adapted for use by teams rather than a technology designed to deal with specific team issues.

One option for the future of virtual teams is the development of virtual reality environments for teams (Priest et al., 2006). Virtual reality can be used to create a team environment where team members can "meet" in a virtual space. This creates a rich media environment for interacting. Research on simulation-based training shows that it can create a sense of involvement, immersion, and presence. This technique may help compensate for the reduced personal experience in virtual teams.

The new generation of workers is more comfortable using a variety of communication technologies and more comfortable forming and maintaining social relationships via technology (Dube & Robey, 2008). From childhood, they have established social relations through communication technologies, such as online gaming and Internet pen pals. They frequently use cell phones and instant messaging for maintaining social connections. Consequently, the younger generation should have less trouble in virtual teams forming social relations and developing trust compared to the older generation.

One of the problems with virtual teams is the lack of informal interactions (Thompson & Coovert, 2006). It is the informal interactions and chance encounters of daily worklife that help build interpersonal relationships and create a solid team identity. The use of more informal and social communication technologies may help deal with this problem. Instant messaging, chat rooms, and other informal communications technologies can allow team members to share their work experience. Facebook and other social networking technologies can help create a social identity for the team. The simple act of sharing of photos by team members can help develop social connections within virtual teams.

Creating team connections via instant messaging or chat rooms can help simulate the informal social interactions of collocated teams (Thompson & Coovert, 2006). When chat room connections are kept open, teams create a virtual environment that is similar to a physical work environment where casual conversations can occur at any time. Users of instant messaging often adopt an informal communication style that is similar to social conversation in person. It leads to briefer communications that are more informal and that occur more often, which is similar to the informal communications that occur in "brick and mortar" work environments.

Summary

The use of communication and collaboration technologies has expanded rapidly and is changing how teams operate. The new technologies increase access to information, support internal and external communication, and help teams manage their task and group processes. Virtual team meetings are no longer constrained by time or place. Differences among communication technologies are related to their speed, interactivity, richness, and ability to document communications.

Communicating via technology has interpersonal effects. Status differences are reduced, and interactions are spread more evenly among participants. People are more anonymous in virtual groups, which can increase negative or emotional messages. Reduction in social and emotional cues increases the chances for miscommunication. Many of these effects reflect the insufficiency of communication norms for regulating behavior.

Virtual teams differ from face-to-face teams. The former perform better on idea generation and problem-solving tasks, but worse on decision-making and negotiation tasks. However, overall team performance is often similar for experienced teams. Although less information is exchanged when virtual teams are making decisions, decision making is sometimes improved in virtual teams because of increased willingness of team members to share unique information. One of the greatest problems for virtual teams is developing trust and social relations among members.

Selecting the right communication technology depends on the characteristics of the technology, task, and team. The most advanced technology may not be the best, given that rich technologies can be distracting. Over time, teams adapt to communication technologies through modification of technologies and the development of new communication norms and procedures. It is important for teams to select the communication and collaboration technologies that are best suited for the task. However, some tasks like negotiating conflicts are difficult to carry out using communication technology.

The two main challenges facing virtual teams are dealing with communications problems and creating effective interpersonal relationships. There are a variety of team-building approaches to help teams deal with these problems. The effectiveness of virtual teams may improve in the future because of the increased use of technology for informal, social communications.

Team Leader's Challenge 15

You are the leader of a virtual team that is coordinating research projects among your corporation's five research centers, distributed around the world. Although you had a coordinators' meeting several years ago, cost and time constraints make it impossible to regularly meet in person. The research centers have videoconferencing equipment, but time differences among the sites make the use of videoconferencing services difficult. Consequently, most of your team's communication is done via email.

The virtual team has worked well at exchanging information and keeping everyone up to date on the progress of research. However, there is a growing conflict between one of the U.S. research centers and the Asian center; they seem to be unable to coordinate activities and negotiate project roles. Their emails are getting more critical and disrespectful, and the rest of the team is tired of reading their back-and-forth bickering.

How can you (the team leader) deal with this communication problem?

Does the solution require either face-to-face or videoconference meetings?

Why might videoconferencing not be as effective as a face-to-face meeting in this situation?

Could establishing new technology communication norms be used to prevent such problems in the future?

ACTIVITY: DEVELOPING NETIQUETTE FOR VIRTUAL TEAMS

Objective: Virtual teams need to develop different norms to regulate team interactions. Norms for virtual teams are sometimes called "netiquette rules."

Activity: Develop a set of norms for a virtual team (Activity Worksheet 15.1). These norms should cover communication, participation, and decision making. What other types of norms are needed to help a virtual team operate effectively? You should try developing norms for the use of email, texting, telephones, and videoconferencing.

Analysis: How do the norms differ for the different types of technology? How are technology communication norms different from face-to-face meeting norms?

Discussion: What are the advantages and disadvantages of virtual teams? Can the development of new norms improve how virtual teams operate? What other actions should be taken to support the use of virtual teams?

ACTIVITY WORKSHEET 15.1
Norms for Virtual Teams

Communication Norms:

Participation/Response Norms:

Decision-Making/Conflict Resolution Norms:

Other Team Norms:

ACTIVITY: EXPERIENCING TEAMWORK IN A SIMULATED VIRTUAL TEAM

Objective: Virtual teams often rely on email for their communications, but performing team tasks using only written communications is more difficult than using face-to-face communications.

Activity: Create three teams. For the first team, divide the members into two separate rooms and have them perform a teamwork task by sending written messages or texting. For the second team, divide the members into two separate rooms and have them perform a teamwork task talking on their cell phones. For the third team, have them meet together face-to-face to perform a teamwork task. The task could be solving a problem, making a decision, or planning an event.

Analysis: Compare the experiences of performing tasks using written versus cell phone versus face-to-face communication. How effective and enjoyable were these approaches?

Discussion: What are the problems created by the reliance on communication technology for teams? What types of tasks are best suited for different communication technologies?

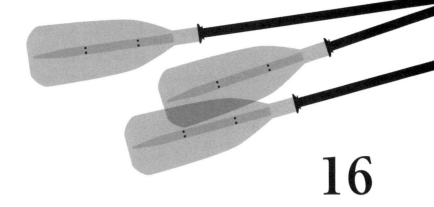

16

Evaluating and Rewarding Teams

An important way to motivate teams is through performance evaluation and reward programs. Performance evaluations communicate to the team how well it is performing. This information may be used to provide direction, motivate performance, and inform the organization's reward system. Team members should participate in the evaluation process, given that they are most aware of the contributions of individual team members.

The shift to teamwork often requires organizations to change the way they reward people. The individual reward programs used in traditional organizations may not reward commitment and participation in teams. Organizations can use combinations of individual, team, and organizational rewards to motivate teams. The best reward program depends on the nature of the task and the type of team.

Learning Objectives

1. How does the performance evaluation system affect teamwork?

2. What are the characteristics of a good team performance evaluation system?

3. What are the advantages of using multirater performance evaluations?

4. How do biases (such as the team halo effect) influence the evaluation process?

5. Why do organizations need to change their reward systems to support teamwork?

6. What are the advantages and disadvantages of individual versus team rewards?

7. What are the main types of individual, team, and organizational rewards that are useful for teams?

8. How does the best type of reward program relate to the type of team?

16.1 Team Performance Evaluations

Team performance evaluations provide feedback to the team to improve the way it operates; they may be linked to rewards to motivate team members. Organizations may evaluate individual team members, the operation of the entire team, or combinations of individual and team. Performance evaluation measures need to be specific and clear, to be identified in advance, and need to relate to behaviors under members' control. The evaluation process should include participation from both supervisors and team members. Although participating in the evaluation process creates biases, multirater evaluations increase the accuracy and acceptance of evaluations.

Developing a team-oriented performance evaluation system and using the information to provide feedback is an important way to improve team operation (Mohrman, Cohen, & Mohrman, 1995). Teams use feedback from performance evaluations to identify and correct problems in operations. In addition, performance evaluations are used to measure the team's success and provide input to the organization's reward system, which motivates the team to better performance.

Performance evaluations are valuable for providing feedback to employees, motivating them, and supporting training and development. Unfortunately, the evaluation process often creates conflict and leads to dissatisfaction rather than motivation and development. Because of this potential for conflict, managers and employees try to avoid conducting performance evaluations. Managers may feel uncomfortable giving feedback to subordinates, and most employees believe their performance is above average so they resent being criticized, even if it is constructive criticism (Lawler, 2000).

Types of Evaluations

Three main approaches to team performance evaluation are traditional individual evaluations, team member evaluations, and evaluations of the team

(Lawler, 2000). In traditional evaluations, the supervisor appraises an individual employee. This evaluation is tied to the organization's compensation system. Performance evaluations are typically done this way in most organizations. In the second approach, team member evaluations, team members instead of a supervisor conduct the performance evaluation. The third approach, evaluations of the team, is used when the work of a team is highly interdependent. Because it may be impossible to evaluate employees individually, the supervisor instead of team members evaluates the operation of the entire team.

There are several factors that affect which type of performance evaluation is appropriate for a circumstance (Lawler, 2000). From a teamwork perspective, the most important factor is work design. Individual evaluations are most appropriate for individual work assignments. When work is highly interdependent or conducted primarily in a team, individual evaluation approaches are not appropriate and may discourage cooperation in the team. However, the type of evaluation used often depends on how the organization operates. Most traditional organizations rely on individual performance evaluations linked to compensation programs, even when employees primarily work in teams.

For some teams, such as sports and action teams, evaluations may include both individual and team performance measures. Individual performance measures relate to the organization's reward system and provide information useful for identifying the assistance needed for specific individuals. For other teams, such as production and project teams, evaluations may measure only the team's performance because of the difficulty in accurately measuring individual performance distinct from team performance.

Types of Measures

The key to developing a good measurement system is making certain that it captures both team and organizational goals. A lack of clear team goals and accountability is one of the main reasons for the failure of work teams (Jones & Moffett, 1999). Team performance measurements should relate to contributions to the organization. It is necessary to ensure the measurements relate to factors that the team has the ability to influence (Zigon, 1997). The measures should focus on the results of the team's performance not on the internal activities of the team, because the team should be free to accomplish its goals in its own way.

Performance evaluations are improved when specific, quantifiable goals are set for the team, and these are identified in advance (Lawler, 2000). To make the performance evaluation process fair and to motivate performance, people need to know, in advance, how their performance will be measured and the acceptable levels of performance. Without goals and accurate measurement criteria, team members cannot know how to act to receive positive evaluations. It is useful to include team members in the development of the performance evaluation system. This increases understanding of the evaluation measures and acceptance of the evaluation process.

Many performance evaluations systems fail because the measures are vague or poorly defined (Lawler, 2000). Rather than evaluating traits, such as reliability, cooperativeness, or leadership, when defining the evaluation structure it is better to use behavioral or outcome-based measures that can be quantified and clearly defined. For example, instead of using a trait like cooperativeness, evaluate based on the frequency of participation in team meetings or the frequency of providing assistance to team members. Vague measures are more vulnerable to stereotypes and other perceptual biases.

When developing a team performance evaluation system, one basic alternative is to use behavioral measures versus the results of performance (Rynes, Gerhart, & Parks, 2005). Behavioral performance measures have advantages: They can be used for any type of job. The rater can deal with factors outside the employee's control that impact results. And they can encourage positive employee behaviors (like cooperation) that are not directly related to the job. Although results-based evaluations are more objective, high-quality objective measures are unavailable for many teams. Consequently, most performance evaluations include a mixture of these two types of measures (Gross, 1995).

Typically, a team performance measurement system contains five to ten different measures (Jones & Moffett, 1999). Because the purpose of measurement is to provide feedback and improve performance, it is preferable to have a simpler system that team members can relate to rather than a sophisticated system that is hard to interpret. Using behavioral scales encourages the rater to focus on the target's behavior rather than on personality. Including team members in the development of behavioral scales is a good way to improve the relevance and credibility of the evaluation system. Table 16.1 presents a simple behavioral scale developed by students for evaluating contributions to team projects (Levi & Cadiz, 1998).

Participation in the Evaluation Process

Traditionally, the employee's supervisor conducts the performance evaluation; however, teamwork evaluations should include more than input from the supervisor (Lawler, 2000). It is difficult for a supervisor to conduct a performance evaluation on someone who works on a team. Teamwork often

Table 16.1   Behavioral Rating Scale to Evaluate Student Team Projects

Use the following rating scale to evaluate your team members' behavior on the class project:

    1 = never   2 = sometimes   3 = usually   4 = always

Did the team member you are rating

A. make commitments to do tasks?
B. do his or her fair share of the work?
C. produce work with acceptable quality?
D. actively participate in team discussions and decision making?

Rate each team member:

Team member	A	B	C	D	Total
1 _____	_____ +	_____ +	_____ +	_____ =	_____
2 _____	_____ +	_____ +	_____ +	_____ =	_____
3 _____	_____ +	_____ +	_____ +	_____ =	_____
4 _____	_____ +	_____ +	_____ +	_____ =	_____

requires a shift to the use of a multirater evaluation approaches like 360-degree feedback, which includes input from team members, customers, and supervisors. Those most qualified to evaluate a team member's performance are the fellow team members. The team's supervisor and customers can evaluate the overall performance of the team, but only the team members can accurately evaluate an individual's role in the team (Gross, 1995).

Multirater performance evaluations are more reliable and valid than supervisor-only evaluations (Rynes et al., 2005). Also, those being evaluated are more likely to believe that feedback from multiple sources is more credible and fair. Sometimes performance evaluations from the supervisor are used for pay decisions, while evaluations from team members are used for feedback and development purposes (Lawler, 2000). This approach makes it easier for the team member raters to be honest, because their feedback does not affect pay decisions for the recipient.

A multirater approach may be used for student team projects. Normally, students evaluate their own performance on team projects more accurately than professors do (Levi & Cadiz, 1998). The professor only sees the final product, while the students observe the performance of each team member. However, professors often are reluctant to use student evaluations because of a belief that students will not accurately evaluate one another. Nevertheless, the use of student evaluations of team projects reduces social loafing by giving students the ability to influence their teammates' behavior and increases the perceived fairness of the evaluation system.

Problems and Biases With Team Evaluations

Team performance evaluations should not encourage competition among team members. Many organizations use evaluation systems that require a fixed distribution of good and poor performance (for example, 20% higher performers, 60% moderate performers, and 20% poor performers). These practices are inappropriate for teams (Lawler, 2000). Ranking employees against one another encourages competition and reduces teamwork. If the team is performing well and everyone is doing his or her fair share, ranking team members against one another is inappropriate and can damage team operations. A team that works well together should not have performance gaps among team members.

Including team members in the performance evaluation process raises questions about fairness and accuracy (Gross, 1995). Personal relationships and favoritism are a problem in evaluations, regardless of whether they come from a supervisor or a team member. Team members often do not have experience or training conducting performance evaluations, so they require assistance to complete them. Although there are problems with team members' ratings, the main limit on use of team member evaluations is that managers are often reluctant to give up the power to conduct performance evaluations.

Although it is valuable to include team member evaluations in the performance evaluation system, some team members are uncomfortable evaluating coworkers' performances, especially when the evaluations are related to pay increases (Lawler, Mohrman, & Ledford, 1995). Team members feel more comfortable evaluating one another when they can use objective performance standards and the ratings remain confidential.

All evaluation systems that use people rather than purely objective scores may suffer from bias. Peers are no more likely to reflect biases than supervisors, but some biases are more likely to affect peer evaluations. For example, inflation bias refers to the effect that more positive evaluations are given when raters expect to have to present feedback to others. Therefore, inflation bias results when the members experience both empathy and fear of creating conflict in the team during the evaluation (Antonioni, 1994). Reciprocity bias occurs when people feel obligated to give positive ratings after they received positive ratings from others.

One type of bias is unique to teams. The team halo effect describes how team members view the success and failure of teams (Naquin & Tynan, 2003). When teams are successful, team members view success as caused by the team; when they are unsuccessful, they tend to blame individual members for the failure. This type of scapegoating is likely to affect team members' evaluations of one another. When the team is successful, there is a tendency to rate every team member as a good performer. When teams fail, members are more likely to give negative performance evaluations to selected members.

16.2 Reward Systems

An organization's reward system is an important way of encouraging a team to improve the way it operates. Team rewards have the potential to influence the motivation of individual team members, the level of coordination in the team, and the quality of the group process. More organizations are beginning to use some type of team rewards to encourage team effectiveness (DeMatteo, Eby, & Sundstrom, 1998). Most Fortune 1000 companies use some degree of team-based incentives (Merriman, 2009).

The shift to teamwork creates problems with traditional compensation systems (Lawler, 2000). An organization needs to change its compensation practices to support teamwork, because pay is a communication device that tells employees what is important. However, compensation programs are typically conservative, so they are rarely used to lead organizational change. As organizations become more team oriented, existing compensation practices either get in the way or are modified to support the use of teams (Lawler, 1999).

In traditional companies, pay systems focus on individuals, people are paid based on their position in the organization's hierarchy, and bonuses are reserved primarily for managers. These companies rely on increases in base pay (often by seniority) and promotions as a way of rewarding and motivating employees. But, in team-based organizations, with flatter hierarchies and flexible job assignments, this traditional approach to compensation is not effective (Gross, 1995).

Types of Approach

The three approaches to rewarding performance are individual, team, and organizational. Individual reward systems are good for motivating high performers, but may discourage cooperation and teamwork. Team and organizational approaches are better at encouraging teamwork and are appropriate when the tasks are highly interdependent (Cohen & Bailey, 1997). There also are in-between options. For example, production workers and professionals are often evaluated and rewarded for individual performance. However, information about their participation in teams may be included in their individual performance evaluations.

Most U.S. employees prefer individual rather than team-based rewards. This is particularly true of employees who have high levels of achievement motivation (Rynes et al., 2005). Team rewards tend to have less incentive effect than individual rewards; however, individual reward programs may not encourage sufficient cooperation among team members. When teams are rewarded collectively, the team has the right incentive to deal with members who are not doing their fair share. On the other hand, not offering rewards for individual performance can reduce the motivation of high-performing team members (Lawler, 2000).

Although team rewards are valuable motivational tools, their use may create problems. An emphasis on team rewards may encourage social loafing, discourage the performance of good workers, and create inequity problems (DeMatteo et al., 1998). Individuals who are high performers may have negative attitudes toward team rewards because they perceive them as inequitable. However, this is somewhat mitigated if high performers believe that teamwork is necessary to accomplish important tasks (Haines & Taggar, 2006). Inequity problems also arise from inconsistencies in how organizations evaluate and reward teams (Merriman, 2009). Finally, team members vary in how much of their rewards they want from team rather than individual performance.

Hybrid Approaches

The types of problems that result with the use of individual and team rewards are the reason organizations often use hybrid approaches that combine both types of rewards. In some studies, teams that are rewarded for a mix of individual and team performance perform better than teams rewarded solely for either individual or team performance (Fan & Gruenfeld, 1998). However, mixing individual and team rewards is not always effective.

Mixing individual and team rewards can create a social dilemma for team members (Barnes, Hollenbeck, Jundt, DeRue, & Harmon, 2011). Should they act for the team or their individual self-interest? Research on social dilemmas suggests that mixing individual and team rewards may not be the best approach since team members respond more strongly to the individual rewards.

The best approach may depend on the type of tasks the team is performing (Barnes et al., 2011). Individual incentives encourage the team members to put in more effort and work faster, but may decrease accuracy because of reduced support, cooperation, and coordination of knowledge. Focusing on one's own work may reduce cooperation and back-up behaviors by team members. Team rewards are often needed when teams have high levels of interdependence because of greater needs for coordination and information sharing. When accuracy, coordination, and back-up behaviors are important to team success, team incentives alone may be the best approach.

Culture may affect how team members respond to different types of rewards. Team members from individualistic cultures prefer individual rewards, while collectivists prefer team rewards (Duarte & Snyder, 2006). Cultural differences also affect team members' beliefs about what constitutes good performance. Individualists focus on task success, while collectivists value the working relationships that have been developed. These differences make it difficult to reward virtual teams with members from different cultures.

In a student teamwork experiment, hybrid rewards worked better than individual or team rewards because they encouraged task-oriented communication and reduced social loafing (Pearsall, Christian, & Ellis, 2010). Team rewards motivated social helping and coordination, but reduced individual effort and accountability. Individual rewards had a stronger focus on individual effort and outcomes, but did not encourage helping behavior in a team. Hybrid rewards were effective in this experiment because they rewarded two different actions, so team members did not have to make trade-offs. They could focus on one goal or both goals.

Creating the right mix of individual and team rewards can be difficult. For example, when evaluating and rewarding student team projects, what percentage of the grade should be student ratings of each other's performance versus the teacher's evaluation of the quality of the project? The proportion of the students' team member evaluations should be large enough to make a difference (at least 10% of the grade), but not so large that it distracts the students from focusing on the task (35% or less of the grade). When students understand the advantages and disadvantages of different reward approaches, they often select about 25% for the team member evaluations proportion of the project's grade.

16.3 Rewarding Individual Team Members

In most organizations, rewards are based on job descriptions (Lawler, 1999). Specific jobs have salary ranges attached to them, and employees are paid on the basis of their jobs and periodic performance evaluations from their managers. One approach to making individual reward systems more responsive to teamwork is to change the performance evaluation system by including factors, such as cooperation and team participation. Because managers often are unaware of the internal operations of a team, this requires input from team members in the evaluation process. Other approaches to supporting teamwork through individual rewards are changing how base pay is calculated (e.g., adopting a skill-based pay program).

Changing Base Pay

Team members' base pay should be fair and equitable. Because they share work, support one another, and respond flexibly to work situations, their base pay should be similar (Gross, 1995). In traditional organizations, each job has a different base pay. When people shift to teamwork, the distinctions among jobs can disappear. In team-oriented organizations, people do not have specific jobs, but rather have roles and temporary task assignments (Lawler, 2000). Consequently, it makes more sense to pay people for what they are capable of doing (their skills and knowledge) than for the changing tasks they perform. This is why team-based organizations shift to broad pay bands rather than salaries for specific jobs. The policy reduces pay distinctions among team members, improving perceived fairness.

The primary benefit of the team-oriented salary approach is that it gives the organization more flexibility for managing teams (Manufacturing Studies Board, 1986). Issues such as cross-training, job rotation, and teamwork do not cause compensation problems because salary is not based on the type of work performed on a given day. It gives the organization the option of deciding—without considering salary implications—how much cross-training will be done, who and when to train, and where to assign employees. In this scenario, individuals who prefer to perform limited job activities may continue to do so while employees who seek job variety and want to learn new skills may be accommodated, achieving flexibility for both the organization and the individual.

The main problem associated with a team-oriented salary approach is that it eliminates one of the organization's means of rewarding individual performance. In the traditional compensation system, employees had an incentive to work hard and learn new skills in order to be promoted to a new job. The lack of an incentive for harder work is a significant problem, which often requires adopting a system of individual or team bonuses to motivate employees.

Skill-Based Pay

An alternative approach for supporting teamwork is to pay an employee for the skills or competencies he or she possesses (Lawler, 1999). Skill-based pay encourages employees to learn new skills, which makes them more flexible and increases their understanding of the work process (Gross, 1995).

The primary benefit of this approach is to improve the flexibility of the team in performing its task. It is most commonly used when the team member skills are not too widely divergent and the team's actions are highly interdependent. For example, factory workers who are multiskilled can take over one another's jobs when bottlenecks occur or when team members are absent. Professional teams that provide an integrated service to customers, such as in the insurance or banking industry, use multiskilled workers to improve customer service.

The primary advantage of skill-based pay is organizational flexibility. However, several problems may occur with skill-based pay programs (Luthans & Fox, 1989). Training costs rise because of skill-based pay. There can be quality and productivity problems because employees are working on new jobs in order to gain new skills. Promotions may be limited after a few years because employees have learned all the skills offered by the company. Therefore, skill-based pay is often used to make the transition into work teams and then abandoned once most of the workers have completed their skills training (Gross, 1995).

Knowledge-based pay or career ladders are a type of skill-based pay for professional workers (Lawler, 2000). Multiskilled professionals are a benefit to professional teams. Cross-training will not create the skills, but job rotation helps an organization nurture the development of professionals with skills and knowledge that cross traditional professional boundaries. Knowledge-based pay, which rewards employees for depth of knowledge in an area, is a useful organizational tool for developing and retaining technical experts.

16.4 Team and Organizational Reward Programs

Team rewards are based on a successful team performance. Organizations are adopting team rewards because using work teams makes it difficult to accurately evaluate individual performance as distinct from that of the team (DeMatteo et al., 1998). The effectiveness of team reward programs depends on the characteristics of the rewards, the organization, and the team (Gross, 1995; Lawler, 2000). Team rewards should be large enough to make a noticeable difference in the member's pay; they are often assumed to be about 10% of the salary. To encourage cooperation, rewards should be distributed equally among all team members. Team rewards are more effective when the organizational culture supports teamwork and when teams are integrated into the operation of the organization. Effective team rewards require clear team goals, measurable performance standards, and a task that requires integrated teamwork.

It can be difficult to develop appropriate team rewards for some types of teams. For example, project teams can be difficult to reward. An organization often rewards project team members when they successfully complete the project, which is a good team incentive. However, team members come and go during the course of a project, so it is difficult to determine who should share in the rewards. One approach is to use team recognition programs to reward project teams at important milestones in a project. An alternative is to rely on organizational rewards like profit sharing to reward successful teamwork.

Team Recognition Programs

Most companies do not have special reward programs for teams. When they do, the most common type is the use of recognition awards (Gross, 1995). Special awards and recognition programs may be used to reward successful team performance. Although recognition programs are a valuable way of acknowledging effort beyond expectations, these programs supplement, but do not substitute for team reward programs (Lawler, 2000).

Recognition awards are one-time events that acknowledge team and individual success (Gross, 1995). Recognition awards may be either cash or noncash. Surveys show that about one-third of large U.S. companies use recognition awards to reward successful team performance. Noncash awards should be appropriate for the specific employees and given in a manner that publicly recognizes team accomplishments. Cash awards should be large enough (several hundred dollars or more) to have an impact.

When establishing a team recognition program, the decision must be made whether to give cash or noncash rewards. There should be several levels of awards or amounts to recognize different levels of contribution. To ensure fairness, there should be an organization-wide system for nominating and selecting teams for recognition. Awards should be given as close as possible to the time of a team success. The awards presentation should be a positive experience that publicizes the success of the team.

Organizational Rewards

A potential problem with team incentive programs is that they may inadvertently create competition among teams within an organization (Lawler, 2000). When an organization's work requires coordination among teams, the use of team rewards may reduce overall organizational performance. In addition, measuring the performance of individual teams may be difficult in some organizations. Profit sharing, gain sharing, and other organizational reward programs are a useful approach for dealing with these problems.

Such organizational programs reward teams for helping an organization succeed or for achieving an organizational performance goal (such as quality, productivity, or customer service goals).

Profit-sharing programs are based on meeting profitability targets for the organization (Rynes et al., 2005). The large number of employees involved and factors outside of employees' control affecting profits may limit the motivational effects of these programs. Gain-sharing programs link pay to collective results at a level smaller than the entire organization. For example, they may be linked to the performance of a specific facility or production unit. This can make them more motivating, given that fewer employees are involved. They provide a way to give incentives to teams when jobs are interconnected and individual incentive programs cannot be used. Gain-sharing programs are powerful incentives that encourage teamwork throughout an organization (Rynes et al., 2005).

Organizational reward programs may be calculated and distributed to people in a variety of ways (Thomas & Olson, 1988). The success of the programs depends more on the organizational context and participants' beliefs than on the specific formulas used to calculate rewards. The biggest problem with organizational reward programs is the difficulty in establishing a connection between a team member's actions and the performance of the organization. This is especially true in larger organizations.

In U.S. culture, it is difficult to get away from individual reward systems. However, organizations may use multiple performance reward programs (DeMatteo et al., 1998). Most organizations use individual salary systems as their primary methods of compensation. Additional compensation may be based on skills, individual merit, team incentives, and organizational incentives. It is not really a matter of choosing which system is best, but rather of selecting the right combination of approaches. The right combination is likely to depend on the characteristics of the organization.

16.5 Relationship of Rewards to Types of Teams

The reward program an organization uses to support teamwork depends on the type of team.

Types of Teams

The type of team and its organizational level affect the reward program. Teams vary in whether they perform the basic work of the organization or supplemental work and whether the teams are temporary or permanent. The three basic types of teams are parallel, process (or work), and project teams (see Table 16.2). Organizational level affects teams because of skills (common versus specialized) and power (ability to impact the organization). Skill-based pay makes sense for a factory team, but not for a professional team. Profit sharing may be useful for a management team, but inappropriate for a service team.

Parallel teams are typically part-time, temporary teams that supplement the regular work system and perform problem-solving and improvement functions (Lawler, 2000). An example of a parallel team is a quality improvement team that meets to analyze and discuss issues of quality. Parallel teams often meet regularly, follow predesigned systems for problem solving, receive teamwork training, and make recommendations for approval by management. They provide recommendations for change, but do not implement them. Such teams often have a limited lifespan and disband after working on a particular topic. Parallel teams are widely seen in industry, with more than 85% of large U.S. companies using them.

Parallel teams are an excellent way to encourage employee participation in the organization. However, they create an evaluation and reward problem for the team members (Gross, 1995). There is an inherent conflict between commitment to the team's task and commitment to the member's primary job functions. Members of parallel teams spend limited work time in the team and most of their time working for a supervisor who is not part of the team. Because of these dual loyalties, parallel teams often have problems motivating members. Including an employee's work on the parallel team in his or her performance evaluation helps deal with this dilemma.

A process team or work team is a full-time, permanent team that is the major part of the members' work. Process or work teams are responsible for producing a product or providing a service (Lawler, 2000). Process teams

Table 16.2   Types of Teams

Type of Team	Use	Characteristics
Parallel team	• Problem solving	• Temporary
	• Improvement	• Partial commitment
Process or work team	• Make a product	• Permanent
	• Provide a service	• Full commitment
Project team	• Design a product	• Temporary
	• Implement a program	• Full commitment

range from factory workers assembling products to airline crews and surgical teams. Employees may have similar skills and training or be cross-functional. Process teams are used by 78% of large U.S. companies. They typically control how the task is performed, but vary in how much control they have over selection of tasks, personnel issues, and other work aspects.

The use of process teams produces many benefits when performing complex tasks and providing social support to team members (Gross, 1995). However, this type of team creates an evaluation and reward problem because it is often difficult to evaluate and reward individual behaviors in the team, given that the tasks are interdependent. Measurement of performance of these teams is inherently at the team level. Organizations may use team rewards to motivate the entire team, but it is important to recognize individual contributions as well. This often requires including team members in the performance evaluation process.

Project teams are typically composed of a diverse group of knowledge workers who come together to perform a project in a defined period (Lawler, 2000). One example is a new product development team. Project teams work on unique and uncertain tasks that require creativity and decision making. Project teams are temporary structures whose membership may change during a project and disband when the project is completed.

Project teams often require full-time commitment from team members, but are of limited duration. Although they complete a project, team members' quality of work is difficult to measure because its value may not be known until long after the work is completed. Project teams are often cross-functional and can include team members with a variety of skills and expertise. Forming a project team can be a highly effective way to accomplish certain types of tasks for an organization. However, this type of team creates evaluation and reward problems given that there is often no supervisor capable of evaluating the specialized performances of the team members (Gross, 1995).

Linking Rewards to Types of Team

Table 16.3 shows the relationship between types of teams and rewards. Rewards for performance may not be needed for parallel teams; however, incentive programs may help motivate teams (Lawler, 2000). Organizational reward programs, such as profit-sharing and gain-sharing programs fit well with the use of parallel teams. However, there is a weak link between the success of a parallel team and improved performance of the organization. Not only is it difficult for the team to see the connection between its work and organizational success, but success is shared with other organization members who are not on the team.

Table 16.3   Relationship of Rewards to Types of Team

Type of Team	Reward Programs
Parallel team	• Team recognition awards
	• Organizational rewards
Process (or work) team	• Salary-based compensation
	• Skill-based pay
	• Individual, team, and organizational rewards
Project team	• Team recognition awards
	• Team and organizational rewards

The alternative to organizational rewards is to give the team bonuses or recognition awards. One problem with using bonuses is that it is often difficult to estimate the value of the recommendations made by parallel teams, and the value is dependent on whether the ideas are accepted and implemented by management. Recognition awards are a popular alternative for rewarding parallel teams. The key to recognition programs is to give the team something it values when it has accomplished significant work.

Process or work teams benefit from the use of a variety of individual and team reward programs. Individual-based programs like skill-based pay encourage the development of important team skills. Shifting to salary-based compensation rather than paying people for the job they perform, encourages equality among team members. Team and organizational incentive programs motivate coordinated actions. Finally, individual incentives based on team member evaluations help motivate team members when the work is not highly interdependent.

Project teams may be the most difficult type of team to reward (Lawler, 2000). A common approach is to give the team a bonus or recognition award when its task has been completed. However, project teams may work for a long time on a project, and team membership may change during the project. In addition, member participation on the team may vary so that giving each team member the same reward may be inappropriate. One alternative is to give team rewards or bonuses during project milestones. Team bonuses can be given equally or relative to the level of participation. Organizational reward programs like profit sharing may be a useful way to reward project teams in smaller organizations.

Summary

Performance evaluations provide important information to help a team improve its operations and motivate performance by linking to the organization's reward system. Evaluations may focus on individual performance, team member evaluations of one another, or evaluations of the entire team. They may measure either the team members' behavior or the results of the team's performance. Evaluation measures should be developed through a participative process and be linked to both team and organizational goals. Participation of team members in the evaluation process is important because supervisors are often unaware of the internal operations of the team. Multirater approaches to evaluations that include team members increase the accuracy and perceived fairness of the evaluations.

There are problems and biases with any performance evaluation system. Using concrete behavioral measures reduces the impact of stereotypes and perceptual biases of raters. Confidentiality of evaluations reduces the reluctance of some team members to negatively evaluate others. Teams can suffer from the halo effect where they give everyone high ratings when the team is successful and scapegoat selected members with bad performance ratings when the team fails.

Rewards may motivate individual and team performance. Often the traditional individual compensation system used by organizations gets in the way of teamwork. Individual reward systems are good at motivating individual performance, but may reduce cooperation and commitment to the team. Team rewards encourage cooperation, but may not encourage individual motivation. Organizational reward systems encourage cooperation among teams and commitment to the overall goals of the organization.

Team-oriented reward programs use a combination of individual, team, and organizational reward programs. The best approach to rewarding teams depends on the type of task and team. When tasks are interdependent, the organization should use team or organizational rewards. Parallel, process (or work), and project teams differ in the amount of time and commitment to the team. This factor affects the best way to reward team participation.

Process teams require changes in how individuals are compensated to promote flexibility and skill development. Team reward programs are useful when the work of the team is so interrelated that individual performance evaluations and rewards are inappropriate. Team recognition awards are valuable ways of rewarding parallel and project teams, where team participation is not a full-time, permanent activity. Organizational reward programs, such as profit sharing or gain sharing, encourage teams in an organization to work together and reward teams that help the organization succeed.

Team Leader's Challenge 16

You are the leader of a quality improvement team that has worked to redesign your organization's work processes. The team is composed of members from various parts of the organization. Although this project is important for the organization, the team members only spend part of their time working on the project. The team has met regularly for the past six months. The commitment and motivation levels of the participants have been highly variable. Some team members complain that their managers do not consider the work of the team to be important.

The team presented its proposed changes last week to management, and the response was mixed. Clearly, it will be easier for some sectors of the organization to adopt and implement the recommendations than others. The benefits of the proposed changes primarily help improve customer service, so it is difficult to measure the financial impact of the proposal. Your team has put in a lot of effort to develop this proposal, and you would like to see the members rewarded for their effort.

How should the team's performance be evaluated?

What is the best way for you (the team leader) to reward the team members?

How should the rewards be distributed?

SURVEY: INDIVIDUAL VERSUS TEAM REWARDS

Purpose: Understand how you think teams should be rewarded and what best motivates your performance on a team project. When people work on teams, their performance can be rewarded using individual or team rewards or a combination of both types of rewards. Organizations vary on which types of rewards they use, and individuals vary on which type of rewards they prefer.

Directions: Using the scale below, indicate the amount of agreement with each of the following statements about how teams should be rewarded.

| 1 | 2 | 3 | 4 | 5 |

Strongly Disagree   Strongly Agree

_____ 1. I am more motivated when rewards are based solely on the team's performance.

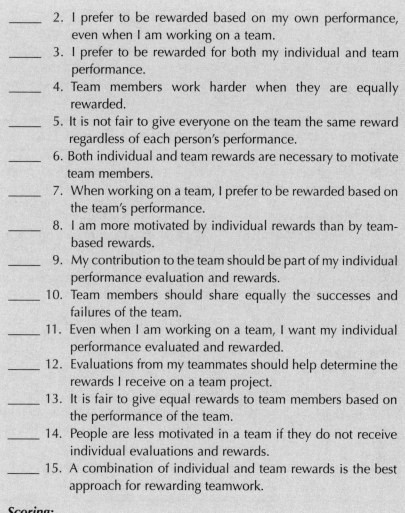

_____ 2. I prefer to be rewarded based on my own performance, even when I am working on a team.

_____ 3. I prefer to be rewarded for both my individual and team performance.

_____ 4. Team members work harder when they are equally rewarded.

_____ 5. It is not fair to give everyone on the team the same reward regardless of each person's performance.

_____ 6. Both individual and team rewards are necessary to motivate team members.

_____ 7. When working on a team, I prefer to be rewarded based on the team's performance.

_____ 8. I am more motivated by individual rewards than by team-based rewards.

_____ 9. My contribution to the team should be part of my individual performance evaluation and rewards.

_____ 10. Team members should share equally the successes and failures of the team.

_____ 11. Even when I am working on a team, I want my individual performance evaluated and rewarded.

_____ 12. Evaluations from my teammates should help determine the rewards I receive on a team project.

_____ 13. It is fair to give equal rewards to team members based on the performance of the team.

_____ 14. People are less motivated in a team if they do not receive individual evaluations and rewards.

_____ 15. A combination of individual and team rewards is the best approach for rewarding teamwork.

Scoring:

Add questions 1, 4, 7, 10, and 13 to obtain your preference for team rewards score.

Add questions 2, 5, 8, 11, and 14 to obtain your preference for individual rewards score.

Add questions 3, 6, 9, 12, and 15 to obtain your preference for a combination of individual and team rewards score.

Discussion: What are the pros and cons of individual or team-based rewards? What problems are created when you work in a team with only individual or team rewards? What do these results say about your attitudes toward working in teams?

SOURCE: Adapted from Shaw, J., Duffy, M., & Stark, E. (2001). Team reward attitude: Construct development and initial validation. *Journal of Organizational Behavior, 22,* 903–917.

ACTIVITY: EVALUATING AND REWARDING A PROJECT TEAM

Objective: Developing effective evaluation and reward programs for project teams can be one of the most difficult assignments. It is important to balance evaluations of the results of the team's work with the contributions of individual team members. Finding the right balance and ways to measure these factors is key in a successful evaluation and reward program.

Activity: Use Activity Worksheet 16.1 to develop a performance evaluation and reward program for a project team. Select either a student project team or a professional new product design team as a specific example to use.

Analysis: Do the evaluation criteria provide sufficient direction to team members so that they know how to act in order to be successful? Will the reward program that you selected motivate team members to perform well? What problems are you likely to encounter if you use this program?

Discussion: What are the effects of using team member ratings to evaluate team performance? What is the right balance between individual and team rewards?

ACTIVITY WORKSHEET 16.1
Activity: Evaluating and Rewarding a Project Team

Team Goals: What are the main goals of the team?

_____

_____

_____

_____

Team Evaluation: What criteria should be used to evaluate overall team performance?

_____

_____

_____

_____

Member Evaluation: What criteria should be used to evaluate each team member's performance?

_____

_____

_____

_____

Reward Program: How should the team's work be rewarded?

_____

_____

_____

_____

What percentage of the reward should be based on the team's project versus the behavior of the individual team members?

_____ % team reward—based on supervisor's evaluation of the team project

_____ % individual reward—based on team members' evaluations of individual performance

Activity: Team Halo Effect

Objective: The team halo effect is a major type of bias encountered when assessing team member evaluations. This bias can be demonstrated in a simple class activity.

Activity: Create two or more teams and have the teams complete solving anagrams. Give one team easy anagrams to solve and the other team difficult anagrams. After the competition, have the participants anonymously rate their team members on a numeric scale.

Analysis: Compare the team member evaluations of the winning and loosing teams. Were there uniformly positive evaluations for the winning team? Did the losing team members give negative evaluations to some of their teammates?

Discussion: How does the team halo effect impact the way you evaluate your teammates? How can you conduct the performance evaluation of a team project in order to reduce the halo effect? How does the team halo effect relate to team cohesion?

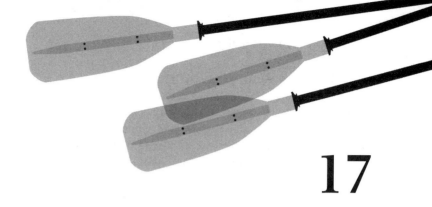

17

Team Building and Team Training

Team building is the term used to describe approaches to improving the operation of teams. Team-building programs typically focus on improving teamwork skills, developing social relations, and solving problems that disrupt team performance. Teamwork training programs teach specific teamwork skills like assertiveness; cross-train team members to improve coordination; and promote organizational learning through the use of problem-solving teams.

Learning Objectives

1. What are some of the different definitions of team building?

2. What are some reasons why organizations do not use team building?

3. What are the criteria of effective teams and the symptoms of ineffective teams?

4. What are the main types of team-building activities?

5. What skills are taught in teamwork training programs?

6. What factors relate to the effectiveness of teamwork training?

7. What are the main types of teamwork training?

8. How does action learning develop and improve teams in an organization?

17.1 What Is Team Building?

Organizational development is a set of social science techniques designed to promote changes in organizations that enhance personal development and increase organizational effectiveness. Team building is an organizational development intervention that focuses on improving the operations of work teams. Team building means regularly taking time to evaluate the performance of teams to identify obstacles and develop patterns of work that are more productive. To be effective, team building must be viewed as an ongoing activity.

A variety of perspectives on team building emphasize different goals and approaches. Rather than trying to combine these perspectives to create a single view, the following is a sample of the different perspectives on team building:

- Team building is a problem-solving process that focuses on the following three issues: (1) What keeps the team from being effective? (2) What changes could improve the team's effectiveness? (3) What is the team doing effectively now that it wants to continue to do (Dyer, Dyer, & Dyer, 2007)?
- Team building means making sure the team has common goals and that members can work together to achieve them. The main priority in team building is developing a strong sense of belonging to the team. Unless team members identify with one another and see themselves as a team, it is impossible to organize them to accomplish a common goal (Hayes, 1997).
- What does it mean to develop a team? It means creating a team with the appropriate mix of skills, including technical and group process skills. It also means improving performance by changing the way the team operates. The team development process includes organizing work and roles, acquiring the necessary skills and resources, establishing the necessary relationships inside and outside the team, and changing the situation to facilitate performance (Mohrman, Cohen, & Mohrman, 1995).
- Team building is a set of approaches designed to improve the team's social relations and interactions in order to make the team more effective. The primary approaches include goal setting, interpersonal relations skills, role clarification, and problem solving. Selecting the right approach to use depends on a diagnosis of the team's problems (Shuffler, DiazGranados, & Salas, 2011).

Organizational Context of Team Building

Team building requires examination of the organizational context of the team (Hayes, 1997). Many organizations trying to implement teamwork fail to appreciate how their current practices and culture limit the ability of teams to operate. Effective teamwork requires a supportive organizational environment. It is not useful to focus on the internal problems of a team if the source of the problems lies in the surrounding organization. For example, it is difficult to promote cooperation among team members when the organization only rewards individual performance.

The context in which the team operates has a greater impact on performance than the internal competencies of team members (Mohrman et al., 1995). Therefore, team development must focus on building the relationship between the team and its organizational context. Too often, a team-building program focuses on internal development when the key to performance problems is external.

A central organizational issue for a team is the organization's performance evaluation and reward system. Performance evaluation systems have the potential to provide a team with feedback that can be used to improve team performance. Reward systems provide motivation for the team members to work together. The performance evaluation and reward system is an effective way for an organization to motivate a team to improve the way it operates.

The organization's culture impacts support for team-building programs (Dyer et al., 2007). Cultures vary on how much they value open communication and participation, support for collaborative work, and willingness to invest in people. Team-oriented organizational cultures recognize the importance of developing teamwork skills. Top management provides support for teamwork and team-building programs. Team-building programs take time, so organizations need to have the patience to let their teams develop and practice new ways of working together. This takes a long-term focus on teamwork: Time must be made available for teams to engage in team-building activities.

Evaluating Team-Building Programs

Although many organizational leaders say that team building is an important activity, their actions do not necessarily support their words (Dyer et al., 2007). Most companies that use teams offer little in the way of team development. They fail to include teamwork in their goals and reward systems. Top management focuses on financial issues, often ignoring the value of teamwork as a means of improving performance. The result is mixed signals about teamwork and the value of team building.

Organizations overlook the importance of team-building activities for several reasons: They are limited by lack of expertise in team building and the availability of competent professionals who can run team-building programs. Managers often do not understand the benefits of team building, so they do not reward teams that spend time involved in team-building exercises. Finally, team members are also skeptical about the value of team building, so they are reluctant and view these activities as a waste of time.

Part of the problem in gaining organizational support for team-building programs is their reputation. Organizational programs are subject to fads, and team-building programs have suffered from this perception (Shuffler et al., 2011). During the 1960s, encounter groups encouraged people to share their true feelings with one another. Establishing good social relations among team members requires open communication, but the approach can be carried too far. Overemphasis on self-disclosure may create embarrassing problems for group members in work settings. For example, perhaps a member should not reveal inner feelings about his or her boss. Team building through wilderness experiences or ropes courses—another fad—is enjoyable, but it can be difficult to translate these experiences into solving work problems (Franz, 2012). Rumors about poorly run team-building programs of the past limit current support for team building.

Research demonstrates the effectiveness of team-building programs (Klein et al., 2009). Evaluation studies measure the impacts of team building on the following criteria: cognitive (knowledge of teamwork), affective (trust and team potency), team process (coordination and communication), and performance. Goal setting and role clarification are the most effective techniques, with impacts primarily for affective and process outcomes. Team-building interventions that focus on task issues are more effective at improving performance than morale-boosting activities (Cotton, 1993).

17.2 Does Your Team Need Team Building?

The first step in developing a team-building program is to assess the problems the team is facing (Franz, 2012). It is important to recognize that there is not one best approach to team building for all teams (Shuffler et al., 2011). Different approaches are effective for different team needs, so assessment is crucial.

To determine whether team building is needed, you need criteria for effective teams and an understanding of the problems that may interfere with team performance. Table 17.1 presents a set of criteria that can be used to evaluate the effectiveness of teams.

Effective teams have clear goals and values that are understood and accepted by all team members. Team members must understand their assignments and how their roles fit into the team's activities. The team climate provides trust and support among team members so they are willing to share ideas and feelings. All team members participate in the team's communication processes, and the team strives to make most decisions through consensus. Once decisions have been made, team members accept them and commit to implementing the decisions. Leaders are supportive of team

Table 17.1   Criteria for Effective Teams

- Clear and measurable performance goals
- Roles and assignments that are accepted by team members
- Climate of trust, psychological safety, and support
- Open and participative communication environment
- Effective problem solving and decision making
- Supportive leadership
- Constructive handling of conflict
- Supportive organizational culture and structure
- Ability to monitor performance and make needed changes

SOURCE: Adapted from Dyer, W., Dyer, W., & Dyer, J. (2007). *Team Building: Proven Strategies for Improving Team Performance* (4th ed.). San Francisco, CA: John Wiley.

members and help facilitate team processes. Differences of opinion are recognized and handled rather than ignored. The team's organizational culture and structure are consistent with how the team operates and what it wants to accomplish. Finally, the team regularly monitors its performance and has the ability to make needed changes.

Table 17.2 presents a set of symptoms of team problems that indicate when team building is needed. Many of these symptoms identify the effects rather than the causes of problems (Dyer et al., 2007). In many cases, the two causal factors are conflicts between team members and leaders and difficulties among team members. Conflicts with team leaders often lead to overconformity, resistance to leaders, an authoritarian leadership style, and lack of trust. Problems among team members often lead to bickering, lack of trust, personality conflicts, disagreements (with limited attempts to resolve them), cliques or subgroups, and missed deadlines.

Table 17.2   Symptoms of Ineffective Teams

- Decrease in team performance
- Increase of complaints from team members
- Evidence of unproductive conflicts among members
- Confusion about assignments, roles, and relationships
- Decisions misunderstood or not enacted
- Lack of involvement from team members
- Lack of initiative, creativity, or effective problem solving
- Ineffective meetings with low participation
- High dependency on the leader

SOURCE: Adapted from Dyer, W., Dyer, W., & Dyer, J. (2007). *Team Building: Proven Strategies for Improving Team Performance* (4th ed.). San Francisco, CA: John Wiley.

Team members may blame individuals for team problems rather than recognizing that the team process is responsible. Team conflicts and confusion are good examples of problems blamed on individuals, but that are really the responsibility of the team. Such problems can be addressed through team building.

For example, how does one deal with two team members who are constantly arguing with each other? If the conflict seems to be due to a "personality clash," there is no solution except to get rid of one or both of the team members. An individual's personality cannot be simply rearranged to prevent future clashes. A more useful approach is to view conflict as a violation of expectations about what is to be done. Expectations focus on behavior, and behavior is open to change. The team can discuss its expectations about performance and can negotiate an agreement that allows conflicting team members to work together.

Similarly, confusion among team members typically arises from unclear assignments and relationships. Solving this problem focuses not on individual team members, but on the team processes. Teams have to do a better job of clarifying the roles of all team members instead of attributing blame to individuals for failing to perform unclear assignments.

17.3 Types of Team-Building Programs

Categorizing the programs typically used in team building is difficult because there is no agreed-on set of techniques. The following subsections describe five different types of team-building programs: goal setting, role clarification, interpersonal process skills, cohesion building, and problem solving.

Goal Setting

The goal-setting process is designed to clarify the purpose of the team (Klein et al., 2009). This approach involves clarifying the team's goals and developing objectives that are more specific. This typically is done through consensus building to create agreement about and commitment to the team's goals. Objectives are developed to further define the team's tasks and establish action plans that include team member assignments. The final step in a goal-setting program is to develop an evaluation and feedback system so the team can monitor the attainment of its goals (Locke & Latham, 1990).

A goal-setting program may be narrowly focused on the team's immediate performance or broadly focused on the values and mission of the team and organization. The broader view is designed to develop a common vision for the team by exploring the team's underlying values and purpose. The broader approach is useful for teams that will exist for a long time and for teams whose members come from diverse backgrounds (Hayes, 1997).

Role Clarification

The role clarification approach focuses on clarifying individual roles, team norms, and shared responsibilities of team members (Klein et al., 2009). Conflict between roles and ambiguity about roles create stress and disrupt performance. Team members need to be clear on both their own roles and the roles others perform. In clarifying duties and task relationships among team members, coordination is improved and the team is better prepared to perform its task.

Several approaches can be used to enable a team to define its roles (Hayes, 1997). The negotiation approach asks team members to analyze their work situations and identify what other people could do to improve their effectiveness, which can include a list of behaviors that they appreciate and advocate and those that they want reduced or eliminated. The team members then negotiate changes in one another's behaviors to get what they want from the other team members.

An alternative approach asks team members to interact and group process observers to analyze the roles they perform. These observations are used to evaluate the team's performance. The typical result of analysis shows the team is underusing certain behaviors and relying on a limited range of behaviors. This information may be used to help improve team interactions.

The value of role clarification approaches is that they allow team members to see themselves from the outside, through the eyes of an observer or other members. This allows members to develop a new perspective for understanding how they operate and teaches them how to adjust their interaction styles in ways that improve team operations.

Interpersonal Process Skills

Team members need to learn how to coordinate their efforts with other members and work together as a team. Decision making, problem solving, and negotiating are some of the team process skills members can learn. If a team's problems are related to a lack of these teamwork skills, teaching members interpersonal process skills is one approach to team building.

Teaching group process skills is more than just lecturing. In team building, a team typically is given simulated activities or exercises to perform to practice these skills and analyze the results (Scholtes, 1988). For example, instead of waiting until an important project decision has to be made, the team may practice decision-making techniques in a desert survival exercise.

Process consultants are often used to facilitate these team exercises, observe how the team operates, and comment on the group process (Forsyth, 1999). Feedback from these outside observers is viewed as key in the learning experience. This approach to learning has traditionally been viewed as the best way to improve teamwork skills.

Cohesion Building

The purpose of cohesion building is to foster team spirit and build interpersonal connections among team members. When successful, it strengthens the team's morale, increases trust and cooperation, and develops team identity. Cohesion building is accomplished through techniques that create unity, a sense of belonging, and pride in the team (Hayes, 1997). The goal is to increase the sense of being a part of the team. Once team members have firmly established this relationship, they are more committed to the team goals and more supportive of the actions of other members.

Creating unity helps develop a sense of cooperation and belonging. One technique is to identify team boundaries so team members have a greater sense of being part of something unique. Once they begin to perceive the team in this way, they notice more similarities among fellow team members and more differences from outside groups. These psychological distinctions encourage team identification and commitment.

One popular cohesion-building activity is an outdoor experience program. In this program, the team leaves its work environment and meets in an outdoor setting. Team members are presented with a series of challenges they must deal with as a team, such as crossing a river using ropes or climbing a mountain. In working together to meet these challenges, the team develops a sense of cohesion and accomplishment. In recent years, organizations have shifted to using charity activities, such as house building for Habitat for Humanity, to encourage pride in the team-building activity.

Problem Solving

Team building is designed to improve team operations. Rather than starting with an approach to team building, the team may start with an analysis of its problems (Klein et al., 2009). The problem-solving approach to team building starts with problem identification and analysis. The problems may come from performance data, objective outside sources, or internal team communication. Information about team problems is gathered through surveys, interviews, or group discussions. This information is organized and shared with the team. Early on, a diagnostic session clarifies the problems and identifies the team's strengths and weaknesses.

The diagnosis stage ends with a discussion of how the team should proceed to take action on solving its problems. A standard problem-solving approach is used to generate alternatives and develop solutions. An action plan is developed for implementing the proposed changes in how the team operates.

This sounds like a fairly straightforward approach to solving a team's problems, but it may be difficult for a team to conduct (Dyer et al., 2007). By the time the team recognizes it has a problem, the underlying conflict may make resolution difficult. Outside consultants are often needed to help the team analyze itself, develop alternatives, and negotiate acceptable solutions.

17.4 Team Training

Because of the lack of training in how to operate, teams do not always live up to expectations (Marks, Sabella, Burke, & Zaccaro, 2002). Team training focuses on developing the skills the team needs to perform its tasks (Shuffler et al., 2011). This includes developing the skills, knowledge, and attitudes needed, practicing those skills, and providing feedback to improve the team's ability to use them. Team training requires identifying the specific knowledge and skills needed for effective performance and then developing approaches for these specific objectives.

To be effective, team members must understand their roles, coordinate their actions with others, and understand how their actions interact with others (Goldstein & Ford, 2002). Training is required to develop task-related skills and knowledge, teamwork skills, and knowledge of the roles of the other team members. Finally, teams need training on process improvement skills so they can learn how to improve performance.

A training program starts with a needs assessment to determine a team's training needs and objectives (Arthur, Bennett, Edens, & Bell, 2003). The assessment analyzes the goals of the team, the requirements of the members, the tasks they must perform, and the types of coordination needed. The information is used to create training objectives and design training programs. After training is conducted, evaluations are used to determine whether training objectives have been met.

The effectiveness of training programs depends on the method of training, the type of skill to learn, and the training environment (Arthur et al., 2003). Teamwork training is more effective when it focuses on identified training competencies or skills, when the team is trained together, when they have an opportunity to practice their new skills, and when they receive feedback about their performance. This methodology ensures that the training is transferred from the training session to the work environment. Two important issues related to effective teamwork training programs are training the team together and planning for the transfer of training.

Training the Team Together

Training of team members should be done with the team as a whole; this develops the team's mental model and transactive memory. A team's mental model is a common understanding by team members of how the team operates (Klimoski & Mohammed, 1997). Effective teams have a shared understanding of the team's goals, norms, and resources, including understanding of the roles, knowledge, and skills of each team member. This shared understanding is essential for coordination among team members, especially for tactical teams (teams that carry out a procedure, such as a surgery or aircraft team).

The team climate refers to the degree to which the team supports attempts to use the newly learned skills. Conducting the training with the people in their assigned teams creates a supportive team climate for new skills performance. The supportiveness of the work environment has a substantial effect on whether the newly learned skills are applied (Edmondson, Bohmer, & Pisano, 2001).

Planning for the Transfer of Training

Transfer of training refers to the extent that the new skills learned in training are used in the work environment (Salas & Cannon-Bowers, 2001). Factors that affect transfer of training include the environment where the training occurs, the time lag between the training and opportunities to apply the skills, cues in the job environment that prompt applying the new skills, and supervisor support for their application. The problem of training transfer is important; research suggests that only 10% of training actually transfers to the work environment (Smith-Jentsch, Salas, & Brannick, 2001).

Several training strategies may be used to encourage transfer of training, such as practice and feedback in simulated environments, encouraging supervisor support of the application of new skills, and creating a supportive team climate. Transfer of training is easier when the application environment is similar to the training experience. The team leader may provide opportunities to perform the newly learned skill, model the skill, and reinforce attempts at performance.

17.5 Types of Training

Team members may only receive training in generic teamwork skills. This training is similar to other types of training provided by organizations. Several types of training have been developed specifically for teams, three of which are presented here: team resource management training, cross-training and interpositional training, and action learning.

Team Resource Management Training

Team Resource Management (TRM) (also called Crew Resource Management) is a training program to develop a defined set of teamwork competencies so a team can operate without error under stressful circumstances (Goldstein & Ford, 2002). This approach was developed for the aviation industry and has application to other action teams that perform in stressful situations, such as military and surgical teams.

TRM begins with a methodology for analyzing the team to identify its mission requirements and coordination demands. The information is used to develop a set of team competencies for training. A training method is then selected and exercises are developed for team members to practice their new skills. The exercises provide an opportunity to evaluate the effectiveness of the training program and to provide constructive feedback to the participants. The teamwork competencies and skills needed by teams that are often the focus of training are presented in Table 17.3.

Table 17.3   Teamwork Competencies and Skills

Competencies and Skills	Definition
Adaptability	The ability to use information from the environment to change how the team operates
Shared situational Awareness	The development of an understanding of the team's internal and external environment and dynamics
Performance monitoring and feedback	The ability to accurately monitor performance, provide constructive feedback, and use this information to improve operations
Leadership and team management	The ability to direct and coordinate the activities of the team

(Continued)

Table 17.3   (Continued)

Competencies and Skills	Definition
Interpersonal relations	The ability to facilitate interactions to resolve disputes and motivate performance
Coordination	The ability to organize the team's resources and actions so that performance is effective
Communication	The ability to effectively exchange information with other team members
Decision making	The ability to gather and analyze information and use this information to solve problems

SOURCE: Adapted from Cannon-Bowers, J., Tannenbaum, S., Salas, E., & Volpe, C. (1995). Defining competencies and establishing team training requirements. In R. Guzzo & E. Salas (Eds.), *Team effectiveness and decision making in organizations* (pp. 330–380). San Francisco, CA: Jossey-Bass.

TRM training combines classroom training with practice in simulators with feedback (Salas, Bowers, & Edens, 2001). It focuses on developing identified teamwork competencies necessary to the team and has developed a set of tools and methods for identifying and teaching needed competencies. TRM training strategies use evaluations to encourage development of effective training programs. This training has been shown to be successful in reducing errors and accidents, improving teamwork, and increasing efficiency. The approach to training is effective because it focuses on specific teamwork competencies and provides trainees with opportunities to practice their skills and receive feedback.

Assertiveness training is an example of the type of training that is part of TRM. Problems with teamwork are a chief cause of major air carrier accidents (Jentsch & Smith-Jentsch, 2001). For example, accidents occur when crew members are unwilling to communicate problems to their superiors. This lack of assertiveness is a major problem for airline crews, medical teams, and police and firefighting teams, which is why assertiveness training is a standard element of TRM training.

Assertiveness is both a skill and an attitude. Consequently, training programs focus on both developing assertive communication skills and changing attitudes about when assertiveness is appropriate. Assertiveness is a situation-specific behavior. People's willingness to be assertive depends on the situation they are in and their relationship with the other people involved in the same situation. This is why it is important to conduct assertiveness training in environments that match the same type of occasion with the assertive behavior application. A member's willingness to act assertively is highly dependent on the team culture established by the team leader. Training programs also teach team leaders how to appropriately acknowledge assertive communications from subordinates.

Cross-Training and Interpositional Training

Cross-training is used to increase the flexibility of team members (Goldstein & Ford, 2002). In cross-training, team members are trained in the technical skills of two or more jobs, allowing the team to assign members to the tasks that need to be performed. In some cases, a pay-for-skills program is used to reward team members for learning new skills. A typical example of cross-training is a manufacturing team where members learn multiple roles. This allows the team to flexibly respond to changes in the work environment and to personnel changes. Cross-training programs often use on-the-job training, with experienced team members training other members.

The goal of interpositional training is to allow team members to better understand the working knowledge and roles of other team members and the interconnections among the actions of team members (Goldstein & Ford, 2002). This type of training leads to shared mental models of how the team operates and the coordination needs of the team. An example of interpositional training is teaching a flight crew to better understand each other's roles and abilities, but not to replace each other's positions.

Interpositional training is designed to develop shared knowledge structures among team members (Marks et al., 2002). This is especially significant for action teams with highly interdependent work arrangements. Action team members have specialized skill sets (such as the members of a surgical team), rely on coordination to complete their tasks, and operate in challenging environments. Because of their interdependence, effective performance requires coordination among team members.

Three types of interpositional training vary in depth of knowledge and method. Positional clarification simply provides team members with information about the tasks and roles of other team members. Positional modeling adds observation of team members' duties to this information. Positional rotation has a team member perform another member's job to gain experience with the other's duties. The most appropriate form of interpositional training depends on the level of interdependence in the team roles. Positional clarification is useful when there is some interdependence; positional modeling may be preferable when teams are highly interdependent.

Interpositional training improves team performance because the training develops shared mental models among team members. Shared mental models improve team coordination, which improves performance, especially in interdependent tasks. Interpositional training is not designed to teach members to perform each other's tasks, but to raise awareness of all the team roles. Interpositional training increases "back-up" or assistance to team members in performing tasks. Although interpositional training is especially important for action teams, it is beneficial for other teams, too. Service teams, for example, benefit from having a greater understanding of one another's roles to coordinate service to customers.

Action Learning

The action learning approach is based on the belief that most learning occurs when people are dealing directly with real-life issues (Goldstein & Ford, 2002). The focus of action learning is to develop teams that can analyze and solve important, real-life problems in their organizations. Action learning combines training with developing innovative solutions to existing organizational problems. In the process of solving the problem and reflecting on the team's problem-solving strategies, team members learn how to create and operate as effective problem-solving teams. The components of an action learning program are presented in Table 17.4.

Action learning is self-managed learning (Marquardt, 2002). The team gains skills and knowledge, then shares this knowledge with the organization. Team learning includes generating knowledge by analyzing a complex problem, taking action to solve it, then evaluating the results. The team is able to perform better in the future because it has learned how to experiment with new approaches to problems and how to communicate its knowledge. It is a strategy that develops a team and promotes learning throughout an organization. Through thoughtful, innovative action, teams learn how to effectively use their resources.

The action learning approach simultaneously solves a complex organizational issue while developing teamwork skills in people and organizations (Marquardt, 2004). It is an approach to continual learning that encourages experimentation, allows mistakes, offers support, and promotes feedback. It is a shift from a culture of training (where someone else determines what you need to know) to a culture of learning (where you are responsible for your own development).

Table 17.4   Components of an Action Learning Program

1. Problem or challenge	Learning is built around a problem or issue, a task that needs solving that is important to the team and organization. Teams learn best from taking action and then reflecting on the results. The problem must be real and valuable and be capable of being affected by the team's efforts. Examples of problems include reducing turnover, improving quality, reorganizing a department, or improving an organizational process.
2. Learning team	Teams should be relatively small, optimally from four to eight members. It is important to have a diverse perspective, so cross-functional or cross-organizational teams are best. Teams must have the ability to implement actions and affect the organizational issue they are working on.
3. Learning coach	The learning coach facilitates the group process, encourages reflection, promotes communication, and facilitates problem solving. The coach asks, What are you learning? How can you solve this problem? The coach helps the team solve its problem, but also promotes reflection on the group process and learning teamwork skills.
4. Insightful questioning and reflective listen	The coach encourages questioning and discussing the problem rather than jumping to a solution. This emphasis on analysis of the problem encourages reflection, creativity, and better problem-solving skills.
5. Taking action	There is no learning without action. The implementation and evaluation/feedback process is the key to learning. Learning occurs in the act of reflecting on action.
6. Commitment to learning	Solving organizational problems is good, but the more important organizational benefit is the understanding gained of how to solve problems. Action learning promotes organizational learning and development. It is an approach for dealing with organizational problems; it helps develop people with the skills to solve current and future problems. It promotes learning how to learn.

SOURCE: Adapted from Marquardt, M. *Building the Learning Organization*. Copyright © 2002, Palo Alto, CA: Davies-Black.

Summary

Team building is a type of organizational development that focuses on improving the operation of teams. To be effective, it should be an ongoing team activity. Team building examines both the internal processes and organizational contexts of teams. Although team-building programs have been shown to be effective, organizations and teams are often reluctant to conduct them.

Deciding whether a team needs team building requires criteria for effective and ineffective teams. Effective teams have clear goals and tasks, open communication climates, supportive leaders, and procedures for managing tasks and problems. Ineffective teams have unresolved conflicts and hostilities, confusion about goals and tasks, low levels of motivation, and high dependence on their leaders.

There are many different types of team-building activities. Goal setting is used to clarify a team's goals and objectives. Role definition clarifies individual roles and aids in establishing group norms. Interpersonal process skills use training activities to teach members to work together as a team. Cohesion building tries to create a team identity and improve social relations among team members. Problem solving identifies the team's main problems and works with the team to develop and implement solutions.

Team training programs are used to develop the task-related skills of team members, increase awareness of the roles in the team, and provide skills to improve performance. Training is more effective when based on a needs assessment and improved through evaluations. Team members should be trained together and the training integrated into the work environment.

There are three main types of teamwork training. TRM uses assessment to identify needed teamwork competencies and combines training with practice and feedback to ensure its effectiveness. Cross-training and interpositional training improve team flexibility and coordination by enabling team members to understand the roles and interconnections in the team. Action learning uses participation in facilitated problem-solving teams to develop teamwork skills and solve important organizational problems.

Team Leader's Challenge 17

You are the team leader at a large engineering design firm. The general manager of the firm is extremely frustrated with his attempts to develop and use project teams. He has tried personality testing to improve communication skills, wilderness experiences to improve problem-solving skills, and Japanese culture lessons to improve consensus decision making. None of these approaches has worked, and he now wonders whether engineers can be trained to work in teams.

The most recent team-building program is using "professional" team facilitators who are graduate students in counseling from a nearby university. Their program is getting a mixed reaction from team members. (Maybe learning to better express their feelings wasn't what these teams needed.) The facilitators are often effective in improving the performance of the teams, but they are not encouraging them to learn how to operate independently. The director is looking for advice from his project team leaders about the use of teams and the future of team building in the firm.

What went wrong with the past team-building efforts?

What advice would you (the team leader) give the director about team building in the organization?

How can action learning be used to help promote teamwork in this organization?

ACTIVITY: TEAM BUILDING

Objective. Team-building programs typically promote team development and learning by having the team perform some activity while observers record the group process. After the activity is completed, a facilitator discusses the group process observations with the team and uses this information to help the team improve how it operates.

Activity. Form teams of five to seven people and distribute a copy of the "University Discipline Board Decision" (Activity Worksheet 17.1) to each team. Select one or two observers and give them one of the group process observation forms found at the end of the chapters in this book: for example, Chapter 6: Communication; Chapter 8: Power and Social Influence; Chapter 9: Decision Making; and Chapter 13: Diversity. After the team has discussed the problem in the worksheet and reached a consensus decision, ask the observers to provide feedback to the team.

Analysis. Use the analysis sections in the observation sheets to discuss the group process. This activity may create gender differences, so examine how the gender mix of the teams may have affected their ability to reach an agreement.

Discussion. How can using team-building activities like this example help improve a team's group process? Examine the activity on Norms for Virtual Teams at the end of Chapter 15. What norms should a university develop about the use of information technology?

ACTIVITY WORKSHEET 17.1
University Discipline Board Decision

You are members of a University Discipline Board. You have been asked to review the following case and determine whether the accused student violated the university's Sexual Harassment Code of Conduct or any other relevant University Code of Conduct. If you find the student guilty, you must decide on the appropriate consequence. All decisions made by the University Discipline Board must be unanimous.

Case

John Smith is a sophomore at the university. He is taking an English class in creative writing. He decided to write a series of stories about a serial rapist who violently preys on college women at an anonymous university. In his stories, the names of the women victims are students in his writing class. He decided to "publish" his stories by putting them on the Internet using his electronic homepage (which is based on the university's computer).

Several of the women students in the class have read the stories, were upset by them, and have complained to university administrators.

Decision

1. Is John Smith guilty of violating the university's Sexual Harassment Code of Conduct or any other relevant University Code of Conduct?

   _____ Yes _____ No

2. If yes, what disciplinary action should the university take?

ACTIVITY: APPRECIATIVE INQUIRY OF TEAMWORK

Objective. Appreciative Inquiry is an organizational development technique that is rooted in the positive psychology movement, meaning that it focuses on strengths rather than deficits. It encourages people to think about what is possible, to create a positive image of the future, and to plan on how to make it happen. This activity examines the potential of teamwork by understanding your best teamwork experiences so you can learn how to create better teams in the future.

Activity. Think about the times you worked on teams when you really enjoyed participating and felt the team was very effective. Write a description of your best teamwork experience. It can be from school, work, or other types of organizations. What factors made this your favorite team? Ask group members to share their team experiences and develop a list of Characteristics of Successful Teams. Write your answers on Activity Worksheet 17.2.

Analysis. Review your list of Characteristics of Successful Teams. When you are in a team that lacks these characteristics, what can you do as a team leader or member to improve the team? Write out Action Plans for Improving Teams on the Activity Worksheet 17.2. Try to be as specific as possible with your recommendations.

Discussion. Review your Action Plans for Improving Teams. Have you ever tried to intervene to make your teams better? If so, what happened when you tried to make your team function better? If not, what prevents you from trying to change or improve your teams?

ACTIVITY WORKSHEET 17.2
Appreciative Inquiry of Teamwork

Characteristics of Successful Teams:

Action Plans for Improving Teams:

SOURCE: Adapted from Head, T. (2006). Appreciative Inquiry in the graduate classroom: Making group dynamics a practical topic to address. *Organizational Development Journal, 24*(2), 83–88.

Appendix

Guide to Student Team Projects

One of the best ways to teach teamwork skills is in the context of a large-scale team project that requires team problem solving (Goltz, Hietapelto, Reinsch, & Tyrell, 2008). An unstructured real-world problem can be used as a mechanism for teaching both teamwork and problem-solving skills. The team assignment needs to be challenging and motivating (Rentz, Arduser, Meloncon, & Debs, 2009). When designing team projects, it is important to consider problem design (What are the characteristics of the task?), team design (How do students get chosen for the team?), process design (How do students manage the team process?), and evaluation design (How is student input included in the evaluation?).

Many times, students are assigned team projects with limited preparation or training about how to work in teams (Snyder, 2009). If professors do not provide instruction on how to work in teams, they should not be surprised by poor team performance and dissatisfied students. Student team members need help to deal with the following challenges: understanding the purpose of the project, encouraging participation among team members, planning the project, keeping a project on track, and negotiating conflicts. All these topics are discussed in this book.

This appendix contains advice and tools to help students conduct a team project and learn from the experience. Although there are a lot of activities at the beginning of the project, student teams that spend time planning for teamwork and taskwork are more successful in the long run (Mathieu & Rapp, 2009). The following sections present guidelines on starting the team, planning and developing the project, monitoring the project and maintaining teamwork, performing team writing, and wrapping up and completing the project. It is up to the students to work through this structure and manage their group process in order to successfully complete their team project.

A.1 Starting the Team

Team Warm-Ups

Team warm-ups are social activities designed to help the team members get to know each other. Forming social relations at the beginning of a team project helps build trust and improve communications throughout the project. Building social relations is something teams should do at the very beginning, from the first team meeting. Once the team project gets going, team members don't want to spend time building social relations—they want to focus on the task. So, for the first three weeks of your team project, start your team meetings with a 10-minute warm-up activity (see Figure A.1).

These activities encourage self-disclosure—telling the other team members about yourself. However, this is a limited self-disclosure suitable for a work environment. You have a right to privacy, so be open with your teammates, but do not feel obliged to share more than would be appropriate to share in a work environment.

Development of a Team Contract

An important part of starting a team is to obtain agreement about the purpose or goals of the team, the roles and responsibilities of the team members, norms or operating rules, and expectations about the performance of team members. The contract provides an initial commitment and direction for the team about how members will work together. It focuses on the teamwork process rather than on the task aspects of the team project.

When thinking about team goals, try to develop three to five goals. The goals can be about the task, the group process, or what members hope to accomplish working on the project. For example, is your focus getting a good grade, learning a lot about teamwork, or getting along with the other students? It is better to write specific goals rather than general goals. Objectives are the specific actions or criteria that relate to your goals. Objectives should be written so that they are measurable and the team can evaluate whether the goals were met.

Team members should discuss what they expect from each other. What are the primary roles and responsibilities of team members? This includes

Figure A.1   Team Warm-Ups

Week 1 Team Warm-Up

Each member should introduce herself or himself to the team, in turn. Have each tell name, major, hometown, and other biographic information.

Discuss the following topics by taking turns answering these questions:

- What is your favorite movie? Why?
- What was your favorite class or instructor? Why?
- What do you like most and least about team projects?

Week 2 Team Warm-Up

Have the group members discuss several of the following questions:

- What is one of your favorite jokes?
- Describe your favorite vacation, recreation activity, or sport.
- What is your favorite music? List the top three songs you listen to now.
  (Research shows college students are good at assessing personality from music.)

Have group members discuss these topics about working on team projects:

- What types of work do you like best? What types of work do you like least?
  (This may help you assign roles later in the project.)

Week 3 Team Warm-Up

- Have each team member privately write down three names that would be good for the team.
- List all the team members' ideas.
- Have the team create a new list that does not include any names already listed.
- Try to select a name for your team that is supported by all members.
- If there is time, develop a team logo to go with the name.

SOURCE: Adapted from Scholtes, P. (1988). *The team handbook: How to use teams to improve quality.* Madison, WI: Joiner.

both task and relationship issues. Does the team expect equal commitment and participation from each member? How important is it that assignments are done on time or that work is high quality? How important is working cooperatively and maintaining good social relations? What is important to you as a team member? Try to be specific about these expectations.

Meeting rules or team norms define the appropriate behaviors for the team and its members. There are a variety of issues to consider when establishing norms. How should decisions be made? What are legitimate reasons for missing meetings? What should be done when people miss too many meetings? How important is it that everyone participates in team discussions? When assignments are made, what should be done when team members do not complete them? Who is responsible for the agenda and minutes? How should conflicts and disagreements be handled? How can the team encourage members to listen attentively and respectfully to others? What should the team do to enforce its rules?

One of the main complaints people have about their performance evaluations is that they did not know what was expected of them. You have just discussed the roles and responsibilities of team members and the operating rules for the team. Should these expectations be included in team members' performance evaluations? What criteria should be used to evaluate each team member's performance?

To develop a team contract, team members should think about the team's goals, objectives, roles, norms, and performance expectations. Then, the team should come to an agreement on these topics to create a written team charter. Figure A.2 presents a format for the development of a team contract.

Figure A.2   Team Contract

---

a. *Team Goals:* What are the main goals of your team?

b. *Team Objectives:* What specific actions or criteria relate to these goals? How can these be measured or evaluated?

c. *Team Member Roles:* What are the primary roles and responsibilities of each team member?

d. *Team Norms:* What operating rules does the team need?

e. *Team Member Evaluation:* What criteria will be used to evaluate each member's performance?

SOURCE: Adapted from Herrenkohl, R. (2004). *Becoming a team.* Mason, OH: South-Western.

Leadership and Meeting Roles

Teams often establish meeting roles to help meetings operate more efficiently. The two most common meeting roles are team leader and recorder. The team leader has two functions: set up the agenda and facilitate the team meeting. The team's agenda is designed to structure the meeting and is related to the tasks the team is performing. The leader acts as a facilitator who ensures that information is shared and processed by the team in a supportive and participative environment. This includes keeping the team discussion on track, preventing personal criticism, and ensuring participation by all team members. The team recorder takes notes on key decisions and task assignments in order to provide documentation of the team's activities.

Student teams usually make the mistake of selecting a team leader at the first meeting. Unfortunately, they often pick the most talkative person rather than the person best suited for structuring the team's task or facilitating team meetings. During the first three weeks of a team project, the leader role should be rotated. After that, the team can decide to keep rotating or select a permanent leader. Use the Team Role Analysis (Figure A.3) to help make your decision.

Managing Team Technology

Regardless of whether team members are collocated or are scattered around the world, project teams rely on technology for communication and managing project documents. Even when teams regularly meet face-to-face, they often use technology for both task and social communication.

Successful use of technology by teams requires addressing several issues. First, all team members need to agree on which technologies to use for various functions. Second, the team needs to make sure that everyone has sufficient capacity to use the technologies. This means that all team members have the technologies available to them and they have the skills to use the technologies. Finally, there needs to be agreement about the norms for use of the selected technology.

There are a variety of norms that teams may decide to develop about the use of technology. Here are some of the questions teams should discuss when developing technology norms. Which technology should be used for different types of communication? What is the appropriate length and response time for different technologies (for example, email versus texting)? When should messages or replies be sent to everyone on the team? What are the rules for modifying or editing shared documents? When does an issue, decision, or conflict require a face-to-face meeting?

Figure A.3   Team Role Analysis

For the past three weeks, your team has been rotating the roles of leader and recorder. It is now time to decide how to handle these role issues in the future.

Step 1: Analyze your team's leadership.

Each team member should anonymously write down who has emerged as the informal leader of the team. Compare and discuss the answers:

- Do the team members agree on who is the leader?
- How did someone become the leader or why did a team leader not emerge?

Step 2: How should team leadership operate in the future?

- Should someone be appointed the team's leader?
- Should the role of leader continue to be rotated at each meeting?
- Who should be the leader?

Step 3: Which of the following activities define the team leader's role?

_____ The leader facilitates the team meetings.

_____ The leader coordinates and/or directs the team project.

_____ The leader is the editor of the team project.

_____ Other leader roles _____

Step 4: What other roles should the team have?

- Does the team need a recorder and other meeting roles?
- Who should fulfill these roles?

As a team, complete the Team Project Technology Survey (Figure A.4) in order to develop agreement about your team's use of technology and to identify potential technology problems.

A.2 Planning and Developing the Project

Challenge the Assignment

When given an assignment, most teams jump right in and start to solve what they view as the problem. Often, they work on their initial ideas until it is obvious that their first approach is not working, at which point they go

Figure A.4   Team Project Technology Survey

List the technology and software your team selected to

    communicate task-related information _____

    communicate social-related information _____

    manage your project documents _____

How effective are these technologies at performing the listed functions?

(rate from 1—not at all effective, 2—somewhat effective, 3—effective, 4—very effective)

    _____ Communicate task-related information

    _____ Communicate social-related information

    _____ Manage your project documents

What are the benefits of using technology in your team project?

_____

What problems have you encountered using technology?

_____

Develop norms about the use of technology for your team.

_____

---

back to the beginning and start over. This is a very inefficient and frustrating approach.

Take time at the beginning to understand the assignment. Ask your professor questions about the assignment. Develop an overall plan and then question whether it will work. At the second and third team meetings, review the project assignment and the direction your team is taking. Ask the following questions: What are the benefits of our approach to the assignment? What are the problems with our approach to the assignment? Should we change our approach? It is better to change direction earlier rather than later in the project.

Generation of Project Ideas

Student project teams often face their most difficult decision at the beginning—selecting a project topic or initial direction. If the team is having trouble developing and agreeing to ideas, try using some team creativity techniques. The following is a modified brainwriting approach that is useful.

Brainwriting Method

1. *Write.* Have each team member write down at least five ideas.

2. *Review.* Combine all the ideas into a large list (or use sticky notes and cover a wall). Review the list and combine or link ideas that are related.

3. *Multivote.* Allow each team member to select three alternatives he or she would like to support. Tally the votes and remove items that received no votes or only one vote. Discuss the alternatives that have been selected, and look for new ways to combine or synthesize alternatives. If necessary, repeat this process until there are five or fewer ideas.

4. *Decide.* Use consensus decision making to select an alternative. Avoid arguing for your own position without listening to the position of others. Do not try to reach a quick agreement by voting or tossing a coin. Try to get others to explain their position so that you better understand the differences. Look for creative and collaborative solutions, such as integrating alternatives.

Project Planning

Planning is an ongoing activity for a team. To plan a project, the team needs to break the project down into its basic parts, develop a schedule proposing length of time to perform the parts and the necessary sequence to complete the parts, and assign team members to work on the parts. A project timeline is a simple graphical representation of a team project. Figure A.5 shows a project timeline for a 10-week student research project. You should try to develop a project timeline for your team project and consult it regularly to track your progress. It is useful to include some milestone reviews—times when you will review the team's progress and modify the project plan if needed.

Roles and Assignments

Although we call it teamwork, individuals working alone who use team meetings to coordinate their activities often do most of the work on a team project. Consequently, dividing a project into various tasks, assigning individuals to perform tasks, and monitoring the completion of tasks are important team functions.

Team projects can be divided in a number of ways. The overall project can be divided into report sections (Introduction, Analysis, Discussion), or activities (data gathering, analysis, writing). Individuals can be assigned certain tasks, while the team as a whole may perform other tasks. Team members need to negotiate these role assignments with each other. Remember, equity is less a matter of whether everyone is doing the same amount of

Figure A.5   Project Timeline

Project Activity	Responsible Persons	Weeks									
		1	2	3	4	5	6	7	8	9	10
Develop goals and team contract		■									
Select a project topic			■	■							
Collect research articles			■	■	■						
Write literature review					■	■	■				
Develop research methods					■						
Gather research data						■	■				
Analyze data and create tables							■				
Write research results								■			
Write project paper									■		
Edit paper										■	
Develop presentation										■	■
Conduct presentation											■
Review project at milestones					■			■			

work, and more about whether everyone is pulling his or her own weight and is equally invested in the outcome.

The most common approach used by student teams is to divide the project and assign one person to perform each part. Team meetings are used to monitor progress and coordinate activities. A few parts of the project (making strategic decisions or reviewing the final report) are left to the team as a whole. This is an efficient approach, but it leaves the team vulnerable to a team member who fails to perform his or her role. An alternative approach is the pair system, where at least two people are assigned to each major activity, and everyone works on more than one part of the project. This approach encourages coordination and integration and protects the team from problem team members.

To create roles and assignments, the team needs to discuss the following issues:

Which parts of the project should be divided and assigned to individuals?

Which parts of the project should be done by all team members?

Who should be assigned to work on various parts of the project?

Should there be a project leader to coordinate activities?

Should the team have an editor who is responsible for putting together the final report?

The team should develop an action plan that lists the major team assignments, who is responsible for performing them, and what results are expected. The action plan needs to be periodically reviewed and modified during the course of the project.

Reevaluation of the Project and Approach

Is this a good project topic? How can we improve or refine our definition of the project? Is our approach a good one? Are we headed in the right direction? These are very good questions to ask about the team's initial project decisions. These are even better questions to ask during the second week of a project rather than during a midpoint crisis. Try completing a Force Field Analysis (Figure A.6) to assist the team with these questions and answers.

A Force Field Analysis starts when you list the driving and restraining forces related to your project topic or approach. After you list these forces, highlight the most important ones. Next, review your project by discussing the following issues:

Is this a good project topic or approach? Should we accept it or reject it?

How can we improve or refine our approach?

What additional information do we need to develop our approach to the project?

Figure A.6   Force Field Analysis: Are We Going in a Good Direction?

Driving Forces	Restraining Forces
Factors that make this a good project (i.e., what are the benefits of this project topic or approach?)	Factors that limit the success of this project (i.e., what are the problems with this project topic or approach?)

A.3 Monitoring the Project and Maintaining Teamwork

Team Meetings: Sharing Information, Making Decisions, and Tracking Assignments

Team meetings are used to coordinate activities, track progress, make decisions, and assign tasks. Team meetings should start with sharing information and reviewing progress. Team members check in by updating the team on their activities and work assignments. If the team has developed a project plan and timeline, it can review its progress on meeting the objectives. After reviewing progress, team meetings then focus on decision making. Decisions relate to project topics, management of the team, team activities, task assignments, and coordination of tasks. At the end of the meeting, important decisions are summarized and task assignments reviewed.

Teams need to plan their project by outlining the various tasks, deciding when the tasks need to be completed, and assigning team members to perform the tasks. Once the planning has been completed, the team should regularly review its progress on meeting these objectives. The Weekly Action Plan (Figure A.7) is a good way to record assignments at the end of a team meeting. It also makes a good starting point for reviewing performance at the next meeting.

It is the team leader's job to help structure and facilitate the team meeting. Simple agendas that outline the meeting structure (information sharing, progress check, team decisions, and task assignments) and identify decision topics are useful to keep the team on track. The leader can ask for input on

Figure A.7   Weekly Action Plan

Action	Responsible Person	Expected Result	Completion Date

the agenda either before or at the beginning of the meeting. The recorder monitors progress of the meeting and records the major decisions and task assignments.

Group Process Evaluations

Once the team has started working on its project, the team needs to monitor its progress, manage problems, and improve how it is operating. Student teams fall into behavior patterns fairly quickly. They often adopt patterns they used before in other team projects or classroom settings. These behavior patterns become stable ways of operating, even when they are not adaptive or effective. This is why it is important to set aside time to evaluate how the team is operating.

One of the biggest problems for improving teams is to get beyond scapegoating or blaming individuals (or outside forces) for the team's problems. It is not problem people who are causing difficulties—it is a team process that does not work. Your team has to accept responsibility that they allow problem behaviors to occur and continue. Scapegoating never leads to solutions. It is just a way of blaming others for the problem so the team does not have to work on a solution.

The team must decide whether it wants to live with its problems (and problem people) or whether it wants to evaluate what it is doing and develop strategies to work together more effectively. Team members often ignore problems ("don't make waves") until the problems are very disruptive and difficult to solve. It is better to identify problems early and deal with them before they disrupt the team's operation. Regular group process evaluations are one way to do this.

Group process evaluations are performed at the end of team meetings. They help identify what the team is doing right and encourage dealing with team problems. Have each team member rate the team's performance and then answer the following questions: What is the team doing well? What areas of improvement are needed? (See Figure A.8.) After answering these questions, discuss the responses in the team. Use the discussion to acknowledge accomplishments, identify problems, and develop solutions for the team's problems.

Student teams should conduct group process evaluations about every other week. This helps ensure that problems are identified before they become too difficult to manage. It is useful for students to save their evaluations to track the team's progress. The group process evaluation forms are a good history of the team's performance and are useful for evaluating and learning from the team project experience.

Managing Problem Behaviors

Group process evaluations are good at identifying the problems teams encounter, but how should the team manage these problems? This activity is a method that teams can use to manage problem behaviors. The team can try it on a sample problem to learn how the approach works or use it on a problem the team is trying to resolve. Figure A.9 presents a format for this activity.

Figure A.8   Group Process Evaluation

How well is the team performing?								
Very Poorly	1	2	3	4	5	6	7	Very Well
What is the team doing well?								
What areas of improvement are needed?								

Figure A.9   Managing Problem Behaviors Activity

Defining the Problem Behavior
Discuss examples of when and why this behavior occurs. Write a definition of the behavior below.

Managing Problem Behaviors
Preventive Measures: What can the team do to prevent this behavior from occurring?
Compensatory Approaches: How can the team change how it operates to compensate for the behavior?
Change Approaches: What strategies can the team use to change the behavior?

SOURCE: Adapted from Scholtes, P. (1994). *The team handbook for educators*. Madison, WI: Joiner.

The first step is to select and define the problem behavior. There are many behaviors that can disrupt a team's operation. If the team has discussed team norms, then problem behaviors can be viewed as actions that violate these norms. Common problems for teams are poor attendance, failure to complete assignments on time, dominating team discussions, or interpersonal conflicts among team members. The team should select a problem that it wants to handle better in the future.

After selecting a problem behavior for analysis, try to better define the behavior. Think of specific examples of the problem behavior. Discuss when the behavior occurs and what is causing it. What team norms does it violate? Write a definition of the behavior.

There are several approaches to managing problem behaviors. The team can try to prevent the behavior from occurring, it can compensate for the behavior by changing how the team operates, or it can try to use rewards or punishments to change the behavior. For the problem behavior identified, discuss alternative approaches for the team to manage the problem behavior and write your answers.

After completing this analysis, the team is ready to decide how it wants to deal with the problem behavior. Regardless of whether the team decides to do nothing or adopt one of the strategies identified in the activity, the team should review the status of the problem at its next meeting.

Milestone: Midpoint Evaluation

The midpoint of the project cycle is a time when teams often evaluate what they are doing. Although it is halfway through the project's period, most teams discover that the project is less than half completed. What is worse is that the team may doubt whether they are headed in the right direction. It is time to stop and reevaluate the team's goals and objectives, the direction of the project, and the way the team is operating. You might want to go back and review the team's contract, conduct a Force Field analysis on the project's direction, or review and modify the project timeline so it reflects the team's actual performance. Finally, do a group process evaluation and review how well your team is working together.

A basic midpoint evaluation technique for reflecting on the team's performance is the Start-Stop-Continue Approach (Dyer, Dyer, & Dyer, 2007). Individual team members write down what they think the team should start doing, stop doing, and continue doing in order to be more effective. The team discusses these views and looks for patterns or common responses. The team leader asks for concrete examples of the identified issues. Next, the team discusses ways to change what they are doing to become more effective.

After the midpoint, teams need to make a push toward performance. Working hard to complete the project is only useful if you are heading in the right direction and have a group process that supports teamwork. Now is the time as a team to make sure that this happens and the project moves forward.

A.4 Performing Team Writing

Writing in a team is not easy. There are lots of problems that can arise, from personality clashes to computer incompatibilities. There is no definitive approach that is the best way for a team to write together. The success of various approaches depends on the group size and the personalities and abilities of the team members.

Writing in a team is risky. You have to give up control and learn to accept differences in writing styles. You must also deal with writing and decision-making issues at the same time. This is very confusing because you sometimes do not know whether the disagreement is about what you said or how you are saying it. Added to these problems is fear—the fear that your grade will be affected and you will not get credit for your good work.

Overall Strategy

Writing a team paper usually has three parts: defining and outlining the project, writing the sections, and reviewing and editing. Students often go too quickly through the first stage and end up with a lot of problems and confusion later on. Students also forget about the third stage, so the final project can have the appearance of being thrown together at the last moment. Recognizing the importance of all three stages makes team writing easier and improves the quality of the project.

When defining the nature of the project, the team should discuss the particular content of the final document, which requires development of an outline of the final report and a team discussion about what information is to be presented. Try to anticipate problems, such as dealing with problem team members and keeping on schedule. Establishing a work plan with assignments and due dates helps manage some of these problems.

The team needs to decide how to divide the writing. The next section presents several options to accomplish this task. However, before you send your team members out to write their sections, you need to establish some ground rules. How long should the sections be? Should people submit drafts or relatively finished text? Should the team review the detailed outlines before writing drafts?

Although the team should develop the project's overall outline collaboratively, there are many options for dividing up the writing and editing tasks. Although dividing the assignment is efficient (especially since it reduces meeting times), at some point everyone needs to review and edit the document. You have not done your part if you have not reviewed and agreed with (or offered modifications) to the entire document.

Division of Work

There is no single preferred method to divide up the tasks of writing a report. A team's options range from having one person write the entire report with information provided by team members, to all the team members collaboratively writing the report together. In most cases, teams select an approach between these extremes, where the project is divided and individual team members write sections of the report. Regardless of your selection, there are two additional elements to the divide and write approach: the weak editor system and the strong editor system. Your team should discuss how you want to write the project using these approaches as a starting point for your discussion.

1. *Weak editor:* Divide the paper into sections and assign the writing of parts. This is probably the most common approach to team writing. It makes logical sense because it uses division of labor. However, it often leads to papers that are difficult to read because the sections do not flow smoothly together. Using this approach still requires a good editing system to help deal with the overlaps and missing information that inevitably occurs.

If your team is using this approach, then you need to spend time at the beginning defining what the sections of the paper should look like. Obviously, this includes having a good report outline so the sections do not repeat or overlap. In addition, there need to be rules about how to make the parts as compatible as possible. For example, how should each section end so the next section flows into it smoothly? Some options for writing rules include the size of each section, agreement on the key terms to use throughout the report, typical paragraph length, formatting and layout, and computer compatibility issues.

2. *Strong editor:* In this approach, a central editor controls most of the writing process. Although your team may elect to have individual team members work on separate sections of the report, you may want to take a more centralized approach to writing the final document. For example, the team members submit drafts of their sections of the report to a central editor who finishes the drafts and cobbles the sections together. This approach often leads to a more integrated report, but it puts stress and a lot of responsibility on a key team member.

From the professor's perspective, this is a good approach: The report is easier to read because the writing style is more consistent. However, it does create a few problems for the team. It requires better planning because the drafts of the sections have to be submitted earlier to give time for the editor to put them all together. The editor has to put in extra work, which means that you are using your team's best writer to integrate work rather than to write important sections. Additionally, similar to other centralized approaches, it also creates problems about how to select and reward the team member who takes this central role.

Most student teams select the weak editor approach, where the editor's job is merely to cut and paste parts of the report. This approach is easy for the students, but it can create problems in the paper. Often, student team reports have unexplained gaps between sections or sections that overlap with each other. The terminology used in one part of the report might be different from other parts, as a result the reader is often uncertain if new concepts are really being used. Also, language and writing style differences can make a team paper hard to read. The strong editor approach helps to deal with these writing problems. The main difficulty with the strong editor approach is that it takes time. The parts of the report must be submitted to the editor early enough that the editor can work on the paper and have the team members review the final product. Regardless of which approach a team uses, everyone is responsible for the report. No team member is finished with the assignment until he or she has reviewed the final draft!

The use of technology for team writing allows an alternative approach: reciprocal composition (Duarte & Snyder, 2006). In this approach, an outline of the report is stored in an electronic database that is available to all team members. Team members work on all parts of the report by adding and editing material. Electronic document-writing tools allow the team to monitor each other's participation in the writing process and the changes being made to the report. This approach can be very efficient because it allows all team members to work simultaneously. However, it requires a tightly structured agenda to ensure progress on all parts of the document.

A.5 Wrapping Up and Completing the Project

Milestone: Precompletion Planning

Several weeks before the final project is due, it is time for a review meeting to evaluate the situation and plan for completion of the project. This is similar to the other milestone evaluations (such as the midpoint review), except the focus is on how to complete the project. If all is going well, this evaluation is just reviewing the project plan, coordinating submissions of material to the editor, and arranging a final review meeting. If things are not going as planned, now is the time to decide how to salvage the situation by reassigning tasks, redefining expectations about tasks and activities, or even negotiating a new contract with your professor. Even if you are having problems, your team still has some options in order to finish successfully within the next two weeks.

Team Evaluations

In many student team projects, the professor allows some student input on team member evaluations. This is appropriate, since students know more about the performance of individual team members than the professor. It is time to review the team's contract to see what performance expectations your team decided were relevant. You should use these to evaluate your teammates, since it is not fair to evaluate people on new criteria or to evaluate different team members using different criteria.

Teams have evaluation biases. Teams tend to give everyone high evaluations when the team is successful and to scapegoat or blame a few members when the team performs poorly. Instead, you should try to honestly evaluate your teammates using the criteria your team established. It is fine to give mostly positive evaluations when your team worked well together, but it is not fair to give everyone a high evaluation if that does not reflect individual contributions.

Celebrating Success and Learning From the Experience

Congratulations—you finished your team project. If your team was like most project teams, you had your ups and downs along the way, with challenges and conflicts to manage. Your team should celebrate its success with a social event.

This is not likely to be your last team project as a student or professional, so you should try to learn as much as possible from the experience. If you have been saving your group process evaluations, now is a good time to review them to try to understand the teamwork process. How did your evaluations of the team's performance change during the course of the project? What were the things that your team did well during the project? What were the areas where improvement was needed? Was your team able to resolve its problems along the way?

A final group process evaluation that examines the entire project experience can be a valuable learning tool. Remember that people learn more from positive feedback than they do from negative feedback. Make sure you try to understand what went right about the project so you can repeat it in the future.

References

Adam, H., Shirako, A., & Maddux, W. (2010). Cultural variance in the interpersonal effects of anger in negotiations. *Psychological Science, 21*(6), 882–889.

Adler, N. (1986). *International dimensions of organizational behavior.* Boston, MA: Kent.

Adler, P. (1991). Workers and flexible manufacturing systems: Three installations compared. *Journal of Organizational Behavior, 12,* 447–460.

Alberti, R., & Emmons, M. (1978). *Your perfect right.* San Luis Obispo, CA: Impact.

Allen, J. A., Sands, S. J., Mueller, S. L., Frear, K. A., Mudd, M., & Rogelberg, S. G. (2012). Employees' feelings about more meetings: An overt analysis and recommendations for improving meetings. *Management Research Review, 35*(5), 405–418.

Allen, N., & Hecht, T. (2004). The "romance of teams": Toward an understanding of its psychological underpinnings and implications. *Journal of Occupational and Organizational Psychology, 77,* 439–461.

Allen, V., & Levine, J. (1969). Consensus and conformity. *Journal of Experimental Social Psychology, 5,* 389–399.

Amabile, T. (1996). *Creativity in context.* Boulder, CO: Westview.

Amabile, T., Fisher, C., & Pillemer, J. (2014, January). IDEO's culture of helping. *Harvard Business Review,* 55–61.

Amason, A. (1996). Distinguishing the effects of functional and dysfunctional conflict on strategic decision making: Resolving a paradox for top management teams. *Academy of Management Journal, 39*(1), 123–148.

Ames, D. (2008). In search of the right touch. *Current Directions in Psychological Science, 17*(6), 381–385.

Ancona, D., & Caldwell, D. (1990). Information technology and work groups: The case of new product teams. In J. Galegher, R. Kraut, & C. Egido (Eds.), *Intellectual teamwork: Social and technological foundations of cooperative work* (pp. 173–190). Hillsdale, NJ: Lawrence Erlbaum.

Ancona, D., & Caldwell, D. (1992). Demography and design: Predictors of new product team performance. *Organizational Science, 3,* 321–331.

Antonioni, D. (1994). The effects of feedback accountability on upward appraisal ratings. *Personnel Psychology, 47,* 349–356.

Appelbaum, E., & Batt, R. (1994). *The new American workplace.* Ithaca, NY: IRL Press.

Argyris, C. (1998). Empowerment: The emperor's new clothes. *Harvard Business Review, 76*(3), 98–105.

Armstrong, D., & Cole, P. (1995). Managing distances and differences in geographically distributed workgroups. In S. Jackson & M. Ruderman (Eds.), *Diversity in work teams: Research paradigms for a changing workplace* (pp. 187–215). Washington, DC: American Psychological Association.

Arthur, W., Bennett, W., Edens, P., & Bell, S. (2003). Effectiveness of training in organizations: A meta-analysis of design and evaluation features. *Journal of Applied Psychology, 88*(2), 234–245.

Asch, S. (1955, Winter). Opinions and social pressure. *Scientific American,* 31–35.

Axelrod, R. (1984). *The evolution of cooperation.* New York, NY: Basic Books.

Axley, S. (1996). *Communication at work: Management and the communication-intensive organization.* Westport, CT: Quorum Books.

Ayoko, O., Callan, V., & Hartel, C. (2008). The influence of team emotional intelligence climate on conflict and team members' reactions to conflict. *Small Group Research, 39*(2), 121–149.

Bandura, A. (2000). Exercise of human agency through collective efficacy. *Current Directions in Psychological Science, 9,* 17–20.

Baer, M., & Frese, M. (2003). Innovation is not enough: Climates for initiative and psychological safety, process innovations, and firm performance. *Journal of Organizational Behavior, 24*(1), 45–68.

Barczak, G., Lassk, F., & Mulki, J. (2010). Antecedents of team creativity: An examination of team emotional intelligence, team trust, and collaborative culture. *Creativity and Innovation Management, 19*(4), 332–345.

Barnes, C., Hollenbeck, J., Jundt, D., DeRue, D., & Harmon, S. (2011). Mixing individual incentives and group incentives: Best of both worlds or social dilemma? *Journal of Management, 37*(6), 1611–1635.

Barnlund, D. C. (1970). A transactional model of communication. In K. Sereno & C. Mortensen (Eds.), *Foundations of communication theory* (pp. 83–102). New York, NY: Harper & Row.

Barsade, S. G., & O'Neill, O. A. (2014). What's love got to do with it? A longitudinal study of the culture of companionate love and employee and client outcomes in a long-term care setting. *Administrative Science Quarterly, 59*(4), 551–598.

Bass, B. (1985). *Leadership and performance beyond expectations.* New York, NY: Free Press.

Battaglia, B. (1992). Skills for managing multicultural teams. *Cultural Diversity at Work, 4,* 4–12.

Beal, D., Cohen, R., Burke, M., & McLendon, C. (2003). Cohesion and performance in groups: A meta-analytic clarification of construct relations. *Journal of Applied Psychology, 88*(6), 989–1004.

Becker, J. A., Halbesleben, J. R., & Dan O'Hair, H. (2005). Defensive communication and burnout in the workplace: The mediating role of leader–member exchange. *Communication Research Reports, 22*(2), 143–150.

Beebe, S., & Masterson, J. (1994). *Communicating in small groups.* New York, NY: HarperCollins.

Beersma, B., Hollenbeck, J., Conlon, D., Humphrey, S., Moon, H., & Ilgen, D. (2009). Cutthroat competition: The effects of team role decisions on adaptation to alternative reward structures. *Organizational Behavior and Human Decision Processes, 108,* 131–142.

Beersma, B., Hollenbeck, J., Humphrey, S., Moon, H., Conlon, D., & Ilgen, D. (2003). Cooperation, competition, and team performance: Toward a contingency approach. *Academy of Management Journal, 46*(5), 572–590.

Behfar, K., Mannix, E., Peterson, R., & Trochim, W. (2011). Conflict in small groups: The meaning and consequences of process conflict. *Small Group Research, 42*(2), 127–176.

Belbin, R. (1981). *Team roles at work.* Oxford, UK: Butterworth Heinemann.

Bell, S., Villado, A., Lukasik, M., Belau, L., & Briggs, A. (2010). Getting specific about demographic diversity variable and team performance relationships: A meta-analysis. *Journal of Management, 37*(3), 709–743.

Bendersky, C., & Shah, N. (2013). The downfall of extroverts and rise of neurotics: The dynamic process of status allocation in task groups. *Academy of Management Journal, 56*(2), 387–406.

Bennis, W., & Biederman, P. (1997). *Organizing genius: The secrets of creative collaboration.* Reading, MA: Addison-Wesley.

Bikson, T., Cohen, S., & Mankin, D. (1999). Information technology and high-performance teams. In E. Sundstrom (Ed.), *Supporting work team effectiveness* (pp. 215–245). San Francisco, CA: Jossey-Bass.

Blake, R., & Mouton, J. (1969). *Building a dynamic corporation through grid organizational development.* Reading, MA: Addison-Wesley.

Bradley, B., Postlethwaite, B., Klotz, A., Hamdani, M., & Brown, K. (2011). Reaping the benefits of task conflict in teams: The critical role of team psychological safety. *Journal of Applied Psychology, 97*(1), 151–158.

Brehm, S. S., & Brehm, J. W. (1981). *Psychological reactance: A theory of freedom and control.* New York, NY: Academic Press.

Brescoll, V. L. (2012). Who takes the floor and why: Gender, power, and volubility in organizations. *Administrative Science Quarterly, 56*(4), 622–641.

Brewer, M. (1995). Managing diversity: The role of social identities. In S. Jackson & M. Ruderman (Eds.), *Diversity in work teams: Research paradigms for a changing workplace* (pp. 47–68). Washington, DC: American Psychological Association.

Briggs, R., Kolfschoten, G., Vreede, G., & Dean, D. (2006). Defining key concepts in collaboration engineering. *AMCIS 2006 Proceedings,* Paper 17, 121–128. Retrieved from http:// aisel.aisnet.org/amcis2006/17

Brown, S. (1996). A meta-analysis and review of organizational research on job involvement. *Psychological Bulletin, 120,* 235–255.

Burke, C., Priest, H., Wooten, S., DiazGranados, D., & Salas, E. (2009). Understanding the cognitive processes in adaptive multicultural teams: A framework. In E. Salas, G. Goodwin, & C. Burke (Eds.), *Team effectiveness in complex organizations: Cross-disciplinary perspectives and approaches* (pp. 209–241). New York, NY: Routledge.

Burke, C., Stagl, K., Salas, E., Pierce, L., & Kendall, D. (2006). Understanding team adaptation: A conceptual analysis and model. *Journal of Applied Psychology, 91*(6), 1189–1207.

Burn, S. (2004). *Groups: Theory and practice.* Belmont, CA: Wadsworth.

Burnstein, E., & Vinokur, A. (1977). Persuasive arguments and social comparison as determinants of attitude polarization. *Journal of Experimental Social Psychology, 13,* 315–332.

Burpitt, W., & Bigoness, W. (1997). Leadership and innovation among teams: The impact of empowerment. *Small Group Research, 28,* 414–423.

Bushe, G. (1988). Cultural contradictions of statistical process control in American manufacturing organizations. *Journal of Management, 14,* 19–31.

Cannon-Bowers, J., & Salas, E. (1998). Team performance and training in complex environments: Recent findings from applied research. *Current Directions in Psychological Science, 7,* 83–87.

Cannon-Bowers, J., Tannenbaum, S., Salas, E., & Volpe, C. (1995). Defining competencies and establishing team training requirements. In R. Guzzo & E. Salas (Eds.), *Team effectiveness and decision making in organizations* (pp. 330–380). San Francisco, CA: Jossey-Bass.

Carnevale, A., Gainer, L., & Meltzer, A. (1990). *Workplace basics: The essential skills employers want.* San Francisco, CA: Jossey-Bass.

Carnevale, A., & Stone, S. (1995). *The American mosaic: An in-depth report on the future of diversity at work.* New York, NY: McGraw-Hill.

Carnevale, P. (1986). Strategic choice in mediation. *Negotiation Journal, 2,* 41–56.

Carte, T. A., Chidambaram, L., & Becker, A. (2006). Emergent leadership in self-managed virtual teams. *Group Decision and Negotiation, 15*(4), 323–343.

Caruso, H. M., & Woolley, A. W. (2008). Harnessing the power of emergent interdependence to promote diverse team collaboration. In M. A. Neale, E. Mannix, & K. Phillips (Eds.), *Research on managing groups and teams: Groups and diversity* (Vol. 9). Oxford, UK: Elsevier Science Press.

Casciaro, T., & Lobo, M. (2005). Competent jerks, lovable fools, and the formation of social networks. *Harvard Business Review, 83*(6), 92–99.

Castore, C., & Murnighan, J. (1978). Determinants of support for group decisions. *Organizational Behavior and Human Performance, 22,* 75–92.

Charan, R., & Useem, J. (2002). Why companies fail. *Fortune, 145*(11), 50–62.

Chen, G., Kirkman, B. L., Kanfer, R., Allen, D., & Rosen, B. (2007). A multilevel study of leadership, empowerment, and performance in teams. *Journal of Applied Psychology, 92*(2), 331–346.

Cheng, J. (1983). Interdependence and coordination in organizations: A role system analysis. *Academy of Management Journal, 26,* 156–162.

Choi, K., & Cho, B. (2011). Competing hypotheses analyses of the associations between group task conflict and group relationship conflict. *Journal of Organizational Behavior, 32,* 1106–1126.

Clarke, N. (2010). Developing emotional intelligence abilities through team-based learning. *Human Resource Quarterly, 21*(2), 119–138.

Cohen, B. P., & Zhou, X. (1991). Status processes in enduring work groups. *American Sociological Review,* 179–188.

Cohen, M. A., Rogelberg, S. G., Allen, J. A., & Luong, A. (2011). Meeting design characteristics and attendee perceptions of staff/team meeting quality. *Group Dynamics: Theory, Research, and Practice, 15*(1), 90–104.

Cohen, S., & Bailey, D. (1997). What makes teams work: Group effectiveness research from the shop floor to the executive suite. *Journal of Management, 23,* 239–290.

Cohen, S., Ledford, G., & Spreitzer, G. (1996). A predictive model of self-managing work team effectiveness. *Human Relations, 49,* 643–676.

Cole, R. (1989). *Strategies for learning: Small-group activities in American, Japanese, and Swedish industry.* Berkeley: University of California Press.

Cordery, J., Morrison, D., Wright, B., & Wall, T. (2010). The impact of autonomy and task uncertainty on team performance: A longitudinal field study. *Journal of Organizational Behavior, 31,* 240–258.

Cosier, R., & Dalton, D. (1990). Positive effects of conflict: A field assessment. *International Journal of Conflict Management, 1,* 81–92.

Côté, S., Lopes, P. N., Salovey, P., & Miners, C. T. (2010). Emotional intelligence and leadership emergence in small groups. *The Leadership Quarterly, 21*(3), 496–508.

Cotton, J. (1993). *Employee involvement.* Newbury Park, CA: Sage.

Cox, T. (1994). *Cultural diversity in organizations: Theory, research, and practice.* Oakland, CA: Berrett-Koehler.

Cox, T. (1995). The complexity of diversity: Challenges and directions for future research. In S. Jackson & M. Ruderman (Eds.), *Diversity in work teams: Research paradigms for a changing workplace* (pp. 235–245). Washington, DC: American Psychological Association.

Crotty, S., & Brett, J. (2012). Fusing creativity: Cultural metacognition and teamwork in multicultural teams. *Negotiation and Conflict Management Research, 5*(2), 210–234.

Curseu, P., Schruijer, S., & Boros, S. (2007). The effects of groups' variety and disparity on groups' cognitive complexity. *Group Dynamics: Theory, Research, and Practice, 11*(3), 187–206.

Daft, R., & Lengel, R. (1986). Organizational information requirements, media richness, and structural design. *Management Science, 32,* 554–571.

Dalkey, N. (1969). *The Delphi method: An experimental study of group decisions.* Santa Monica, CA: RAND.

Davis, S. (1984). *Managing corporate culture.* Cambridge, MA: Ballinger.

Davis, L., & Wacker, G. (1987). Job design. In G. Salvendy (Ed.), *Handbook of human factors* (pp. 431–452). New York, NY: John Wiley.

Dawes, R. (1988). *Rational choice in an uncertain world*. San Diego, CA: Harcourt Brace Jovanovich.

Day, D. (2013). Leadership. In S. Koxzlowski (Ed.), *The Oxford handbook of organizational psychology* (696–725). New York, NY: Oxford University Press.

Day, D., Gronn, P., & Salas, E. (2004). Leadership capacity in teams. *The Leadership Quarterly, 15*(6), 857–880.

Deal, T., & Kennedy, A. (1982). *Corporate cultures*. Reading, MA: Addison-Wesley.

Deci, E. (1975). *Intrinsic motivation*. New York, NY: Plenum.

DeChurch, L., Mesmer-Magus, J., & Doty, D. (2013). Moving beyond relationship and task conflict: Toward a process-state perspective. *Journal of Applied Psychology, 98*(4), 559–578.

DeDreu, C. (2007). Cooperative outcome interdependence, task reflexivity, and team effectiveness: A motivated information processing perspective. *Journal of Applied Psychology, 92*(3), 628–638.

DeDreu, C., & Weingart, L. (2003). Task versus relationship conflict, team performance, and team member satisfaction: A meta-analysis. *Journal of Applied Psychology, 88*(4), 741–749.

DeJong, B., & Dirks, K. (2012). Beyond shared perceptions of trust and monitoring in teams: Implications of asymmetry and dissensus. *Journal of Applied Psychology, 97*(1), 1–16.

de Leede, J., & Stoker, J. (1999). Self-managing teams in manufacturing companies: Implications for the engineering function. *Engineering Management Journal, 11*(3), 19–24.

Delbecq, A., Van de Ven, A., & Gustafson, D. (1975). *Group techniques for program planning*. Glenview, IL: Scott, Foresman.

DeMatteo, J., Eby, L., & Sundstrom, E. (1998). Team-based rewards: Current empirical evidence and directions for future research. *Research in Organizational Behavior, 20*, 141–183.

Dennis, A., & Valacich, J. (1993). Computer brainstorms: More heads are better than one. *Journal of Applied Psychology, 78*, 531–537.

Dennis, A. R., & Valacich, J. S. (1999, January). Proceedings of the 32nd Annual Hawaii International Conference in System Sciences: *Rethinking media richness: Towards a theory of media synchronicity*. (HICSS-32). Maui, Hawaii: The Institute of Electrical and Electronics Engineers (IEEE) Computer Society.

Dertouzos, M. (1997). *What will be: How the new world of information will change our lives*. New York, NY: Harper.

Deutsch, M., & Gerard, H. (1955). A study of normative and informational social influence upon individual judgment. *Journal of Abnormal and Social Psychology, 51*, 629–636.

Devine, D., Clayton, L., Philips, J., Dunford, B., & Melner, S. (1999). Teams in organizations: Prevalence, characteristics, and effectiveness. *Small Group Research, 30*, 678–711.

Dewey, J. (1910). *How we think*. New York, NY: Heath.

DeWit, F., Greer, L., & Jehn, K. (2012). The paradox of intragroup conflict: A meta-analysis. *Journal of Applied Psychology, 97*(2), 360–390.

Dibble, R., & Gibson, C. (2013). Collaboration for the common good: An examination of challenges and adjustment processes in multicultural collaborations. *Journal of Organizational Behavior, 34,* 764–790.

Diefendorff, J. M., Erickson, R. J., Grandey, A. A., & Dahling, J. J. (2011). Emotional display rules as work unit norms: A multilevel analysis of emotional labor among nurses. *Journal of Occupational Health Psychology, 16*(2), 170–186.

Diehl, M., & Stroebe, W. (1987). Productivity loss in brainstorming groups: Toward a solution of a riddle. *Journal of Personality and Social Psychology, 53,* 497–509.

DiSalvo, V., Nikkel, E., & Monroe, C. (1989). Theory and practice: A field investigation and identification of group members' perception of problems facing natural work groups. *Small Group Behavior, 20,* 551–567.

Drach-Zahavy, A. (2004). Exploring team support: The role of team's design, values, and leader's support. *Group Dynamics, 8*(4), 235–252.

Drescher, M., Korsgaard, M., Welpe, I., Picot, A., & Wigand, R. (2014). The dynamics of shared leadership: Building trust and enhancing performance. *Journal of Applied Psychology, 99*(5), 771–783.

Driskell, J., Radtke, P., & Salas, E. (2003). Virtual teams: Effects of technological mediation on team performance. *Group Dynamics: Theory, Research, and Practice, 7*(4), 297–323.

Driskell, J., & Salas, E. (2006). Groupware, group dynamics, and team performance. In C. Bowers, E. Salas, & F. Jentsch (Eds.), *Creating high-tech teams* (pp. 11–34). Washington, DC: American Psychological Association.

Druskat, V., & Wheeler, J. (2003). Managing from the boundary: The effective leadership of self-managing work teams. *Academy of Management Journal, 46*(4), 435–457.

Druskat, V., & Wolff, S. (2001). Building the emotional intelligence of groups. *Harvard Business Review, 79*(3), 80–90.

Duarte, D., & Snyder, N. (2006). *Mastering virtual teams* (3rd ed.). San Francisco, CA: Jossey-Bass.

Dube, L., & Robey, D. (2008). Surviving the paradoxes of virtual teamwork. *Information Systems Journal, 19,* 3–30.

Dyer, W., Dyer, W., & Dyer, J. (2007). *Team building: Proven team strategies for improving team performance* (4th ed.). San Francisco, CA: John Wiley.

Eagly, A., Karau, S., & Makhijani, M. (1995). Gender and the effectiveness of leaders: A meta-analysis. *Journal of Personality and Social Psychology, 117,* 125–145.

Earley, P., & Gibson, C. (2002). *Multinational work teams: A new perspective.* Mahwah, NJ: Lawrence Erlbaum.

Earley, P., & Mosakowski, E. (2000). Creating hybrid team cultures: An empirical test of transnational team functioning. *Academy of Management Journal, 43*(1), 26–49.

Edmondson, A., Bohmer, R., & Pisano, G. (2001). Speeding up team learning. *Harvard Business Review, 79*(9), 125–132.

Edmondson, A., & Lei, Z. (2014). Psychological safety: The history, renaissance, and future of an interpersonal construct. *Annual Review of Organizational Psychology and Organizational Behavior, 23–43.*

Edmondson, A., & Nembhard, I. (2009). Product development and learning in project teams: The challenges are the benefits. *Journal of Product Innovation Management, 26,* 123–138.

Edmondson, A., & Roloff, K. (2009). Overcoming barriers to collaboration: Psychological safety and learning in diverse teams. In E. Salas, G. Goodwin, & C. Burke (Eds.), *Team effectiveness in complex organizations: Cross-disciplinary perspectives and approaches* (pp. 183–208). New York, NY: Routledge.

Ellis, S., Carette, B., Anseel, F., & Lievens, F. (2014). Systematic reflection: Implications for learning from failures and successes. *Current Directions in Psychological Science, 23*(1), 67–72.

Emich, K. (2014). Who's bringing the donuts: The role of affective patterns in group decision making. *Organizational Behavior and Human Decision Processes,* 124, 122–132.

Erez, M., & Somech, A. (1996). Is group productivity loss the rule or the exception? Effects of culture and group-based motivation. *Academy of Management Journal, 39*(6), 1513–1537.

Fairchild, J., & Hunter, S. (2013). We've got creative differences: The effects of task conflict and participative safety on team creative performance. *Journal of Creative Behavior, 48*(1), 64–87.

Falbe, C., & Yukl, G. (1992). Consequences for managers using single influence tactics and combination of tactics. *Academy of Management Journal, 35,* 638–652.

Fan, E., & Gruenfeld, D. (1998). When needs outweigh desires: The effects of resource interdependence and reward interdependence on group problem solving. *Basic and Applied Social Psychology, 20*(1), 45–56.

Farh, J., Lee, C., & Farh, C. (2010). Task conflict and team creativity: A question of how much and when. *Journal of Applied Psychology, 95*(6), 1173–1180.

Farh, C., Seo, M., & Tesluk, P. (2012). Emotional intelligence, teamwork effectiveness, and job performance: The moderating role of job context. *Journal of Applied Psychology, 98*(1), 1–11.

Farmer, S., & Roth, J. (1998). Conflict-handling behavior in work groups: Effects of group structure, decision process, and time. *Small Group Research, 29,* 669–713.

Feldman, D. (1984). The development and enforcement of group norms. *Academy of Management Review, 9,* 47–53.

Ferris, W. (2009). Demonstrating the challenges of behaving with emotional intelligence in a team setting: An on-line/on-ground experiential exercise. *Organizational Management Journal, 6,* 23–38.

Fiore, S., & Schooler, J. (2004). Process mapping and shared cognition: Teamwork and the development of shared problem models. In E. Salas & S. Fiore (Eds.), *Team cognition: Understanding the factors that drive process and performance* (pp. 133–152). Washington, DC: American Psychological Association.

Fisher, R., Ferreira, M., Assmar, E., Redford, P., & Harb, C. (2009). Individualism-collectivism as descriptive norms: Development of a subjective norm approach to culture measurement. *Journal of Cross-Cultural Psychology, 40*(2), 187–213.

Fisher, R., Ury, W., & Patton, B. (1991). *Getting to yes: Negotiating agreement without giving in* (2nd ed.). Boston, MA: Houghton Mifflin.

Ford, R., & Fottler, M. (1995). Empowerment: A matter of degree. *Academy of Management Executive, 9*(3), 21–31.

Forsyth, D. (1999). *Group dynamics* (3rd ed.). Belmont, CA: Thompson.

Forsyth, D., & Kelley, K. (1996). Heuristic-based biases in estimates of personal contributions to collective endeavors. In J. Nye & A. Brower (Eds.), *What's social about social cognition? Research on socially shared cognitions in small groups* (pp. 106–123). Thousand Oaks, CA: SAGE.

Franz, C., & Jin, K. (1995). The structure of group conflict in a collaborative work group during information systems development. *Journal of Applied Communication Research, 23,* 108–127.

Franz, R. (1998). Task interdependence and personal power in teams. *Small Group Research, 29,* 226–253.

Franz, T. (2012). *Group dynamics and team interventions.* Chichester, UK: Wiley-Blackwell.

French, J., & Raven, B. (1959). The bases of power. In D. Cartwright (Ed.), *Studies in social power* (pp. 150–167). Ann Arbor: University of Michigan Press.

Gardner, H. (2012, April). Coming through when it matters most. *Harvard Business Review,* 83–91.

Garvin, D. (2013, December). How Google sold its engineers on management. *Harvard Business Review,* 75–82.

Gersick, C. (1988). Time and transition in work teams: Toward a new model of group development. *Academy of Management Journal, 31,* 9–41. Gersick, C., & Davis-Sacks, M. (1990). Summary: Task forces. In R. Hackman (Ed.), *Groups that work (and those that don't)* (pp. 146–153). San Francisco, CA: Jossey-Bass.

Gibb, J. (1961). Defensive communication. *Journal of Communication, 11,* 141–148.

Gibson, C. B., & Gibbs, J. L. (2006). Unpacking the concept of virtuality: The effects of geographic dispersion, electronic dependence, dynamic structure, and national diversity on team innovation. *Administrative Science Quarterly, 51*(3), 451–495.

Gibson, C., Huang, L., Kirkman, B., & Shapiro, D. (2014). Where global and virtual meet: The value of examining the intersection of these elements in twenty-first century teams. *Annual Review of Organizational Psychology and Organizational Behavior,* 217–244.

Gibson, C., & McDaniel, D. (2010). Moving beyond conventional wisdom: Advancement in cross-cultural theories of leadership, conflict, and teams. *Perspectives on Psychological Science, 5*(4), 450–462.

Gibson, C. B., & Zellmer-Bruhn, M. E. (2001). Metaphors and meaning: An intercultural analysis of the concept of teamwork. *Administrative Science Quarterly, 46*(2), 274–303.

Gigone, D., & Hastie, R. (1997). The impact of information on small group choice. *Journal of Personality and Social Psychology, 72*, 132–140.

Gino, F., Argote, L., Miron-Spektore, E., & Todorova, G. (2010). First, get your feet wet: The effects of learning from direct and indirect experience on team creativity. *Organizational Behavior and Human Decision Processes, 111*(2), 102–115.

Glikson, E., & Erez, M. (2013). Emotion display norms in virtual teams. *Journal of Personnel Psychology, 12*(1), 22–32.

Goldstein, I., & Ford, J. (2002). *Training in organizations* (4th ed.). Belmont, CA: Wadsworth.

Goltz, S., Hietapelto, A., Reinsch, R., & Tyrell, S. (2008). Teaching teamwork and problem solving concurrently. *Journal of Management Education, 32*(5), 541–562.

Goncalo, J., Polman, E., & Maslach, C. (2010). Can confidence come too soon? Collective efficacy, conflict and group performance over time. *Organizational Behavior and Human Decision Processes, 113*, 13–24.

Goncalo, J. A., & Staw, B. M. (2006). Individualism–collectivism and group creativity. *Organizational behavior and human decision processes, 100*(1), 96–109.

Graen, G., & Uhl-Bien, M. (1995). Relationship-based approach to leadership: Development of leader-member exchange (LMX) theory of leadership over 25 years. *Leadership Quarterly, 6*, 219–247.

Greenberg, J., & Baron, R. (1997). *Behavior in organizations: Understanding the human side of work* (6th ed.). Upper Saddle River, NJ: Prentice Hall.

Greenberg, J. (2011). *Behavior in organizations* (10th ed.). Boston, MA: Prentice Hall.

Greengross, G., & Miller, G. F. (2008). Dissing oneself versus dissing rivals: Effects of status, personality, and sex on the short-term and long-term attractiveness of self-deprecating and other-deprecating humor. *Evolutionary Psychology, 6*(3), 393–408.

Greer, L., & van Kleef, G. (2010). Equality versus differentiation: The effects of power dispersion on group interaction. *Journal of Applied Psychology, 95*(6), 1032–1044.

Gross, S. (1995). *Compensation for teams: How to design and implement team-based reward programs.* New York, NY: Amacom.

Guzzo, R., & Dickson, M. (1996). Teams in organizations: Recent research on performance and effectiveness. *Annual Review of Psychology, 47*, 307–338.

Gwynne, S. (1990, October 29). The right stuff. *Time*, 74–84.

Hackett, D., & Martin, C. (1993). *Facilitation skills for team leaders.* Menlo Park, CA: CRISP.

Hackman, R. (1986). The psychology of self-management in organizations. In M. Pallak & R. Perloff (Eds.), *Psychology and work* (pp. 89–136). Washington, DC: American Psychological Association.

Hackman, R. (1987). The design of work teams. In J. Lorsch (Ed.), *Handbook of organizational behavior* (pp. 315–342). Englewood Cliffs, NJ: Prentice Hall.

Hackman, R. (1990a). Creating more effective work groups in organizations. In R. Hackman (Ed.), *Groups that work (and those that don't)* (pp. 479–504). San Francisco, CA: Jossey-Bass.

Hackman, R. (1990b). Work teams in organizations: An orienting framework. In R. Hackman (Ed.), *Groups that work (and those that don't)* (pp. 1–14). San Francisco, CA: Jossey-Bass.

Hackman, R. (1992). Group influences on individuals in organizations. In M. Dunnette & L. Hough (Eds.), *Handbook of industrial and organizational psychology* (pp. 199–267). Palo Alto, CA: Consulting Psychologists Press.

Hackman, R. (2002). *Leading teams: Setting the stage for great performances.* Boston, MA: Harvard Business School Press.

Hackman, R. (2012). From causes to conditions in group research. *Journal of Organizational Behavior, 33,* 428–444.

Hackman, R., & Morris, C. (1975). Group tasks, group interaction process, and group performance effectiveness: A review and proposed integration. *Advances in Experimental Social Psychology, 8,* 47–99.

Hackman, R., & Oldham, G. (1980). *Work redesign.* Reading, MA: Addison-Wesley.

Hackman, R., & Wageman, R. (2005). A theory of team coaching. *Academy of Management Review, 30*(2), 269–287.

Hackman, R., & Walton, R. (1986). Leading groups in organizations. In P. Goodman (Ed.), *Designing effective work groups* (pp. 72–119). San Francisco, CA: Jossey-Bass.

Haines, R. (2014). Group development in virtual teams: An experimental reexamination. *Computers in Human Behavior, 39,* 213–222.

Haines, V., & Taggar, S. (2006). Antecedents of team reward attitude. *Group Dynamics: Theory, Research, and Practice, 10*(3), 194–205.

Hambley, L., O'Neill, T., & Kline, T. (2007). Virtual team leadership: The effects of leadership style and communication medium on team interaction styles and outcomes. *Organizational Behavior and Human Decision Processes, 103,* 1–20.

Hare, A. (1982). *Creativity in small groups.* Beverly Hills, CA: SAGE.

Harkins, S., & Jackson, J. (1985). The role of evaluation in eliminating social loafing. *Personality and Social Psychology Bulletin, 11,* 457–465.

Harrison, D., & Humphrey, S. (2010). Designing for diversity or diversity for design? Tasks, interdependence, and within-unit differences at work. *Journal of Organizational Behavior, 31,* 328–337.

Harrison, D., & Klein, K. (2007). What's the difference? Diversity constructs as separation, variety, or disparity in organizations. *Academy of Management Review, 32*(4), 1199–1228.

Harrison, D., Price, K., Gavin, J., & Florey, A. (2002). Time, teams, and task performance: Changing effects of surface and deep level diversity on group functioning. *Academy of Management Journal, 45*(5), 1029–1045.

Harvey, J. (1988). *The Abilene paradox and other meditations on management.* Lexington, MA: Lexington Books.

Harvey, S. (2014). Creative synthesis: Exploring the process of extraordinary group creativity. *Academy of Management Review, 39*(3), 324–343.

Hatfield, E., Cacioppo, J. T., & Rapson, R. L. (1993). Emotional contagion. *Current Directions in Psychological Science, 2,* 96–99.

Hayes, N. (1997). *Successful team management.* London, UK: International Thomson Business Press.

Head, T. (2006). Appreciative Inquiry in the graduate classroom: Making group dynamics a practical topic to address. *Organizational Development Journal, 24*(2), 83–88.

Helper, S., Kleiner, M., & Wang, Y. (2010). Analyzing compensation methods in manufacturing: Piece rates, time rates, or gain-sharing? (Working Paper 16540). Cambridge, MA: National Bureau of Economic Research.

Hempel, P., Zhang, Z., & Han, Y. (2012). Team empowerment and the organizational context: Decentralization and the contrasting effects of formalization. *Journal of Management, 38,* 475–501.

Hemphill, J. (1961). Why people attempt to lead. In L. Petrullo & B. Bass (Eds.), *Leadership and interpersonal behavior* (pp. 201–215). New York, NY: Holt, Rinehart & Winston.

Herrenkohl, R. (2004). *Becoming a team.* Mason, OH: South-Western.

Herrenkohl, R., Judson, G., & Heffner, J. (1999). Defining and measuring employee empowerment. *Journal of Applied Behavioral Science, 35,* 373–389.

Hersey, P., & Blanchard, K. (1993). *Management of organizational behavior: Utilizing human resources.* Englewood Cliffs, NJ: Prentice Hall.

Hertel, G., Geister, S., & Konradt, U. (2005). Managing virtual teams: A review of current empirical research. *Human Resource Management Review, 15*(1), 69–95.

Hewstone, M., Rubin, M., & Willis, H. (2002). Intergroup bias. *Annual Review of Psychology, 53*(1), 575–604.

Higgins, M., Weiner, J., & Young, L. (2012). Implementation teams: A new lever for organizational change. *Journal of Organizational Behavior, 33,* 366–388.

Hirak, R., Peng, A. C., Carmeli, A., & Schaubroeck, J. M. (2012). Linking leader inclusiveness to work unit performance: The importance of psychological safety and learning from failures. *The Leadership Quarterly, 23*(1), 107–117.

Hirschfeld, R., & Bernerth, J. (2008). Mental efficacy and physical efficacy at the team level: Inputs and outcomes among newly formed action teams. *Journal of Applied Psychology, 93*(6), 1429–1437.

Hirschfeld, R., Jordon, M., Field, H., Giles, W., & Armenakis, A. (2006). Becoming team players: Team members' mastery of teamwork knowledge as a predictor of team task proficiency and observed teamwork effectiveness. *Journal of Applied Psychology, 91*(2), 467–474.

Hoch, J., & Kozlowski, S. (2014). Leading virtual teams: Hierarchical leadership, structural supports, and shared team leadership. *Journal of Applied Psychology, 99*(3), 390–403.

Hoever, I., Knippenberg, D., Ginkel, W., & Barkema, H. (2012). Fostering team creativity: Perspective taking as key to unlocking diversity's potential. *Journal of Applied Psychology, 97*(5), 982–996.

Hofstede, G. (1980). *Culture's consequences: International differences in work-related value*. Beverly Hills, CA: SAGE.

Hofstede, G. (2011). Dimensionalizing cultures: The Hofstede model in context. *Online readings in psychology and culture, 2*(1), 8.

Hofstede, G., Hofstede, G. J., & Minkov, M. (2010). *Cultures and organizations: Software of the mind* (3rd. ed.). New York, NY: McGraw-Hill.

Hogg, M. (1992). *The social psychology of group cohesiveness: From attraction to social identity*. New York, NY: New York University Press.

Hollander, E., & Offerman, L. (1990). Power and leadership in organizations. *American Psychologist, 45*, 179–189.

Hornsey, M. J., Robson, E., Smith, J., Esposo, S., & Sutton, R. M. (2008). Sugaring the pill: Assessing rhetorical strategies designed to minimize defensive reactions to group criticism. *Human Communication Research, 34*(1), 70–98.

Huang, R., Kahai, S., & Jestice, R. (2010). The contingent effects of leadership on team collaboration in virtual teams. *Computers in Human Behavior, 26*, 1098–1110.

Huckman, R., & Staats, B. (2013, December). The hidden benefits of keeping teams intact. *Harvard Business Review, 91*(12), 27–29.

Huffmeier, J., & Hertel, G. (2011). Many cheers make light the work: How social support triggers process gains in teams. *Journal of Managerial Psychology, 26*(3), 185–204.

Humphrey, S., & Aime, F. (2014). Team microdynamics: Toward an organizing approach to teamwork. *Academy of Management Annals, 8*(1), 443–503.

Ilgen, D., Hollenbeck, J., Johnson, M., & Jundt, D. (2005). Teams in organizations: From input-process-output models to IMOI models. *Annual Review of Psychology, 56*, 517–543.

Ilies, R., Wagner, D. T., & Morgeson, F. P. (2007). Explaining affective linkages in teams: Individual differences in susceptibility to contagion and individualism-collectivism. *Journal of Applied Psychology, 92*(4), 1140–1148.

Insko, C., Schopler, J., Graetz, K., Drigotas, S., Currey, K., Smith, S., . . . Bornstein, G. (1994). Interindividual–intergroup discontinuity in the prisoner's dilemma game. *Journal of Conflict Resolution, 38*, 87–116.

Jackson, A., & Ruderman, M. (1995). Introduction: Perspective for understanding diverse work teams. In S. Jackson & M. Ruderman (Eds.), *Diversity in work teams: Research paradigms for a changing workplace* (pp. 1–13). Washington, DC: American Psychological Association.

Jackson, S. (1992). Team composition in organizational settings: Issues in managing an increasingly diverse workforce. In S. Worchel, W. Wood, & J. Simpson (Eds.), *Group process and productivity* (pp. 138–173). Newbury Park, CA: SAGE.

Janis, I. (1972). *Victims of groupthink*. Boston, MA: Houghton Mifflin.

Janis, I., & Mann, L. (1977). *Decision making*. New York, NY: Free Press.

Janz, B., Colquitt, J., & Noe, R. (1997). Knowledge worker team effectiveness: The role of autonomy, interdependence, team development, and contextual support variables. *Personnel Psychology, 50*, 877–905.

Jehn, K. (1995). A multimethod examination of the benefits and detriments of intragroup conflict. *Administrative Science Quarterly, 40,* 256–282.

Jehn, K., & Shaw, P. (1997). Interpersonal relationships and task performance: An examination of mediating processes in friendship and acquaintance groups. *Journal of Personality and Social Psychology, 72,* 775–790.

Jentsch, F., & Smith-Jentsch, K. (2001). Assertiveness and team performance: More than "just say no." In E. Salas, C. Bowers, & E. Edens (Eds.), *Improving teamwork in organizations* (pp. 73–94). Mahwah, NJ: Lawrence Erlbaum.

Johnson, D., & Johnson, F. (1997). *Joining together: Group theory and group skills* (6th ed.). Boston, MA: Allyn & Bacon.

Johnson, D., Maruyama, G., Johnson, R., Nelson, D., & Skon, L. (1981). Effects of cooperative, competitive, and individualistic goal structures on achievement: A meta-analysis. *Psychological Bulletin, 89,* 47–62.

Johnson, S. K., Bettenhausen, K., & Gibbons, E. (2009). Realities of working in virtual teams: Affective and attitudinal outcomes of using computer-mediated communication. *Small Group Research, 40*(6), 623–649.

Jones, G., & George, J. (1998). The experience and evolution of trust: Implications for cooperation and teamwork. *Academy of Management Review, 23,* 531–546.

Jones, S., & Moffett, R. (1999). Measurement and feedback systems for teams. In E. Sundstrom (Ed.), *Supporting work team effectiveness* (pp. 157–187). San Francisco, CA: Jossey-Bass.

Jong, J., Curseu, P., & Leenders, R. (2014). When do bad apples not spoil the barrel? Negative relationships in teams, team performance, and buffering mechanisms. *Journal of Applied Psychology, 99*(3), 514–522.

Jordan, P., & Troth, A. (2004). Managing emotions during team problem solving: Emotional intelligence and conflict resolution. *Human Performance, 17*(2), 195–218.

Joshi, A. (2014). By whom and when is women's expertise recognized? The interactive effects of gender and education in science and engineering teams. *Administrative Science Quarterly, 59*(2), 202–239.

Karau, S., & Williams, K. (1993). Social loafing: A meta-analytic review and theoretical integration. *Journal of Personality and Social Psychology, 65,* 681–706.

Karau, S., & Williams, K. (1997). The effects of group cohesion on social loafing and social compensation. *Group Dynamics: Theory, Research, and Practice, 1,* 156–168.

Katzenbach, J., & Smith, D. (1993). *The wisdom of teams.* Cambridge, MA: Harvard Business School Press.

Katzenbach, J., & Smith, D. (2001). *The discipline of teams.* New York, NY: John Wiley.

Kayser, T. (1990). *Mining group gold.* El Segundo, CA: Sherif.

Kemery, E., Bedeian, A., Mossholder, K., & Touliatos, J. (1985). Outcomes of role stress: A multisample constructive replication. *Academy of Management Review, 28,* 363–375.

Kerr, N., & Bruun, S. (1983). Dispensability of member effort and group motivation losses: Free rider effects. *Journal of Personality and Social Psychology, 44,* 78–94.

Kerr, N., & Tindale, R. (2004). Group performance and decision making. *Annual Review of Psychology, 55,* 623–655.

Keysar, B., & Henly, A. (2002). Speakers' overestimation of their effectiveness. *Psychological Science, 13*(3), 207–212.

Kidder, T. (1981). *The soul of the new machine.* New York, NY: Avon.

Kilmann, R., & Saxton, M. (1983). *The Kilmann-Saxton culture gap survey.* Pittsburgh, PA: Organizational Design Consultants.

Kipnis, D. (1976). *The powerholders.* Chicago, IL: University of Chicago Press.

Kipnis, D., & Schmidt, S. (1982). *Profiles of organizational influence strategies: Influencing your subordinates.* San Diego, CA: University Associates.

Kipnis, D., Schmidt, S., Swaffin-Smith, C., & Wilkinson, I. (1984). Patterns of managerial influence: Shotgun managers, tacticians, and bystanders. *Organizational Dynamics, 12*(3), 58–67.

Kirkman, B., & Rosen, B. (1999). Beyond self-management: Antecedents and consequences of team empowerment. *Academy of Management Journal, 42*(1), 58–74.

Kirkman, B. L., & Shapiro, D. L. (1997). The impact of cultural values on employee resistance to teams: Toward a model of globalized self-managing work team effectiveness. *Academy of Management Review, 22*(3), 730–757.

Kirkpatrick, S., & Locke, E. (1991). Leadership: Do traits matter? *Academy of Management Executive, 5,* 48–60.

Kivlighan, D., & Jauquet, C. (1990). Quality of group member agendas and group session climate. *Small Group Research, 1,* 205–219.

Klein, C., DiazGranados, D., Salas, E., Le, H., Burke, C., Lyons, R., & Goodwin, G. (2009). Does team building work? *Small Group Research, 40*(2), 181–222.

Klein, J. (1984, September). Why supervisors resist employee involvement. *Harvard Business Review,* 87–93.

Klimoski, R., & Mohammed, S. (1997). Team mental model: Construct or metaphor? *Journal of Management, 20*(2), 403–437.

Knight, G., & Dubro, A. (1984). Cooperative, competitive, and individualistic social values. *Journal of Personality and Social Psychology, 46,* 98–105.

Koman, E., & Wolff, S. (2008). Emotional intelligence competencies in the team and team leader. *Journal of Management Development, 27*(1), 55–75.

Kruger, J., Epley, N., Parker, J., & Ng, Z. (2005). Egocentrism over e-mail: Can we communicate as well as we think? *Journal of Personality and Social Psychology, 89*(6), 925–936.

Langfred, C. (2000). Work group design and autonomy: A field study of the interaction between task interdependence and group autonomy. *Small Group Research, 31,* 54–70.

Larson, C., & LaFasto, F. (1989). *Teamwork: What must go right/what can go wrong.* Newbury Park, CA: SAGE.

Latane, B., Williams, K., & Harkins, S. (1979). Many hands make light the work: The causes and consequences of social loafing. *Journal of Personality and Social Psychology, 37,* 822–832.

Laughlin, P., & Hollingshead, A. (1995). A theory of collective induction. *Organizational Behavior and Human Decision Processes, 61,* 94–107.

Lawler, E. (1986). *High involvement management.* San Francisco, CA: Jossey-Bass.

Lawler, E. (1999). Creating effective pay systems for teams. In E. Sundstrom (Ed.), *Supporting work team effectiveness* (pp. 188–214). San Francisco, CA: Jossey-Bass.

Lawler, E. (2000). *Rewarding excellence: Pay strategies for the new economy.* San Francisco, CA: Jossey-Bass.

Lawler, E., Mohrman, S., & Ledford, G. (1995). *Creating high performance organizations: Practices and results of employee involvement and quality management in Fortune 1000 companies.* San Francisco, CA: Jossey-Bass.

Lea, D., & Brostrom, L. (1988). Managing the high-tech professional. *Personnel, 65*(6), 12–22.

Lee, C., Farh, J., & Chen, Z. (2011). Promoting group potency in project teams: The importance of group identification. *Journal of Organizational Behavior, 32,* 1147–1162.

Lehrer, J. (2012). *Imagine: How creativity works.* Boston, MA: Houghton, Mifflin, & Harcourt.

Levi, D., & Cadiz, D. (1998). *Evaluating teamwork on student projects: The use of behaviorally anchored scales to evaluate student performance* (ERIC Document Reproduction Service No. TM29122). East Lansing, MI: National Center for Research on Teacher Learning.

Levi, D., & Lawn, M. (1993). The driving and restraining forces which affect technological innovation. *Journal of High Technology Management Research, 4,* 225–240.

Levi, D., & Rinzel, L. (1998). Employee attitudes toward various communications technologies when used for communicating about organizational change. In P. Vink, E. Koningsveld, & S. Dhondt (Eds.), *Human factors in organizational design and management* (Vol. 6, pp. 483–488). Amsterdam, The Netherlands: Elsevier Science.

Levi, D., & Slem, C. (1995). Team work in research and development organizations: The characteristics of successful teams. *International Journal of Industrial Ergonomics, 16,* 29–42.

Levi, D., & Slem, C. (1996). The relationship of concurrent engineering practices to different views of project success. In O. Brown & H. Hendrick (Eds.), *Human factors in organizational design and management* (Vol. 5, pp. 25–30). Amsterdam, The Netherlands: Elsevier Science.

Levine, J. (1989). Reaction to opinion deviance in small groups. In P. Paulus (Ed.), *Psychology of group influence: New perspectives* (pp. 187–232). Hillsdale, NJ: Lawrence Erlbaum.

Levine, J., & Choi, H. (2004). Impact of personnel turnover on team performance and cognition. In E. Salas & S. Fiore (Eds.), *Team cognition: Understanding the factors that drive process and performance* (pp. 153–175). Washington, DC: American Psychological Association.

Lewin, K. (1951). *Field theory in social science.* New York, NY: Harper.

Lewis, K. (2004). Knowledge and performance in knowledge-worker teams: A longitudinal study of transactive memory systems. *Management Science, 11,* 1519–1533.

Li, N., Kirkman, B., & Porter, C. (2014). Toward a model of work team altruism. *Academy of Management Review, 39*(4), 541–565.

Likert, R. (1961). *New patterns in management.* New York, NY: McGraw-Hill.

Locke, E., & Latham, G. (1990). *A theory of goal setting and task performance.* Englewood Cliffs, NJ: Prentice Hall.

Lord, R. (1985). An information processing approach to social perceptions, leadership, and behavioral measurement. *Research in Organizational Behavior, 7,* 87–128.

Lorinkova, N., Pearsall, M., & Sims, H. (2013). Examining the differential longitudinal performance of directive versus empowering leadership in teams. *Academy of Management Journal, 58*(2), 573–596.

Lott, A., & Lott, B. (1965). Group cohesiveness as interpersonal attraction: A review of the relationships with antecedent and consequence variables. *Psychological Bulletin, 64,* 259–309.

Lumsden, G., & Lumsden, D. (1997). *Communicating in groups and teams.* Belmont, CA: Wadsworth.

Luthans, F., & Fox, M. (1989, March). Update on skill-based pay. *Personnel,* 26–31.

Lyons, S., & Kuron, L. (2014). Generational differences in the workplace: A review of the evidence and directions for future research. *Journal of Organizational Behavior, 35,* 139–157.

Mannix, E., & Neale, M. (2005). What differences make a difference? The promise and reality of diverse teams in organizations. *Psychology in the Public Interest, 6*(2), 32–55.

Manufacturing Studies Board. (1986). *Human resources practices for implementing advanced manufacturing technology.* Washington, DC: National Academy Press.

Manz, C. (1992). Self-leading work teams: Moving beyond self-management myths. *Human Relations, 45,* 1119–1140.

Marks, M., Mathieu, J., & Zaccaro, S. (2001). A temporally based framework and taxonomy of team processes. *Academy of Management Review, 26*(3), 356–376.

Marks, M., Sabella, M., Burke, C., & Zaccaro, S. (2002). The impact of cross-training on team effectiveness. *Journal of Applied Psychology, 87*(1), 2–13.

Marquardt, M. (2002). *Building the learning organization.* Palo Alto, CA: Davies-Black.

Marquardt, M. (2004, June). Harnessing the power of action learning. *Training & Development,* 26–32.

Martin, J., Knopoff, K., & Beckman, C. (1998). An alternative to bureaucratic impersonality and emotional labor: Bounded emotionality at the body shop. *Administrative Science Quarterly*, 429–469.

Mathieu, J., Gilson, L., & Ruddy, T. (2006). Empowerment and team effectiveness: An empirical test of an integrated model. *Journal of Applied Psychology*, 91(1), 97–108.

Mathieu, J., Maynard, T., Rapp, T., & Gilson, L. (2008). Team effectiveness 1997–2007: A review of recent advancements and a glimpse into the future. *Journal of Management*, 34(3), 410–476.

Mathieu, J., & Rapp, T. (2009). Laying the foundation for successful team performance trajectories: The roles of team charters and performance strategies. *Journal of Applied Psychology*, 94(1), 90–103.

Mathieu, J., Tannenbaum, S., Donsbach, J., & Alliger, G. (2014). A review and integration of team composition models: Moving toward a dynamic and temporal framework. *Journal of Management*, 40(1), 130–160.

Mayer, J., & Salovey, P. (1997). What is emotional intelligence? In P. Salovey & D. Sluyter (Eds.), *Emotional development and emotional intelligence: Educational implications* (pp. 3–32). New York, NY: Basic Books.

Maynard, T., Mathieu, J., Gibson, L., & Rapp, T. (2012). Something(s) old and something(s) new: Modeling drivers of global virtual team effectiveness. *Journal of Organizational Behavior*, 33, 342–365.

Mayo, E. (1933). *The human problems of an industrial civilization*. Cambridge, MA: Harvard University Press.

McAllister, D. (1995). Affect and cognition-based trust as foundations for interpersonal cooperation in organizations. *Academy of Management Journal*, 38, 24–59.

McCallin, A., & Bamford, A. (2007). Interdisciplinary teamwork: Is the influence of emotional intelligence fully appreciated? *Journal of Nursing Management*, 15, 386–391.

McClelland, D., & Boyatzis, R. (1982). Leadership motive pattern and long-term success in management. *Journal of Applied Psychology*, 67, 737–743.

McComb, S., Green, S., & Compton, W. (1999). Project goals, team performance, and shared understanding. *Engineering Management Journal*, 11(3), 7–12.

McGrath, J. (1984). *Groups: Interaction and performance*. Englewood Cliffs, NJ: Prentice Hall.

McGrath, J. (1990). Time matters in groups. In J. Galegher, R. Kraut, & C. Egido (Eds.), *Intellectual teamwork: Social and technological foundations of cooperative work* (pp. 23–62). Hillsdale, NJ: Lawrence Erlbaum.

McGrath, J., Berdahl, J., & Arrow, H. (1995). Traits, expectations, culture, and clout: The dynamics of diversity in work groups. In S. Jackson & M. Ruderman (Eds.), *Diversity in work teams: Research paradigms for a changing workplace* (pp. 17–45). Washington, DC: American Psychological Association.

McGrath, J., & Hollingshead, A. (1994). *Groups interacting with technology*. Thousand Oaks, CA: SAGE.

McIntyre, R., & Salas, E. (1995). Measuring and managing for team performance: Lessons from complex environments. In R. Guzzo & E. Salas (Eds.), *Team effectiveness and decision making in organizations* (pp. 9–45). San Francisco, CA: Jossey-Bass.

McKenna, E. (1994). *Business psychology and organizational behavior.* Hillsdale, NJ: Lawrence Erlbaum.

Meindl, J., & Ehrlich, S. (1987). The romance of leadership and the evaluation of organizational performance. *Academy of Management Journal, 30,* 91–109.

Menges, J. I., & Kilduff, M. (2015). Group emotions: Cutting the gordion knots concerning terms, levels-of-analysis, and processes. *The Academy of Management Annals, 9*(1), 849–932.

Merriman, K. (2009). On the folly of rewarding team performance, while hoping for teamwork. *Compensation Benefits Review, 41,* 61–66.

Mesmer-Magnus, J., DeChurch, L., Jimenez-Rodriguez, M., Wildman, J., & Shuffler, M. (2011). A meta-analytic investigation of virtuality and information sharing in teams. *Organizational Behavior and Human Decision Processes, 115,* 214–225.

Milgram, S. (1974). *Obedience to authority.* New York, NY: Harper & Row.

Milkman, K., Chugh, D., & Bazerman, M. (2009). How can decision making be improved? *Perspectives on Psychological Science, 4*(4), 379–383.

Mills, M., Fleck, C., & Kozikowski, A. (2013). Positive psychology at work: A conceptual review, state-of-practice assessment, and a look ahead. *Journal of Positive Psychology, 8*(2), 153–164.

Minton-Eversole, T. (2012). Virtual teams used most by global organizations, survey says. *Society for Human Resource Management, 19,* 157–190.

Mittleman, D., & Briggs, R. (1999). Communication technologies for traditional and virtual teams. In E. Sundstrom (Ed.), *Supporting work team effectiveness* (pp. 246–270). San Francisco, CA: Jossey-Bass.

Miville, M., Gelso, C., Pannu, R., Liu, W., Touradji, P., Holloway, P., & Fuertes, J. (1999). Appreciating similarities and valuing differences: The Miville-Guzman Universality-Diversity Scale. *Journal of Counseling Psychology, 46*(3), 291–307.

Mohammed, S., Ferzandi, L., & Hamilton, K. (2010). Metaphor no more: A 15 year review of the team mental model. *Journal of Management, 36,* 876–910.

Mohrman, S. (1993). Integrating roles and structure in the lateral organization. In J. Galbraith & E. Lawler (Eds.), *Organizing for the future* (pp. 109–141). San Francisco, CA: Jossey-Bass.

Mohrman, S., Cohen, S., & Mohrman, A. (1995). *Designing team-based organizations.* San Francisco, CA: Jossey-Bass.

Moreland, R., Argote, L., & Krishnan, R. (1996). Socially shared cognition at work. In J. Nye & A. Bower (Eds.), *What's social about social cognition?* Thousand Oaks, CA: SAGE.

Moreland, R., & Levine, J. (1982). Socialization in small groups: Temporal changes in individual-group relations. *Advances in Experimental Social Psychology, 15,* 137–192.

Moreland, R., & Levine, J. (1989). Newcomers and old-timers in small groups. In P. Paulus (Ed.), *Psychology of group influence* (pp. 143–186). Hillsdale, NJ: Lawrence Erlbaum.

Moreland, R., & Levine, J. (1992). Problem identification by groups. In S. Worchel, W. Wood, & J. Simpson (Eds.), *Group process and productivity* (pp. 17–48). Newbury Park, CA: SAGE.

Morgeson, F. (2005). The external leadership of self-managing teams: Intervening in the context of novel and disruptive events. *Journal of Applied Psychology, 90*(3), 497–508.

Morgeson, F., Reider, M., & Campion, M. (2005). Selecting individuals in team settings: The importance of social skills, personality characteristics, and teamwork knowledge. *Personnel Psychology, 58,* 583–611.

Moscovici, S. (1985). Social influence and conformity. In G. Lindzey & E. Aronson (Eds.), *The handbook of social psychology* (pp. 347–412). Hillsdale, NJ: Lawrence Erlbaum.

Mueller, J., Melwani, S., & Goncalo, J. (2012). The bias against creativity: Why people desire but reject creative ideas. *Psychological Science, 23*(1), 13–17.

Mullen, B., & Copper, C. (1994). The relation between group cohesiveness and performance: An integration. *Psychological Bulletin, 115,* 210–227.

Mullen, B., Johnson, C., & Salas, E. (1991). Productivity loss in brainstorming groups: A meta-analytic integration. *Basic and Applied Psychology, 12,* 3–24.

Mullen, B., Salas, E., & Driskell, J. (1989). Salience, motivation, and artifacts as contributors to the relationship between participation rate and leadership. *Journal of Experimental Social Psychology, 25,* 545–559.

Murnighan, J. (1981). Group decision making: What strategies should you use? *Management Review, 25,* 56–62.

Myers, D., & Lamm, H. (1976). The group polarization phenomenon. *Psychological Bulletin, 83,* 602–627.

Nadler, J., Thompson, L., & Morris, M. (1999, August). *Schmooze or lose: The efforts of rapport and gender in e-mail negotiations.* Paper presented at the annual meeting of the Academy of Management, Chicago, IL.

Naquin, C., & Tynan, R. (2003). The team halo effect: Why teams are not blamed for their failures. *Journal of Applied Psychology, 88*(2), 332–340.

Nemeth, C. (1979). The role of an active minority in intergroup relations. In W. Austin & S. Worchel (Eds.), *The social psychology of intergroup relations* (pp. 348–362). Pacific Grove, CA: Brooks/Cole.

Nemeth, C., & Staw, B. (1989). The trade-offs of social control and innovation in groups and organizations. In L. Berkowitz (Ed.), *Advances in experimental social psychology* (pp. 195–230). San Diego, CA: Academic Press.

Nickerson, R. S. (1998). Confirmation bias: A ubiquitous phenomenon in many guises. *Review of General Psychology, 2,* 175–220.

Nkomo, S. (1995). Identities and the complexity of diversity. In S. Jackson & M. Ruderman (Eds.), *Diversity in work teams: Research paradigms for a changing workplace* (pp. 247–253). Washington, DC: American Psychological Association.

Northcraft, G., Polzer, J., Neale, M., & Kramer, R. (1995). Diversity, social identity, and performance: Emergent social dynamics in cross-functional teams. In S. Jackson & M. Ruderman (Eds.), *Diversity in work teams: Research paradigms for a changing workplace* (pp. 69–95). Washington, DC: American Psychological Association.

Nye, J., & Forsyth, D. (1991). The effects of prototype-based biases on leadership appraisals: A test of leadership categorization theory. *Small Group Research, 22,* 360–379.

O'Dell, C. (1989, November 1). Team play, team pay: New ways of keeping score. *Across the Board,* 38–45.

Offner, A., Kramer, T., & Winter, J. (1996). The effects of facilitation, recording, and pauses on group brainstorming. *Small Group Research, 27,* 283–298.

O'Neill, T., Allen, N., & Hastings, S. (2013). Examining the "pros" and "cons" of team conflict: A team-level meta-analysis of task, relationship, and process conflict. *Human Performance, 26,* 236–260.

Orsburn, J., Moran, L., Musselwhite, E., Zenger, J., & Perrin, C. (1990). *Self-directed work teams: The new American challenge.* Homewood, IL: Business One Irwin.

Osborn, A. (1957). *Applied imagination.* New York, NY: Scribner.

Ouchi, W. (1981). *Theory Z: How American business can meet the Japanese challenge.* Reading, MA: Addison-Wesley.

Park, G., & DeShon, R. (2010). A multilevel model of minority opinion expression and team decision-making effectiveness. *Journal of Applied Psychology, 95*(5), 824–833.

Park, N., Rhoads, M., Hou, J., & Lee, K. (2014). Understanding the acceptance of teleconferencing systems among employees: An extension of the technology acceptance model. *Computers in Human Behavior, 39,* 118–127.

Parks, C. (1994). The predictive ability of social values in resource dilemmas and public good games. *Personality and Social Psychology Bulletin, 20,* 431–438.

Parks, C., & Sanna, L. (1999). *Group performance and interaction.* Boulder, CO: Westview.

Parks, M. R. (1977). Relational communication: Theory and research. *Human Communication Research, 3*(4), 372–381.

Pascale, R., & Athos, A. (1981). *The art of Japanese management.* New York, NY: Simon & Schuster.

Paulus, P. (1998). Developing consensus about groupthink after all these years. *Organization Behavior and Human Decision Processes, 73,* 362–374.

Paulus, P. (2000). Groups, teams, and creativity: The creative potential of idea-generating groups. *Applied Psychology: An International Review, 49*(2), 237–262.

Paulus, P. (2002). Different ponds for different fish: A contrasting perspective on team innovation. *International Association for Applied Psychology,* 394–399.

Pavit, C. (1993). What (little) we know about formal group discussion procedures. *Small Group Research, 24,* 217–235.

Pearsall, M., Christian, M., & Ellis, A. (2010). Motivating interdependent teams: Individual rewards, shared rewards, or something in between? *Journal of Applied Psychology, 95*(1), 183–191.

Pelled, L., Eisenhardt, K., & Xin, K. (1999). Exploring the black box: An analysis of work group diversity, conflict and performance. *Administrative Science Quarterly, 44,* 1–28.

Penarroja, V., Orengo, V., Zornoza, A., & Hernandez, A. (2013). The effects of virtuality level on task-related collaborative behaviors: The mediating role of team trust. *Computers in Human Behavior, 29,* 967–974.

Peters, T., & Waterman, R. (1982). *In search of excellence.* New York, NY: Harper & Row.

Peterson, R., & Nemeth, C. (1996). Focus versus flexibility: Majority and minority influence can both improve performance. *Personality and Social Psychology Bulletin, 22,* 14–24.

Pettigrew, T. F., & Martin, J. (1987). Shaping the organizational context for black american inclusion. *Journal of Social Issues, 43*(1), 41–78.

Pieterse, A., Knippenberg, D., & Dierendonck, D. (2013). Cultural diversity and team performance: The role of team member goal orientation. *Academy of Management Journal, 56*(3), 782–804.

Podsakoff, P., & Schriesheim, C. (1985). Field studies of French and Raven's bases of power. *Psychological Bulletin, 97,* 387–411.

Pokras, S. (1995). *Team problem solving.* Menlo Park, CA: CRISP.

Priest, H., Stagl, K., Klein, C., & Salas, E. (2006). Virtual teams: Creating context for distributed teamwork. In C. Bowers, E. Salas, & F. Jentsch (Eds.), *Creating high-tech teams* (pp. 185–211). Washington, DC: American Psychological Association.

Prochaska, R. (1980). The management of innovation in Japan: Why it is successful? *Research Management, 23,* 35–38.

Pruitt, D. (1986). Trends in the scientific study of negotiation. *Negotiation Journal, 2,* 237–244.

Quoidbach, J., & Hansenne, M. (2009). The impact of trait emotional intelligence on nursing team performance and cohesiveness. *Journal of Professional Nursing, 25*(1), 23–29.

Rahim, M. (1983). A measure of styles of handling interpersonal conflict. *Academy of Management Journal, 26,* 368–376.

Rains, S. A. (2005). Leveling the organizational playing field—virtually a meta-analysis of experimental research assessing the impact of group support system use on member influence behaviors. *Communication Research, 32*(2), 193–234.

Rajaram, S. (2011). Collaboration both hurts and helps memory: A cognitive perspective. *Current Directions in Psychological Science, 20*(2), 76–81.

Raven, B., Schwarzwald, J., & Koslowsky, M. (1998). Conceptualizing and measuring a power/interaction model of interpersonal influence. *Journal of Applied Social Psychology, 28,* 307–333.

Reichwald, R., & Goecke, R. (1994). New communication media and new forms of cooperation in the top management area. In G. Bradley & H. Hendrick (Eds.), *Human factors in organizational design and management* (Vol. 4, pp. 511–518). Amsterdam, The Netherlands: Elsevier Science.

Rentz, K., Arduser, L., Meloncon, L., & Debs, M. (2009). Designing a successful group-report experience. *Business Communication Quarterly, 72,* 79–84.

Rice, R., Instone, D., & Adams, J. (1984). Leader sex, leader success, and leadership process: Two field studies. *Journal of Applied Psychology, 69,* 12–31.

Rico, R., Sanchez-Manzanares, M., Antino, M., & Lau, D. (2012). Bridging team faultlines by combining task role assignment and goal structure strategies. *Journal of Applied Psychology, 97*(2), 407–420.

Richardson, J., & West, M. (2010). Dream teams: A positive psychology of team working. P. Linley, S. Harrington, & N. Garcea (Eds.), *Oxford handbook of positive psychology and work* (pp. 235–249). New York, NY: Oxford University Press.

Ridgeway, C. L. (1997). Interaction and the conservation of gender inequality: Considering employment. *American Sociological Review,* 218–235.

Roch, S., & Ayman, R. (2005). Group decision making and perceived decision support: The role of communication medium. *Group Dynamics, 9*(1), 15–31.

Rogelberg, S. G., Allen, J. A., Shanock, L., Scott, C., & Shuffler, M. (2010). Employee satisfaction with meetings: A contemporary facet of job satisfaction. *Human Resource Management, 49*(2), 149–172.

Rogelberg, S. G., Scott, C., & Kello, J. (2007). The science and fiction of meetings. *MIT Sloan management review, 48*(2), 18–21.

Rogelberg, S. G., Shanock, L. R., & Scott, C. W. (2012). Wasted time and money in meetings: Increasing return on investment. *Small Group Research, 43,* 236–245.

Rohlen, T. (1975). The company work group. In E. Vogel (Ed.), *Modern Japanese organization and decision making* (pp. 185–209). Tokyo, Japan: Tuttle.

Rosenberg, L. (1961). Group size, prior experience, and conformity. *Abnormal and Social Psychology, 63,* 436–437.

Ross, L., & Ward, A. (1995). Psychological barriers to dispute resolution. In M. Zanna (Ed.), *Advances in experimental social psychology* (Vol. 27, pp. 255–304). San Diego, CA: Academic Press.

Rothwell, J. D. (2015). *In mixed company: Communicating in small groups and teams* (9th ed.). Boston, MA: Cengage Learning.

Rudman, L. A., Moss-Racusin, C. A., Phelan, J. E., & Nauts, S. (2012). Status incongruity and backlash effects: Defending the gender hierarchy motivates prejudice against female leaders. *Journal of Experimental Social Psychology, 48*(1), 165–179.

Rynes, S., Gerhart, B., & Parks, L. (2005). Personnel psychology: Performance evaluation and pay for performance. *Annual Review of Psychology, 56,* 571–600.

Sakuri, M. (1975). Small group cohesiveness and detrimental conformity. *Sociometry, 38,* 340–357.

Salas, E., Bowers, C., & Edens, E. (2001). Research and practice of resource management in organizations. In E. Salas, C. Bowers, & E. Edens (Eds.), *Improving teamwork in organizations: Applications of resource management training* (pp. 235–240). Mahwah, NJ: Lawrence Erlbaum.

Salas, E., & Cannon-Bowers, J. (2001). The science of training: A decade of progress. In S. Fiske, D. Schacter, & C. Zahn-Waxler (Eds.), *Annual review of psychology* (pp. 471–499). Palo Alto, CA: Annual Review Press.

Sawyer, R. (2012, January 25). What Mel Brooks can teach us about "group flow." *Greater Good.* Retrieved from http://greatergood.berkeley.edu/article/item/ what_mel_brooks_ can_teach_us_about_ group_flow#

Schein, E. (1988). *Process consultation: Its role in organizational development.* Reading, MA: Addison-Wesley.

Schein, E. (1992). *Organizational culture and leadership* (2nd ed.). San Francisco, CA: Jossey-Bass.

Scholtes, P. (1988). *The team handbook: How to use teams to improve quality.* Madison, WI: Joiner.

Scholtes, P. (1994). *The team handbook for educators.* Madison, WI: Joiner.

Schwenk, C. (1990). Effects of devil's advocacy and dialectical inquiry on decision making: A meta-analysis. *Organizational Behavior and Human Decision Processes, 47,* 161–176.

Seibert, S., Wang, G., & Courtright, S. (2011). Antecedents and consequences of psychological and team empowerment in organizations: A meta-analysis review. *Journal of Applied Psychology, 96*(5), 981–1003.

Shaw, J., Duffy, M., & Stark, E. (2001). Team reward attitude: Construct development and initial validation. *Journal of Organizational Behavior, 22,* 903–917.

Shaw, M. (1981). *Group dynamics: The psychology of small group behavior.* New York, NY: McGraw-Hill.

Sherif, M. (1966). *In common predicament: Social psychology of intergroup conflict and cooperation.* Boston, MA: Houghton Mifflin.

Shuffler, M., DiazGranados, D., & Salas, E. (2011). There's a science for that: Team development interventions in organizations. *Current Directions in Psychological Science, 20*(6), 365–372.

Simon, H. (1979). *The science of the artificial* (2nd ed.). Cambridge, MA: MIT Press.

Slavin, R. (1985). Cooperative learning: Applying contact theory in desegregated schools. *Journal of Social Issues, 41,* 45–62.

Slem, C., Levi, D., & Young, A. (1995). Attitudes about the impact of technological change: Comparison of U.S. and Japanese workers. *Journal of High Technology Management Research, 6,* 211–228.

Smith, K., Carrol, S., & Ashford, S. (1995). Intra- and interorganizational cooperation: Toward a research agenda. *Academy of Management Journal, 38,* 7–23.

Smith-Jentsch, K., Cannon-Bowers, J., Tannenbaum, S., & Salas, E. (2008). Guided team self-correction: Impacts of team mental models, processes, and effectiveness. *Small Group Research, 39*(3), 303–327.

Smith-Jentsch, K., Salas, E., & Brannick, M. (2001). To transfer or not to transfer? Investigating the combined effects of trainee characteristics, team leader support, and team climate. *Journal of Applied Psychology, 86*(2), 279–292.

Snell, S., Snow, C., Davison, S., & Hambrick, D. (1998). Designing and supporting transnational teams: The human resource agenda. *Human Resource Management, 37*(2), 147–158.

Snow, C., Snell, S., Davison, S., & Hambrick, D. (1996). Use transnational teams to globalize your company. *Organizational Dynamics, 24*(4), 50–67.

Snyder, L. (2009). Teaching teams about teamwork: Preparation, practice, and performance review. *Business Communication Quarterly, 72*(1), 74–79.

Somech, A., Desivilya, H., & Lidogoster, H. (2009). Team conflict management and team effectiveness: The effects of task interdependence and team identification. *Journal of Organizational Behavior, 30,* 359–378.

Somech, A., & Drach-Zahavy, A. (2013). Translating team creativity to innovation implementation: The role of team composition and climate for innovation. *Journal of Management, 39*(3), 684–708.

Spitzberg, B. H. (1983). Communication competence as knowledge, skill, and impression. *Communication Education, 32*(3), 323–329.

Spreitzer, G., Cohen, S., & Ledford, G. (1999). Developing effective self-managing work teams in service organizations. *Group and Organization Management, 24,* 340–367.

Sproull, L., & Kiesler, S. (1991). *Connections: New ways of working in the networked organization.* Cambridge, MA: MIT Press.

Srull, T., & Wyer, R. (1988). *Advances in social cognition.* Hillsdale, NJ: Lawrence Erlbaum.

Staples, D. S., & Zhao, L. (2006). The effects of cultural diversity in virtual teams versus face-to-face teams. *Group Decision and Negotiation, 15*(4), 389–406.

Stasser, G. (1992). Pooling of unshared information during group discussions. In S. Worchel, W. Wood, & J. Simpson (Eds.), *Group process and productivity* (pp. 17–48). Newbury Park, CA: SAGE.

Stasser, G., & Titus, W. (1985). Pooling of unshared information in group decision making: Biased information sampling during discussion. *Journal of Personality and Social Psychology, 48,* 1467–1478.

Stein, M. (1975). *Stimulating creativity.* New York, NY: Academic Press.

Steiner, I. (1972). *Group process and productivity.* New York, NY: Academic Press.

Stewart, G. (2010). The past twenty years: Team research is alive and well at the Journal of Management. *Journal of Management, 36*(4), 801–805.

Stewart, G., Courtright, S., & Barrick, M. (2012). Peer-based control in self-managing teams: Linking rational and normative influence with individual and group performance. *Journal of Applied Psychology, 97*(2), 435–447.

Stogdill, R. (1974). *Handbook of leadership.* New York, NY: Free Press.

Stoner, J. (1961). *A comparison of individual and group decision making involving risk* (Unpublished master's thesis). Massachusetts Institute of Technology, Cambridge, MA.

Sundstrom, E. (1999). The challenges of supporting work team effectiveness. In E. Sundstom (Ed.), *Supporting work team effectiveness* (pp. 2–23). San Francisco, CA: Jossey-Bass.

Sundstrom, E., DeMeuse, K., & Futrell, D. (1990). Work teams. *American Psychologist, 45,* 120–133.

Sundstrom, E., McIntyre, M., Halfhill, T., & Richards, H. (2000). Work groups: From the Hawthorne studies to work teams of the 1990s and beyond. *Group Dynamics: Theory, Research, and Practice, 4*(1), 44–67.

Sunstein, C., & Hastie, R. (2014). Making dumb groups smarter. *Harvard Business Review,* December, 91–98.

Swaab, R., Schaerer, M., Anicich, E., Ronay, R., & Galinsky, A. (2014). The too-much-talent effect: Team interdependence determines when more talent is too much or not enough. *Psychological Science, 25*(8), 1581–1591.

Sweeney, J. (1973). An experimental investigation of the free rider problem. *Social Science Research, 2,* 277–292.

Tajfel, H. (1982a). Social psychology of intergroup relations. *Annual Review of Psychology, 33,* 1–39.

Tajfel, H. (1982b). *Social identity and intergroup relations.* New York, NY: Cambridge University Press.

Tajfel, H., & Turner, J. C. (1979). An integrative theory of intergroup conflict. *The social psychology of intergroup relations, 33*(47), 74.

Tajfel, H., & Turner, J. (1986). The social identity theory of intergroup behavior. In S. Worchel & W. Austin (Eds.), *Psychology of intergroup relations* (pp. 2–24). Chicago, IL: Nelson-Hall.

Takeuchi, J., Kass, S., Schneider, S., & Van Wormer, L. (2013). Virtual and face-to-face teamwork differences in culturally homogeneous and heterogeneous teams. *Journal of Psychological Issues in Organizational Culture, 4*(2), 17–27.

Tannen, D. (1991). *You just don't understand: Women and men in conversation.* London, UK: Virago.

Tannenbaum, S., Mathieu, J., Salas, E., & Cohen, D. (2012). Teams are changing: Are research and practice evolving fast enough? *Industrial and Organizational Psychology, 5*(1), 2–24.

Tauer, J., & Harackiewicz, J. (2004). The effects of cooperation and competition on intrinsic motivation and performance. *Journal of Personality and Social Psychology, 86*(6), 849–861.

Taylor, F. (1923). *The principles of scientific management.* New York, NY: Harper.

Tekleab, A., Quigley, N., & Tesluk, P. (2009). A longitudinal study of team conflict, conflict management, cohesion, and team effectiveness. *Group and Organizational Management, 34*(2), 170–205.

Thomas, B., & Olson, M. (1988). Gain sharing: The design that guarantees success. *Personnel Journal, 67*(5), 73–79.

Thomas, K. (1976). Conflict and conflict management. In M. Dunnette (Ed.), *Handbook of industrial and organizational psychology* (pp. 889–935). Chicago, IL: Rand McNally.

Thompson, L. (2004). *Making the team: A guide for managers* (2nd ed.). Upper Saddle River, NJ: Pearson.

Thompson, L., & Coovert, M. (2006). Understanding and developing computer-supported cooperative work teams. In C. Bowers, E. Salas, & F. Jentsch (Eds.),

Creating high-tech teams (pp. 213–241). Washington, DC: American Psychological Association.

Thompson, L., & Hastie, R. (1990). Judgment tasks and biases in negotiation. In B. Sheppard, M. Bazerman, & R. Lewicki (Eds.), *Research on negotiations in organizations* (Vol. 2, pp. 1077–1092). Greenwich, CT: JAI.

Thompson, L., & Hrebec, D. (1996). Lose-lose agreements in interdependent decision making. *Psychological Bulletin, 120,* 396–409.

Tjosvold, D. (1995). Cooperation theory, constructive controversy, and effectiveness: Learning from crisis. In R. Guzzo & E. Salas (Eds.), *Team effectiveness and decision making in organizations* (pp. 79–112). San Francisco, CA: Jossey-Bass.

Tjosvold, D., Wong, A., & Chen, N. (2014). Constructively managing conflicts in organizations. *Annual Review of Organizational Psychology and Organizational Behavior,* 545–568.

Todd, A., Hanko, K., Galinsky, A., & Mussweiler, T. (2011). When focusing on differences leads to similar perspectives. *Psychological Science, 22*(1), 134–141.

Todorova, G., Bear, J., & Weingart, L. (2014). Con conflict be energizing? A study of task conflict, positive emotions, and job satisfaction. *Journal of Applied Psychology, 99*(3), 451–467.

Tolbert, P., Andrews, A., & Simons, T. (1995). The effects of group proportions on group dynamics. In S. Jackson & M. Ruderman (Eds.), *Diversity in work teams: Research paradigms for a changing workplace* (pp. 131–159). Washington, DC: American Psychological Association.

Tost, L., Gino, F., & Larrick, R. (2013). When power makes others speechless: The negative impact of leader power on team performance. *Academy of Management Journal, 56*(5), 1465–1486.

Triandis, H. (1994). *Culture and social behavior.* New York, NY: McGraw-Hill.

Triplett, N. (1898). The dynamogenic factors in pace-making and competition. *American Journal of Psychology, 9,* 507–533.

Tschan, F., Semmer, N. K., Gurtner, A., Bizzari, L., Spychiger, M., Breuer, M., & Marsch, S. U. (2009). Explicit reasoning, confirmation bias, and illusory transactive memory: A simulation study of group medical decision making. *Small Group Research, 40*(3), 271–300.

Tsui, A., Xin, K., & Egan, T. (1995). Relational demography: The missing link in vertical dyad linkage. In S. Jackson & M. Ruderman (Eds.), *Diversity in work teams: Research paradigms for a changing workplace* (pp. 97–129). Washington, DC: American Psychological Association.

Tuckman, B., & Jensen, M. (1977). Stages of small group development revisited. *Group and Organizational Studies, 2,* 419–427.

Turkle, S. (2011). *Alone together.* New York, NY: Basic Books.

Turner, J. C., Hogg, M. A., Oakes, P. J., Reicher, S. D., & Wetherell, M. S. (1987). *Rediscovering the social group: A self-categorization theory.* Oxford, UK: Blackwell.

Uhl-Bien, M., & Graen, G. (1992). Self-management and team-making in cross-functional work teams: Discovering the keys to becoming an integrated team. *Journal of High Technology Management Research, 3,* 225–241.

Uzzi, B. (1997). Social structure and competition in interfirm networks: The paradox of embeddedness. *Administrative Science Quarterly, 42,* 35–67.

Vallas, S. (2003). Why teamwork fails: Obstacles to workplace change in four manufacturing plants. *American Sociological Review, 68,* 223–250.

Van de Ven, A., & Delbecq, A. (1974). The effectiveness of nominal, Delphi, and interacting group decision making processes. *Academy of Management Journal, 17,* 605–621.

Van der Vegt, G., & Bunderson, J. (2005). Learning and performance in multidisciplinary teams: The importance of collective team identification. *Academy of Management Journal, 48*(3), 532–547.

Van der Vegt, G., Emans, B., & Van de Vliert, E. (1998). Motivating effects of task and outcome interdependence in work teams. *Group and Organization Management, 23,* 124–144.

Van Gundy, A. (1981). *Techniques of structured problem solving.* New York, NY: Van Nostrand Reinhold.

Van Gundy, A. (1987). *Creative problem solving: A guide for trainers and management.* New York, NY: Quorum Books.

Van Knippenberg, D., & Schippers, M. (2007). Work group diversity. *Annual Review of Psychology, 58,* 515–541.

Van Maanen, J., & Barley, S. (1985). Cultural organization: Fragments of a theory. In P. Frost, L. Moore, M. Louis, C. Lundberg, & J. Martin (Eds.), *Organizational culture* (pp. 31–54). Beverly Hills, CA: SAGE.

Van Maanen, J., & Kunda, G. (1989). "Real feelings": Emotional expression and organizational culture. *Research in organizational behavior, 11,* 43–103.

Vangelisti, A. L., Knapp, M. L., & Daly, J. A. (1990). Conversational narcissism. *Communications Monographs, 57*(4), 251–274.

Vashdi, D., Bamberger, P., & Erez, M. (2013). Can surgical teams ever learn? The role of coordination, complexity, and transitivity in action team learning. *Academy of Management Journal, 56*(4), 945–971.

Vignovic, J., & Thompson, L. (2010). Computer-mediated cross-cultural collaboration: Attributing communication errors to the person versus the situation. *Journal of Applied Psychology, 95*(2), 265–276.

Villado, A., & Winfred, A. (2013). The comparative effect of subjective and objective after-action reviews on team performance on a complex task. *Journal of Applied Psychology, 98*(3), 514–528.

Visser, V. A., van Knippenberg, D., van Kleef, G. A., & Wisse, B. (2013). How leader displays of happiness and sadness influence follower performance: Emotional contagion and creative versus analytical performance. *The Leadership Quarterly, 24*(1), 172–188.

Vorauer, J, Gagnon, A., & Sasaki, S. (2009). Salient intergroup ideology and intergroup interaction. *Psychological Science, 20*(7), 838–845.

Vroom, V., & Jago, A. (1988). *The new leadership: Managing participation in organizations.* Englewood Cliffs, NJ: Prentice Hall.

Vroom, V., & Yetton, P. (1973). *Leadership and decision making.* Pittsburgh, PA: University of Pittsburgh Press.

Wageman, R., Hackman, J., & Lehman, E. (2005). Team diagnostic survey: Development of an instrument. *Journal of Applied Behavioral Science, 41*(1), 373–398.

Walker, H., Ilardi, B., McMahon, A., & Fennell, M. (1996). Gender, interaction, and leadership. *Social Psychology Quarterly, 59*, 255–272.

Wall, V., & Nolan, L. (1987). Small group conflict: A look at equity, satisfaction, and styles of conflict management. *Small Group Behavior, 18*, 188–211.

Walton, R., & Hackman, J. (1986). Groups under contrasting management strategies. In P. Goodman & Associates (Eds.), *Designing effective work groups* (pp. 168–201). San Francisco, CA: Jossey-Bass.

Walton, R., & McKersie, R. (1965). *A behavioral theory of labor negotiations.* New York, NY: McGraw-Hill.

Wang, D., Waldman, D., & Zhang, Z. (2014). A meta-analysis of shared leadership and team effectiveness. *Journal of Applied Psychology, 99*(2), 181–198.

Wanous, J. (1980). *Organizational entry: Recruitment, selection, and socialization of newcomers.* Reading, MA: Addison-Wesley.

Wanous, J., & Youtz, M. (1986). Solution diversity and the quality of group decisions. *Academy of Management Journal, 29*, 149–159.

Wech, B., Mossholder, K., Steel, R., & Bennett, N. (1998). Does work group cohesiveness affect individuals' performance and organizational commitment? *Small Group Research, 29*, 472–494.

Wegner, D. (1986). Transactive memory: A contemporary analysis of the group mind. In B. Mullen & G. Goethals (Eds.), *Theories of group behavior* (pp. 185–208). New York, NY: Springer-Verlag.

Wellins, R., Byham, W., & Wilson, J. (1991). *Empowered teams.* San Francisco, CA: Jossey-Bass.

Wellins, R., & George, J. (1991). The key to self-directed teams. *Training and Development Journal, 45*(4), 26–31.

West, M. (2004). *Effective teamwork: Practical lessons from organizational research* (2nd ed.). Malden, MA: Blackwell.

West, M. (2012). *Effective teamwork: Practical lessons from organizational research* (3rd ed.). London, UK: Blackwell.

Wheelan, S. (2005). *Group process: A developmental perspective* (2nd ed.). Boston, MA: Allyn & Bacon.

Wiedow, A., & Konradt, U. (2011). Two-dimensional structure of team process: Team reflection and team adaptation. *Small Group Research, 42*(1), 32–54.

Wilder, D. (1986). Social categorization: Implications for creation and reduction of intergroup bias. In L. Berkowitz (Ed.), *Advances in experimental social psychology* (Vol. 19, pp. 291–355). San Diego, CA: Academic Press.

Williams, J., & Best, D. (1990). *Measuring sex differences: A multination study.* Newbury Park, CA: SAGE.

Witeman, H. (1991). Group member satisfaction: A conflict-related account. *Small Group Research, 22*, 24–58.

Woolley, A., Chabris, C., Pentland, A., Hashmi, N., & Malone, T. (2010). Evidence for a collective intelligence factor in the performance of human groups. *Science, 330*, 686–688.

Worchel, S., Andreoli, V., & Folger, R. (1977). Intergroup cooperation and intergroup attraction: The effect of previous interaction and outcome of combined effort. *Journal of Experimental Social Psychology, 13*, 131–140.

Yang, J., & Mossholder, K. W. (2004). Decoupling task and relationship conflict: The role of intragroup emotional processing. *Journal of Organizational Behavior, 25*(5), 589–605.

Yilmaz, G., & Peña, J. (2014). The influence of social categories and interpersonal behaviors on future intentions and attitudes to form subgroups in virtual teams. *Communication Research, 41*(3), 333–352.

Yong, K., Sauer, S., & Mannix, E. (2014). Conflict and creativity in interdisciplinary teams. *Small Group Research, 45*(3), 266–289.

Youngs, G. (1986). Patterns of threat and punishment reciprocity in a conflict setting. *Journal of Personality and Social Psychology, 51*, 541–546.

Yukl, G. (1989). Managerial leadership: A review of theory and research. *Journal of Management, 15*, 251–289.

Yukl, G. (1994). *Leadership in organizations* (3rd ed.). Englewood Cliffs, NJ: Prentice Hall.

Yukl, G., & Guinan, P. (1995). Influence tactics used for different objectives with subordinates, peers, and supervisors. *Group and Organization Management, 20*, 272–297.

Zaccaro, S., Heinen, B., & Shuffler, M. (2009). Team effectiveness and team leadership. In E. Salas, G. Goodwin, & C. Burke (Eds.), *Team effectiveness in complex organizations: Cross-disciplinary perspectives and approaches* (pp. 83–112). New York, NY: Routledge.

Zaccaro, S., & Klimoski, R. (2002). The interface of leadership and team processes. *Group and Organization Management, 27*(1), 4–14.

Zaccaro, S., & Marks, M. (1999). The roles of leaders in high-performance teams. In E. Sundstrom (Ed.), *Supporting work team effectiveness* (pp. 95–125). San Francisco, CA: Jossey-Bass.

Zaccaro, S., Rittman, A., & Marks, M. (2001). Team leadership. *The Leadership Quarterly, 12*(4), 451–483.

Zander, A. (1977). *Groups at work*. San Francisco, CA: Jossey-Bass.

Zander, A. (1994). *Making groups effective*. San Francisco, CA: Jossey-Bass.

Zarraga, C., & Bonache, J. (2005). The impact of team atmosphere on knowledge outcomes in self-managed teams. *Organizational Studies, 26*(5), 661–681.

Zhang, Z., Hempel, P., Han, Y., & Tjosvold, D. (2007). Transactive memory system links work team characteristics and performance. *Journal of Applied Psychology, 92*(6), 1722–1730.

Zigon, J. (1997, January–February). Team performance measurement: A process for creating performance standards. *Compensation and Benefits Review*, 38–48.

Zigurs, I., & Khazanchi, D. (2008). From profiles to patterns: A new view of task-technology fit. *Information Systems Management, 25*, 8–13.

Zuboff, S. (1988). *In the age of the smart machine*. New York, NY: Basic Books.

Index